QUEER LONDON

THE CHICAGO SERIES
ON SEXUALITY, HISTORY, & SOCIETY

EDITED BY JOHN C. FOUT

Also in the series:

QUEER LONDON

Perils and Pleasures in the Sexual Metropolis, 1918–1957

MATT HOULBROOK

The University of Chicago Press
Chicago and London

The University of Chicago Press, Chicago 60637
The University of Chicago Press, Ltd., London
© 2005 by The University of Chicago
All rights reserved. Published 2005
Paperback edition 2006
Printed in the United States of America

14 13 12 11 10 09 08 07 06   2 3 4 5

ISBN: 0-226-35460-1 (cloth)
ISBN-13: 978-0-226-35462-0 (paper)
ISBN-10: 0-226-35462-8 (paper)

Library of Congress Cataloging-in-Publication Data

Houlbrook, Matt.
    Queer London : perils and pleasures in the sexual
  metropolis, 1918–1957 / Matt Houlbrook.
        p.   cm. — (The Chicago series on sexuality,
  history, and society)
    Includes bibliographical references and index.
    ISBN 0-226-35460-1 (cloth : alk. paper) 1. Gay
  men—England—London—History—20th century.
  2. Homosexuality—England—London—History—20th
  century. 3. Sex customs—England—London—History—
  20th century. 4. London (England)—Social life and
  customs—20th century. I. Title. II. Series.
      HQ76.2.G72L655 2005
      306.76′62′094210904—dc22

                                              2005004166

This is London, not Antarctica.
—Hefner, *We Love the City*

CONTENTS

ILLUSTRATIONS

ACKNOWLEDGMENTS

A few months ago a friend told me that I practice the historian's equivalent of method acting. Looking back, I'm not convinced that this was meant as a compliment. I've lived this book for the past eight years. My friends have had to cope with me drifting in and out of conversations in the pub, lost in whatever bit of history I was working on; not coming out because I was busy; talking endlessly about powder puffs; thinking PRO reference numbers would make great tattoos; dragging them down alleyways to check out where a urinal once stood. They've humored me, encouraged me, and tolerated my obsessions. They've taken the piss often enough to keep me vaguely connected to reality and reminded me that there are more important things than MEPO files. They've been there when I needed them. For what it's worth, I offer my thanks to Michelle Atkinson, Rachel Buxton, Ann Deary, Claire Hibbitt, Bryn Jeffries and Clare Samuelson, Tom Kingston, Han Maddox, Cath Rothon, Dave Scales, Caroline Thomas, and Paul Watson. The late Vanessa Coombe would have been delighted to see this book in print. I miss her.

Amazingly, institutions have funded my obsessions: postgraduate studentships from the University of Essex and the Arts and Humanities Research Board of the British Academy; a Junior Research Fellowship at New College Oxford; and most recently, a job in the School of History at the University of Liverpool. At New College, Alan Ryan gave unwavering and appreciated support. At Liverpool, I've found a new energy from colleagues and students alike. Thanks to Dmitri van den Bersselaar, Miriam Dobson, Martin Heale, and Dan Scroop. Andy Davies has listened, advised, and kicked me into action again.

This book started out as my Ph.D. dissertation under the supervision of Geoff Crossick and Pam Cox. Their constant encouragement and insights pushed me farther than I ever imagined. Ken Plummer offered perceptive suggestions. As examiners, Mike Roper and John Tosh forced me to look again at ideas I had taken for granted.

I've been lucky enough to have worked on this project at the same time as a generation of historians has begun to reshape the ways in which we think about queer British history. It is an exciting time to be working in this field, and I have benefited from a remarkably generous and open exchange of ideas with Harry Cocks, Paul Deslandes, Laura Doan, Frank Mort, and Alison Oram, amongst others. Matt Cook and Morris Kaplan read the manuscript;

their scribbled comments made me reconsider and rework. This is a much better book as a result. My biggest intellectual and personal debt is to Chris Waters: he's a much-loved friend, a constant source of encouragement, and an infuriating and compelling intellectual challenge in equal measure. He's an absolute star. Along the way Marcus Collins, Richard Dennis, Lesley Hall, Steven Maynard, Malcolm Shifrin, and Frances Spalding have shared ideas or references and commented on various works.

And now it's a book. Credit here has to go to Douglas Mitchell, my editor at Chicago. It's impossible to say how much I've benefited from his remarkable talent for communicating energy and enthusiasm via e-mail. He's supported and cajoled, kept me on track, and made me laugh out loud. Seth Koven and Martin Francis read my manuscript for the press. I thank them for their constructive suggestions and hope they can see the results. I'm extremely grateful to the production and editorial team at Chicago— particularly Tim McGovern and Maia Rigas—for working so hard to make this book what it has become. Thanks also to Sandra Mather from the Department of Geography at the University of Liverpool for drawing the map.

Finally, I owe a unique debt to my family. My brother, Adam, has done more than he probably had to. He's read my work; he's been on too many nights out with me; he's refused to put up with my angst. As selfless as ever, he's done more than his fair share of piss taking. My parents, Malcolm and Joyce, have simply been there and been themselves. They all mean the world to me.

If I *am* a method historian, then right now I'm between jobs. To all of you: until the next book kicks off in earnest, I'm back in the here and now, so let's celebrate.

NOTE ON TERMINOLOGY

Finding an appropriate vocabulary with which to discuss the historical organization of male sexual practices and identities is notoriously difficult. The contemporary terms "gay"/"homosexual" and "straight"/"heterosexual" position such practices within a particular interpretive framework that cannot be imposed straightforwardly on the past. Where possible, I thus use the conceptual categories deployed by the men I study, exploring the meanings such terms carried. In general discussion, I use the rubric "queer" to denote all erotic and affective interactions between men and all men who engaged in such interactions, and "homosex" as an "amalgam . . . [that] indicates sexual activities of various sorts between two males" (John Howard, *Men Like That: A Southern Queer History* [Chicago and London, Chicago University Press, 1999], xviii). I use both terms without making any assumptions about the conceptualization or organization of those activities—without, for example, viewing the individuals involved as "gay" in the way we would use the term today. Given that "queer" was also part of everyday discourse in the early twentieth century denoting a historically and culturally specific understanding of male sexual practices, it carries a dual meaning throughout this book. I hope that my intended meaning will be clear from the context.

CLRO   Corporation of London Record Office
CHP   Departmental Committee on Homosexual Offences and Prostitution (1954–57)
CRIM   Central Criminal Court
DE   *Daily Express*
DM   *Daily Mail*
DPP   Director of Public Prosecutions
Emp   *Empire News*
EN   *Evening News*
ES   *Evening Standard*
FL   Fawcett Library, London
GH   Guildhall Justice Room
GLC   Greater London Council
HO   Home Office
IPN   *Illustrated Police News*
JB   *John Bull*
LCC   London County Council
LMA   London Metropolitan Archive
MA   *Morning Advertiser*
MEPO   Metropolitan Police
Met   Metropolitan Police
MH   Mansion House Justice Room
NSA   National Sound Archive, London

NVA   National Vigilance Association
NW   *News of the World*
PRO   Public Record Office, The National Archives, London
PMC   Public Morality Council
PS   London Metropolitan Magistrate's Court

BOW   Bow Street
CLE   Clerkenwell
GRE   Greenwich
HAM   Hampstead Petty Sessions
LAM   Lambeth
MAR   Marylebone
MS   Marlborough Street
NLO   North London
OLD   Old Street
SWE   South Western
TH   Thames
TOW   Tower Bridge
WES   Westminster
WLN   West London
WOO   Woolwich

RCPPP   Royal Commission on Police Powers and Procedures
SOC   Street Offences Committee

INTRODUCTION
THIS IS LONDON

This is Cyril's story.

He moved to London in 1932 at the age of twenty. There he became a young man about town, enjoying the privileges and possibilities that an independent income created in a modern consumer society. At first he stayed at the Montague Hotel in Bloomsbury, though he later took a furnished room in Leicester Chambers off Lisle Street, in the heart of the West End, that bustling realm of shops, theaters, restaurants, and bars. Cyril seems to have found his way around quickly. He began to frequent certain commercial venues, making a kind of home for himself in places like the Caravan, a basement club in Endell Street. Here he made friends and socialized, found sex and, eventually, embarked on a series of passionate affairs. In 1934, he wrote to Morris, one of these men:

> I was very disappointed to find that you were not coming to the club tonight, as ever since I phoned you on Monday and made arrangements with you I just lived for tonight . . . I stayed in bed all day yesterday, didn't even get up to eat and just thought of you and counting the hours until I should see you . . . I love you Morris darling . . . I only wish that I was going away with you, just you and I to eat, sleep and make love together.[1]

Tortured with the exquisite agony of a new love, Cyril was, still, happy. Also in 1934, he reflected on these experiences in a letter to his friend Billy, who ran the Caravan. Seventy years later, Cyril's excitement at the world in which he had only just begun to move and its importance to him remains tangible. He talked about his relationships, his feelings, and the life he was

My Dear Billy,

      just a note to say that I am very disappointed about you, I honestly thought that you were queer, ~~and~~ but different from the others, and I liked you very much. I didnt intend coming to the Club last night only I felt that I must see you. I have only been queer since I came to London about two years ago, before then I knew nothing about it, as I told you I am married and have a little girl two years of age, and I still like girls occasionally, there are veryfew boys with whom I want to have an affair with, I like them all as friends but nothing more. I have a boy staying with me and who is really my affair, we have been together now since I came to town and I like him very much, and I think he is a better pal to me than any woman could ~~xx~~ ever be, altho' sometimes I wish that I was still normal as queer people are very temperamental and dissatisfied. I honestly hoped to have an affair with you Billy, and I shall only come to the Club to see you. Well it is now 10.p.m. and I have just got up out of bed so must close down and have a bath and dress, and hope that you will excuse my telling you all this only as I say, I like you very very much and feel that I can talk this way to you. Please be a dear boy and destroy this note, and do not mention it to anyone as this is just between you and I. I shall look forward to seeing you in about a couple of hours. Until then.

         Your Very Sincere friend always,

           Cyril ████████

Figure 1. Photograph of Cyril's letter to Billy, 1934. The National Archives of the UK (PRO), ref no. MEPO 3/758. Material in the National Archives in the copyright of the Metropolitan Police is reproduced by permission of the Metropolitan Police Authority.

forging in the city. He wrote, "I have only been queer since I came to London about two years ago, before then I knew nothing about it" (see fig. 1).[2]

On one level, it is easy to interpret this story because it seems so very familiar, so instantly recognizable. In many ways Cyril's story is all "our" stories. In mapping his own changing sense of self and sexual practices onto his encounter with London, he establishes a productive relationship between space, the social, and subjectivity. Geographical, temporal, and subjective movements blend together. "Being queer" is equated with the cultural experience of urban life—"coming to London about two years ago." Retrospectively, self-knowledge—self-realization—is correlated with that moment of migration. London is both a symbolic and experiential rupture, a productive space that generates and stabilizes a new form of selfhood and way of life. Cyril's story pivots upon an implicit opposition between silence and speaking out, repression and fulfillment, nonbeing and being. This can easily be a recognizable tale of the big city as a space of affirmation, liberation, and citizenship—the city as a queer space.

This story can be taken further. Cyril found himself within networks of public and commercial sociability constructed by men like him. For the "homosexual," we are told, this was a period of social intolerance, legal repression, and cultural marginalization. London was, nonetheless, the site of a vibrant, extensive, and diverse queer urban culture. Overlapping social worlds took hold in parks, streets, and urinals; in pubs, restaurants, and dancehalls; in Turkish baths; in furnished rooms and lodging houses. Across this city, men met in these places, brought together by their desires for sex or sociability. By participating in this world, they were able to forge social ties and ways of being that belied their nominal exclusion from metropolitan life. Little wonder that Cyril's letters are marked by a profound sense of belonging.

In linking sexual selfhood and place Cyril thus illustrates a familiar theme: the association between "homosexuality" and the city. It is this broad historical, historiographical, and conceptual issue that *Queer London* addresses. Stories of the city as a queer space—stories like this—have become a cultural and academic commonplace over the past century. As Matt Cook recently observed, "think of 'gay' men and 'gay' culture and we think of cities."[3] Such patterns of thought have permeated popular culture through TV series like *Queer as Folk* or books like Maupin's *Tales of the City*.[4] In that proliferation of historical studies of sexual difference since Michel Foucault's groundbreaking *History of Sexuality,* there has, moreover, been an overwhelming focus on the organization of queer sexualities in their urban setting. Together, the work of George Chauncey, Marc Stein, and others comprises a dynamic queer urban history.[5]

In many senses this focus on the city is understandable. It is, after all, in the modern city that queer lives have assumed their characteristic contemporary forms—think of Old Compton Street or San Francisco's Castro. It is here that the novelists, autobiographers, and historians who write about such practices have made their home. It is, moreover, in the city that regulatory agencies and newspapers have generated the most extensive and vivid evidence of such practices in the past. The city appears important because, as Neil Bartlett's compelling *Who Was That Man?* illustrates, it is here that we can see the accumulated historical traces of queer male networks, both visually and through the surviving historical record.[6] The world that Cyril was beginning to explore so eagerly in the 1930s can be traced back through the late nineteenth-century cases of Oscar Wilde or Cleveland Street to the early eighteenth-century Molly Houses. If the links between these different worlds are problematic, London's importance to queer men and public knowledge of "homosexuality" was long established.[7]

This focus on the city, moreover, reflects current trends in critical academic thought, particularly the "spatial turn" within the fields of history, cultural studies, and human geography. As the work of David Harvey, Henri Lefebvre, or Edward Soja suggests, space—the city—is not simply a passive backdrop against which social and cultural processes are enacted but a "constitutive part of the cultural and social formation of metropolitan modernity." Male sexual practices and identities do not just take place *in* the city; they are shaped and sustained *by* the physical and cultural forms of modern urban life just as they in turn shape that life.[8]

In this context, it is unsurprising that *the* dominant paradigm in historical analyses of male sexualities has been the correlation of the emergence of visible queer cultures with the experiential dimensions of urban modernity. Just as Cyril mapped "being queer" onto "coming to London," so historians taking their cue from Foucault have mapped the "great paradigm shift" of the "making of the modern homosexual" onto the process of urbanization. In the early work of John d'Emilio or Jeffrey Weeks, for example, urbanization—by disrupting structures of authority, weakening the family, and offering the anonymity of the modern metropolis—is a precondition of the emergence of the "homosexual" as an identity, state of being, and social world from the mid-nineteenth century onwards.[9]

Such analyses of the temporal conjunction of space and sexuality reach their apogee in Henning Bech's *When Men Meet* (1997). Bech's starting point is the notion that "being homosexual . . . is not primarily a matter of discourse and identity but a way of being." He locates this particular "homosexual form of existence" within modern experiences of urbanity, in particular, the flux, anonymity, and visuality of the crowd. Here the city is a productive space, generating specific forms of desire and conventions of social interaction. Bech concludes with an axiom: the city is "the social world proper of the homosexual . . . to be homosexual he must get into the city." Simultaneously, this is a suggestive historical analysis and a profound cultural imperative.[10]

Such arguments are compelling because they seem to be commonsense. They are, however, deeply problematic. Simplistic invocations of urbanization as a liberating agent or the city as a queer space efface very real experiences of the city as alienating, disruptive, and dangerous. Cyril's letters suggest a life full of happiness and affirmation. Detailed accounts of his behavior in the Caravan suggest its role as a site of private sociability in his life. They offer tantalizing details about his character and appearance. Yet how has this evidence come down to us? Because the British state sought to suppress particular social and sexual interactions between men; because plainclothes police kept the club under observation over several weeks; because they raided the venue and arrested everyone there; because at Bow Street Police Station Cyril was subject to the humiliating ritual of having his cheeks rubbed with blotting paper for evidence of make-up; because he was imprisoned and then brought to trial at the central criminal court, Old Bailey, for aiding and abetting in keeping a disorderly house; because the Metropolitan Police searched his flat, confiscating his letters, a pencil sketch of a naked man, and a photograph of a penis. In the end, Cyril wasn't convicted, but only because he arrived late at court and the director of public prosecutions deemed the week he had already spent in prison "a sufficient lesson to [him] not to associate with such clubs in future."[11]

Entering the public record was a disaster in Cyril's life, as it was in the lives of those countless other men who encountered the law in this period. This disaster was, moreover, compounded by being reported in the national press: Cyril's name and address, his nickname, and his letter to Morris were mentioned in *The Times, News of the World,* and *Illustrated Police News*.[12] That his story is preserved is thus evidence of a momentary failure to negotiate the tensions inherent to queer urban life—a failure to evade the law and public hostility. Simultaneously, however, we can read these sources as I do here: to suggest how men *were* able to create a place for themselves in the city and explore how they understood and organized their desires. This dissonance means we must understand the records of official agencies—on which this book draws—as being produced at the point where public and private, pain and pleasure, intersect. They are, in this sense, paradigmatic sources in understanding the contradictory nature of queer lives in early twentieth-century London, for just as the city opened up certain possibilities for certain men, it closed down other possibilities and left other men marginalized or silenced. We can celebrate the fact that Cyril and men like him created this world, but we must also recognize its exclusions, dangers, ambiguities, and limits.

If established narratives of the "making of the modern homosexual" obscure these often brutal realities, so the singular linearity of this chronology effaces the complexities of men's relationship to urban space and, in particular, the relationship between sexual practices and identities and the city. Attempting to map changes *across time* has obscured the persistent differences and tensions in the organization of queer practices *across space*. Too often, the city is treated as a universalized agent of social change, producing a hegemonic singular "homosexuality." As Scott Bravmann suggests, "the modernist narrative logic of social constructionist accounts of gay identity formation . . . elides the multiple differences among gay men"—differences of class, race, age, gender, and place. Thinking of urbanization as a "grand, universalizing historical process" thus "obscures recognition of effective and meaningful difference within that overarching process of change."[13] The key point is very simple: men are different from one another, and those differences shape their experiences of the city, the lives they lead, and their sense of selfhood.

The apparent familiarity of Cyril's equation between "being queer" and "coming to London" is thus deceptive. Cyril's "London" is most definitely not our London. Moreover, his use of the term "queer" itself cannot easily be mapped onto contemporary categories of queerness. When Cyril went to the Caravan, his face was powdered, lips rouged, and eyebrows plucked. He was called—and referred to himself—by the nickname "the Countess" and the pronoun "she." He was married, had a two year-old daughter, and "still like[d] girls occasionally." Despite this, he thought his current affair "a better pal to me than any women could ever be." It seems Cyril understood the distinction between what he called "normal" and "queer people" in terms very different to our own.[14]

The strangeness of Cyril's story underscores Steven Maynard's emphasis upon the need to explore "the conceptual categories and ways of knowing actually used by actors in the past." What *did* Cyril mean when he used the terms "queer" and "normal"? What did the terms mean to other men, both those who thought of themselves as queer and those who did not?[15] In its simplest sense, queer signified men's difference from what was considered "normal." This difference was, in part, located in their sexual or emotional attraction to—and encounters with—other men. Yet it could also encompass differences in behavior and appearance. Queer, in this sense, could be a mode of self-understanding, a set of cultural practices, and a way of being. Its meanings were, moreover, never self-evident, stable, or singular. Within broader categories of class, race, gender, age, and place, men experienced, understood, and organized their desires very differently; understandings of sexual difference were multiple and contested.

Cyril, for example, located his queerness in an ineffably womanlike character, constructing an "effeminate" public persona consistent with what he assumed to be his inner nature. He was, in contemporary terms, a quean—a flamboyant and striking figure in London's streets and commercial venues and, for many Londoners, the very embodiment of sexual difference.[16] For others, particularly middle- and upper-class men, by contrast, their choice of sexual partner was the *only* thing that made them different. Conventionally masculine and discreet, they neither looked nor behaved "differently" and remained invisible to passersby. All these men might have referred to themselves as queer, but they did not necessarily understand the term in the same way.

If the meanings of queerness diverged, then so too did notions of what it meant to be a "normal" man. To a twenty-first-century observer, the most anomalous figure within queer urban culture in the first half of the twentieth century is the working-class man who engaged in homosex or ongoing emotional relationships with other men, at the same time as with women, and without considering himself—or being considered by other men—to be anything other than "normal." At the time, however, such figures—known variously as men, trade, rough trade, roughs, renters, or to be had—were an integral part of London's sexual landscape. To have sex with or to love another man did not necessarily make a man different. The most remarkable thing about queer urban culture is that it was, to a large extent, composed of and created by men who never thought themselves queer.

The boundaries between sexual difference and "normality" were thus problematic, unstable, and contested, and discrete frameworks for interpreting male sexual practices and identities coexisted, intersected, and overlapped. Being queer was never simply the same as being "homosexual," though it could be. Being "normal" never simply denoted what would today be labeled "heterosexuality," though in specific contexts and for certain men—particularly bourgeois men—it often did. Forms of understanding that we often assume to be timeless—the organization of male sexual practices and identities around the binary opposition between "homo-" and "heterosexual"—solidified only in the two decades after the Second World War. Remarkably, their origins lie within living memory.[17]

Rather than seeking to "rediscover" a "hidden" "gay" culture, this book thus explores the historical production of diverse modes of sexual difference and "normality" and the ways in which these interpretive frameworks shaped how men understood their desires; their sexual, social, and cultural practices; and the urban lives they forged. My interest is, in Joan Scott's terms, "how difference is established, how it operates, how and in what ways it constitutes subjects who see and act in the world."[18] Like earlier generations of historians, I explore the relationship between "being queer" and the city. Rather than conceptualizing the city as constituting a unitary "homosexuality," however, I scrutinize the competing understandings of masculinity, sexuality, and character that shaped men's participation in queer urban culture and relate these to differences of class, race, age, and place. Rather than focus solely on those who identified as queer, I give equal attention to those who considered themselves "normal" but nonetheless socialized with, had sex with, and loved other men. Diverse desires, ways of being, and cultural practices converged upon and were constituted by what I have called queer London.[19]

Just as we must recognize the fragmentation and antagonisms of queer urban culture in the first half of the twentieth century, so we must also, crucially, recognize its difference from London today. The relationship between "being queer" and "coming to London" is so ubiquitous that it can obscure the process of meaningful change over time. Too often the "modern city" is taken as a static category of analysis, creating the impression that the modern "homosexual" and the modern city came into being at the same time—at some point in the mid-nineteenth century—and have remained unchanged ever since. Yet Cyril's unfamiliar life reminds us that the relationship between sex and the city is historically specific. This thing called the modern metropolis is an organic and fluid entity that changes over time. London 1885 is different from London 1918, London 1934, London 1957 or London 2004. And, if the experience of being modern and urban is constantly shifting, then so too are the boundaries between sexual difference and "normality" and the geographical and cultural organization of male sexual practices and identities.

This book is about London. Simultaneously, London existed as a large-scale social unit—a physical area roughly coterminous with the administrative boundaries of the London County Council—and a series of related but discontinuous sites of sociability, danger, and pleasure—public spaces, commercial venues, and private flats. It existed, moreover, as an imagined space, exercising a profound influence on the ways that contemporaries thought about sexual difference. In this sense, London was never isolated or distinct but instead occupied a nodal position in national and international networks of sociability and knowledge. London was an imperial metropolis, and its queer cultures reflected the influence of immigration and racial difference upon metropolitan life. National newspapers reported metropolitan vice more frequently than that of any other urban center, establishing an axiomatic connection between "homosexuality" and the capital. As such, London often occupied a prominent place in the minds of many provincial queer men, representing an enticing space of affirmation and possibility.

This is not to suggest that London represented the limits of queer experiences in early twentieth-century Britain. There were, for example, established public and commercial networks in towns and cities like Blackpool, Liverpool, Manchester, Glasgow, and Brighton from at least the 1920s.[20] Many men, moreover, came to find metropolitan life restrictive, oppressive, and dangerous or found the more public manifestations of queer urban culture distasteful. They sought refuge elsewhere—in the rural idyll evoked by E. M. Forster, or abroad, in the Mediterranean, Berlin, or New York. Queer urban culture took shape within a persistent tension between London's centripetal and centrifugal power.[21]

Just as London occupied a particular place within national queer cultures, so it was also part of a global network of queer cities. Many men—usually, but not only, the wealthy and privileged—moved easily between London and New York, Vienna, San Francisco, Berlin, Rome, or Paris, to work, to live, or simply for pleasure.[22] These transnational connections underscore this book's organizing theme—that relationship between modern urban life and "being queer." In part, by exploring this relationship in London in the first half of the twentieth century, I aim to contribute to the ongoing debate about the generalized cultural and experiential dimensions of urban modernity. This was, after all, one of *the* quintessentially modern metropolises. "London," remarked the progressive urban sociologist Robert Sinclair in 1937, "is a sun among cities in an age when life is almost wholly urban, and by examining London we examine a ringleader, for good and evil."[23]

It would be misleading to assume too close a fit between the histories I tell here and those of other urban centers. In Britain itself, London was unique in terms of its sheer size, its role as a financial, political, maritime, imperial, and cultural capital, and its racial and social composition. It was unique, moreover, in the scale and vitality of the queer world that developed there. Internationally, London had a history and character that distinguished it from anywhere else. If forms of commercial or public sociability look similar and it is possible to discern commonalities in the understanding, organization, and experience of sexual difference between Western cities, all these cities were, nonetheless, unique. As compared to gay New York, for example, queer London was more deeply divided by extremes of wealth and that powerful British sense of class. London's ethnic composition, by contrast, reduced the salience of race as a fault line. London had its East End and its Seven Dials, but neither of those neighborhoods was anything like a Harlem. In London, white, black, or Indian men were more likely to socialize alongside each other. Moreover, London's cultural geography, particularly the West End's status as *the* metropolitan site of commercialized leisure, shaped a queer world that was more obviously centralized. If it is important to draw out parallels in queer urban histories, we must equally remain alive to the particular, the local, and the national—that uniqueness that makes cities different from one another. This book is, above all, about *London*.[24]

This book is about men, not women. Certainly, queer men and women inhabited many of the same commercial venues, and their sense of self took shape within overlapping understandings of gender and sexuality. Yet their experiences of London were fractured by differences of gender. While men were able to move through the public city by day or night, women's access to public space was more problematic. The association between femininity and domesticity, familial and neighborhood surveillance, anxieties surrounding the moral status of public women, and the city's very real dangers constrained women's movements. Women's marginal position in the labor market lessened their ability to access commercial venues or private residential space. In London, queer women negotiated a very different set of problems. While female sexual deviance—particularly prostitution—was inscribed within forms of surveillance that echoed the regulation of male sexualities, lesbianism remained invisible in the law and, in consequence, in the legal sources on which this book draws. Lesbian London demands its own study.[25]

This book starts with the First World War drawing to a close in 1918 and concludes with the publication of the report of the Departmental Committee on Homosexual Offences and Prostitution—more commonly known after its chairman, John Wolfenden—in 1957. In 1918 and 1957 alike, British public life was saturated with anxious debate about the social problem of "homosexuality" in general and metropolitan queer culture in particular. The 1918 "Black Book" libel trial at the Old Bailey, following scarcely veiled allegations of lesbianism aimed at the actress Maud Allen by the proto-fascist member of Parliament (MP) Noel Pemberton-Billing, drew the reading public's attention to the characteristic spaces of queer London.

In those pubs, bathhouses, and cruising grounds where men found sex and sociability, Pemberton-Billing saw Britain's corruption by German "vice" and espionage—a threat to the nation's very existence.[26] In the 1950s, similarly, the Second World War's disruptive impact on British society rendered queer urban culture increasingly problematic, placing London at the center of apocalyptic tabloid exposés of metropolitan "vice." And yet, if we can identify common themes across the four decades separating these moral panics, their outcomes diverged radically: a libel trial—which Pemberton-Billing won—in 1918; the creation of a departmental committee that recommended the decriminalization of private sexual relations between consenting adult men in 1957. This book is, in part, an attempt to understand how the shifting organization of queer urban culture shaped this chronology.

Queer London thus maps the geography, culture and politics of queer life in the period between the "Black Book" trial and Wolfenden—the lives of men like Cyril. Drawing upon an increasingly vibrant literature within history, human geography and cultural studies, it moves beyond simplistic invocations of the city as a queer space, and of a unified "homosexual" experience to explore the complex interrelationship between modern urban life and the organization of sexual and gender practices.

Parts 1 and 2—"Policing" and "Places"—explore queer men's relationship to the broader metropolitan environment, in particular the ways in which modern urban culture generated particular spaces of sociability and sexual encounter. The five chapters here trace the organization and character of queer life within its public spaces (streets, parks, and urinals), the commercial realm of bars, nightclubs, baths, and the operations of the metropolitan housing market. I contextualize this within a detailed analysis of the regulation of this world by the Metropolitan Police, the London County Council, and other municipal authorities. As such, I demonstrate *both* the vitality and diversity of London's queer culture *and* its constraints and exclusions. For while the city could open up possibilities of safety and affirmation, it left many men excluded, isolated, and in danger.

Part 3, "People," turns to the ways in which men understood and organized their practices *and* their engagement with the city. As such, it explores the historical meanings of sexual difference and "normality." Drawing upon critical and theoretical insights derived from feminist and queer theory, it identifies three distinct characters—the effeminate quean, the "normal" working man who had sex with men *and* women, and the respectable middle-class "homosexual." These characters embodied very different understandings of masculinity and sexuality, structured along intersecting lines of class, place, gender, age, and ethnicity. If such men regularly saw each other as they moved through the city—and just as often interacted sexually and socially—their relationships were always uneasy, as likely to encompass rejection as much as commonality.

Part 4 focuses upon the politics of queer life in the period leading up to the Wolfenden Report—looking ahead to the 1967 Sexual Offences Act, which passed Wolfenden's recommendations into law. It explores the construction of the "homosexual" as source of cultural danger and a threat to national stability and, hence, a suitable subject for criminal law. Against this, it traces the emergence of an assertive queer identity politics that challenged the cultural moorings of the sexual offences laws. Rather than being unequivocally affirmative, I argue, this process was consciously exclusionary, encapsulating profound antagonisms *between* queer men.

In mapping queer urban experiences in particular, *Queer London* explicitly scrutinizes a series of issues that are central to our understanding of twentieth-century British history in general. Moreover, the work contributes to ongoing debates about the British experience of "modernity." A number of recent edited collections have identified a sense of living with the new as a key motif throughout the past century, associated with particular forms of social organization and experience. In part, this book explores one aspect of these social forms—the relationship between the city and sexual difference. It contextualizes the organization of masculine sexualities within, for example, modern forms of expert knowledge, municipal government, the urban crowd, a mass media, consumerism, new understandings of selfhood, economic change, and the separation of public and private space. As such it stands as a particular case study in the British experience of modernity, drawing upon these debates to explore queer sexualities and, in turn, subjecting wider historical themes to critical scrutiny.[27]

At around 1:00 A.M. on August 25, 1934, Cyril was wrapped in the arms of Arthur J., a twenty-two-year-old waiter, in the Caravan (fig. 2). As Charlie, the pianist, played, they danced, whispered, and kissed. Suddenly the basement was full of uniformed policemen, and several men around them turned out to be plainclothes detectives. Amazingly, Cyril seems not to have panicked. Indeed, he retained a certain poise and self-possession. Approaching Divisional Detective Inspector (DDI) Campion, the officer in charge, he commented, "I don't mind the beastly raid, but I would like to know if you could let me have one of your nice boys to come home with me. I am really rather good." The inspector asked who he was. Cyril replied, "I am the Countess, you ought to know that." Campion, apparently, "did not want to listen to such rot."[28]

Figure 2. Photograph of the Caravan Club, 1930s. Photographer unknown. The National Archives of the UK (PRO), ref no. DPP 2/224. Material in the National Archives in the copyright of the Metropolitan Police is reproduced by permission of the Metropolitan Police Authority.

Cyril's experiences are my point of departure for exploring queer urban culture in early twentieth-century London, highlighting the themes I take up below. In positioning his own changing sense of self and sexual practices within his encounter with London, Cyril embodies the complex relationship between the city, the social, and the self that is the central focus of *Queer London*. His story suggests queer men's contradictory engagement with urban life, the ways in which they could find the modern city *both* liberating *and* dangerous. His encounter with Campion indicates the role of the law in shaping queer lives and the ways in which men sought to evade and challenge its force. He tells us about what it meant to be "queer" and about the life he forged—about where he went, what he did, how he made sense of his desires, how he looked, who he loved. And he embodies understandings of gender and sexuality very different from our own, opening up ongoing debates about the historicization of sexual difference and "normality." In all these senses, what follows is Cyril's story.

PART 1

POLICING

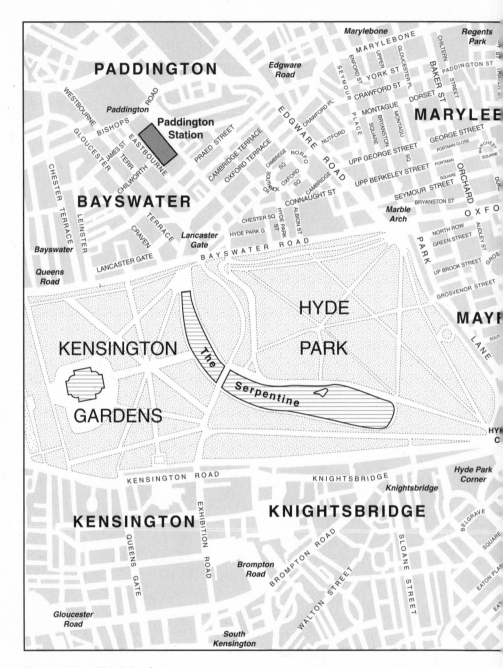

Figure 3. Map, "This Is London."

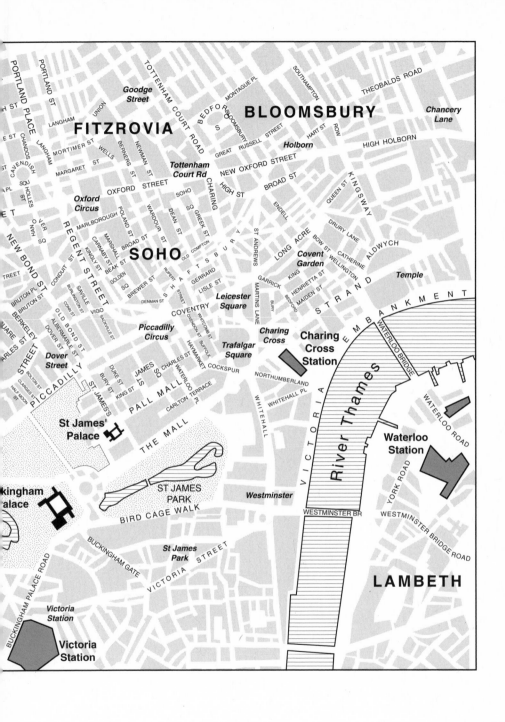

1

THE LAW

It is received wisdom that, as Liz Gill put it in the *Guardian* recently, "being gay was illegal" until the 1967 Sexual Offences Act.[1] If the statement is misleading in its conception of the law, it nonetheless highlights the accumulated battery of legal provisions designed or utilized to suppress sexual, social, or cultural interactions between men in the first half of the twentieth century. As Harry Cocks demonstrates, the offences of buggery and indecent assault evolved within common and statute law from the late eighteenth century to encompass *any* homosexual encounter, *wherever* it had occurred, and whether or not the men involved had consented.[2] These provisions were codified and elaborated in the late nineteenth century. Sections of the Offences against the Person Act (1861) dealing with buggery and indecent assault were followed by the notorious section 11 of the Criminal Law Amendment Act (1885), defining any act of "gross indecency" between men in "public or private" as an offence.[3] Statute law was, moreover, complemented by the offence of "indecency" under many local bylaws.[4]

These narrowly defined sexual offences were supplemented by a series of provisions that targeted wider social and cultural practices. Responding to anxieties about the condition of London's streets, the Vagrancy Law Amendment Act (1898) and the Criminal Law Amendment Act (1912) introduced the public order offence of "persistently importuning for an immoral purpose," which attempted to suppress queer men's use of public space for "cruising" and social interaction.[5] Generalized public order statutes and licensing provisions, moreover, notionally made it an offence for a commercial venue to tolerate queer men's presence. It was never illegal simply "to be gay," but the law criminalized a series of discrete social, sexual, and cultural practices in which men might participate.[6]

The formal regulation of male sexual and social behavior was thus structured around a dual logic. Although the introduction of legislation was often ad hoc and haphazard, in practice the law constituted a pervasive system of moral governance, defining sexual "normality" through the symbolic ordering of urban space. Acceptable sexual conduct was defined around the bourgeois nuclear family—private, between adult "heterosexual" married couples. Legislation against homosex thus echoed that against prostitution or public sex—in Philip Hubbard's phrase, making "dominant moral codes clear, tangible and entrenched, providing a fixed point in the attempt to construct boundaries between good and bad subjects."[7] In so doing, the law collapsed the conceptual distinctions between public and private that, notionally, went to its very heart. As Leslie Moran suggests, public space was understood as the realm of law's full presence—"a space of order and decency through the law." The private, by contrast, was "an alternative place where the law is absent."[8] The law's "absence," however, was contingent upon conforming to notions of normative sexual and social behavior. The "bad subject"—the sexual deviant—remained subject to state intervention, and was deemed sufficiently dangerous as to warrant intrusion into the sanctified private sphere.

For queer men, these provisions had profound implications, for the law threatened to follow them into the intimate, prosaic, and ubiquitous spaces of everyday urban life. If they looked for partners in the street or park or simply had sex in their own home, they could be arrested, prosecuted, imprisoned for up to ten years, and—in certain cases—whipped. If they met friends in a café they could be caught up in a police raid, their names taken, and the venue closed. The formal technology of surveillance institutionalized and embodied by the law suggested that the British state was unwilling to tolerate any expressions of male same-sex desire, physical contact, or social encounter. In all its erotic, affective, and social relations the queer body—and the spaces it inhabited—was a public body, subject to the draconian force of law. De jure, the modern metropolis held no place for the queer.

To read queer men's experiences of the law from its formal provisions, however, fails to comprehend the complex and often contradictory ways in which legislation was implemented. Only through the intermediary agencies of municipal governance established in the nineteenth century—the Metropolitan Police (the Met), the London County Council (LCC), the Metropolitan Borough Councils, and the Military Authorities—did that legislation acquired tangible significance.[9] Rather than what it said, the issue becomes how, and with what effects, was legislation translated into practice on London's streets. How was the law embodied through the daily routine of police operations?

While queer urban cultures were subject to surveillance by a diverse range of agencies, this chapter focuses upon the operations of the Met and, in particular, their enforcement of the sexual offences laws. It was in London's public spaces and through the figure of the policeman that queer men most often encountered the law. The Met were always most active in policing men's behavior, providing information to all other agencies. Moreover, this case study highlights the tensions between legislative pronouncements and the realities of regulation. I will return to the policing of commercial venues and the activities of other official agencies throughout part 2, setting shifting forms of regulation against the changing organization of queer sociability. My argument here—elaborated in the chapters that follow—is simple: policing was idiosyncratic and contingent, rendering specific practices and places invisible while bringing others into sharp relief. The de jure exclusion of queer men from metropolitan London collapsed amidst the operational realities of modern police systems.

THE POLICE

To explore the operationalization of the sexual offences laws means reconstituting the cognitive landscape inhabited by individual policemen, the maps through which they organized and understood their own movements across the city. The legal and administrative rules governing policing, as well as the informal knowledge officers gained through experience on the ground, interacted to produce an imagined geography of sexual transgression that defined whom the queer was, where he was to be found, and how he could be apprehended.

Crucially, while legislation collapsed the conceptual distinction between public and private, that logic did not extend to the procedural rules defining the Met's formal operational domain. The result, in Nick Fyfe's terms, was "a set of significant steering constraints of structural importance for [their] time-space deployment."[10] The physical, cultural, and administrative barriers constructed around the home created a de facto private space. Officers could only enter residential spaces with a search warrant. In detecting private sexual offences, the Met thus relied upon public complaints or secondhand information. That the police never made any concerted attempts to pursue the queer into his home placed men's behavior there almost beyond the law: "such acts," the director of public prosecutions (DPP) admitted in 1954, "are unprosecutable."[11] Access to commercial venues was similarly circumscribed, possible only under particular conditions. These formal "steering constraints" confined the policeman's habitual beat to London's streets and open spaces.[12]

Working within these jurisdictional parameters, senior and divisional officers thus established administrative definitions of importuning, gross indecency, and indecent assault that oriented patrols towards public queer spaces, mapping legal offences firmly onto particular urban sites. In Hyde Park, for example, beat officers were directed to the Meeting Ground and Hyde Park Corner.[13] Under these formal definitions the public urinal was identified as *the* locus of sexual offences. Asked to report on "homosexuality" in the West End in 1952, C Division police officers simply listed the urinals where men could be found.[14] This formal correlation between geography and criminality was, moreover, constantly reproduced at the divisional level. In 1933, for example, the attention of officers at Tower Bridge station was drawn to one Bermondsey urinal "by notes in the rough book."[15] The administrative conventions of policing articulated a narrow operational field that, for the most part, placed alternative sites of queer sexual and social interaction outside surveillance.

Within these formal constraints, the enforcement of the law depended upon the everyday movements of individual officers. Immersed in their operational environment, policemen became ever more familiar with the spatial and cultural organization of queer life, gaining the informal knowledge allowing them to interpret and implement legislation. As one officer was told during a 1932 raid on a ballroom, "you know what kind of boys we are."[16] The importance of knowing these "kind of boys" to policing is clear from the experiences of Police Constable (PC) 89/E Reginald Handford. Handford joined the Met in 1925, transferring to Bow Street station the following year at the age of twenty-two. There he became part of a group of twelve plainclothes policemen employed in the "detection of crime" in the district around the Strand.[17]

Handford learned to police from his more experienced colleagues—Cundy, Mogford, Shewry, Hills, and Slyfield—drawing upon their accumulated experience dealing with sexual offences. In part, officers became increasingly sensitized to the visual signifiers of character that allowed them to differentiate the queer from the fluid urban crowd. The effeminate quean became a working definition both of the queer himself and the perpetrator of a sexual offence, his body a demonstrable sign of deviant intent. While Handford, for example, recognized that "there are different forms of sodomites" and, indeed, arrested one man who "had no outward indication of his nefarious habits," he clearly visualized the transgressive male body in a particular way.[18] When asked, "have these male importuners . . . anything distinctive about them?" he replied immediately, "Yes, painted lips, powder."[19] On the beat, this image oriented officers towards individuals and commercial venues. In 1926, for example, Slyfield and Mogford were inside the Strand Hotel Restaurant when Frank W. drew their attention because of his "heavily powdered" face. They watched him cruising in other bars, on the Strand, and in Villiers Street before arresting him for importuning.[20] Within such mentalities, sexual offences could be defined as transgressions of acceptable masculine styles, leaving conventionally dressed men and the venues they frequented invisible.

The sensitivity of Slyfield and Mogford to the minutiae of self-presentation suggests a further geographical coding of sexual transgression. To put it another way, their experience produced a detailed cognitive map that defined sexual offences as place-specific. While Frank W. may have moved unnoticed outside the West End, in a district imagined as a site of sexual disorder and vice his body drew suspicion. Indeed, the officers' presence in certain venues on the Strand indicates how policing was organized not just by knowledge of *who* the queer was but also *where* he could be found. Sexual deviance—and consequently, police surveillance—was, in part, mapped onto the Strand's commercial spaces and places like the Coliseum Theatre.[21] Despite this, procedural constraints and their immersion in public urban life focused officers' attention upon the streets, parks, and above all, urinals frequented by queer men. If street cruising was fluid and mobile, urinals were fixed and physically bounded—as well as being administratively defined— and therefore easy to keep under surveillance. In 1927, almost all of the arrests made by E Division officers arose in fifteen local urinals—places like Durham House Street, Taylor's Buildings, York Place, and Cecil Court.[22]

This local geography of sexual transgression was clearly established by 1917, inherited and elaborated by successive generations of beat officers, and becoming central to occupational definitions of masculinity and competency. The good policeman, quite simply, knew his "ground."[23] Within this milieu Handford, apparently, learned quickly. Through conversation he became aware of the Coliseum's reputation and the "importuners" around Charing Cross. On the beat, colleagues introduced him to the "public house[s] sodomites are frequenting." He knew of the blackmailers operating in the neighborhood and the men who had sex under the arches of the Adelphi. He recognized the "convicted sodomites" he encountered. He identified "four urinals which are used by these sort of people," having "discussed . . . the prevalence of this particular crime at this particular place with Slyfield [and] Mogford." Drawing upon this remarkable familiarity with local queer culture, he focused his own attentions on one "notorious urinal" in the Adelphi Arches—"always frequented by certain sodomites." The urinal became an established stop in his habitual patrols. In eighteen months he arrested fifteen men there for sexual offences and was commended three times.[24]

E Division's focus on public space—and particularly on local urinals— reflected the broader geography of urban policing. Between 90 and 95 percent of the incidents resulting in proceedings for sexual offences in London's lower courts arose in urinals, parks, or streets. Urinals accounted for between 55 and 70 percent of the total. Indeed, in 1947 18 percent of all incidents (114 out of 637) were detected in the toilets at Victoria Station. In only two periods was there any departure from this pattern. Pressure from purity organizations to "clean up" London's open spaces resulted in a twofold increase in the proportion of incidents arising in parks between 1917 and 1922. And in 1937—coronation year—there was a marked intensification in the surveillance of West End streets, as officers attempted to cleanse London's public face.[25] Both these years were exceptional: policing consistently focused upon London's urinals.

These broad patterns masked significant differences between local police divisions. Between 1917 and 1957 the Bow and Marlborough Street magistrates, responsible for the central districts patrolled by A, B, C, and E Divisions, heard over half the prosecutions for queer offences. In 1922 both courts tried six cases each month, rising to twenty-one in 1952. East End or suburban magistrates, by contrast, heard only a handful of cases each year.[26] In part, this reflected London's queer geography: most incidents arose in the West End since that was where men gathered in greatest numbers. Yet it was also structured by different patterns of police deployment and knowledge. Central London officers encountered queer men more frequently, were oriented towards sexual offences by divisional officers and thus conducted a more active surveillance of public and commercial spaces. Such operations performed an important ideological function. Central London was the symbolic heart of imperial grandeur, mass consumption, and tourism. Here the queer was a dangerous incursion onto the defining spaces of Britishness, his presence striking because he seemed so out of place. The imagined geography of metropolitan life demanded modes of policing that were simply not deemed necessary elsewhere, containing the visibility of disorderly sexualities and "purifying" the West End.[27] The geography of policing embodied in these statistics fundamentally undermined men's nominal exclusion from the city. If the risk of arrest was ever-present in some places, in others it was distant, intangible, and unlikely.

The Met were certainly not the only agency that maintained surveillance over London's queer spaces, operating alongside a disparate range of other municipal authorities. These institutions, moreover, were supplemented by the quasi-official work of organizations like the National Vigilance Association (NVA), the Central South London Free Church Council, and the Public Morality Council (PMC). Drawing upon the campaigning traditions of evangelical Christianity established in the late nineteenth century, such organizations sought to reaffirm London's moral order. Their agents regularly patrolled streets and commercial venues, attempting to purge sexual dissidence from public space. If their focus was primarily upon female prostitution and working-class "heterosexuality," they periodically turned their attention to the queer men they encountered, gathering information and pressing the police to act against offending behavior at particular cruising grounds, cinemas, and venues.[28]

Crucially, however, the activities of these organizations were always constrained *within* official geographies of regulation, supplementing rather than extending the Met's surveillance. Neither the PMC nor NVA ever initiated independent prosecutions against individuals or venues, relying instead upon the Met or LCC officials to respond to pressure and take further action. Patrolling officers focused upon the same public spaces as the police and were unable to gain access to private residences or many commercial venues. The PMC also tended to employ ex-policemen as patrolling officers—seeking advice from Scotland Yard—who drew on their accumulated experience and replicated police beats.[29] By the 1940s even the PMC—traditionally the most active organization—simply watched London's streets, noting arrest figures and describing the activities of local police. Their active focus shifted away from the streets and toward the propriety of magazines, radio, and theater.[30]

THE "WAYS AND MEANS"

Knowing who the queer was and where he could be found did not, however, make policing straightforward. When Reginald Handford began plain-clothes police work, he received "no definite instructions" from his superiors on how to maintain surveillance over queer men. Just as knowledge of his district was derived from fellow officers, so were the operational tactics he adopted: "My colleagues Slyfield and Mogford used to tell me how to conduct these cases."[31] In performing their duties, such officers forged a flexible set of working rules for orientation. What was known as the "Ways and Means Act" encompassed the informal practices that allowed officers to operate effectively on the street. This was a culture of knowingness, emphasizing the practical utility of beat officers' immersion in the realities of metropolitan lowlife, crime and vice, and of getting the job done over adherence to the formal conventions of policing.[32]

Such tactics were crucial against queer men, whose awareness of and attempts to evade the law presented particular problems of detection. Encounters in urinals, for example, were—as Brigadier General Horwood noted—"very hard . . . to detect . . . You have practically to catch the individual in flagrante delicto."[33] In acting against public sexual cultures and commercial venues alike, officers drew upon their familiarity with urban queer life, utilizing "invisibility, or more specifically . . . dissimulation, making the police presence appear to be something other than it [was]."[34]

Whilst plainclothesmen patrolled streets and parks and kept urinals under external surveillance, making arrests usually demanded a more intimate and active relationship with suspects. Officers regularly entered urinals, discarding the visual signifiers of official status and participating in a public sexual exchange, deliberately replicating men's movements to encourage them to approach or even touch them. In 1954, for example, Detective Constable (DC) Martin entered a urinal in West India Dock Road, standing in the stall next to a suspect, exchanging eye contact and uttering a few words. When the man stroked Martin's penis he arrested him for indecent assault and importuning. Using his own body as bait, Martin became an agent provocateur—a "pretty policeman." From the 1920s onwards, in urinals and on the streets, such tactics were ubiquitous.[35]

Officers, particularly those from E Division or C Division's Clubs Office, used similar tactics against West End cafés and pubs frequented by queer men, entering in plainclothes, observing customers' behavior and participating in queer sociability. In 1932, for example, police constables Chopping and Labbatt were "sent to spy out the land" at a drag ball in Holland Park Avenue.[36] To access this space, they became a part of it. Labbatt "made himself up to look like one of the defendants and adopted their jargon."[37] While drinking in the Mitre, opposite the ballroom, their appearance prompted a man to smile at them. Chopping smiled back. The man approached, asking, "Are you going to the drag tonight?" When Chopping suggested that he was waiting for a friend, the man replied, "Don't wait my dears . . . go over and tell them Betty sent you." He accompanied the constables to the ballroom, introducing them as "two camp boys, friends of mine."[38]

What followed was a remarkable performance, through which Labbatt and Chopping created the illusion of their immersion in queer culture.

Labbatt apparently wore drag, "act[ing] as PC Chopping's Queenie" for
"obvious reasons."[39] They danced together and with other men and participated in several sexual encounters. Chopping danced with "The Bitch," who
"placed his hands inside my trousers."[40] Both drew upon an evident knowledge of queer "jargon." Asked "Have you traded tonight," Labbatt replied,
"Twice with my boyfriend," pointing to Chopping.[41] At the door to the
ballroom—or the urinal—social identities were temporarily unfixed. The
policeman became a mere man, or more accurately, a queer man. Effecting
the transition from outsider to insider, officers opened queer space to surveillance, drawing upon a well-practiced knowledge of queer bodies and
spaces to temporarily enter that world.

Yet a successful prosecution rested upon officers' ability to reestablish the
proper demarcations between police and policed in court, rendering their
informal tactics invisible. Before the Old Bailey, for example, Labbatt and
Chopping sought to remove themselves from their public narratives. Whilst
Labbatt admitted passing as queer, he vehemently denied provoking the men's
actions.[42] Courtroom officials colluded in this all-pervasive silence. The written
notes of the depositions before the West London magistrate included Chopping's
account of John P.'s comment: "Indicating Labbatt he said 'oh hasn't he got a
lovely colour tonight?' Labbatt's face was made up and so was mine." The
information was strangely omitted from the typed transcripts submitted to
the Old Bailey. In mapping the queer for public consumption, the participating figure of the policeman had vanished. The queer was no longer a familiar
urban presence, but a dangerous other. These were policing techniques that,
in Frank Mort's terms, "made homosexuals visible and knowable in ways
which invariably preserved a sense of cultural distance."[43]

Many observers found the dissonance between formal conventions and
informal tactics that was periodically revealed in London's courts problematic. The perils of undercover policing were many: as officers mimicked
queer men to entrap them, mimicry became menace. Magistrates, particularly, were often troubled by a sense that officers had somehow incited
offences within urinals. The police, it seemed, were profoundly implicated
in the commission of the very offences they were supposed to prevent. In a
series of cases between the wars, magistrates expressed growing disquiet
with police practices, particularly the deployment of uncorroborated and
standardized forms of testimony, the apparent fabrication of evidence, and
the use of agents provocateurs, discharging defendants or passing sentence
reluctantly.[44] This critique was strongest in the 1920s, when it intersected with
a "deeper and more serious malaise in the relations between the police . . .
respectable public" and magistracy. Recurrent cases involving "respectable"

men and women arrested for "street offences" suggested instances of police malpractice. The ensuing outcries generated a series of Home Office and Met inquiries into the gap between working rules and legal conventions, culminating in the Street Offences Committee (SOC; 1927) and the Royal Commission on Police Powers and Procedures (RCPPP; 1928).[45]

The case of Frank Champain, combining as it did suggestions of entrapment, uncontrolled working rules, and uncorroborated evidence, brought this "malaise" to a head in 1927. Champain—a schoolmaster, war hero, and former Oxford cricket blue—had been arrested for importuning in urinals around the Adelphi. Convicted at Bow Street and sentenced to three months' hard labor, Champain successfully appealed to the County of London Sessions.[46] The case caused such public controversy that Home Secretary William Joynson-Hicks instructed the SOC, which had been set up to investigate the regulation of female solicitation, to consider the allegations of malpractice against E Division's plainclothesmen.[47] Whilst Champain declined to appear before the committee, Reginald Handford, the constable at the eye of the storm, was subjected to a severe cross-examination.

Handford testified as he had done in court: he had entered the Adelphi Arches urinal to relieve himself, rather than detect queer offenders. It was only Champain's behavior that led him to keep the schoolmaster under observation. Yet his own account implicated Handford in Champain's "offence." Entering the urinal, he stood in the adjacent stall. When Champain spoke to him, offering him a cigarette, he said nothing but left—waiting outside, and then following Champain along the Strand. After walking a short distance Champain turned and walked past Handford, back towards the urinal, beckoning him with his head. Handford again followed him inside, standing in the adjacent stall "to see what happened."[48] The men again spoke, Handford following Champain between urinals before arresting him.[49]

The committee was well aware of the implications here. "This was," observed the chairman, "the third time [Champain] had seen you in the urinal . . . he might very well conclude that you were going to a urinal for an improper purpose too."[50] They remained, however, sympathetic: "The task you have to perform is about as unpleasant as any I can imagine, and I think you have to show considerable tact in performing it."[51] They fudged the issue:

> The detection and suppression of this odious form of crime is attended with peculiar difficulties . . . the offender is likely to refrain from importuning unless he is alone with the person whom he selects . . . It is also difficult . . . if [the

constable] is to bring offenders to justice to avoid stepping the line which divides the detection of a crime which has been committed from the Agent Provocateur who is a party to the commission of the crime.[52]

Whilst "it might be said that by following Mr. Champain about [Handford] led him to believe that he would be a willing participant and placed temptation in his way," the committee did not see the need to "discuss here this large and difficult topic":

> We do not suggest here that a principle can be laid down to cover all cases and all classes of crime. In particular we are not to be taken as finding fault with the course which Constable Handford . . . adopted.[53]

Despite this, their report clearly envisaged a tighter formal control over officers' conduct. "The duty of dealing with cases of male importuning," they noted, "should be entrusted only to police officers who have received very careful instruction from their superiors as to the manner in which they should discharge their very difficult task."[54]

With this proviso, the committee's report both vindicated Handford and tacitly condoned police operations against urinals. The following year the RCPPP endorsed these conclusions. Whilst acknowledging public hostility—agents provocateurs were "objectionable"—they manufactured a discreet silence around their deployment: "There is no evidence of any practice of initiating offences with a view to inducing or entrapping members of the public into committing breaches of the law." They went further, accepting such methods where third-party observation was impossible.[55]

The unease with which many observers viewed informal police tactics was further exacerbated by concern surrounding the effects of officers' contact with vice and criminality. That officers were often unable to fully effect the separation of police and policed in court was, for magistrates, the press, and senior policemen, disquieting. In maintaining surveillance over the city, plainclothesmen seemed to come into dangerous proximity to sexual and moral deviance, their ability to "pass" through this world "expos[ing] them to greater temptations than when they are in uniform."[56] Discarding the visual signs of status threatened an individual's official role and identity. When C Division officers were sensationally exposed taking bribes from West End club owners in 1928, such concerns escalated, dominating the RCPPP:

> Apart . . . from the danger of corruption there is the risk . . . that habitual employment in visiting clubs . . . is likely to have a demoralising effect in the police concerned . . . chosen for their youth . . . dressed in clothes to

which they are unaccustomed and given money to spend freely . . . [offi-cers] are brought into contact with a mode of life very different from their own.[57]

For the young working-class policeman London's glittering nightlife was a dangerous temptress.

The policeman's immersion in queer life was thus a particularly resonant embodiment of wider anxieties, invested with overtones of sexual corruption and moral danger. Habitually, it seemed, officers approached a contagion so strong that it threatened to seduce them to evil, destroying their identities as men. Participating in sexual encounters in urinals was, in this context, a chilling threat. In 1933 W. Oulton, Tower Bridge magistrate, reacted an-grily to a case arising in Bermondsey:

I would protest against [this] method of obtaining evidence . . . While appre-ciating the difficulty of securing reliable testimony and the personal sacrifice of those making it, it is . . . a sacrifice a police officer should not be required to make . . . to invite and endure an insult to his manhood of a gross character. His own self-esteem must suffer and it affects the dignity of the force.[58]

As Oulton's comments suggest, the public revelation of the strategic unfixing of police identities profoundly disrupted the Met's image and sta-tus, threatening to undermine the "self-esteem," masculinity, and in-tegrity of the individual officer and—by implication—the "dignity" of his unit.

There were similar concerns surrounding officers' presence in commercial venues. At the conclusion of the Holland Park trial, Roy remembered:

The judge called these two detectives and praised them. "I am going to rec-ommend your promotion for dealing with this horrible case. I feel so sorry, it must have affected you mentally . . . under no circumstances must you ever be involved in a case again of any description with homosexual men . . . no human being could stand it."[59]

Indeed, as the *News of the World* reported, both Labbatt and Chopping "were so revolted at their experiences that they . . . asked to be relieved of further observation."[60] Their request is significant. Many officers operated on this interface for years, constantly crossing and recrossing the boundaries between police and policed. Such tactics were, moreover, essential to their ability to operate successfully. Labbatt and Chopping's anxiety thus revolved around the adoption of gendered signifiers that undermined their own notions of manliness, particularly when newspaper coverage disrupted the silences that normally existed around police practice. Once their immersion in this milieu became public, the affront to their manhood seemed intolerable.

Throughout the interwar period the terms upon which plainclothes officers could be safely deployed—against all classes of offence—were thus subject to ongoing internal debate. In minimizing the risks inherent to policing sexual offences, some divisional officers had, indeed, tacitly adopted the RCPPP's recommendation that officers be rotated rapidly as early as 1914.[61] This principle was formalized by Lord Trenchard's operational reforms in the early 1930s, which emphasized the importance of rotation, capped the maximum period of deployment, and made covert observation in commercial venues subject to senior officers' authorization.[62] When the boundaries between police and policed were indistinct and unstable, the Met remained, in Superintendent Franklin's terms, "fully alive to the necessity of not keeping men on this unpleasant duty for too long."[63]

THE CHRONOLOGY

The explosive debates of the 1920s had a tangible impact upon the policing of public queer spaces. Between 1922 and 1927, around eighty men were arrested for importuning each year. In 1928, however, arrests dropped dramatically—to fifteen, then to ten in 1929.[64] This was not a response to directives from the Home Office, Scotland Yard or divisional officers but instead reflected the actions of individual policemen. As Assistant Commissioner Norman Kendal recognized

> After the "Champain" case the view of the general rank and file . . . was that if persons were arrested for this particular class of offence the police might be attacked and called liars . . . therefore the duty was unpopular [and] . . . prosecutions were not frequent.[65]

Facing magisterial hostility and a public outcry that deemed their tactics unacceptable, the "rank and file" were simply unwilling—or unable—to enforce the law. Handford's own changing priorities represented this broader shift. Champain's acquittal "was rather a blow," leaving him "hurt" at his own "failure." Before the SOC he initially denied that he had "slacked in [his] efforts to stamp out this sort of crime." His official record told a different story. In the eighteen months before encountering Champain, Handford made around fifteen arrests in the Adelphi Arches. In the following five months he made none. He responded awkwardly to questioning: "I have not seen anyone around there . . . I have concentrated my efforts on suspected persons and pickpockets." He was asked again: "Then you have rather dropped this business?" And his reply was, "Yes sir . . ."[66]

The *institutional* legacy of this experience, moreover, left senior officers remarkably reluctant to police queer men more vigorously. In 1931, Kendal rejected London District Command's demand for greater action: "He did not want to have a very intensive campaign i.e. more intensive than that which [was already ongoing] . . . which would result in a large number of arrests."[67] Despite this, the SOC and RCPPP went a long way toward placating public opinion, creating the foundations for an administrative reorganization of policing. In the 1920s queer men were operationally identified as part of generalized public order concerns, not as a specific problem: plainclothes officers patrolled urinals, streets, and parks only within their wider beats. This changed when plainclothes deployment was reconfigured in the early 1930s, as senior officers attempted to preclude the resurgence of public criticisms by formalizing the structures within which queer space was policed.

In 1930, Kendal thus noted that

> Brigadier Whitehead obtained a squad of men and a CID officer of experience to deal with this class of offence . . . The police employ . . . men who are regarded as absolutely reliable . . . for one month upon this class of work . . . [they] are taken off for the following month.[68]

After this date, C Division had two plainclothes officers "continually employed on this unpleasant duty," periodically increasing their number according to public complaints and local officers' perceptions.[69] What came to be called the "vice squads" had two implications. First, the queer's incursion into the West End was marked as a specific operational concern, requiring an organized response. Second, the formalization of surveillance and the enhanced control of divisional officers coincided with the "sudden revival of police activity," observed by the vigilance campaigner Mrs. Neville-Rolfe. Arrests for importuning rose from 10 in 1929 to 113 in 1930 and 78 in 1931.[70]

If this microanalysis suggests the administrative and cultural basis of changing police activity, there are significant problems in reading changing patterns of surveillance from long-term trends in recorded queer offences—as many historians have attempted. As Pam Cox suggests, "frequent changes in law, court organization and methods of categorizing and recording offences, frustrate statistical continuities."[71] The legal categories within which "crime" was tabulated did not correspond precisely to the statutes used against queer men. Moreover, official data recorded the number of *offences* or *offenders,* when an individual could be charged on multiple counts

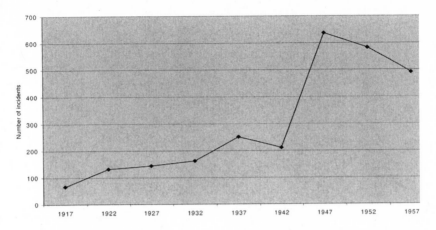

Figure 4. Queer incidents resulting in proceedings at the Metropolitan Magistrates' Courts and City of London Justice Rooms, 1917–57.

and police action on any one occasion could lead to one, two, or more men being arrested. Official figures were highly sensitive to changing charging policies and, as such, represent an inadequate proxy for levels of police surveillance.

It is, however, possible to draw out such chronological shifts from the registers of the Metropolitan Magistrates' Courts and City of London Justice Rooms, which list all cases heard before London's lower courts. This material enables us to calculate the number of queer *incidents:* those individual moments at which a man or men concerned together in an act were arrested and then tried. This focus upon incidents approximates more closely to the intensity with which officers acted against queer spaces, filtering out the statistical distortions inherent to offences and offenders data. The results of my survey of the registers at five-year intervals between 1917 and 1957 are outlined in figure 4 and the appendix.[72]

This survey underscores the importance of operational, administrative, and cultural shifts at the divisional and beat level to the intensity of policing. When the Met returned to peacetime strength and duties at the end of the First World War, the number of queer incidents increased—doubling between 1917 and 1922. Police surveillance remained relatively constant throughout the 1920s, then rose in the 1930s after the operational reorganization discussed above. As officers were called up and resources concentrated on essential duties during the Second World War, attention was deflected from sexual disorder—although C Division retained their "vice squads." Surveillance was, moreover, hindered by the peculiar conditions of the Blitz. In 1940 the PMC noted how "the blackout has led to an increase in street importuning in the West End . . . [since] the difficulties of control have been greatly enhanced."[73]

The most striking trend, however, was the dramatic intensification in police activity after the Second World War. Between 1942 and 1947 the number of incidents tripled—from 211 to 637, remaining throughout the 1950s twice as high as the interwar level. To contemporaries and historians alike, the British state seemed to have embarked upon a "witch hunt" against the "homosexual." This notion of an unprecedented persecution draws upon two key assumptions. First, that it was driven by politicians and senior officials, coinciding with the "devoutly Catholic" Theabald Mathew's tenure as DPP from 1944 and peaking with the appointment of David Maxwell-Fyffe as home secretary and John Nott-Bower as commissioner of police in 1953. Second: that the geography of law enforcement was qualitatively different—agents provocateurs were deployed for the first time and more efforts were made to prosecute private sexual offences.[74]

I do not want to dispute the very real experience of the 1950s as, in Michael S.'s words, the "intolerant period."[75] Yet the assumptions underpinning the "witch hunt" are problematic, overstating the differences between pre- and postwar policing and obscuring the exact mechanisms whereby the number of incidents increased. The intensification of surveillance did not coincide with Mathew's appointment but rather followed the Met's return to peacetime operations. The appendix suggests that police activity peaked in the late 1940s and was—as Nott-Bower observed at the time—actually being relaxed by 1953.[76] Moreover, the geography of policing remained unchanged. Agents provocateurs had operated for decades; most incidents arose in urinals, parks, and streets; private spaces remained practically invisible. There was nothing unprecedented about this: officers targeted the same people and places they always had.

The narrative's epistemological bases are equally shaky, relying, as it does, upon the explanatory power of senior officials' and politicians' "homophobia"—implicit in Weeks's characterization of Maxwell-Fyffe as "fervently anti-homosexual."[77] Certainly, official rhetoric was suffused with vitriolic hostility towards the queer. But the relationship of public pronouncements to street policing was more complex than this allows. The comments Weeks takes as evidence of Maxwell-Fyffe's "anti-homosexual[ity]" were not expressed as a *reason* to increase police surveillance but represented his *response* to rising prosecution figures—they followed rather than pre-ceded policing shifts. In November 1953, for example, Maxwell-Fyffe "called a private meeting of Metropolitan Magistrates . . . to discuss moral offences in London" since "judges and magistrates were *commenting upon the apparent increase in vice*."[78] Patrick Higgins similarly reads Mathew's anxious reflection on this "increase in vice" before the Wolfenden Committee retro-spectively. Here, Higgins found the "smoking gun" he was looking for: "The piece of the jigsaw which explains why the number of . . . homosexual offences rose so dramatically . . . a highly-placed moralist with a very spe-cific axe to grind."[79] Certainly, this public discourse justified and fed back into police operations, but it cannot fully explain them.

There is simply no evidence that the DPP, home secretary, or commis-sioner of police ordered officers to target queer men more vigorously. Indeed, their ability to do so was limited, as they themselves recognized. In 1931 Archibald Bodkin, then DPP, outlined how

> The DPP is not . . . generally concerned with this class of offence until *after* evidence has been obtained which would warrant a prosecution . . . even then [he] was not ordinarily concerned except in indictable cases of sodomy or acts of gross indecency. Most of the charges arising . . . have been . . . for the summary offence of importuning.[80]

In 1954 Mathew himself noted the "relatively few" cases his department handled—those of "special gravity, difficulty and importance": 260 out of 1052 "unnatural offences," 246 out of 1129 "attempted offences," and 73 out of 2597 cases of "male indecency" in the previous four years.[81]

So what happened after the Second World War? The key changes occurred at the divisional level, reflecting the prosaic operational decisions made by district officers, their perception of local streets, and the consequent redeployment of beat officers. In the mid-1940s, C Division officers began to express concern at queer men's increasing visibility on West End streets. As they returned to peacetime operations the existing "vice squads" were thus enlarged. The result was a twofold increase in the number of incidents charged at Bow Street between 1942 and 1947.

C Division had always acted vigorously against queer spaces. The inten-sification in policing in the 1940s, however, gained greatest impetus through operational changes within F and B Divisions. In 1949 Nott-Bower noted a "considerable increase" in the number of arrests in B Division "due to the increased police activity . . . increased patrols having been authorised because it was suspected that the situation in that division was becoming worse."[82] Whilst officers had patrolled Victoria Station since

1918, they stepped up their activities after the war: the number of incidents occurring there rose from 18 to 114 between 1942 and 1947. Simultaneously, officers' developing knowledge of local queer cultures meant surveillance expanded to include previously unpoliced locations—a cluster of urinals around South Kensington Tube Station. This process was echoed in F Division, where officers began to patrol a similar group of urinals in Hammersmith for the first time.[83]

The result of these changes was an unprecedented increase in the number of incidents charged before the West London magistrate: six in 1942 increased to 100 in 1947 and 168 in 1952. Around 95 percent of these arose in urinals. The court's share of the number of incidents for London as a whole increased from 3 percent to 30 percent.[84] In this sense the notion of a "witch hunt" is misleading. The "persecution" of queer men worked from the bottom of the criminal justice hierarchy up, not the top down. And if there were faint echoes of increased police activity in other London courts, the rising number of incidents was overwhelmingly driven by local operational changes in only three police divisions. To a remarkable extent their activities were, moreover, geographically confined.

CONCLUSION

Between 1917 and 1957 hundreds of men were imprisoned for sexual or public order offences committed in London's public, commercial, or residential spaces. Many more encountered the law informally—warned by policemen in a urinal, witnessing a nightclub raid, hearing news from friends, or reading the court cases that regularly appeared in the *News of the World* or *Illustrated Police News*. The risk of arrest could seem ever-present, bracing many men's everyday lives with a crippling perpetual anxiety. In December 1935 Edwin H., a fifty-nine-year-old taxi driver, and Thomas P., a bank messenger, aged forty-four, were arrested whilst "committing an act of grave impropriety in H.'s taxi in Lambeth Palace Road." After being remanded on bail, their case came before the Lambeth magistrate. "Counsel . . . stated that H. had been found dead in the Thames and that P., suffering from the effects of immersion in the river, was in hospital." Rather than risk public exposure, imprisonment, ostracism by friends and family, and dismissal at work, Thomas and Edwin chose to take their lives together in the icy waters of the Thames.[85]

It is hard to see beyond individual tragedies like this. To focus solely on such suffering, however, overestimates the homogeneity of the law's impact upon queer urban culture. Certainly, formal legislation implied a mode of surveillance that was draconian, pervasive, and repressive. Yet the assumption that the British state engaged in a concerted campaign against queer men, culminating in the "witch hunt" after the Second World War, misrepresents the organization and nature of police operations. Even when the number of incidents resulting in court proceedings began to rise again in the late 1940s there was no attempt to suppress "homosexuality" per se, and the vagaries of policing on the ground level continued to attenuate the law's potential force. Quite simply, there was no witch hunt. The result, as this chapter has suggested, was that the law's impact was ambiguous and contradictory. Rather than being constant and universal, the extent and intensity of surveillance varied according to an individual's location within the city, the time of day, his appearance, and his demeanor. The risk of encountering the law was greater in the West End rather than the East End, in the urinal rather than the furnished room, at night rather than during the day, if wearing makeup rather than conventionally masculine in appearance. In these respects, the geographical and cultural organization of policing was remarkably consistent.

Men thus experienced the law very differently—an unfelt force or a blighting ever-present danger—depending on their class, age, and status, the lives they led, and the spaces they frequented. Policing fell most heavily upon those who relied on public space for sex and sociability, because they were working-class, young, or married. Those who could afford private rooms, join exclusive clubs, or rejected the disreputable public realm could remain officially invisible. If keenly aware of the legal situation, the law could be a nebulous, distant presence, not affecting them, their friends, or the places they frequented—an irritant more for the stigma it conferred rather than any tangible risk.

If personal experience, gossip, and newspaper reports highlighted London's perils, they simultaneously offered queer men some indication of where and how they could evade surveillance. Police procedures produced and institutionalized a particular geography of danger and safety, publicity and privacy, secrecy and disclosure, within which queer urban culture could take hold and develop. The law was not the only influence on that culture—or even the most important one. Despite this, it exerted a profound influence upon the cultural and geographical organization of queer urban life. Not all may have realized it—though most did—but on entering queer London men also entered an ongoing relationship with the agencies that sought to regulate it.

PART 2

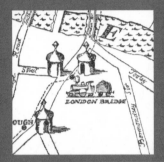

PLACES

"London," Hunter Davies observed in 1966, "is the magnet which attracts queers in Britain."[1] His impression was born out in contemporary sociological investigations. In the late 1950s and early 1960s, Michael Schofield interviewed a number of men for the studies that became *A Minority* (1960) and *Sociological Aspects of Homosexuality* (1965). Thirty-nine of what Schofield labeled his homosexual-others sample group lived in London. Of these, 69 percent were born elsewhere and had moved to the capital, compared to an average of 54 percent in the 1951 census. Out of the twenty-four men he interviewed who had been born in small towns and villages, twenty-one had moved to London.[2]

What drove these migration patterns? In the mid-1950s, John Chesterman was a student in York, "educating" himself in being queer.

> It was a difficult business because there were no signposts . . . to tell you what to do or where to go. I used to go to London . . . with the . . . crazy attitude that I just had to go in and I would let whatever happened to me happen.

Through his trips Chesterman learned "that I wasn't alone . . . I knew that the next step was to find as many other gay people as I could. And it eventually meant living in London—*it had to*." London exercised a captivating hold on Chesterman's imagination, as on that of many other young men. Through the press and his own travels, he encountered a vibrant world of street life and commercial venues—places to meet other men. This was a world he simply "*had to*" become part of. Despite having an established social circle, he and his friends found the provincial atmosphere "suffocat-

ing," and would "talk endlessly about how we were going to escape . . .
escape meant London." In the early 1950s, Chesterman did "escape," moving into a flat in Notting Hill Gate. Like Cyril L., he experienced this as a
turning point, at which "the whole world widened all the way round me."[3]

For men like Chesterman, London's allure was its status as the site of a
rich queer urban culture. But how did this world come to exist and take the
shape it did? Historians have mapped the formation of queer social worlds
onto the process of urban material and cultural change, connecting the
"modern homosexual" and the modern city. If this macrolevel analysis is
suggestive, however, in treating the city primarily as a large-scale and singular unit, it obscures the specificities of the relationship between urban culture and sexual practices. The four chapters that follow attempt to develop
a more nuanced, complex, and microlevel geography of queer London.
Exploring the ways in which modern urban culture generated particular
spaces of sociability and sexual encounter between men, I conceptualize the
city as a series of related but discrete sites of interaction, danger, and pleasure: the flux and transience of the urban crowd—that public world of
streets, parks, and urinals; the sites of modern consumer culture—the commercial realm of bars and nightclubs; the unique commercial space of
London's bath houses; and residential spaces and the separation between
public and private life which, for many observers, was a defining trait of
modern British culture. In sum, I delineate four characteristic spheres
within the modern city, tracing how each of these shaped the organization
and character of queer life in different ways—and how the results were both
liberating and exclusionary.

The distinction between public and private space is, indeed, a theme that
runs throughout part 2. My taxonomy of the sites of sex and sociability is, in
part, organized around that distinction: in moving from the urinal to the
bachelor flat, the chapters move across the putative boundaries between public and private life. In exploring the geography of queer urban culture, however, we need to rethink this binary opposition, for these boundaries were
unstable and problematic. The queer body was a public body, subject to the
potential force of the law even in the nominally private realm of the home.
By contrast, many men were often able to find precarious moments of privacy
for sexual encounters in the most public of urban spaces. Queer lives always
occupied spaces that were simultaneously and to varying degrees public *and*
private, subject to surveillance *and* invisible, dangerous *and* safe. Throughout
I explore how these tensions were worked out at different sites, how men
reworked the boundaries between public and private in seeking the space to
socialize or have sex in safety, and how their ability to do so varied massively.

As this discussion suggests, queer urban culture could only take shape within the constraints generated by the operations of the Met and those other agencies that sought to regulate the city. I focus below on how the modern city shaped the geography of queer life but continue to emphasize the role of municipal authorities in structuring where men met and how they moved through the city. If London became a "magnet" for queer men, it was only through these intersecting processes, and the outcome was never unequivocally affirmative.[4]

2

~~~~~~~~~~~~~~~~~~~~~~~

GEOGRAPHIES
OF PUBLIC SEX

ROBERT'S STORY

As a young student during the First World War, Robert Hutton regularly wandered the bustling streets of London's West End.

> Men in uniform, hucksters, hawkers, prostitutes and people like myself, killing time and enjoying the crowds, jostled and strolled from the Pavilion to Leicester Square and back again . . . When dusk fell a feeling of restlessness and excitement crept over me.[1]

Like those soldiers, "hucksters," and "people like myself" he glimpsed in the crowds, Hutton was drawn by the district's imaginary status as a space of pleasure, leisure, and consumption, a public realm opened up by the underground railway and omnibus since the 1870s. Its unrivalled concentration of retail outlets and sites of commercialized leisure—bars, theaters, restaurants, and cinemas—meant the West End embodied modern consumer culture, its status emblematized by the neon advertising billboards that transformed Piccadilly Circus into a kaleidoscope of light and color. In this new urban landscape men and women of all classes found opportunities for public sociability, spectatorship, and pleasure. As H. V. Morton noted in 1932, "the bright lights call them night after night, if only to saunter for an innocent hour in the slow, exciting crowds."[2]

For Hutton, his immersion in these "slow, exciting crowds" generated the heightened sensations of arousal evident in the "excitement and restlessness" recalled years later. Amidst the bustling flow of humanity his gaze was fleetingly yet repeatedly drawn to the men who passed by, anonymous and distant yet tantalizingly close. His experiences of London's streets actuated disconcerting desires; gripped by an unexplainable longing, Hutton never wanted to return to his parent's suburban home.

> Some day I promised myself I would stay as long as I liked and mingle with the crowds instead of being . . . an onlooker . . . I would have liked to get into conversation with one or other of the young men in uniform and once or twice, I tried it, but did not get much response. They were looking for something and in a vague way so was I. I hoped that some day I might meet someone who felt the same way.[3]

In 1916 he did "meet someone." Browsing at the bookstall in Victoria Station, Hutton glanced at a "well-dressed man of 35." The man returned his gaze, and they entered into conversation. From this apparently unnoticed exchange in one of London's busiest stations, the men found a transient moment of privacy elsewhere. Walking up to Belgrave Square, they had sex amongst the trees. In so doing they echoed the movements of countless young working-class heterosexual couples as they negotiated the constraints of the family home. "Only in the misty corners of the thickening streets," suggested Thomas Burke in 1922, "can [such couples] attain the solitude they seek . . . For the young lover . . . the street is more private than the home."[4]

In Hutton's brief encounter lie the foundations of a complex and vibrant public queer culture. If this culture intersected and overlapped with wider forms of urban sociability it remained, nonetheless, distinctive in its social and spatial organization. Men's use of London's streets, parks, and urinals echoed the role of public space within urban life per se. Just as the West End drew crowds in their thousands, so the streets of crowded working-class neighborhoods were also bustling centers of communal interaction. Ruth Bowley noted how "among the free amusement centres . . . an important place must be given to the streets . . . which in the evenings present a gay appearance . . . the main roads are full of people."[5] Here young men and women gathered on street corners or walked the parks or local high streets, talking, gazing at shop windows and each other in the ritual courtship "monkey parade."[6]

If queer men were drawn into the public domain for reasons identical to those with whom they shared London's parks and streets—because they were excluded from commercial or private space—the perils they encountered there were unique. In public, men negotiated pervasive networks of formal and informal surveillance, and the city's possibilities were tempered by ever-present risks. Subject to ongoing surveillance by policemen, purity campaigners, and park-keepers, London's public spaces held the ubiquitous danger of arrest. Hutton himself was imprisoned twice after being arrested in the West End. Such pressures were reinforced by the potentially hostile reactions attendant on being identified as queer by other occupants of public space. Between the wars violent late-night assaults in Hyde Park were regularly reported in the press, leaving little doubt as to the victim's sexual character. In 1936, for example, DDI Kidd noted the "doubtful character" of two men who had refused to make official complaints to police, fearing the consequences of a court appearance: an elderly gentleman mugged at the meeting ground and a butler found badly beaten.[7]

Awareness of such risks gained from newspapers, direct experience and informal gossip profoundly influenced the shape of the world men forged in London's public spaces. As they moved through the city, men constantly made tactical decisions on where to meet and how to comport themselves. Operating on the precarious border between invisibility (to passersby and police) and visibility (to each other), such practices temporarily reconfigured the boundaries between public and private, resolving the tension between peril and possibility to ensure that men *could* meet and interact in safety. This was the basis upon which they forged an equivocally vital world that interwove opportunities for sex and sociability.

Such practices made public space central to *both* metropolitan queer cultures *and* pejorative notions of sexual difference. For many bourgeois observers the regular newspaper reports of men arrested having sex in urinals or parks positioned the queer within a realm coded as sordid and loveless. Yet their vitriol effaced the ways in which many men experienced public queer culture as a very tangible—if ambiguous—site of communality and affirmation. Through their perpetual repetition, even the most fleeting and anonymous encounters established a transient yet enduring sense of affiliation. Despite his later arrests, Hutton reflected upon that first encounter in Belgrave Square in terms far removed from those articulated by contemporary observers:

> It was as if a curtain had been drawn back . . . I could see clearly what had been partially obscured before. . . . this was what . . . I had been looking for . . . I knew now . . . that other people . . . felt the same way as I did. I was no longer alone.[8]

STREETS

As Hutton's experiences suggest, the West End was the heart of public queer life in the first half of the twentieth century. Following established metropolitan trajectories, the district drew men from across London and beyond. In the busy thoroughfares and circulating crowds they found a legitimate reason for their public presence, just like the female prostitutes who also walked the district. Some men exploited these opportunities and the West End's reputation as a cosmopolitan and transgressive space in order to assert a highly visible presence. In 1939, for example, officers from the PMC observed twenty-two men "painted and powdered and . . . wearing high-healed shoes" as they patrolled Piccadilly.[9]

Yet if the West End was the characteristic habitat of what were termed queans, screamers, or pansies, most of those drawn out on the town—"up west"—preferred to avoid risking such visibility. The hegemonic image of the "West End poof" meant that those who conformed to the dominant sartorial and cultural demands of masculinity remained hidden from the public gaze even as they occupied the streets in considerable numbers. Bourgeois gentlemen strolled the streets looking for partners, conventionally attired and never drawing attention. Working-class youths met on street corners and picked up middle-class "steamers." Invisible—for the most part—to passersby and policemen, they developed tactics that ensured they remained visible to each other. In the perpetual flux and movement of strangers, queer men could move unnoticed while making the streets bustling centers of queer life. Passing in the crowd, they exchanged recognition signals of movement, gesture, and gaze, in a complex spatial poetics that utilized the conventions of street life to simultaneously reveal and conceal their actions.

Such practices cohered upon the gaze men exchanged as they passed each other—Edward Stevenson's "psychic-sexual interrogation."[10] Within the crowd, the ability to see—and be seen by—other men animated specific forms of social interaction. Those men interviewed by the sociologist Michael Schofield in the 1950s repeatedly attested to this. Two-thirds believed they could recognize other queer men, citing signals like their "liquid" or "searching" eyes. In describing how they identified each other, the eyes or a look were mentioned 62 times, followed by gestures (36), intuition (28), walk (25), clothes (14), and vocabulary (8).[11]

Alongside such exchanges, men utilized the social organization of street life, concealed in the crowds yet signaling intent through their movements in relation to others. John Alcock explained:

> You'd see somebody . . . look at them and . . . stop and look in a shop window . . . let them pass you and if they looked in the next window you knew that you were fairly on . . . Go up to the next shop window and . . . make some comment . . . if you were interested . . . then off you'd go.[12]

In 1937 Ashley P. was thus in Piccadilly "looking at a shop window when a young man came up and spoke to me. We talked about things exhibited for sale . . . and walked together [towards] . . . Leicester Square."[13] Retail districts legitimized the complex interplay between motion and immobility demanded by cruising. On busy streets—defined legally and culturally as avenues of movement—loitering in a doorway or on a corner disrupted the normative order of urban space, risking unwanted attention. Plate glass display windows provided reason to stand. It was, perhaps, no coincidence that men were regularly found cruising on busy shopping streets like Piccadilly, Regent Street, and Oxford Street.

They also relied upon legitimate everyday social interactions between strangers, transforming requests for a light, directions, or the time into recognized approaches designed to ascertain whether another man were interested. In 1935 Ernest R. followed a man onto Hampstead Heath, looking, asking for the time, and then offering a cigarette.[14] Since most men smoked the offer of a cigarette or asking for a light was commonplace—a queer version of the romantic cliché of gentlemen lighting a lady's cigarette.[15] In 1922 the clergyman Thomas R. was thus walking across Hyde Park when he passed "a young man sitting . . . taking a cigarette from a packet [he] . . . asked me if I had a match." Thomas lit the cigarette, sitting down with the man and kissing him.[16] The ubiquity of asking a stranger for a light ensured such interactions never appeared out of the ordinary.

Their necessary sensitivity to such visual minutiae meant men often assumed they possessed some magical ability to recognize each other. If doctors and officials occasionally recognized this, they found it mystifying. Such issues absorbed the Wolfenden Committee. They heard how Police Constable Butcher

> watched one [homosexual] for an awful long time . . . and never saw him speak to a soul. When I did eventually get him and asked him how he accosts these men he said, "I can tell if a man is interested in me just by looking at him." There is a certain look among these people and if they look and the look is returned that is quite enough.[17]

When questioned, Carl Winter and Peter Wildeblood drew a discreet veil over the exact processes at work, citing a generalized "telepathy" or "instinct."[18] Whatever they implied, approaching a stranger was always a tense and potentially dangerous moment, occasionally with near-comical results. Alcock, walking along Regent Street, exchanged glances with a man ahead of him. The man stopped before a shop window. Alcock approached: "'Have you got a light?' . . . 'Yes. It's twenty to nine.'"[19]

Through such practices men transformed the capital's busiest streets into places they could find partners—or simply see other men—without most Londoners ever being aware of their presence. Crowded West End streets brought very different men together—symbolized by the trade, queans, and respectable queers who walked Piccadilly. This broad convergence, however, masked the divergent character of different streets. Soldiers from the Brigade of Guards, for example, may have walked Piccadilly but tended to remain around Hyde Park Corner at its western end or on the terrace below the National Gallery in Trafalgar Square. Queans, by contrast, gathered further east—in the Circus itself or on Soho's narrow streets—where they drew less attention. The Embankment and Trafalgar Square, where many destitute men gathered or slept, were known haunts of rough trade.[20]

The microgeography of public queer life was reconfigured constantly as men reacted to police operations and the West End's changing character. Pat remembered how "every rent boy would vanish" from Piccadilly Circus periodically.[21] Sites of public interaction were, in part, determined by the shifting geography of queer commercial sociability. In the 1920s, for example, the concentration of venues on the Strand drew many men to the surrounding streets and alleys, particularly those around Charing Cross and the Adelphi.[22] Similarly, in 1953 the MP William Field had moved between urinals in Leicester Square and nearby bars like the Standard and Queen's. The Standard's popularity drew so many men to Coventry Street that police nicknamed it the "Standard Front."[23]

If other streets were known cruising grounds, particularly around the rooming districts off Bayswater Road and Praed Street, the only district that approached the West End's importance was around Waterloo Station.[24] While Waterloo Road itself was a bustling thoroughfare and local commercial center, the station and railway created a honeycomb of narrow alleyways, often thrown into darkness by the tracks passing overhead. After the opening of the Union Jack Club—a military leave hostel—in 1907, the district altered significantly, "the neighbourhood becom[ing] infested with women who tempted young soldiers," in one magistrate's words.[25] The huge numbers of servicemen frequenting the surrounding streets and coffee stalls simultaneously attracted many queer men, transforming the area into a renowned cruising ground between the wars. In 1926, for example, the local magistrate railed against those "pests of society" inhabiting Waterloo Road after a policeman had observed William K. and William L. "and others of their kind standing about together near the [Union Jack] Club at all hours."[26]

COTTAGES

Although men met in London's busiest streets, they could never have sex there. For those excluded from residential space, the public city thus became the necessary locale of tenuous moments of privacy. Negotiating the ever-changing risk of observation, they sought out the fissures within the urban landscape, gleaning contingent moments of safety where surveillance collapsed in the darkness or built environment, generating a mobile realm of illicit sexuality. Walking down Whitechapel High Street, John G. asked Michael R., "Is there any dark corners?" They found an alleyway "in complete darkness."[27] Such transient niches of privacy—where men *could* have sex—were thus created across the city, on South West India Dock Quay,[28] or Shadwell Park Stairs in the Rotherhithe Tunnel, for example.[29]

Yet they also forged networks of sites where the sexual possibilities were institutionalized, if precarious: London's public urinals. The urinals constructed in streets and stations by municipal authorities in the late nineteenth century were a liminal social space in which a unique interplay between public and private sustained complex opportunities for privacy and sexual encounter. Placed on public avenues of movement to allow Londoners to circulate within the city, moral and sanitary sensibilities positioned urination and defecation at one remove from this flow—in an alleyway and/or physically partitioned from the street. Partially concealed from public view, the urinal was somewhere it was legitimate to stand still amidst perpetual movement, where there would always be other men, and where it was a prerequisite to have one's cock out.[30]

The constant use of urinals allowed men looking for homosex to enter and leave without arousing suspicion. Simultaneously, however, there was always the risk of unwanted observers entering. To insulate themselves from this danger, men deployed tactics that allowed them to meet and forge transient moments of privacy. In 1933, for example, four men were in the urinal at the Black Lion pub on Kilburn High Road. Two left. "C. watched the[m] walk out from the yard through some ornamental holes in the iron sheets which form the front of the urinal." Alone, the men began to kiss, still watching through the holes. When a man entered the yard they parted, entering separate stalls.[31] Such reverse surveillance could be more elaborate, with one man acting as lookout. Police knew of such problems. The urinal on Fair Street (Bermondsey) was "of such a nature . . . as to lend itself to acts of indecency . . . [a] round iron structure with small holes from which any approach can be observed."[32]

Within the urinal men insinuated a word, gesture, or movement into public space, demonstrating their desires to those in the know through established modes of symbolic exchange. In the Fair Street urinal two plainclothes policemen were standing in the stalls when S. entered. He "left the stall in which he was standing and went round towards PC Cooper, stopping in the stall on his left hand side . . . S. said to PC Cooper, 'will you give me a light please?'" When Cooper lit the cigarette, S. touched his penis.[33] Movement, gaze, and gesture constituted an effective urinal etiquette, appraising the other man's interest, temporarily rendering the public private.

Men's movements between urinals were further informed by their awareness of the need for invisibility. A friend told John to "do one at a time . . . [and] take a bus to the next one. Not like . . . the silly queans . . . who go in and out like the weatherman."[34] Michael S. recounted a salutary story about Baker Street underground toilets:

> The police . . . used to come and look underneath the doors . . . if there were four feet . . . they'd bash it down . . . This man . . . always took two carrier bags . . . he told his partner to stand with his feet in the . . . bags . . . when the police looked all they saw were two feet and two carrier bags.[35]

The persistent reproduction of such tactics created a complex and extensive network of sexual opportunities. Many of these were in West End streets or tube stations like Piccadilly Circus and Victoria.[36] Unlike commercial venues, however—overwhelmingly concentrated in central London—men used urinals across the city, often in local parks or pubs like Deptford's Railway Tavern.[37] If urinals were thus the most geographically accessible queer space, they differed greatly in their social and cultural organization. In the 1950s, for example, dozens of men were arrested in urinals in the City—London's financial center—particularly Bank and Blackfriars stations. All of them worked in nearby banks and offices, often living in suburban London. Most were clerks, but there were several businessmen, stockbrokers, and solicitors, many of who were married. Most were cruising *during* the working day—at lunch or immediately after work.[38] By contrast, most men arrested in urinals within the jurisdiction of Old Street Police Court—Victoria Park, Islington Green, and Grove Road—were from nearby working-class neighborhoods like Dalston or Islington and were usually found late at night. There was also a small number of men from nearby Jewish neighborhoods. This intersection between class, ethnicity, and locality was evident in one case from Woods Buildings (Stepney) in 1947: Aaron G. was a Jewish shop assistant from Raven Road, Charles B. a laborer from Newington Crescent.[39]

As they moved between London's urinals, men's experiences thus generated finely calibrated cognitive maps, imaginary and habitual sexual geographies. Billy W., for example, walked between Taylor's Buildings, Leicester Square, and Rose Street in November 1932.[40] Tom Driberg had his established circuit—from the Astoria, via urinals opposite the Garrick Club and by the Coliseum, finishing in "Of Alley."[41] Some produced more formal guides, hand-drawn maps of the queer city. In 1928 Emlyn Williams heard of an antique dealer, nicknamed "Miss Footsore," who had mapped London's urinals, calling them "Comfort Stations of the Cross."[42]

The most remarkable of these documents—perhaps the first queer city guide—was published by Routledge in 1937: *For Your Convenience: A Learned Dialogue Instructive to all Londoners and London Visitors*. Ostensibly it records a conversation between Mr. Mumble, "doyen of the Theleme Club," and a young commercial traveler. Mumble is seeking enlightenment on "some of the things a man often wants to know . . . [like] what to do if one were walking through Wigmore Street after three cups of tea." He is fortunate. His companion is preparing "section plans of the London streets, suitable for the pocket . . . marking with a green dot the precise location of every refuge."[43]

Written pseudonymously by the urban observer Thomas Burke, *For Your Convenience* offers an ironic—if heavily veiled—indictment of contemporary sexual mores: "It's queer that this shyness persists."[44] If never spoken aloud, "homosexuality" is a pervasive open secret in the text. Mumble is toasted "to you sir and another kind love." An "aesthetic revulsion" towards the urinal recalls Wilde. Pilsner or Munchner, the young man's favorite drinks, denote Berlin's notorious queer subculture, although he admits, "I do not partake with the freedom of the German student."[45] In positioning the reader within queer cultural traditions, such signs enable an alternative reading—a gleefully knowing play on the urinal's manifest function. Mumble's quest can be read as a justified concern not to be caught short, within a humorous exposition on municipal services. Burke guided men to London's urinals safe in the knowledge that most readers would not comprehend anything else.

Yet those in the know found an alternative. Mumble heard how

> Places of that kind, which have no attendants, afford excellent rendezvous to people who wish to meet out of doors and yet escape the eye of the Busy . . . to exchange information out of earshot of their friends, or the observation of the Dicks.[46]

Placed beyond "earshot" and "observation" by plainclothes "Dicks," London's urinals were revealed as potentially private sites for the enactment of queer desire. Burke even offers a guided tour, starting from Ludgate Circus

> up Fleet Street . . . at the foot of Fetter Lane . . . between the Law Courts and St. Clement Danes . . . Wellington Street . . . Charring Cross Station or the Trafalgar Square Subway . . . Villiers Street in Embankment Gardens . . . Charring Cross Road by the Garrick Theatre . . . Leicester Square . . . Piccadilly Circus Subway . . . Oxford Circus . . . Great Marlborough Street . . . Green Park Gate . . . [47]

The tour is complemented by a hand-drawn map, framed by a louche pair of reclining sweeps: amidst the familiar sites of metropolitan power, culture, and grandeur, London's urinals are marked as small green enclosures (figure 5).

Just as he formalized men's geographical knowledge of these sexual possibilities, so Burke also codified their knowledge of the tactics needed to use these sites safely. Mumble is warned of the dangers—"they set watchers on the spot they are considering"—and told how to avoid them.[48] Urinals on Euston Road and the Victoria Embankment were "visible to natives and foreigners."[49] He is redirected to safer sites in "Buckingham Gate alongside the Albert Tavern . . . hidden behind two . . . telephone booths."[50] This was, he noted, "a game for the steady and contemplative temperament . . . the leisurely step and quiet eye."[51]

PARK LIFE

Like all Londoners, many queer men relied on the city's open spaces as sites of public sociability. During daylight they strolled with friends or relaxed on the grass, by the ponds, or on benches. After dusk they looked for partners and found moments of privacy. LCC keepers regularly encountered men having sex in parks across London, including Battersea Park, Peckham Rye, Hackney Marshes, and Clapham Common.[52] In so doing, such men were part of that far wider public sexual culture forged by young men and women escaping the constraints of the family home. Between February 1918 and August 1919, for example, sixty-nine "heterosexual" couples were prosecuted for indecency offences on Hampstead Heath, while there were only two instances involving same-sex couples.[53] Here, unlike the urinals, queer men shared their sites of public sociability with disparate other groups.

Of all these open spaces, Hyde Park and Hampstead Heath stood out for their longevity and the scale of the public culture that developed within their bounds. Hyde Park, for example, had been a meeting place since 1800.

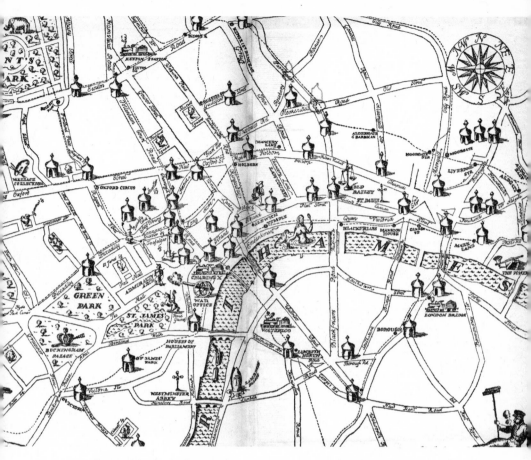

Figure 5. Endpaper, [Thomas Burke], *For Your Convenience: A Learned Dialogue, Instructive to all Londoners and London Visitors, Overheard in The Thélème Club and Taken Down Verbatim by Paul Pry* ([London]: George Routledge and Sons Ltd., 1937).

By 1932 police detected around thirty queer incidents there each year.[54] Both were massive, covered with trees and undergrowth that made it easy to find a secluded spot off the busy paths that crisscrossed the grass. Often—if careful—men could find concealment during daylight. Emlyn Williams regularly met men in Hyde Park, "drift[ing] towards the casual fraternisation when stealth had to set in and newspapers were flung negligently across."[55] Yet it was at night, when the crowds thinned, the darkness cloaked men's movements and the risk of surveillance abated, that the parks fully came alive. In 1915, for example, police watched two men "proceed to a secluded part of the park where they were lost sight of."[56]

This case suggests the productive ways in which the parks' cultural and physical organization informed a distinctive sexual microgeography, predicated upon the interplay between public and private. One of the men had been

> walking up and down amongst the crowd at the Lecture Ground . . . looking into the faces of well-dressed men . . . [then] st[anding] at the entrance to the Gents Lavatory . . . repeatedly smil[ing] in the faces of men entering and leaving.[57]

Amidst the crowds watching the speakers or strolling the walks, men could move unnoticed yet pass close enough to exchange glances. They picked each other up along West Carriage Road or the Monkey Walk, at the Meeting Ground, Hyde Park Corner or Marble Arch, before seeking safety elsewhere.[58] Men met at the fixed sites on the Heath's fringes, like the seating enclosure near Whitestone Pond, before moving further into the wilderness.[59]

Through such movements men carefully negotiated the city's possibilities and dangers, maintaining a precarious balance between meeting others (a selective publicity) and finding moments of safety. In 1929, Stephen L. and Herbert W. met at Hyde Park Corner. Exchanging glances, Herbert asked for a light. Inviting Stephen into the park he told him "we will enter by the Albert Gate—there are too many nosy parkers at Hyde Park Corner." Within the park he reiterated his concern for concealment: "We will cross Rotten Row—it's not so light there the other side." They walked to chairs opposite the Serpentine under a tree away from the paths.[60] This was a distinctly queer topography that enabled their successful movements through the park, a matrix of functional spaces that interwove public and private in very different proportions.

If men could never fully escape the risk of arrest or assault, their *relative* safety made London's open spaces notorious for their sexual possibilities. In streets and urinals, where the risk of observation was always greater, sexual interactions were usually limited to mutual masturbation, avoiding the need to remove clothing. The parks, by contrast, afforded the time and space for more intimate encounters: they were the only place where men were regularly found having oral, intercrural, or anal sex. In 1926, for example, a policeman patrolling the Heath saw "B. sitting on a chair with his trousers undone [and] his person . . . out. C. was kneeling down in front of him with his head between B.'s legs [and his] person . . . in his mouth."[61] The proliferation of such practices generated a tangible sense of license and excess. Paul Lanning remembered the "orgies in the undergrowth" in 1930s Epping Forest: "Everything happened . . . Trousers down, cocks up, cocks in . . .

Masturbation, sodomy, sucking."[62] The Thames towpath between Hammersmith and Putney was another "riverside brothel" until police operations in the 1950s.[63]

To focus upon the sexual interactions within the parks, however, fails to adequately comprehend their place within public queer cultures. As for all Londoners, the parks were important sites of sociability. Hyde Park, in particular, was popular on weekends, part of an established social round where men strolled, met friends, and discreetly admired each other. After a night out in the West End, Alex Purdie would regularly walk there with friends on Sunday mornings, before lunch at Lyons' Coventry Street Corner House.[64] Kenneth Williams' diary similarly suggests the range of functions the park fulfilled. In January 1951 he went with L. for "traditional fun"—a code for sex. On other occasions he took two friends and "camped in the park," or reveled in the opportunity to eye-up other walkers, noting "a fabulous gylrig."[65]

Open-air queer culture assumed its most distinctive form around the bathing ponds provided by municipal authorities as part of the nineteenth-century drive for improving leisure facilities. Screened by a fence and—following the dictates of public morality—open only to men, the stipulation that bathers should be naked offered men an institutionalized and highly enjoyable opportunity to relax and watch each other—what Michael Davidson termed a "wonderful lot of juvenile nudity."[66] Between the wars, the architect Montague Glover roamed the Serpentine, Hampstead Ponds, and Victoria Park, photographing the bathing youths he saw in a visual record of outdoor queer life.[67] Park officials, apparently aware of this, sought to suppress these opportunities. Hyde Park regulations stipulated that "males [could] enter the bathing area for no purpose other than that of bathing." Davidson was thrown out in 1922—apparently watching for too long.[68]

After the Second World War the Serpentine and Hampstead Ponds became, if anything, even more popular. In 1953, for example, the PMC noted "several cases of bathers at the . . . Lido behaving in an offensive manner."[69] Schofield described the "excessively masculine" exhibitionist who found the ponds an ideal opportunity. There were, he noted, "certain bathing places in London . . . where homosexuals congregate to admire and be admired." As one man admitted, "I go to display myself as much as to see others."[70] The ponds became a place where men could see and be seen, a site of a public culture that valued the strength and beauty of the male body.

London's parks were never free from danger. Violent attacks, blackmail, and robberies were common; police and keepers patrolled regularly. On occasion surveillance was intensified. In 1932 the PMC noted how one sweep "secured . . . the absence from [Hyde] Park of a number of known men who frequented that area for very undesirable purposes."[71] If men may have temporarily rethought their movements, however, the authorities could never fully control such large areas, and the parks remained far safer than other outdoor spaces. As the magistrate Paul Bennett implicitly recognized: "After dark [Hyde Park] is an unsavoury place . . . *homosexuals regard it as their own particular place.*"[72] When policing made urinals and streets increasingly dangerous in the 1950s, parks became the most important sites of outdoor cruising.

INDOORS

These outdoor public cultures also extended indoors—to London's cinemas, theaters, and music halls. Here, for a small fee, men could remain for hours, warm, dry, and in a space far safer than the urinal or street. Such sites were outside the Met's habitual operational field. When pressed to increase surveillance by purity organizations during the First World War, officers refused to do so, noting how they would only "keep occasional observation in individual cases when there was reason to believe that immorality was habitual."[73] This safety was enhanced by the physical nature of cinemas or theaters. As Superintendent West noted in 1917, "it is an established fact that acts of indecency take place in cinemas . . . but owing to the darkness such acts are not easy to detect unless a complaint is made by the person assaulted." Concealed from police, staff, or other cinemagoers, men were unlikely to draw attention since "[offences] are generally committed with the consent of both parties."[74] Of fifty-one cinema cases tried by magistrates in nine sampled years between 1917 and 1957, forty-four followed complaints from men and youths about unwanted sexual advances.[75]

London's theaters and music halls had been meeting places since the 1870s, offering considerable opportunities for sexual and social interaction. With a half-crown Rover ticket, men could enter the large promenades at the Empire, Alhambra, and Palladium, for example, circulating amongst those socializing and watching the shows, meeting friends and approaching prospective partners without ever drawing attention—just like the prostitutes who also occupied these spaces.[76] They were particularly popular during the First World War, when Robert Hutton would see "as much or as little of the show as one wished . . . stroll[ing] behind the seats or dawdl[ing] at the bars."[77] As Taylor Croft noted in 1932, some promenades became sites of open queer display. On Saturday night in the "notorious" "standing room portions of a certain music hall," it was no uncommon sight to see literally hundreds of young men, dressed in the unmistakably conspicuous way that inverts affect, walking about, talking in high-pitched voices, recognising each other.[78]

In 1925, the populist weekly journal *John Bull* similarly noted how "better dressed and more presentable ["painted boys"] frequent popular West End music halls."[79]

Simultaneously, however, the darkened galleries afforded opportunities for those who wanted to remain invisible. Standing in the crowd at the back of the Islington Music Hall, John Binns found "someone undone me . . . flies and started pulling me out . . . While they were doing it to me someone pushed themselves up against me and expected me to do it to them."[80] Binns had accidentally stumbled upon a vibrant public sexual culture that made the cheaper halls like the Prince of Wales and Collins one of the most important cruising sites in the early twentieth century. In 1916, for example, police heard of "indecent behaviour among men in the standing gallery in the Coliseum" in St. Martin's Lane.[81] The hall had been a known haunt of "male importuners" for several years, generating several complaints from the NVA to the LCC. Despite this—and regular patrols by staff—it remained a popular meeting place well into the 1920s, although few cases ever came to police attention.[82]

After the First World War—and particularly from the late 1920s—the geographical and cultural organization of these practices was radically reconfigured through changing leisure practices and official interventions. When the PMC investigated "complaints of trouble in the galleries of places of entertainment" in 1935, they found no evidence of "regular use of these places . . . [though] at times men known to importune have been present."[83] Their observations reflected a broader decline in music hall audiences, as Londoners flocked to the new—aggressively modern—cinemas constructed around the city. In 1927 the Empire itself was converted into a cinema—a move that emblematized wider cultural transformations. Almost simultaneously the LCC responded to anxieties about prostitution by closing the promenades.[84]

Just as the cinema generated new opportunities for working-class courtship, so did it have a similar impact on public queer culture. Although purity organizations' anxieties focused upon the unfettered heterosociability and opportunities for "immorality," prostitution, and extramarital liaisons within the auditorium, in 1916 the seasoned vigilance campaigner F. N. Charrington turned his attention to queer men's presence in London's cinemas. After visiting cinemas across the city, Charrington and his agents filed a series of reports to the Met, Home Office, and LCC, demanding action against a fast-growing "evil." The Met responded by directing the National Union of Women Workers to survey cinemas, particular those with "doubtful reputation[s]."[85]

Their surveillance revealed a remarkable, unabashed, and extensive sexual culture. Men were seen having sex in West End cinemas including the Cyril, Cinema de Paris, and Cupid (Leicester Square), the Paper (Cambridge Circus), Gaiety (Tottenham Court Road), Arena (Villiers Street), and Super (Charing Cross Road)—as well as in many suburban cinemas.[86] Their interactions centered upon crowded gangways, not the seats themselves. In the Carlton and Majestic, the "worst cinemas" in Tottenham Court Road,

> the chief immorality . . . goes on in the queues adjacent the wall inside . . . A lad or young fellow standing sideways against the wall would place his linked hands behind him with his fingers turned outwards . . . over and over again the men would come to such lads, generally with a mackintosh or overcoat on their arm thus screening their actual movements.[87]

Access routes enabled movement, while crowds, toilets, boxes, or the casual use of an overcoat offered partial concealment.[88] If many cinema staff thus remained unaware of such practices, some clearly profited from Londoners' demands for privacy, ignoring or actively encouraging courting couples or queer men. In the Arena, NUWW officers were mystified by a rigid separation between men and women. On several occasions Charrington's agent had seen men giving the attendant sixpence but "had no idea why this was so." When he did this himself the "young attendant . . . at once said, 'would you like to sit among boys or girls sir?'"[89]

The LCC responded to these concerns by elaborating their regulation of cinemas. From 1916 licensing provisions demanded "shaded lights along the side so audiences can see each other" and supervision by trained staff—"each with an electric torch to frequently patrol the gangways, switching the light along the rows of seats to detect any improper acts." In official circles, the cinema's darkness was assumed to underpin the existence of sexual transgression. "The moral question," one civil servant noted, "was largely bound up with the lighting question." Standing in gangways and around the auditorium was also prohibited. Ostensibly driven by safety concerns, the moral bases of this policy were always explicit. Closing gangways, Superintendent West commented, "would go far towards preventing . . . improper behaviour which . . . take place while persons are standing in these parts of the halls." The modernization of London's cinemas through these new regulatory regimes was predicated an attempt to constrain public forms of intimacy.[90]

Men did not stop meeting in London's cinemas because of these regulations, but the geography of their interactions shifted subtly—focused upon the seats themselves and movements along aisles and rows. Llewellyn R., for example, in a Wandsworth Bridge Road cinema in 1937, was "continually changing his seat, always to sit beside a youth."[91] Many cinemas, particularly in the West End, thus became known for the possibilities they held. In 1942, for example, Robert N., a clerk and George A., a Canadian soldier, were arrested at the Monseigneur in Leicester Square.[92] The twenty-four-hour rolling program of news and shorts provided by news cinemas like the Monseigneur or Piccadilly News Theatre allowed men to remain for hours—often overnight, which ensured that they were particularly popular. In 1937, the valet Rudolph J. stayed at the Center News Cinema in Great Windmill Street until 3.10 A.M., having sex with other men inside the auditorium before taking a pick-up home.[93]

By the 1960s the most famous of these was the Biograph, near Victoria Station. The district—though not the cinema—had been a popular cruising circuit for decades, and became even more popular during the Second World War. When the Met responded by increasing their surveillance of urinals, men appear to have moved towards the Biograph's relative safety. Kenneth Williams clearly expected to find sex in 1952, visiting "in the hope of traditional entertainment" and complaining bitterly after finding it "terribly desolate."[94] Ironically renamed the Biogrope because of the increasingly public sexual activity, it become one of 1960s queer London's landmarks.[95] Indoors yet public, commercial yet open, music halls and cinemas sustained a sexual culture unlike anywhere else. None of the outdoor locations where men found sex were as safe. In none were the sexual opportunities as concentrated.

PUBLIC AND PRIVATE

For many bourgeois observers the wider forms of public urban culture in which men participated were a source of potent anxieties. Left alone, the unfettered sociability of London's streets and open spaces threatened to corrupt working-class men, women, and youths, seducing them away from normative forms of public "respectability." Such anxieties coalesced around the intrusion of sex into the public realm. Set against the ideological correlation of sexual intimacy and domestic space, public sex was defined as dangerous, immoral, and promiscuous. In the 1920s this moral politics of space was articulated most powerfully around London's parks. Here the "immoral" spectacle of working-class couples, prostitution, and queer men seemed to threaten the nation's youth and armed forces, generating repeated demands for official action from purity organizations. In 1922, for example, the Reverend Peel complained of the "scourge of immorality" to the Office of Works:

> One only has to walk through Hyde Park . . . to see couples . . . lying on top of each other . . . the sights to be seen near Marble Arch are disgusting. The harm being done to young people . . . is serious beyond words. That Park is little less than a brothel . . . a disgrace to a civilised country.[96]

Just as municipal authorities and purity organizations sought to suppress street recreations and working-class heterosociability, so they also reacted with hostility when encountering public queer cultures. Within wider attempts to delineate the proper boundaries between public and private conduct, regulation cohered around articulating a singular notion of the appropriate location of sexual intimacy.[97] Queer men's use of public space, in this context, was simply intolerable. In 1950, one magistrate responded wistfully to cases arising from the Providence Court and George Yard urinals: "I wish they could be blown-up."[98] The Met and LCC did, indeed, go some way to meeting his wishes from the 1930s onwards, closing or demolishing urinals in Babmaes Street, Brydges Place, and Ramillies Place and contemplating fencing and locking parks overnight. On occasion authorities were prepared to physically dismantle the sites of queer interaction.[99]

These operations, however, sat uneasily against notions of the citizen's right to move through the city and local government's concomitant responsibilities. The LCC could never demolish every urinal or close ever park. Unable to *remove* such sites, the Met thus policed the ways in which they were *used*. Law enforcement was informed by dominant understandings of acceptable public practices, articulating a moral politics of space that precluded the possibility of homosex. Individual actions against urinals, for example, suggested the productive influence of commonplace assumptions regarding their appropriate function. These could be written as a set of strict injunctions:

1. Do not urinate too often.
2. Do not stand next to anyone when there are other stalls free.
3. Do not talk to anyone.
4. Do not look or smile at anyone.
5. Do not undo your fly or have your penis on display more than is necessary.

The golden rule: be seen to urinate at all costs.[100]

These assumptions were persistently contested in court, particularly the legitimate frequency of urination. One man, arrested in 1954 after entering a West India Dock Road urinal five times in forty minutes, appealed to nature, citing his "weak bladder."[101] In a striking elaboration on this, medical experts testified how Frank Champain "suffered from an infection of the bladder causing him to urinate frequently . . . [his] large prostate gland . . . account[ed] for him desiring to make water frequently."[102]

Alongside the micropractices of individual policemen, municipal authorities sought to police the boundaries between public and private by reconstructing London's built environment. As the regulation of cinemas suggests, this process was predicated upon reconfiguring physical space to extend surveillance into those urban niches where men regularly engaged in homosex. In 1926, for example, police asked the LCC for "material assistance" in controlling "indecency on Clapham Common" by "improving the lighting of the Parish Path, Bishop's Walk and . . . vicinity of the bandstand."[103] Two years later, an Office of Works official identified "certain areas [in Hyde Park] which are notoriously the haunts of loose characters . . . increased lighting in these areas will be a discouragement to these people."[104] The movement from darkness to light was also the symbolic movement from disorder, depravity, and dangerous privacy to order, morality, and the purity of full publicity.

The most deliberate manifestation of this process was the LCC's gradual reconstruction of London's urinals from the 1920s onwards, in response to public or police complaints about their "misuse."[105] As they sought to suppress men's use of public space, many officials found the "old-fashioned" nineteenth-century cast-iron urinals (fig. 6) an active hindrance to surveillance. As PC Butcher testified before the Wolfenden Committee, "the badly lit urinals and been out of the way, that is our trouble." He proposed a solution:

> With the large toilets [with] . . . white tiles [homosexuals] do not like them and do not use them . . . If [the old-fashioned urinals] were done away with or re-sited in a more obvious place and modernised . . . it would prevent the average man in the street from being importuned.[106]

That LCC officers had begun to address these problems much earlier was evident in their lengthy discussion of the Downshire Hill urinal from 1927 to 1930. Concealed within a "triangular shrubbery," unattended, open overnight, and close to a popular pub, this was "greatly abused." There was an "urgent need for larger and more modern sanitary accommodation."[107]

Figure 6. Photograph, The "old-fashioned" urinal in Popes Road, opposite Brixton Station, 1932. Photographer unknown. The National Archives of the UK (PRO), ref no. CRIM 1/617.

The components of modernization were delineated in other LCC reconstruction projects. In 1930, for example, they supported the application of the St. Pancras Metropolitan Borough Council (MBC) to construct new lavatories on Parliament Hill, providing they build "a gate which shall be kept locked after sunset except [when] . . . attendants are on duty . . . and light the paths well and efficiently."[108] Similarly, in 1950 the Heath Street urinal was moved to "a more suitable position," and "the entrance path . . . fenced and provided with a gate and lock."[109]

Like the introduction of bright lighting, white tiles, deeper stalls, and partitions reaching to the floor between closets, such changes inscribed dominant notions of the urinal's use into London's built environment. From the 1940s, British Rail responded to pressure from the PMC by remodeling station toilets and extending the employment of lavatory attendants. In 1949, they noted "good results follow[ing] the installation of opaque glass panels in the doors at Paddington Station."[110] Through the glass, men could never hope to find privacy. Ironically, the final impetus for this process followed the Luftwaffe's bombs. After being damaged during the Blitz, urinals in Southwark and Archbishops Park—built in 1895—were demolished and replaced by urinals "of a modern type."[111]

The interplay between queer practices and a bourgeois moral politics of space thus had a productive impact on modern urban planning. In 1933–34, for example, a House of Commons committee discussed the redevelopment of group of buildings known as the Adelphi Estate. Built on sloping ground between the Strand and the Thames, the Adelphi was raised to a horizontal plane by a series of vaulted arches. Above and below ground it was a rabbit warren of narrow alleys and passageways. By the 1920s it was, noted Inspector Woods, a well-established "resort of persons of the sodomite class" because of its "position and surroundings"—adjacent to Charing Cross, Villiers Street, and the Strand—and since "the locality is badly lighted" and housed several notorious urinals.[112] In debating "the desirability of closing the lower roads under the Adelphi . . . on the grounds of good order, decency and public morality," the committee proceedings were thus driven by their engagement with one particular queer space.[113] Placed outside the metropolitan "public," defined as a threat to "good order" and "decency," the operations of municipal power in redeveloping the modern city were predicated upon the coordinated exclusion of queer men.

That many men transgressed bourgeois conceptions of public and private through their reliance on London's public spaces thus figured the queer within pejorative categories of sexual immorality. Such representations cohered around the apparent correlation between homosex and the urinal— the most abject and marginal of all public spaces, associated with intolerable bodily functions. The discursive production of person and place was a mutually constitutive process, in which notions of the queer's character were derived from the nature of that site at which he was most often arrested. Embedding the queer in the dirt and defecation of the urinal, the magistrate Harold Sturge thus defined homosex as "morally wrong, physically dirty and progressively degrading."[114] Butcher took this to its logical extreme:

> Urinals have a certain odour . . . a staleness [which] . . . excites [queer men] . . . When a urinal has been cleaned out with Dettol and scrubbed clean and smells clean they will not go anywhere near it . . . once the smell of cleanliness has worn off you can see these people . . . working themselves up to a frenzy . . . they are on heat . . . it is like the bitch, once they have the scent there is no holding them, they are oblivious to anything else.[115]

Butcher neatly linked the abject urinal to the supposed anonymity of the encounters that took place there, defining the queer as incapable of love and driven by inescapable, threatening lust. The indecent assault charges generated by agents provocateurs only served to reinforce this construction. The predatory, promiscuous, and immoral queer emerged in contradistinction to bourgeois notions of public and private conduct, part of a wider spatial morality that stigmatized those who found intimacy in public. He was, in Anomaly's terms, "an abnormally lustful person of more or less insatiable and uncontrollable impulses . . . [a] moral leper, corrupt, obscene and monstrous."[116]

SILENCED COMMUNITIES

The association between public space and impersonal sexual encounters is, however, misleading. If many men found fleeting moments of pleasure in doorways or parks, others entered a vibrant queer world in which accumulated interactions between men sustained unique histories, folklore, and landmarks. Never fully able to escape the risk of arrest or assault and always conscious of the stigma attached to their practices, men nonetheless socialized, formed lasting friendships, and fell in love. Roy, growing up in 1920s Brixton, had his first sexual encounter in a local cinema. Later, while watching local street traders, a man pushed himself into Roy: "I'd got my hands behind my back. I thought this is lovely . . . *it was then I realised that I was very much that way.*" After starting work he continued to meet men in cinemas and urinals. He learnt of the galleries after visiting the Prince of Wales with his aunt. Realizing this "was a scene which I wanted to join," he returned and began to find friendship as well as sex. Learning of other meeting places through these acquaintances, he met his lover—George—at the Coliseum in 1927, and entered wider friendship circles.[117]

Although the public city could thus allow access to safer networks, men forged social connections by simply walking London's streets—as Roy himself realized. In their individual encounters in cinemas and urinals or in the men moving through the West End crowds, men saw themselves as part of something far larger. Even if men did not exchange names or see each other again after sex, public queer life could be a powerful counter to feelings of isolation, offering a potent sense of companionship. Dudley Cave "realised that I belonged to *this great freemasonry of . . . queers*" after a fleeting urinal encounter.[118] In his 1942 report on Arthur C., the medical officer at Feltham Prison began to discern how public space underpinned this "freemasonry": "There have been previous experiences in cinemas of this kind. *His ideas on homosexuality have largely developed because he has frequently observed similar incidents in public lavatories in the Camberwell district.*"[119] If in search of companionship, men always knew where to look: when "bored and lonely," Robert Hutton "wandered aimlessly about the streets, hoping that I would meet someone with whom I could forget . . . my situation."[120]

As they forged ad hoc moments of sexual intimacy and connection, men thus repeatedly reconfigured the putative boundaries between public and private. In so doing they remapped London's familiar spaces, investing them with meanings far removed from those manifest in popular guidebooks or envisaged by municipal authorities. They produced a metropolitan geography that was uniquely queer. In 1935 Harold C. spoke to a man who had followed him onto Hampstead Heath from a nearby urinal: "It is a nice night for a bit of fun but the cottage is full up."[121] Like Cave, Harold had "learnt that what I thought were lavatories were in fact called cottages."[122] Recorded by Emlyn Williams in 1927, and in a glossary of queer slang published in 1932, this simple renaming—urinal equals cottage—marked a symbolic appropriation of everyday urban space. Like the Dilly (Piccadilly) or the Meat Rack (the terrace below the National Gallery), this was, noted Taylor Croft, powerful testimony to London's "distinct urning society."[123]

Repeated practice thus generated a map of a public queer world with its own landmarks, histories, and possibilities. If Burke's *For Your Convenience* was the most remarkable version of this, all men possessed similar cognitive maps, within which certain places were iconic. The "famous" Dansey Place urinal—nicknamed Clerkson's Cottage—attracted patrons from across the world and was rumored to have been bought by a wealthy American and rebuilt across the Atlantic after the war.[124] Here London's public spaces represented "a sense of being part of history though the experience of place . . . imagined, recreated and consumed through the narratives of collective identity."[125]

Men's participation in this world and their engagement with those they encountered was, however, more problematic than the notion of a singular public queer *culture* allows. London's streets, urinals, parks, and cinemas certainly enabled opportunities for a democratic sociability and encounters between very different men. In 1943, for example, the earl of L.—a fifty-two-year-old married man—and Robert W.—a young single kitchen porter—were arrested together in a Leicester Square alley.[126] Burke stressed such unifying operations:

> Differences . . . cannot be created by uniforms or possessions or other artificial means. Particularly in this matter, which . . . brings all men to equality . . . on those occasions all men, whatever their actual or artificial rank[,] are named as members of the genus Homo.[127]

Burke's "genus Homo" was predicated upon the assumed commonality of those engaging in public homosex.

Paradoxically, however, this sense of connection was tempered by a nagging awareness of the ineffable differences of class, ethnicity, age, and cultural style between the men encountering each other in urinals or streets. These social boundaries structured very different engagements with public queer life. Many—particularly young workingmen excluded by poverty and familial expectations from private space—relied on parks and urinals as sites of sexual possibility. Others, especially those conscious of the prescriptions of bourgeois respectability, repudiated public queer life, distancing themselves from practices and places defined as dangerous, distasteful, and abject. Still others invested excitement in this very danger, their flirtatious relationship to the city embodied by the playful tone of *For Your Convenience*.

For those who had nowhere else to go, however—unaware of other meeting places or without queer friends because they were young, lived outside London, or were married—the commonplace link between public space and homosex enabled the expression of what could be troubling desires. "The street corner," noted Michael Schofield, "is the most open homosexual society. It can easily be found . . . and entry . . . can be made without formality."[128] Some passed through this world quickly, meeting men who introduced them to more private spaces and rejecting the cottage or park as "sordid and nasty."[129] Yet others, particular married men, maintained their only contact with queer life through these spaces, attracted by the transient opportunities for sexual satisfaction through encounters that were not considered adulterous or holding any wider significance. Sixteen of the thirty-six men arrested in city urinals in 1952 and 1957 were married.[130] Thomas C. was a forty-eight-year-old clerk with two children. The court extended him leniency since his offence was "a moral lapse."[131]

When one man remembered cottages as "the most important meeting places for homosexuals of all and every kind," it was perhaps the "all and every kind" that should be emphasized.[132] London's public spaces were the site of diverse intersecting queer cultures, coalescing around desires for homosex, sociability, and privacy. The meanings they invested in this realm diverged radically, sustaining a fragmented and often antagonistic community of space rather than of identity.

CONCLUSION

Through their individual movements men transformed London's public spaces into an established yet precarious and ever-changing site of urban queer culture, a vital and vibrant social realm. Never simply about sexual encounters, this realm was about seeing and being seen, about desiring and being desired. However dangerous—which it undoubtedly was—public space interwove sex, sociability, culture, and conflict. Beyond the minute geographical and cultural shifts described above, however, these practices were being displaced to an increasingly marginal position within urban life in general, and queer life in particular. If in the 1920s men's use of parks and streets mirrored that of young men and women of the working class, *public* cultures of heterosexuality were disappearing by the 1950s, as affluence shifted interactions between men and women away from such locales. The monkey parade—cruising's counterpart—gave way to the coffeehouse. The "knee trembler" in park or alley gave way to sex in private. And, responding to intensified postwar policing, street prostitution gave way to the call girl's flat. Against such changes, queer men's continued public presence seemed increasingly unacceptable, increasingly distant from the spatial organization of respectable "heterosexuality."

At the same time, moreover, a similar interplay between economic and cultural change and police operations, displaced public life to the margins of respectable "homosexuality." The ongoing intensification of police surveillance, particularly after the Second World War, raised the dangers of cruising to prohibitive levels. "The only thing," Schofield heard, "is to keep out of public lavatories."[133] As a stable network of bars and clubs developed and men made increasing attempts to articulate a respectable "homosexual" politics, the spatial and cultural movement *away* from public cultures marked a specific—postwar—moment in London's queer history. If men continued to frequent parks, streets, and cottages, by the 1950s sociologists increasingly found that they were those excluded from more stable and respectable sites by wealth, knowledge, or desire: men who were young, married, out-of-towners, or working-class.

3

THE PINK
SHILLING

This chapter maps the commercial sites of queer sociability—the pubs, cafés, restaurants, and nightclubs where men met and interacted. It explores the cultural and geographical organization of this world, as well as its relationship to urban culture, consumer markets, and municipal governance. My starting point is the experiences of the actor Emlyn Williams after he moved to London in 1927. Almost immediately, Emlyn calculated his future budget. Setting aside money for rent—on a furnished room with no kitchen—he provided for food: "Breakfast—cornflakes . . . other meals at ABC's, Lyons and coffee stalls." These eating places quickly became central to Emlyn's life. He met friends in the Strand Corner House; he dined with actor Charles Laughton in the Perroquet—a "chic little restaurant in Leicester Square." Later, he enjoyed a comfortable routine with his partner, Bill Cronin-Wilson:

> We came back to the flat to sit about and . . . read, then we would walk over for dinner at the Little Alexis in Lisle Street, or eggs in "Mary and Mums," the café in the court behind Wyndhams.[1]

More than "dinner," Emlyn's money bought him the *space* for an active social life—access to the sites of public drinking, dining, and entertainment that had developed from the late nineteenth-century. Persistently repeated, these transactions underpinned the world men forged in cafés and bars, meeting friends and creating temporary sites of queer sociability. Within a commercialized leisure market, being a consumer meant power. Particularly if they were discreet, men could find such opportunities anywhere;

socializing alongside other Londoners in backstreet pubs or the most fashionable nightspots they attracted little, if any, attention.

This ad hoc sociability coexisted with an extensive network of known queer meeting places. A venue's reputation depended upon accumulated individual movements, as men socialized with friends, who in turn took their friends. Knowledge circulated further through word of mouth. While still new to London, Emlyn met Angus Rae, an Oxford acquaintance, in the British Museum. Rae directed him towards the Trocadero's Long Bar, the Tea Kettle (Wardour Street), and the Chalice Bar. So armed, Emlyn began to explore London's nightlife, discovering more venues to visit. He found pickups in the Fitzroy Tavern; he celebrated a friend's birthday in the Long Bar; he reveled in the opportunity to watch other men in the Criterion.[2]

Commercialized leisure thus created new opportunities for queer sociability. Men moved through a world that was deeply embedded in modern urban culture—that took hold in everyday sites and was shaped by the social, cultural, and economic landscape inhabited by all Londoners. Where they chose to socialize was informed by shared ideas of fashionability, and common financial constraints. As such, queer commercial sociability overlapped with that forged by disparate other groups. Men's relationship to those with whom they shared London's commercial spaces was contradictory, as likely to encompass amusement and acceptance as hostility.

This world, however, was never a homogenous and democratic "scene." Rather, it was deeply segregated, rent by differences of class, age, gender, and style that drove men towards worlds that could be miles apart. In a capitalist marketplace the key difference was class: not all consumers were created equal. The East End pub may have been cheap and relatively open; the exclusive Mayfair nightspot certainly was not. These differences underpinned *the* critical tension within queer commercial sociability, focused upon the contradictory ways in which consumerism was understood and organized. For some, consumerism opened up potentially *private* spaces, allowing them to meet friends discreetly in restaurants or bars while remaining invisible to onlookers. For others, it meant access to sites of *public* sociability— venues where they could be openly different. Such distinctions shaped profound differences *both* between venues *and* between individual men's behavior inside a venue. Always conventionally respectable, Emlyn initially moved between these worlds, watching the camp "male trash" in the Criterion or drinking in the unequivocally respectable Long Bar. Quickly, however, he decided that "the 'amusing' resorts were not for me," confining his social orbit to more discreet venues.[3]

This persistent tension between public and private forms of sociability was, moreover, exacerbated by men's relationship with the state and the management of individual premises. In London's commercial spaces men entered into an ongoing conflict with the Met and LCC. While they never sought to prevent men meeting, both agencies tried to render them invisible. In a very real sense, policing operated to impose a privatized commercial sociability. Proprietors' responses reinforced this impetus, as they sought to avoid police attention and construct viable commercial concerns. Access to the enabling resources of consumerism was always equivocal, contingent on looking and behaving in certain ways.

SOCIABILITY

During 1934 a small advertising card circulated the West End: "After the day's routine spend your evening at the Caravan, 81 Endell Street." Apparently addressing a queer audience, the card promised a space physically, culturally, and temporally outside the "day's routine." This basement club was "London's Greatest Bohemian Rendezvous . . . the most unconventional spot in town." By deliberately invoking the cultural codes of "Bohemianism" and a disregard for "convention," the card suggested that here men could socialize in safety, their difference accepted. Outside the constraints of work or public life, they could behave freely and openly, "dancing to Charlie" in an atmosphere of "all night gaiety" (fig. 7).[4] The advertisement's language underscores the importance of commercial space within queer lives. At work, most men had to wear a "mask" of normality; on the streets, surveillance was an ever-present risk. At home, men could be isolated from wider social networks. In certain venues, by contrast, they could meet or make friends, find sex or sociability, or simply relax.

Writing in 1952, the sociologist Michael Schofield thus described the pub's role in many men's lives:

> It is only when they come here in the evening that they can let their hair down and feel at home . . . meet other homosexuals, gossip about other people's affairs and talk about their own adventures.[5]

Two decades earlier, an observer watched two friends talking in a nightclub off Tottenham Court Road:

> "You do look worried tonight darling, whatever is the matter with you?" . . .
> "My sweetie has let me down, he promised to come to my flat this evening and I waited in for him. He didn't even phone me, the darling bitch. I feel so lonely now."[6]

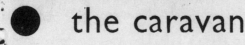

AFTER THE DAY'S ROUTINE SPEND YOUR EVENING AT

the caravan

81 ENDELL ST.

ENTRANCE IN COURT
(Corner of Shaftesbury Avenue, facing
Princes Theatre)
Phone: Temple Bar 7665

*London's Greatest Bohemian Rendezvous
said to be the most unconventional spot in town*

ALL NIGHT GAIETY   **Dancing to Charlie**

PERIODICAL NIGHT TRIPS TO THE GREAT OPEN
SPACES, INCLUDING THE ACE OF SPADES, ETC.

Figure 7. Advertising flyer for the Caravan Club, 1934. The National Archives of the UK (PRO), ref no. MEPO 3/758. Material in the National Archives in the copyright of the Metropolitan Police is reproduced by permission of the Metropolitan Police Authority.

Like Schofield's descriptions, this exchange embodied a real sense of "home," mirroring B. D. Nicholson's characterization of pubs in working-class neighborhoods as "community centres":

> Local gossip is exchanged . . . everyone meets, arranges most of his common activities, lets his personal cares aside and satisfies some of his social cravings.[7]

This opportunity to satisfy "social cravings" meant that, as for all Londoners, commercial space was integral to the formation of queer social networks. Such was its importance that, during 1932, the film extra Sidney C. visited the Palladium Theatre's Circle Bar—a popular meeting place—on over thirty occasions, often three times a week.[8]

If, in this sense, men's use of commercial venues was culturally familiar, they simultaneously transformed London's pubs and restaurants into the site of a visibly different world. One Saturday night in 1932, Taylor Croft visited the Criterion bar, in Piccadilly Circus, to "see the gathering of homosexuals." He left "amazed by the blatancy with which they behave, the utter disregard of normal people . . . or the café management." There were:

Nearly 200 perverts present, noticeably dressed as usual, some with berets on the backs of their heads . . . some with coloured sweaters rolled to their necks, many . . . painted and rouged, one boy actually in women's clothes . . . one man took out a lipstick and openly used it.

As he watched, a "boy crossed to speak to a friend and kissed him on the lips . . . everywhere urnings were going from table to table greeting their friends, discussing forthcoming parties."[9]

In the Criterion, as in countless other venues, men's physical distance from the street and the presence of other queer men generated a tangible sense of release.[10] Implicit in what Croft labeled a "blatant" "disregard" of "normality" was a sense that this was *their* space. In this space the conventions of "normal" urban culture were temporarily suspended. Here men could dress "noticeably," wear makeup, socialize openly with friends, and talk about issues that mattered to them. Here they could flirt with those they found attractive. The entrance was a wide sweeping staircase that, as Emlyn recalled, "caused every charry head to crane and give any new arrival the once over." His friend Angus "once had the doubtful luck to descend to the strains of 'Five Foot Two, Eyes of Blue,'" played by the resident orchestra.[11] Croft, similarly, noticed that "as men entered several . . . were cheered and applauded by the people seated at the tables . . . when two sailors accompanied by older urnings came down the stairs there was general applause." In the evening, what Muirhead's *Blue Guide* described as "London's most fashionable resort for afternoon tea" became somewhere to celebrate masculine beauty.[12] The Criterion had been what George Ives called "a great centre for inverts" since around 1905. By the 1920s, this sense of ownership and history was so pronounced that it was renamed to reflect its camp atmosphere: the "Witches' Cauldron" or "Bargain Basement."[13]

While Croft applied the label "blatancy" to the sight of camp men socializing, in certain venues the "disregard" of "normality" went even further. The result was a public sociability which, to observers and participants alike, seemed like another world. In the Caravan, police watched "men . . . dancing together . . . pausing to caress each other's buttocks . . . go[ing] through the motions of sexual intercourse . . . embracing and kissing."[14] Between the wars, this was certainly not the only place where men could dance. Other possibilities included nightclubs like Billie's in Little Denmark Street (fig. 8), or the weekly events held in rented working-class dancehalls—Selina Hopps's Baker Street functions or Betty's Archer Street dances. In January 1927, Bill thus wrote to Bert L.—"Honey Bunch"—to arrange their weekend: "I will be outside Lees Hall at 8 o'clock on Saturday

Figure 8. Photograph, Billie's Club, Little Denmark Street, 1937. The National Archives of the UK (PRO), ref. no. CRIM 1/903.

and we can easily find a dance . . . we have fixed nothing yet but there are plenty of dances so don't forget to come." Bill's confidence in finding somewhere to dance "easily," as well as the number of functions that weekend, is striking, suggesting the vibrant opportunities for public queer sociability in interwar London.[15]

That sociability also included the spectacle of men openly cruising, particularly within the working-class milieu of the pub. John Lehmann, Rodney Garland, and Peter Wildeblood's memories all suggest how pubs were known for both the availability of casual sexual encounters and the openness of men's exchanges. Places like the York Minster, the Swiss, or the Marquis of Granby in Soho were all, in Wildeblood's terms "less [than] discreet," rough, and cruisy.[16] Throughout the 1930s, for example, respectable men in evening dress and camp queans solicited sailors and workmen in the Running Horse.[17]

These public interactions existed alongside the more private worlds forged, primarily, by middle-class men. Operating within the prescriptive demands of respectability, such men drew upon the privileges of class to construct extensive but invisible social networks in London's more exclusive nightspots. Here a group of friends or a couple dining together, conventionally masculine, wearing a suit and tie, and restrained in their mannerisms would never attract attention. Joe Ackerley's social circle met regularly at Gennaro's in New Compton Street in the 1930s and at the Hungry Horse and Chez Victor's in Wardour Street in the 1950s.[18] The downstairs bar at the Ritz Hotel was similarly appropriated by men from metropolitan high society. Exclusive and unequivocally respectable, it was affectionately nicknamed l'Abri—the shelter.[19]

Most important was the Trocadero's magnificent Long Bar, on the corner of Shaftsbury Avenue and Piccadilly Circus, opened by Lyons in 1896. This was, noted M. Joseph,

> the most famous bar in London . . . It was all marble with pillars support-ing arches down each side and it had a kind of mosaic roof. The bar ran the entire length and there were plenty of tables.[20]

Exclusive, expensive, and "for gentlemen only," the privileges of masculine homosociality sustained an enduring site of queer sociability, frequented by men like the theatre critic James Agate.[21] Emlyn found it "outwardly the most respectable rendezvous in the most respectable of all capitals." He saw "little tables clustered with Gentlemen only . . . in the old uniform of bowler, dark suit, rolled umbrella and starched collar."[22] Amidst these grand surroundings, men could socialize, converse, and form new friend-ships, while being entertained by the resident orchestra and nightly supper reviews. In 1932, the *Evening Standard* announced the new song of the maitre d'—"Make Way, Boys—Here Comes a Sailor."[23]

While ostensibly public, such venues offered elite men the opportunity to forge social worlds that were, effectively, private. They created a com-mercial "home" appropriate to their class and status—respectable, discreet, and exclusive, the basis for enduring friendship networks. After 1916, for example, Robert Hutton began to move in one circle's established social round: "One very soon knew everyone."

> Sunday morning at the Trocadero Long Bar . . . was a recognised gathering place . . . one heard news of friends, swapped experiences of the previous evening and usually ended up in a luncheon party, going on afterwards to pass a lazy afternoon at Alex's hotel in Covent Garden.[24]

"There was," he remembered, "nothing in the nature of an orgy about these Sunday afternoons. Many of the company would be on leave and wanted to enjoy the comforts of civilisation and the company of their fellows."[25] This world was far removed from the spectacle of public cruising or camp men gossiping.

The relationship between these divergent social forms was complex. Many middle-class men deliberately distanced themselves from spaces coded as disreputable, promiscuous, and dangerously visible. Despite this, public and private sociability often overlapped within the same venue. In the respectable yet affordable surroundings of Lyons's Coventry Street Corner House, for example, clerks, shop assistants, and workmen gathered alongside civil servants and the metropolitan intelligentsia, "painted boys" alongside the discreet queer.[26] Middle-class men, moreover, regularly frequented pubs or cafés in central London or the East End looking for working-class pickups. Yet even as they moved through this public realm, their appearance persistently suggested their distance from it. In remaining conventionally masculine, they were effectively invisible, disassociated from those around them.

The privileges of elite masculinity thus allowed certain men to move through the city unnoticed, crossing established social boundaries and exploiting an extensive network of social and sexual opportunities. Yet such mobility depended upon money. Shop assistants or laborers could neither afford—nor were allowed—to enter places like the Ritz. Public and private sociability were thus often separate. The distance between the Long Bar and the Soho café was massive, often solidifying into an impermeable cultural, economic, and spatial boundary that rent queer commercial sociability along lines of class. Yet whatever their choice of venue, simply being amongst other men in a milieu where their desires were accepted offered a compelling sense of affirmation. As one quean entering the Running Horse exclaimed delightedly, "There are quite a lot of us GIRLS here tonight."[27]

REGULATION

When contemporaries surveyed the city, their gaze was inevitably drawn to the arresting spectacle of public queer sociability. Set against these most blatant transgressions, those socializing discreetly remained invisible. In 1920, touring London's "night haunts," Sydney Moseley thus entered a café containing "a crowd of young men so made up that it is not easy to guess their sex . . . Their perfume, carriage and high-pitched voice would make a normal man sick."[28] Reacting with all the symptoms of physical repulsion, Moseley saw in this scene a reflection of London's moral decay. Like Taylor Croft, writing twelve years later, he attributed this dangerous visibility to the relationship between London's "urning meeting places" and the law. Such venues were, wrote Croft:

Perfectly public . . . since no steps can be taken against them . . . If a great number of people of a certain kind use one particular café there is no law to prevent it . . . [although] the sexual lives of urnings may be . . . contrary to the law.[29]

If Croft and Moseley identified the problems facing municipal authorities—the absence of any legislation *directly* prohibiting "urning meeting places"—their conclusions were misleading. The Met and LCC regularly targeted queer venues, using generic licensing and regulatory powers. Places like Melodies Bar in Shepherd's Market or the Adelphi Rooms in Edgware Road, for example, were closed between the wars, ostensibly for unlicensed liquor sales or public dancing.[30] On occasion, the proprietor and habitués of a venue were prosecuted under statutory charges of "keeping a disorderly house" and "aiding and abetting." As Nott-Bower put it in 1954, "a large number of homosexuals behaving in a disorderly way can constitute the premises a disorderly house."[31]

Despite this, the policing of queer commercial sociability was strikingly uneven: certain venues remained open for years without ever drawing attention; others were closed within months. At no time did the municipal authorities attempt to shut every venue. Nott-Bower elaborated on the operational mentalities structuring these idiosyncrasies. The *presence* of "a large number of homosexuals," he implied, was not sufficient cause for action. Surveillance was thus displaced to the ways that men "*behaved*," organized around a distinction between orderly—and thereby acceptable—and "disorderly" practices. He listed unacceptable behaviors: "Paint and powder . . . made-up eyebrows . . . waved hair . . . calling each other girl's names . . . kissing . . . cuddling . . . sitting on each others knees . . ."[32]

Just as discreet social forms remained hidden from casual observers, so they were thus also invisible to official surveillance. That "disorderly" behavior that risked drawing police attention was mapped firmly onto visible queer sociability. Definitions of "disorderly" conduct thus underpinned an operational distinction between private and public sociability, demarcating both the target and the limits of policing. In *every* instance in which a venue was raided or prosecuted, initial observation and the evidence deployed in court focused upon the quean's visible presence. Regulation was thus both narrowly focused and pervasive, moving beyond the suppression of queer venues to demarcate acceptable forms of public sociability. Police operations coalesced around a singular notion of the orderly, respectable masculine consumer—who *could* be queer. As long as men did, said, or wore nothing that overtly signaled their character, they and the places they frequented were beyond the law. As Nott-Bower noted, "a certain public house may become known as a haunt of homosexuals [but] if the men behave properly . . . no action is taken."[33]

These operational definitions were initially elaborated through the use of statute law against nightclubs in the 1920s. In the 1930s, however, this experience sustained a marked shift in the Met's regulation of pubs in response to anxieties surrounding the Running Horse in Shepherd's Market. Before 1937, officers had never prosecuted a landlord for allowing men to congregate on his premises, preferring to keep venues under surveillance and prosecute individuals for importuning inside.[34] Despite having had the Running Horse under observation since 1933, officers repeatedly refused to initiate formal proceedings. While, noted SDI Gavin,

> men of an effeminate nature do regularly use the house . . . [who] may be of sodomist tendencies . . . [But there is] nothing taking place . . . to which police can take exception. The appearance of these effeminately-dressed young men may be repugnant to certain people but their conduct . . . is such that no objection can be taken.[35]

After vociferous complaints from the Canadian Military and Admiralty in 1936, this position became untenable. Following protracted debate, officers fell back on section 44 of the 1839 Metropolitan Police Act (MPA), forbidding a proprietor to "willfully and knowingly permit . . . disorderly conduct in [a] . . . place of public resort." The landlord was cautioned for permitting drunkenness and serving convicted importuners, then prosecuted when he failed to remedy this situation.[36] Despite renewing his license over the winter, the justices deliberately stated that they

> view[ed] this class of offence with the greatest concern. It is of the utmost importance that brewers exercise proper supervision over their houses . . . in any such case in future the bench will refuse to renew the license.[37]

In spring the landlord was prosecuted, convicted, and fined, and the pub was closed. At the 1938 Brewster Session the license reapplication was refused since the pub was "frequented by persons of bad character."[38]

In using the MPA, the Met established a precedent that fundamentally reconfigured the relationship between the state and sites of queer commercial sociability. Rather than bring expensive and time-consuming cases against the habitués of a venue, they targeted the proprietors—the place, not the people. In the 1940s and 1950s, officers became increasingly active, using the MPA to prosecute owners of pubs like the Fitzroy and White Horse, or Bill's Snack Bar on Bouchin Street and the Ham Yard Café.[39] That their operations were rarely reported suggests the flexibility the MPA afforded—since raids were regular, if not frequent. Rather than initiate formal prosecutions, the Met relied on informally cautioning landlords. As one noted in 1936, "officers [had] warned proprietors that they must discourage the attendance of . . . certain types."[40]

The contrast between the policing of pubs and nightclubs before 1937 foregrounds the divergent regulation of different commercial spaces. In part, this followed from procedural constraints on policing. Officers could enter pubs, cafés, or restaurants freely, and they approved premises and the landlord's character *prior* to licensing. Their ability to keep clubs under surveillance, however, was tightly constrained: initial observation required senior officers' authorization; a venue could only be raided with a magistrate's warrant. Once a club had been raided and struck off the clubs register, it could simply reopen under a new name. Given these constraints clubs were relatively secure—almost invisible.[41] These powers intersected with definitions of "disorderly conduct" to focus official attention on the backstreet cafés and bars where queans mingled with prostitutes, "criminals," and recent immigrants—where raids were a constant risk. In 1936, for example, Harry's Restaurant in Lisle Street—"resort of perverts and women of ill-repute"— was fined for harboring prostitutes. A year later it was closed.[42]

Despite being familiar with many venues, Met officers were remarkably reluctant to act formally, often only doing so in response to public complaints. The Caravan, for example, was raided after letters from Holborn Council and "some ratepayers of Endell Street": "Frequented by sexual perverts, lesbians and sodomites . . . an absolute sink of iniquity, your prompt attention is respectfully craved."[43] More insistent were the demands of London District Command, exercised by the threat of servicemen being "corrupted." Military police patrolled venues, placing "undesirable premises" out of bounds. They liaisoned closely with the Met, regularly demanding the closing of venues. Operations in Shepherd's Market in the late 1930s, for example—including raids on the Running Horse and Melodies—followed pressure from the Admiralty and the Royal Air Force.[44]

In the early 1930s these pressures were accelerated by the Public Morality Council's changing priorities. Although they had patrolled commercial venues for decades—and often observed men importuning—the PMC had always focused upon female prostitution. In 1930, however, officers surveyed twenty-five West End pubs "by special request." After reporting eleven for "irregular conduct," "special measures by the police resulted in a large number of male prostitutes being convicted for using these houses for importuning."[45] This focus persisted: in 1933, bolstered by two donations of £100 made specifically to fund this campaign, they again demanded action against a great increase in the attendance at certain places of men and boys for the purposes of importuning other males . . . a list of houses of public resort . . . harboring these men and boys has been compiled . . . police have promised utmost attention to an abuse, the dangers of which they fully appreciate.[46]

The Caravan, dancehalls in Baker and Archer Streets, and a ballroom in Holland Park Avenue were all prosecuted after this quasi-official pressure. If the PMC returned to traditional concerns after 1934, they continued to draw attention to queer venues periodically.[47]

These external pressures intersected with the reorganization of police procedures to bring particular forms of commercial sociability under increasing surveillance after the mid-1930s. The Second World War enhanced this tendency, as anxieties around the "corruption" of servicemen sustained a massive expansion of police powers. Under the Defence Regulations and Emergency Powers Acts (EPA), officers could close "disorderly" premises *without* legal process. Surveillance of nightclubs was tightened: officers could enter without a warrant and refuse to register a club if unsatisfied by the proprietor's character.[48] If these powers were primarily used against heterosocial disorder, they were also deployed against queer venues. Sam's Café in Rupert Street—"resort of criminals, male and female prostitutes"—was closed between 6 P.M. and 6 A.M. under the EPA in 1941.[49] Pubs including the Swiss Hotel on Old Compton Street and the Crown and Two Chairmen on Dean Street were cautioned for "harbouring sodomites" in 1944.[50] As regulation became increasingly effective, the PMC discerned a new nocturnal morality:

> The beneficial effects of the closing orders . . . are beginning to bear fruit . . . such places . . . are putting their houses in order . . . [and] showing less inclination to run against the law.[51]

Municipal authorities thus never sought to prevent men frequenting London's bars, cafés, or restaurants. Indeed, this would have been impossible, since the individuals and venues that conformed to notions of "normal" masculine behavior were effectively invisible. Rather, regulation sought to demarcate acceptable forms of public behavior, imposing a form of sociability through which queer men were rendered invisible. In so doing the law was applied selectively and symbolically, and prosecutions orchestrated for maximum impact. Through a string of sensational "pansy cases" in the 1930s, for example, the Met repeatedly dramatized the intolerable nature of "disorderly" queer practices, after arresting as many as one hundred men in raids on nightclubs. Officials sought to wring the most dramatic lesson from proceedings, placing men in court still in drag and makeup, identifying the defendants by numbered placards around their necks, delivering punitive penal sentences and vitriolic summations.[52] The manager of the Adelphi Rooms—not even present when his premises were raided—was imprisoned for twelve months in 1927. Leslie K., who ran the dances there, served twenty-one months.[53] Reiterated at regular intervals, such awful spectacles constituted an adequate control on queer men's visibility: officers did not act against every café and bar because they did not need to. "It is to be hoped," noted SDI Welley of the Running Horse, "that the conviction will effect a cleansing in other . . . premises where such perverts congregate."[54]

MANAGEMENT

The "cleansing" Welley envisaged implied a form of regulation integral to modern consumer culture. Paradoxically, the elaboration of policing systems focused upon a venue's owner massively enhanced the authorities' ability to control public sociability, just as it reduced their need for direct intervention. Through periodic newspaper reports, proprietors learned only too well of the risks to their person, profits, and commercial existence attendant on accepting certain men's custom, even if they were never directly singled out through a raid, prosecution, or warning. In this context most licensees, noted Nott-Bower, "are only too anxious to keep their house free from . . . disorderly conduct." While they may "occasionally . . . fail in their responsibilities" through "weakness or fear of losing trade . . . the [MPA] provisions . . . are useful in keeping the situation under control despite the low penalty (five pounds) since the effective sanction is the fear of losing the license."[55] When queer men began to frequent the White Horse in Rupert Street in 1951, the licensee Edward S. thus went straight to the police. Officers refused to act, advising him to employ a commissionaire and maintain a strict door policy. When Edward's own attempts to maintain order failed, the pub was raided.[56] Responsibility for the surveillance of commercial sociability was partially displaced onto the marketplace, impressing a pervasive self-regulation upon individual proprietors.

Despite this, many were willing to accept men's paying custom. Often—particularly when men looked conventionally masculine—they may not have even realized that their premises had acquired a reputation as queer. Even if this were not the case, men remained consumers with money to spend, however they may have looked or behaved. Selina Hopps, for example, managed a Baker Street dancehall. In 1933, a court heard how she "knew the sort of people who frequented the place and by gathering them in large numbers . . . *was making considerable profits out of their disgusting behaviour.*"[57] The pink shilling was a potentially lucrative market, and men's demand for a "home" always ripe for exploitation.

If the state sought to constrain men's sociability within peculiarly narrow limits, the amorality of the marketplace allowed queer commercial networks to develop. Some proprietors simply accepted men's custom. Others deliberately cultivated a queer clientele. Jack Neave, for example, ran several West End nightclubs, including the Jamset and Cosmopolitan (Wardour Street), in the early 1930s. He was, in his own words, "very popular among bohemian people." In 1934, he met William Reynolds, who was looking to invest a recent inheritance. Together they rented a basement in Endell Street for £300 from "one of the many shady estate agents in the West End who specialise in letting premises to shady clubs and prostitutes." The Caravan opened in July, charging admission of 1s for "members" and 1s 6d on the door. Decorated in an oriental style and advertised through Neave's contacts and the flyer discussed above, it was unambiguously intended to draw queer men's patronage. Inside they could dance, kiss, and have sex. In six weeks it acquired 445 members and was visited by 2004 people.[58] Billie Joice similarly set out to turn her club in Little Denmark Street into a queer nightspot. Opening in October 1935, she allowed men to dance and employed camp cabaret acts, like Fred Barnes, the famous music hall artist.[59]

Like Billie's or the Caravan, many bars and cafés tried to retain their queer clientele, creating a supportive environment, even if they had not initially sought their custom. The Running Horse staff, for example, knew their customers well—they were on first name terms with regulars and regularly participated in their camp banter. When a "manly type woman" entered one evening and asked the waiter, "Has my wife been in this evening?" he replied immediately, "No, not yet."[60] Moreover, they often protected queer patrons from harassment. One waiter watched five men of "ordinary type . . . engaged in cross talk" with a number of queans. When they became increasingly drunk and violent—one shouting, "They're all fucking poufs in here"—he ushered the "ordinary" men to the door, saying, "It's a good job you are leaving."[61]

This kind of positive acceptance coexisted with a more ambiguous—perhaps more common—commercial laissez-faire: part deliberate ignorance, part grudging toleration, part scarcely veiled hostility. Whatever their attitude, all proprietors realized the potential risks, negotiating a precarious balance between profit and avoiding closure—between the market and the state. Most took men's money while seeking to minimize the dangers, carefully policing their behavior in order to ensure their premises could never be deemed "disorderly." If men's custom could be accepted if they were discreet in pubs like the White Bear, Michael S. found, "any sort of show or camp was frowned upon."[62] Men could eat, drink, or socialize as long as they did nothing that transgressed the informal boundaries tacitly constructed around their visibility.

In part, this involved preventing *open* cruising. At the Corner House, Frank Oliver remembered, "the management had a beady eye on everybody . . . [so] you had to be careful."[63] Surveillance focused upon those who visibly transgressed normative masculinity. Many venues simply refused to accept the risks drawn by the flamboyantly effeminate. In the 1930s, Alex Purdie was thus "barred from nearly every pub in the West End."[64] The boundaries between intolerable visibility and acceptable discretion were, however, more amorphous than Purdie's experiences suggest. That the proper limits on masculine self-presentation were never self-evident created a space in which men could push at the constraints placed on their visibility. In 1953, for example, the doorman of the White Horse was sacked as he struggled to decode the semiotics of self-presentation. As his employer noted, "He made so many mistakes turning away perfectly respectable people . . . half our customers . . . they only had to be wearing a coloured or painted tie or a coloured sweater."[65]

If they were not denied entry, men thus *could* be flamboyantly camp in many venues until a member of staff decided they had gone too far. Even in the Running Horse, a waiter spoke firmly to four youths "of effeminate appearance" who were "very noisy and jostling people about." After this they "quietened down considerably."[66] Such direct interventions were often only periodic, marking a moment when proprietors abandoned a passive laissez-faire, responding either to a sense that their customers had become too visible *or* to informal police pressures. The Running Horse licensee told police how "since . . . you cautioned me it has been the strictest run house in the whole of England"—to the extent that his weekly takings had fallen by over £100.[67]

Just as proprietors tried to contain their customers' visibility, many also constructed impermeable spatial boundaries around them, attempting to reduce the risk of complaints or observation by police. Some physically distanced queer men from the "normal" public. In the Corner House, for example, men met only in the first-floor restaurant. "There was nothing to say it was different," noted Gerald Dougherty, "but the waitresses knew it and wouldn't let a woman sit anywhere near."[68] The territorial separation of queer and "normal" was also temporal. The Criterion, Emlyn noted, "was staid enough . . . until ten P.M. By then the great ornate hall . . . had been emptied of respectable clientele and filled with well-behaved male trash."[69]

Other proprietors—particularly those who deliberately targeted a queer clientele—sought to protect themselves through a form of counter-surveillance designed to exclude police officers, rendering their premises functionally private. This required the flexibility to respond to rumors of surveillance. In 1932, for example, Betty cancelled dances planned in Archer and Baker streets after learning of plainclothes observation on her premises.[70] It also led many proprietors to join protection rackets, bribing Criminal Investigation Department (CID) officers to prevent or warn them of raids. In the 1920s officers from C Division's Clubs Office were heavily implicated in such networks, culminating in the sensational prosecution of one sergeant and a number of club and restaurant owners.[71] The Fitzroy Tavern remained free from prosecution despite officers knowing of its reputation for over a decade: it was, according to John Heath-Stubbs, "common knowledge that Charlie Allchild [the landlord] had bribed the police."[72]

These tactics coalesced in the nightclubs that emerged after 1930. Entrepreneurs sought to configure rigid boundaries between public and private in order to construct viable, enduring, and respectable commercial concerns. Places like the Festival (Dean Street) and Careless Stork (Denman Street) first appeared in the mid-1930s. Muriel Belcher and Dolly Mayers opened the Sphinx in Gerrard Street, followed by the Music Box in Leicester Place in 1937. Others, like le Boeuf sur le Toit (Orange Street), followed in response to increased demand during the Second World War. In 1941, Stan Cowley opened the Arts and Battledress Club, also in Orange Street. In 1952 the club—now the A&B—moved to Rupert Street, becoming one of London's best-known venues, appearing as the Alciabades in Lehman's *In the Purely Pagan Sense* and the Aldebaran in Garland's *Heart in Exile*. Clubs continued to open throughout the 1950s: Toby Roe's Rockingham (Archer Street), Bill Criber's Spartan (Tachbrook Street), and Ted Rodgers Bennett's Festival (Brydges Place).[73]

Such venues represented a novel—yet lasting—development. Unlike most premises, they were queer-run, and catered for an exclusive clientele while deliberately operating within the limits demarcated by official surveillance. In so doing, they relied upon their status as members clubs, enforcing a strict door policy and membership terms to exclude both the "disorderly" queer and potentially hostile members of the public. Doormen allowed only members and guests to enter. New members were accepted only upon introduction. Membership fees were prohibitively high, and there were strict dress codes—shirt and tie.[74] Quentin Crisp noted how these venues developed from the early 1930s through lessons learned from places like the Caravan:

> Every year they grew more respectable . . . more restrained. Even at the beginning when they were slightly sordid I never felt at home. The management feared that my arrival . . . might draw the unwelcome attention of officials . . . amongst the clientele my arrival caused a hush, clamorous with resentment.

The result was that "an evening spent in one of them would almost always be quiet—even cosy."[75]

If the discretion that so exasperated Crisp followed partly from the deliberate exclusion of the quean or working-class trade and the tacit prohibition of kissing or dancing, it was also inherent to the respectable sociability associated with the clubs' market. The Rockingham, for example, looked and felt like a gentleman's club—striped Regency wallpaper, paneling, reading room with leather armchairs, and a large white piano. It was, like similar venues, "piss elegant."[76] Their ambience and prohibitive cost made the clubs what Michael Schofield termed London's "most exclusive homosexual society," attracting "well-educated cultured persons . . . capable of holding responsible high salaried positions in all walks of life."[77]

Amongst nonmembers such venues had a reputation for being staid—"the pouf's Athenaeum" or "elephant's graveyard."[78] It was, however, precisely this that made the clubs so important to bourgeois men, relaxing away from the disreputable public realm.[79] They did so, moreover, in an orderly, safe, and exclusive space that existed beyond the operations of the law. As Nott-Bower noted, "as long as a club were conducted properly . . . we would not raid it."[80] Deliberately designed to be physically and culturally private—invisible—both the Rockingham and A&B remained open for forty years, an enduring commercial basis for queer sociability.

These venues were, however, exceptional and their clientele limited. Most places where men gathered were not queer-run. Most did not cater for an exclusive clientele; most proprietors, moreover, were unable or unwilling to construct such a secure space. In London's commercial venues the consumer, the market, and the state thus engaged in an ongoing conflict over the nature of queer commercial sociability. If some men constantly probed the limits placed on their behavior, this complex interaction underpinned a key trajectory in the emergence of modern forms of queer consumption—the implicit privatizing logic of the commercialized leisure market. In nego-

tiating the dangers posed by official regulation, constructing viable busi-
nesses and safe meeting places, proprietors—and many men themselves—
partially colluded in attempts to render men invisible, seeking to construct
a queer consumer who was not obviously queer.

GEOGRAPHY

John Alcock identified one venue as the "absolute Mecca of the gay scene"
in the middle of the twentieth century—Lyons's Coventry Street Corner
House.[81] For more than four decades after it opened in 1909, the Corner
House was one of queer London's landmarks. In the evenings and on weekends it attracted men from all classes and neighborhoods. They often queued
patiently for hours for the opportunity to drink, eat, listen to the resident
band, and socialize in what one man called a "great garden party atmosphere." By the 1950s, even the waiters were flamboyantly queer. Thus
appropriated, it was also renamed—the Lilypond. Ostensibly referring to
the flowers painted on the walls, the name also embodied a sense of belonging—this "pond" was the "lilies'" "natural home."[82]

Why did the Corner House acquire such status within queer urban culture? Why did men meet here rather than in other venues or districts? In
short, what shaped the geography of commercial sociability? In 1949, the
Lyons Journal suggested a partial answer, identifying the Corner House's
"pronounced cosmopolitan atmosphere" as that which made it "one of the
most popular and busy rendezvous in the West End."[83] This correlation
between particular cultural forms—"cosmopolitanism"—and place—the
"West End"—is significant. Certainly, queer men flocked to central
London's commercialized leisure districts because of the concentration of
theatres, bars, and restaurants. These opportunities, moreover, were imagined in ways that enhanced their attraction. Cosmopolitanism, as Judith
Walkowitz argues, was associated with "transnational forms of commercialized culture"—the "foreign practices, bodies and spaces" thought
to characterize central London. Cosmopolitanism evoked assumptions
about the opportunities to temporarily transgress boundaries of class or
gender. The intersection between the urban economy and its imaginative
representation marked the West End as an alluring space of consumerist
pleasures.[84]

The West End thus exercised a powerful centripetal influence on the
geography of queer commercial sociability. For many men, the cosmopolitan
world in which classes, races, and genders blurred together was their proper
"home"—somewhere they would be less noticeable. Venues thus attracted

diverse constituencies. The Caravan, for example, drew clerks, shop assistants, or waiters from Maida Vale and Pimlico; laborers from Bermondsey; domestic servants living with employers in Pall Mall, wealthy men from prestigious residential districts, and visitors from the suburbs and beyond.[85]

If the idea of cosmopolitanism concentrated queer commercial sociability in the West End, it also drew men to particular venues. In 1920, for example, SDI Collins described the Café Royal on Regent Street—Wilde's former haunt—as a "high-class establishment" attracting "the most Cosmopolitan crowd in London."[86] Its "Bohemianism" underpinned the tangible sense of license observed by Thomas Burke in 1922:

> Here and there may be seen queer creatures . . . an hermaphroditic creature with side-whiskers and painted eyelashes . . . things in women's clothes that slide cunning eyes upon other women. Male dancers who walk like fugitives from the City of the Plain. Hard-featured ambassadors from Lesbos and Sodom.[87]

It was in this context that the Café Royal—and venues like it—remained an informal "home" for queer men from the theatre, literature, and arts well into the 1940s.[88]

The West End retained its importance throughout the period although the streets and venues where men gathered changed constantly. In the 1920s, for example, queer commercial sociability focused upon the Strand and Leicester Square. "The Strand's business," Burke noted, "is the business of leisure"—and its attractions were powerful. Pubs like the Bunch of Grapes, Wellington, Griffin, and Windsor Castle or the Villiers Street and Strand Hotel restaurants attracted servicemen on leave, workingmen and clerks, and respectable gentlemen.[89] Leicester Square—the heart of London's nightlife and a notorious site of cosmopolitan pleasures—was similarly important. Men socialized in the busy galleries of the Empire and Alhambra, Jack Bloomfield's pub, Russell's Bar, and the Cavour—an elegantly upmarket bar frequented by respectable gentlemen and aspirational chorus boys.[90]

Both neighborhoods declined in importance during the 1920s. In part, this was engineered by the Met and LCC. Responding to the spectacle of "heterosexual" vice and pressure from purity organizations, they mounted a concerted attack on disorderly local venues, initially using DORA regulations, and later licensing legislation. The official attempt to "clean up" Leicester Square was reinforced by commercial decision making. Notorious venues like the Alhambra or Leicester Lounge closed; continental restaurants and beer halls were replaced by teashops, targeting a safer and more profitable market of tourists, shoppers, and families. In 1927, the *News of the World* thus lamented the Square's "decay . . . [its] conversion . . . from gay Bohemianism to ultra-respectability."[91] Within this heterosocial "respectability," queer men's presence became less acceptable, and there were simply fewer places for them to go.[92]

The result was that Piccadilly Circus became *the* focus for queer commercial sociability until the 1950s. Baedecker's *London and Its Environs* (1923) described the Circus as "for the pleasure seeker, the centre of London." It was, moreover, the center of queer London, the point at which the vibrant commercial networks explored in this chapter converged.[93] To the southeast was the Lilypond; on the south side, the Criterion. To the north, on Glasshouse Street, was the Regent's Palace Hotel—where the bar was popular for four decades. The Trocadero was to the northeast on Shaftsbury Avenue. And the pubs around the Circus—places like the White Bear and Ward's Irish House—were known queer venues. In Piccadilly Circus, queer commercial sociability existed in all its diversity, as working-men socialized alongside flamboyant queans, discreet middle-class men, and servicemen.[94]

This vibrant social world was, however, precarious. Even in the 1930s, venues were either closing or declining in visibility as managers responded to an increasingly pervasive official regulation. In 1937, for example, Lyons replaced the "men only" Long Bar with the Salted Almond Cocktail Bar, which *did* admit ladies. The "painted boys" Taylor Croft had watched in the Criterion similarly disappeared. The venue survived as the Standard Bar through the 1950s, but was muted, masculine, and discreet.[95] Through the interventions of the state and the protective instincts of the marketplace queer commercial sociability was gradually displaced from the center of metropolitan life.

By the 1950s, queer venues were increasingly confined to marginal districts like Soho, hidden in backstreets and alleys. As an enduring locus of immigrant, underworld, and working-class sociability, Soho represented a cosmopolitan nocturnal space in which the conventions of respectable urbanity could be discarded. Men of all classes were drawn by the allure of illicit sexual and social pleasures, as were writers and artists rejecting bourgeois convention.[96] Amidst this colorful milieu, queer men's presence was less visible and more acceptable. They were clearly an established presence by the late 1920s, as queans, servicemen, and middle-class queers gathered alongside immigrants, underworld gangs, prostitutes, and the metropolitan literati in cafés. The Black Cat in Old Compton Street, for example, was opened by an Italian immigrant in the 1920s. In 1926, *John Bull* attacked it as a site of undesirable immigrant sociability and prostitution. Yet it also catered for "struggling artists, writers and musicians," and provided a comfortable "home" for Quentin Crisp and his friends.[97] After the Second World War, as Piccadilly Circus declined, Soho cafés like the Little Hut (Greek Street), the Alexandra (Rathbone Place), and Bar-B-Q (Frith Street) became increasingly important centers of queer sociability.[98]

As this suggests, the geography of queer commercial sociability shifted constantly, shaped by commercial and economic changes and the policing of particular locales. That geography was further shaped by changing consumer fashions—a compelling sense of where was hot and where was not. The Lilypond's popularity, for example, reflected the growing fashionability of public eating, represented by the cafés opened by chains like Lyons, the ABC, and the Express Dairy Company. In the 1920s, indeed, queer men frequented most Lyons's premises—including the Piccadilly Popular Restaurant and the Marble Arch and Strand Corner Houses—as well as the Victoria ABC Empire and Express Dairy Co. cafés in Waterloo and Charing Cross Road.[99]

The role of fashion in shaping men's choice of meeting place cannot be overestimated. The growing number of queer dance venues in the 1920s, for example, reflected the nightclub "craze" that gripped metropolitan society in general.[100] Similarly in 1960, Michael Schofield noted how "the coffee houses have taken the place of the licensed bar . . . among younger homosexuals" since the war. Influenced by the growing centrality of American consumerism within metropolitan youth cultures, venues like the Mousehole (Swallow Street), the Haymarket Coffee House, and the Matelot (Panton Street) became increasingly popular amongst young queer men.[101]

While queer venues were concentrated in the West End, there were other clusters elsewhere. In part, these reflected where queer men lived. The most distinctive venues were in working-class neighborhoods in east and south London—dockside pubs like the Prospect of Whitby (Wapping Stairs) or Charlie Brown's—(West India Dock Road). Dock laborers, sailors from across the world, and families mingled freely with flamboyant local queans and slumming gentlemen in a protean milieu where queer men and casual homosexual encounters were an accepted part of everyday life. The White Horse in Brixton was thus, one observer noted, "full of prostitutes . . . with coloured men . . . and perverts of a very low type."[102]

In part, these venues were popular because they were also sites of a rough masculine sociability. There were similar commercial enclaves within other working-class neighborhoods, particularly around military facilities. Between the wars, places like the Old World Hotel, the Wellington and Lord Hull pubs, and the Express Dairy Co. Café on Waterloo Road were packed with servicemen staying at the Union Jack Club. As a result, they were hugely popular with middle-class queers and queans looking for trade. In 1930, Bill Cronin-Wilson thus visited "a pub in the Waterloo Road awash with seamen, most of whose bodies . . . were not only able but willing."[103] Pubs like the Grenadier (Wilton Place), Tattershall's Tavern (Knightsbridge Green), the Alexandra Hotel (Hyde Park Corner) and the Packenham and Swan were similarly noted for the opportunities to pick up guardsmen from the nearby barracks.[104]

Queer commercial sociability was, above all, highly peripatetic. Men moved between venues constantly, responding to police activities or purges by staff. "Meeting places," Rodney Garland observed, "changed all the time":

> The underground first took up a pub and met there regularly . . . the "obvious" . . . pansies . . . got into high spirits, let down their hair and screamed; —and the underground was given away . . . the pub . . . soon gained an unsavoury reputation . . . [and] was raided . . . and the publican . . . told to be more careful in future . . . he heeded the warning and if next day a too obvious looking person turned up he refused . . . to serve him.

The result was that "there were comparatively few pubs which had not at one time or another been taken up by the underground."[105]

CONCLUSION

Edgware Road was—indeed, still is—a busy commercial thoroughfare, running northwest from Marble Arch to connect central and north London. It was, moreover, a physical and cultural frontier, upon which distinct districts converged: to the north and west residential districts like Paddington, Bayswater, and Maida Vale, home to a transient working-class and migrant population; to the southeast the West End; Hyde Park directly south; to the east prestigious residential areas like Mayfair. As a result, local bars and cafés attracted a diverse clientele, crossing boundaries of class, ethnicity, gender, and sexuality in a nocturnal world noted for its protean and cosmopolitan character. Throughout the 1920s, the Adelphi Rooms, for example, were regularly hired for local dances—by the Irish Clan Na' Heirran for its Saint Patrick's Day Ball or by Laurie F. for black men and white women.[106]

In the decade after the First World War this neighborhood culture sustained a distinctive queer enclave. The street's proximity to the barracks in Regent's Park and Knightsbridge made its pubs popular amongst soldiers from the Brigade of Guards. Drawn by the opportunities to pick up rough trade, bourgeois men like John Lehmann simultaneously made the short journey up from Mayfair. This conventionally masculine homosociality, however, coexisted uneasily with the scene surveyed by Thomas Burke in 1922:

> The painted boys . . . to be seen in certain rendezvous in Edgware Road . . . You may know these places by the strong odour of scent when you enter them, and the absence of women. The sweet boys stand at the counter, or lounge, beautifully apparelled and groomed in chairs, under the wandering eyes of middle aged grey faced men.[107]

Burke encountered a vibrant public world forged by workingmen from nearby rooming districts. In 1927, for example, police watched a "typical 'Nancy'"—a youth in a "dress blue suit . . . long hair brushed back"—visit a coffee shop before going to the cinema opposite.[108] Leslie K.—a waiter living in Westbourne Grove—similarly hired the Adelphi Rooms for fortnightly dances throughout 1926 after being barred from halls in other neighborhoods. Selling tickets via friends and acquaintances, his events attracted up to three hundred men—clerks, cabinet makers, a coach painter—"painted and powdered . . . [wearing] earrings and low necked dresses." By winter 1926 such events seem to have become simply too visible, too vibrant, too extensive. After several letters of complaint, local police raided the Adelphi Rooms and prosecuted Leslie, sparking a series of "grave dance hall scandals." This dramatic intervention, and the ensuing responses of local proprietors, reconfigured the district's character. While men continued to socialize discreetly in local pubs long after 1927, the "painted boys'" rendezvous disappeared and Edgware Road's reputation faded.[109]

This microhistory suggests the critical change in the spatial and cultural organization of queer commercial sociability after the First World War. For while their interactions with the state and the marketplace enabled men to forge a place for themselves in London's cafés and bars, this simultaneously underpinned a long-term trajectory towards a specific kind of commercial scene—a process of privatization. If this tendency was evident between the wars, it was reinforced by wider cultural and economic changes in the 1940s and 1950s. Paradoxically, as the unique conditions of wartime and the reinvigorated consumerism associated with 1950s "affluence" sustained a marked expansion in the number of queer venues, so official regulation became more effective in rendering those venues—and the men who frequented them—invisible. Clubs like the Rockingham emblematized a wider transformation of queer consumer culture, which rendered increasingly anachronistic and marginal those backstreet Soho cafés and pubs where many men continued to contest the limits on their visibility.

By the 1950s, queer commercial sociability was thus a faint shadow of what it had been between the wars. As places like the Caravan, where flamboyantly camp men had danced, disappeared, as venues retreated from Piccadilly Circus to the alleys of Soho and became evermore exclusive, this world faded towards invisibility, and the possibilities for public interaction were confined within peculiarly narrow spatial and cultural limits. Queer sociability was increasingly discreet and separate from "normal" urban life, the ongoing negotiations between official regulation, individual proprietors, and men's own demands for a secure "home" structuring what might be termed a commercial closet, outside of which it was dangerous to step.

When Tricky Dicky and Ron Storme began organizing queer dance nights in the late 1960s, they thus saw themselves—and were widely perceived—as creating new opportunities for public sociability in the "permissive society." For Richard Smith, Storme's Porchester Hall dances were "where British gay life finally emerged from the shadows . . . where the modern gay club scene began"—the "first opportunity for . . . men to meet in large numbers in public."[110] In postwar London it seemed inconceivable that men had *ever* been able to dance together, to kiss, embrace, or be openly queer in commercial venues. Venues like the Adelphi Rooms had simply vanished from collective memory, forced into historical invisibility through the contested imposition of a commercial closet that by the 1960s seemed to have existed forever. Rather than a new departure, however, Tricky Dicky and men like him were engaging in an ongoing negotiation over the limits of queer commercial sociability—a process far more complex than "emerging from the shadows."

The effects of this process were contradictory, simultaneously *both* liberating *and* exclusionary. For some men the emergence of venues like the Rockingham was unequivocally affirmative, offering them opportunities to socialize in a safe, respectable and semiprivate space. They built their own closet, so that they could disappear from public view. Many others, however, existed outside this realm. They continued to meet in London's cafés and pubs, engaging in an ongoing struggle over the terms upon which they could socialize in public—risking exclusion should their behavior exceed the informal parameters of acceptability and facing the constant risk of a police raid.

If these divergent experiences coalesced upon visual differences in cultural style and behavior they were, crucially, overdetermined by the cruder operations of the market economy, particularly men's differential access to capital. Throughout the period, those venues that offered the greatest degree of safety were always the most expensive—and thereby most exclusive—high society restaurants, bars, and members clubs. Privacy came at a price. Venues like the Rockingham simply consolidated the privileged position of the wealthy, cementing a radical divide in access to secure social space along lines of class. This is not to say that poorer men were unable to participate in queer commercial sociability. Yet their consumer choices were tightly constrained and in the—relatively—more open world of backstreet cafés and pubs they entered into a radically different relationship with the law, individual proprietors, and each other. As queer lives slowly moved away from the public sites of urinal, street, and park, the commercialization of queer cultures inscribed profound social differences and antagonisms into the geography of urban life.[111]

4

THE BATHS

In July 1931, unable to find a room at his club, Mr. Otter-Barry decided to spend the night at the Savoy Turkish Baths at 92 Jermyn Street. He arrived just after midnight and was allocated a bed in a ground-floor cubicle. After bathing and a massage, he was in the plunge pool "when a man entered . . . and stared intently at him." Returning to his cubicle, Otter-Barry received a glass of water from an attendant, who covered him with a blanket and drew a curtain across the entrance.

> The man who had stared at him pulled the curtain aside and thrust his face in the aperture. [Otter-Barry] made no movement and the man withdrew his head . . . pacing up and down outside . . . during the next quarter of an hour the man put his head inside the curtain about three times . . . He went to sleep but was awakened by another man who pulled the curtain aside and looked at him.

Later he woke to find a naked man in his bed "attempting to force his penis . . . into . . . [his] hand." He "pushed the man off and told him to get out. As the man scrambled off he said . . . 'Are you quite sure that is nothing you want to do?'"[1]

This was, apparently, an unnerving experience. Unexpectedly, Otter-Barry had stumbled into a nocturnal otherworld where the conventions of a "normal" bourgeois existence seemed no longer to apply, where men interacted freely and without fear, where it was possible to get into bed with a complete stranger—a queer world in every sense. This was a moral inversion symbolized by crossing from the quintessential Englishness of Jermyn Street and its gentlemen's outfitters to an establishment where the walls were painted red and the décor was "Oriental," "Arabic," or "Turkish." In Otter-Barry's story—later narrated to an LCC official—it is possible to discern how the space behind this threshold sustained a distinctive sexual culture, which many other men found far from unnerving. Michael S. visited the Savoy regularly throughout the 1950s. This was an era in which the risk of arrest or assault seemed ever-present to many men as they moved through London's public and commercial spaces. Yet amidst "quite an air of intolerance . . . there was this little place . . . where everything *was* tolerated."[2] Like countless other men in the decades after 1918, Michael experienced London's baths as an enduring sanctuary. Here they forged a world with its own sexual conventions, social character, protocols, and geography that was almost impermeable to hostile surveillance. Here they could meet friends, relax, and have sex. When asked if he went to the baths often, Barry's reply was immediate and emphatic: "As often as I can . . . It was terrific. It really was."[3]

In many ways London's baths were an anomaly. Thanks to their longevity—the Savoy remained open until 1975—they occupy a prominent place in the contemporary queer imagination: Neil Bartlett, for example, weaves his wonderfully evocative novel *Mr. Clive and Mr. Page* (1996) around a bath in Jermyn Street.[4] Yet they have left relatively few traces in the historical record. The legal sources on which much of my work draws are scant in this respect since the baths were simply beyond the knowledge of most Londoners—including the Met and LCC for long periods of time. This is, in itself, a remarkable testament to the security the baths offered: this was a commercial space in which men felt safe enough to have sex relatively openly—a public space which was, in effect, private. There is a further anomaly in the intersection between social class and this kind of sexual culture. While many workingmen, shop assistants, or clerks frequented the baths, their clientele was primarily drawn from the professions, business, or high society. Indeed, as Pat recalled, for such men the baths were a "very strong [source] of gayness . . . the main scene if you weren't in with a party."[5] Yet these were not the sort of men who normally dropped their "masks" in a commercial venue, or often, indeed, risked engaging in public sex. Again, we are brought back to the baths' status as a sanctuary—offering a privacy that approximated the bourgeois home while simultaneously allowing men to meet. This chapter explores these contradictions. My question is simple: how could this world exist?

SEX AND SOCIABILITY

This world was, in part, an unexpected by-product of the Victorian obsession with the health, purity, and cleanliness of the male body—an obsession manifested through both the provisions of municipal government and fashionable forms of bourgeois leisure. From the 1840s onwards, anxieties surrounding the physical and moral condition of London's poor impelled local authorities to construct public baths in an attempt to cleanse and civilize the urban "residuum." Bermondsey Metropolitan Borough Council, for example, first opened baths for local dockers in 1853. In 1927 they replaced these with a "modern establishment" in Grange Road, which contained two swimming baths, 126 slipper baths in cubicles, and Turkish and Russian baths (fig. 9).[6] The arrival of increasing numbers of Eastern European Jewish immigrants in the East End intensified this process from the 1880s. In Whitechapel, for example, vapor baths like Schewschick's in Brick Lane— offering ritual Sabbath cleansing—supplemented the public baths.[7]

These developments paralleled the increasing popularity of private steam baths and Turkish baths amongst bourgeois men, particularly after the 1860s. As Malcolm Shifrin has documented, the number of such establishments increased rapidly in the last decades of the nineteenth century. This was a new commercial arena of fashionable masculine homosociality in which men could relax, cleanse and purify the body, and meet with friends. Indeed, in many ways the Turkish bath was an informal gentleman's club, providing refreshments and sleeping cubicles alongside an array of steam rooms, massage parlors, and plunge pools. In 1916 there were twenty-five, including nine operated by William Cooper's Savoy Turkish Baths Company and nine owned by the rival Nevill Company. Although this had fallen to fourteen by 1931—and continued to decline—steam baths remained a feature of cultural life for the metropolitan cognoscenti well into the postwar decades, when the guidebook *London Night and Day* could recommend a visit for those "a little heavy in the head."[8]

Queer men had clearly established a distinct presence within the baths' wider clientele by 1900, when the itinerant American Edward Stevenson identified "a small group well-recognised as homosexual rendezvous."[9] From Stevenson's time into the 1960s, three private Turkish baths were known "homosexual rendezvous." The Savoy opened in the late nineteenth century. The baths under the Imperial Hotel in Russell Square were open from 1913 until 1966, when the hotel itself was demolished. Both were large, ornate, and highly reputable premises. The third "rendezvous" was smaller, cheaper, and less prepossessing, built behind a normal shop front with a plain red

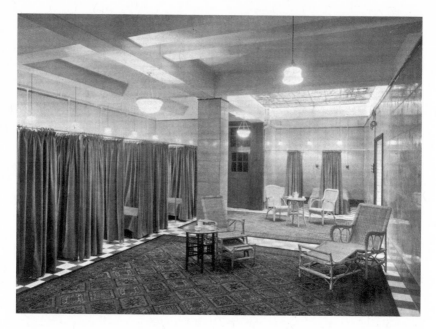

Figure 9. Photograph, Bermondsey Turkish Baths, 1927. Photographer unknown. London Metropolitan Archives.

door at 16 Harrow Road. Owned by the Nevill Company from 1880 to 1947, it was known as the Edgware Road Turkish Baths. It then survived two quick changes of management, remaining open as Tyler's and then the Metro Turkish Baths until 1963, when it was demolished to build the West Way flyover.[10]

The long-standing reputation of these establishments ensured their importance to successive generations of queer men. That they acquired the reputation as "homosexual rendezvous" in the first place reflected two broader aspects of their character. In functioning as an arena for bourgeois homosociality, the baths were equivalent to the Victorian East End settlements or the Bolton Whitmanite circle: single-sex cultural spaces that sustained intense emotional attachments and friendships—often articulated in near-erotic terms—between men.[11] In the baths, moreover, such interactions occurred in a space devoted to the cultivation of bodily health and physicality that brought naked male bodies into close proximity. The Savoy, A. J. Langguth recalled,

> represented a twilight arena for elderly men who came to sweat poisons from their systems and youths who came to strike beguiling poses in Turkish

towels . . . they provided a discreet place to inspect a young man before offering a cup of tea at Lyons.[12]

As Langguth suggests, the male body became subject to a pervasive gaze,
through which the conventions of bathing actuated a particular form of
spectatorship. Many found these opportunities to see and be seen by other
men irresistible. Similarly the swimming pool of the Central London
YMCA in Great Russell Street—founded in the mid-nineteenth century to
provide young men with accommodation and leisure facilities—was, according to Bernard Dobson,

> for men only and . . . full of young fellows . . . I thought this was great. You
> weren't allowed to wear swimming trunks—it was considered unhygienic—
> so as you can imagine a lot of people who were gay were members of the
> YMCA.[13]

Homosociality blended into homoeroticism, admiration into desire. For
Otter-Barry—"stared at in an unpleasant manner"—becoming the subject
of this sexualized gaze was profoundly disconcerting.[14]

When Stevenson visited London's baths around 1900, he echoed this
emphasis on the erotics of spectacle. The baths could not, he recalled, "be
utilised then and there for homosexual practices . . . [being] merely establishments for anatomic inspections: for making appointments to meet elsewhere."[15] Within two decades, however, the baths' reputation had shifted
discernibly and they became known as the site of an open and unabashed
sexual culture. By 1918, Beverley Nichols—who regularly visited the
Imperial while on leave—could grumble to his diary after an "uneventful
night."[16] The tangible expectations that lead to Nichols's disappointment
were echoed in Robert Hutton's ironic account of his experiences after the
Armistice. Hutton

> decided that London would be gay . . . [and] was not mistaken. The next
> three weeks came as near to killing me as the war ever had . . . I slept for a
> week in a Turkish bath, which meant, virtually, that I did not sleep at all.[17]

The interactions that precluded Hutton's sleep were, moreover, replicated
outside the private baths, particularly in the public baths run by the
Bermondsey and West Ham borough councils. As Michael S. suggested,
"most of the baths put up for the benefit of the poor to wash—if they had a
steam bath—would turn into a gay bath."[18] By the 1950s, Bermondsey was
"famous" in queer circles, achieving literary acclaim in Rodney Garland's *The
Heart in Exile* (1953).[19] Kenneth Williams, who "went [there] for traditional

interest" in 1958, found it "quite fabulous."[20] If Bermondsey and West Ham were the best known, other municipal baths offered more ad hoc opportunities. In February 1952, for example, four men were discovered having sex at the Greenwich Baths in Trafalgar Road.[21] It was also—as Dobson and Tony Garrett learned in the 1940s—"easy to pick people up" at the YMCA, where there were "all kinds of goings on in the showers and in and out of the bath."[22] And after the Second World War these institutional opportunities were joined by a handful of smaller saunas, deliberately run by queer men for a queer clientele. Michael S. knew of two, including a "fairly unlikely place [with] no sign outside or anything" in Vauxhall Bridge Road, where there was "a bit of sex."[23]

This "bit of sex" took place within a culture that was simultaneously unabashed and institutionalized, deeply enmeshed in the wider spatial and temporal organization of London's baths. For Hunter Davies, writing in the mid-1960s, the central feature of this culture seemed clear: the baths were a "sure fire set up for homosexuals . . . because it is possible to stay all night."[24] Harrow Road, for example, was open from 9:00 A.M. Monday until 9:00 A.M. Sunday. Like all the large private baths, it had the reputation that "everything used to go on at night."[25] During the day, queer men were part of a mixed—primarily bourgeois—clientele, and their behavior was constrained. At night, by contrast, when this clientele left and with fewer staff on duty, the baths came alive. As Pat recalled, "especially late all sorts of things used to go on . . . [during] the night time it was very high percentage gay."[26]

If this sexual culture had its own temporal rhythms, it was also shaped by the baths' physical structure. Central was the distinction between the public rooms and the individual cubicles provided for changing and sleeping. The Savoy, for example, was on two floors: a reception desk with lockers and cubicles on the ground floor, and the treatment rooms and more cubicles downstairs in the basement. All the cubicles contained two beds and were curtained. While most treatment rooms were visible from the center of the basement, the steam and hot rooms were screened by a glass partition "through which the blurred silhouettes of bathers can be seen" and a brick wall.[27]

It was these partially concealed public rooms, where men met in the steam or around the pool, that were the site of remarkably open sexual advances. In 1930, for example, an LCC inspector was approached twice in the vapor room. One man "expos[ed] and strok[ed] his person." Another "partially clothed . . . beckoned . . . with his finger, exposed his person and made suggestive gestures."[28] Cruising also took place along the public avenues of movement, with men "strolling the corridor of the cubicles" exchanging glances.[29] "You just used to watch other people eyes," recalled Pat, then "you knew full well they were gay."[30]

Most sexual encounters took place in the cubicles themselves, creating a distinctive microgeography predicated upon the movement between public and private space. Mr. A., for example, "stood in the entrance to his cubicle with his person exposed and in an excited condition," watching passersby. He exchanged glances with one man, taking him into the cubicle and drawing the curtain. The man left "shortly afterwards wiping his person." Mr. A. returned to the corridor: "A further customer approached him and entered the cubicle with him . . . both of them came out from the cubicle shortly afterwards, wiping their persons and thighs as they did so."[31]

These interactions, replicated at Harrow Road and the Imperial, suggest the dual basis of the baths' popularity. First, they were a secure space in which men could have sex—at length and often with multiple partners—without fear of detection, arrest, or expulsion. Pat found that "you could easily slip into bed with the other bloke without any trouble": "You used to hear grunts, groans and God knows what going on."[32] Second, as the very audibility of these encounters and the confidence with which men moved around the premises suggests, they experienced this space as exclusively theirs. Like Pat, they automatically assumed that "because [a man] stayed the night there it was almost certain [he was] gay."[33]

Shedding their inhibitions—discarding the masks that structured their public lives—men thus approached complete strangers in the public rooms and individual cubicles, clearly expecting a positive response, or at least confident that neither they—nor anyone watching—would react violently. While the LCC inspector mentioned above was in his cubicle, for example, another man entered and "asked whether he had all the satisfaction he wanted."[34] On a later observation, "a bather who had been walking up and down the passage ways between the cubicles with his rear fully exposed entered [his] cubicle . . . and asked whether he was too tired . . . putting out his hand and touching . . . [his] person."[35] The assumed congregation of queer bodies provided an opportunity for sexual fulfillment and pleasure, guaranteed a degree of security, and functioned as a powerful affirmation that one was not alone. In sharp contrast to London's streets, parks, or commercial venues, in the baths, Pat remembered, "no one worried a damn."[36]

Access to this space of erotic pleasure and affirmation was only available at a price. Baedecker's 1923 guidebook *London and Its Environs* provided a full list of charges. A daytime visit to the Savoy or Imperial cost 3s 6d, an overnight stay 6s. The Harrow Road baths were somewhat cheaper—3s and

2s, respectively.[37] By 1951 the Savoy's charges had risen to 6s and 10s 6d.[38] The private Turkish baths were, by any standards, an expensive luxury, and one that many could not afford. The national serviceman John Alcock was initially treated to a night at the Imperial by a wealthy RAF officer in the late 1940s. While he enjoyed the experience immensely, Alcock returned only "as often as I could afford it, it was expensive."[39] Such commercial barriers reinforced the baths' status as—primarily—an elite masculine leisure space, with access fractured along class lines. The regular clientele tended to be professionals, businessmen, and writers—men like the stockbroker Lawrence B.[40] On moving to London in 1929, for example, the writer William Plomer was taken round the baths by a French aristocratic acquaintance, Rene Janin.[41]

For many upper and middle-class men this exclusivity and social respectability was part of the baths' attraction. High admission charges went a long way to enhancing their personal security, deterring potential blackmailers or muggers, and those seeking to "tap" the wealthy clientele. They were drawn, moreover, by the promise of a safe and private space, distanced from the disreputable and dangerous public city, and where the risk of arrest or assault was minute. The baths allowed such men to find sexual encounters or forge social ties, while all the time avoiding the risks associated with public queer life, functioning as a key resource in managing a rigidly compartmentalized double life. Even men like Robert Hutton, who had few qualms about cruising London's streets, regularly visited the baths. That the baths' security was such a commonplace in elite circles meant they attracted many men who would not normally have participated in queer urban life. The Savoy, recalled Michael S., was "very well known," and "one of the attractions was that so many famous people were seen there"—men like the film star Rock Hudson.[42]

Although the baths' notoriety often rested upon the sexual opportunities they offered, it would be wrong to see this simply as a realm of promiscuous and impersonal encounters. Certainly, the atmosphere could be highly charged, to the extent that some men found it off-putting. Michael S., for example, who was looking for a lifelong friend, "didn't go often . . . perhaps I was a bit fussy or something."[43] Yet for many others the baths continued to sustain an exclusive masculine homosociality, functioning as an informal club where they could socialize with friends and forge new social ties. Hugh Walpole thus regularly bathed with his friends, Arnold Bennett and CFG Masterman.[44] One LCC inspector gestured towards precisely this kind of communality in 1931, when he described the "sounds of men talking . . . all the time he was awake."[45]

The intersection between masculine communality and the opportunity to be amongst other men in an environment where their desires could be expressed freely and without shame or fear meant that many individuals experienced the baths as a powerful source of affirmation. Before John Alcock's "first introduction . . . to the Turkish Baths" he was young, naive, and new to London, "very furtive and careful" in public, and unsure about his desires in private. At the Imperial he seems to have undergone something of an epiphany. This was the moment when Alcock realized that he was not alone: "Everybody was looking and everybody was at it . . . particularly at the Turkish Baths." Armed with a newfound confidence, Alcock's life was transformed.[46]

The baths' central position within this narrative of emergent selfhood was surprisingly common. When asked by an affair "if he had always been that way inclined," Lawrence B. replied immediately: "Yes . . . he had known several boys and usually found them at the Turkish Baths." Going to the baths, for Lawrence, *both* affirmed a broader sense of sexual subjectivity *and* allowed him to forge intimate relationships.[47] Given this, it was, perhaps, no coincidence that when Christopher Isherwood was undertaking what Humphrey Carpenter calls "the process of bringing [Benjamin] Britten out" in 1937, he took him to spend a night at the Savoy. Again the near-therapeutic quality of such an evening seems obvious. "Whether or not anything happened . . . that night," Carpenter observes, Britten "seems to have felt more ready to become sexually active."[48]

The contrast between this world and the more protean municipal baths is instructive. The men arrested in the Greenwich Baths in 1952, for example, included a twenty-six-year-old traveler, fifty-three-year-old caterer, thirty-six-year-old waiter, and forty-eight-year-old actor.[49] Such establishments, noted Hunter Davies,

> vary a lot in comfort and cleanliness but they are all comparatively cheap and the customers are generally a lot younger—many of them the local dockers and factory workers who genuinely go the baths to avail themselves of the facilities but are not averse to enjoying the other facilities . . . [50]

At places like Bermondsey, Barry suggested, "there were always one or two boys on the make, but one got to recognise them."[51] Indeed, it was precisely this dangerous edge, the thrill of social transgression and the opportunities to pick up rough trade that often propelled those middle-class men—men like Kenneth Williams—to make the journey south of the river.

In the postwar decades even the private Turkish baths lost much of their exclusivity, respectability, and grandeur. Their physical deterioration—by the 1960s the furnishings were "rather faded and threadbare"—represented their declining popularity and the owners' unwillingness to invest in everyday maintenance.[52] As demand fell, the cost of admission was reduced. Simultaneously, the baths became more accessible *and* less secure. It was in this context that men like Barry began to find the Imperial "rather dangerous and mercenary."[53] In October 1952, for example, the police were called to deal with an assault on a bather, Hugh S. His assailant was discharged after Hugh apparently refused to give evidence.[54] By the late 1950s the Harrow Road baths, which had always been cheaper than the Savoy or Imperial, were, in Eric Wright's words, "rather downmarket." Despite this, they remained

> very popular with the night owls who often queued waiting to get in after the pubs closed . . . [It was] very much cheaper than finding a hotel room . . . Not that many people managed to get much sleep with all that to-ing and fro-ing going on.[55]

Even if the baths retained their reputation well beyond the 1950s, their golden age seemed to have passed.

COMMERCIAL TOLERANCE

This world could only exist with the tacit acceptance of the management and staff—their willingness to ignore customers' behavior in the interests of profit. If none of the large baths were ever owned by—or deliberately run for—queer men, they were, nonetheless, remarkably tolerant. In the 1940s Barry regularly went to Harrow Road. One night, another man entered his cubicle:

> Harry . . . the old man in charge of the place got on the rampage for some reason. He'd never done so before and I never knew him to after . . . he said, "here, come on, you can't do that. You'd better leave" . . . it was very awkward and . . . wasn't my initiative at all. I was furious. Just took no notice. Pushed the man out and went to sleep and stayed the night.[56]

As Barry himself recalled, the attendant's actions on this occasion were unique. Despite being asked to leave, however, he felt comfortable enough in both the baths and his relationship with the attendant—with whom he was on a first name basis—to remain overnight and continue to frequent the establishment.

By the 1940s, such commercial laissez-faire was a well-established and widely recognized characteristic of all the large Turkish baths. At the Savoy in 1930, for example, LCC inspectors described how "no attempt was made to supervise or control the conduct of customers . . . it seemed almost impossible that the attendant could have been unaware of what was going on."[57] Later this became even more explicit when "at least one attendant passed on several occasions" while men were having sex in a corridor.[58] In the 1950s, Pat recalled "only one bloke . . . sleeping upstairs . . . people used to wander round more or less at will . . . without any trouble whatsoever."[59] The result was what Michael S. called "quite an orgy place," with increasingly open sexual encounters in the steam room.[60] That men were prepared to have sex publicly and did not, apparently, fear exclusion or arrest again suggests that the baths had become *their* space.

This is not to say that their actions were wholly unfettered. Rather, the staff patrolled an informal boundary between public and private encounters, attempting to limit men's visibility and reinforcing a sexual microgeography that, for the most part, situated cruising within corridors and public rooms while confining sexual interactions to individual cubicles. Such a place-specific form of regulation relied not on excluding queer men— though that threat was ever-present—but on informal warnings when they became too indiscreet. Pat thus "never heard of anybody being turfed out . . . [although] you sometimes heard of an attendant raising his voice."[61] These tacit geographical limits on acceptable behavior were, moreover, mirrored by temporal shifts in internal policing, when staff decided that sexual encounters had become too visible or reacted to external pressure by temporarily clamping down. In 1947, following representations to the Savoy's management, the LCC noted with satisfaction

> four attendants are ordinarily on duty in the public part of the baths and . . . exercise a reasonably close supervision over all bathers . . . The secretary of the Licensee Company . . . make[s] frequent visits . . . [to] all parts of the establishment. Notices in the following terms were put up in the changing room and in the public part of the baths between 10th May and 25th June . . .—"any person mis-conducting himself in the baths will be handed over to the police."[62]

The result, Hunter Davis noted, was that "staff mostly turn a blind eye to much of the midnight prowling . . . if the activity is not too blatant."[63]

This kind of ambiguous and contingent tolerance, together with the increasingly exclusive character of certain baths, was, moreover, reinforced by complex historical changes. As early as the 1930s, although places like the Savoy retained a conventionally respectable clientele—including senior police officers—many "normal" men were beginning to be put off by the highly charged sexual atmosphere. In 1931, for example, Alfred Craig noted, "I myself have stopped using these baths owing to the [indecent] conduct."[64] This process was reinforced by developments in domestic sanitation and shifting metropolitan fashions, which reduced the need for municipal baths and the demand for private steam baths. In response, bath owners appear to have tried to guarantee their continued profitability by retaining the queer market, further relaxing their internal policing. As places like the London and Provincial Baths (76 Jermyn Street) closed and large-scale concerns like Nevill's and the Savoy Company folded during the 1940s, it was, perhaps, no accident that those baths that survived had acquired an almost exclusively queer clientele. Indeed, when the Savoy Company collapsed in 1947, the Jermyn Street establishment was one of only two to remain open—albeit under new management.[65] Guidebooks like the *New London Spy* continued to direct the cosmopolitan man-about-town to the baths well into the 1960s. Nonetheless, they acknowledged that this was a strange, disorienting, and potentially dangerous otherworld: "If you adopt the Boy Scouts' motto Be Prepared you should be able to spend a night at the Turkish Baths . . . the steam has a peculiar effect on some chaps."[66]

HOW?

That the baths acquired such a reputation for security and, indeed, that they remained open for so long is, in many senses, surprising—particularly since the Met was at times only too aware of what was going on. In 1930, for example, DI Sands told an LCC hearing that the Savoy's day manager had been "informed that complaints had been received . . . alleging indecent conduct" in October 1917, March 1920, and August 1925. All three complaints were made in writing—two anonymously.[67] On each occasion, however, officers took no action beyond issuing the manager an informal verbal warning, preferring to pass the matter on to the LCC for investigation.[68] By 1931, Alfred Craig could note angrily that "I have made endless complaints to . . . the police over the conduct of the bathers but with no avail."[69]

Craig's frustration was, in part, self-inflicted: he was complaining to the wrong people, since the baths were not formally the Met's concern. During the First World War the National Vigilance Association (NVA) conducted a sustained campaign against the "social evil" of West End steam baths and massage establishments operating as fronts for commercialized "heterosexual" vice. Under the General Powers Acts of 1915 and 1920—products of the NVA's insistent lobbying—such establishments were brought under the licensing authority of the LCC's Public Control Committee (PCC). As well as stipulating certain material standards, licenses provided for revocation—and hence closure—if "the person carrying on . . . such establishment is of bad character" or the premises were "used for any immoral purpose."[70]

As the NVA themselves noted, these provisions had unexpected results.

> To begin with all requests were referred to the police for report since at [the start of the First World War] they had certain information . . . With the passing of the act the police ceased to make inquiries on their own [and] to obtain the information. Control is now entirely in the hands of the LCC who inspect through their own inspectors.[71]

This diffusion of power had profound implications for the ways in which baths were regulated, opening up a space within which the Savoy, Harrow Road, and Imperial could continue to function as queer meeting places for decades. For while the police visited smaller establishments like the Vauxhall Bridge Road sauna in the 1950s and retained responsibility for regulating the municipal baths, they never investigated or raided these larger establishments. Even against the municipal baths police action was rare, usually following a complaint from a man who had been "indecently assaulted" or the activities of members of staff. The municipal bath was outside the Met's normal operational realm. Baths like Bermondsey or West Ham, moreover, tried to deflect potential scrutiny through a complex protection racket. They were, Michael S. recalled, "protected from the police by gangsters . . . the Kray brothers and so on . . . the [baths] paid the gangsters to keep the police away."[72]

Insulated from police surveillance by the formal structures of municipal governance, the private baths benefited further from the severe constraints that the PCC's inspection procedures placed upon their own regulatory capacity. In 1931 the chief officer described how

> it has not been the practice to visit the hot rooms. Moreover it is obvious that a visit, necessarily of short duration made in the ordinary way by an Inspector cannot be of much value for . . . determining whether or not irregular practices are carried on.[73]

As the officer recognized, it was unlikely that a prearranged annual inspection, particularly if it took place during daytime, would ever find anything amiss. Despite this, he did not think alterations were necessary: "The present arrangements should be continued unless a complaint is made to the Council . . . [when] the question of making special arrangements for inspection . . .

would be submitted to the Committee."[74] The anxieties generated by the possibility of homosex were simply insufficient to justify a proactive, rather than reactive, form of surveillance. Relying upon public complaints when the baths were becoming increasingly queer rendered the PCC's regulation extraordinarily impotent. The three occasions when officials confronted the Savoy's manager about the "indecent conduct" that took place on his premises were all prompted by such complaints. But, as DI Sands admitted, "the number of complaints . . . was undoubtedly very small considering the length of time"—and, he might have added, the bath's growing notoriety.[75]

The result was that baths were almost invisible to the official gaze for long periods of time. "There has never," observed the NVA in 1930, "been a big attack on Turkish baths." Yet as the discussion above suggests, this did not mean that they were entirely free from surveillance. "Individual establishments," the NVA continued, "*have* been prosecuted from time to time for irregularities due to perverts."[76] It is possible that opposition to Harrow Road's application for a new license in 1941 was prompted by concerns surrounding such "irregularities," though this is unclear from the surviving evidence.[77] Certainly, the Savoy became subject to sustained official attention on two separate occasions. In 1947 a disgruntled dismissed employee made allegations of "misconduct between bathers" to the PCC. They responded by sending inspectors into the premises on seven occasions: posing "as ordinary bathers . . . [they did] not disclose their identities and remained at the premises all night."[78] On the first instance the plunge bath was found unattended. Informal pressure forced the company to increase their night staff. As a result, "the arrangements made for supervision appeared to be adequate and working satisfactorily [and] nothing was seen during the visit to suggest that anything improper was going on." No further action was taken.[79]

Both the PCC's reluctance to initiate formal proceedings and the management's hasty compliance were reactions to an earlier attempt to revoke the Savoy's license, in the most notorious scandal to affect any bath. While the PCC appears to have taken no action following the complaints made in 1917 and 1920, further complaints in November 1925 and February 1928 forced the committee to conduct covert observations inside the premises.[80] Although nothing came of these visits, Mr. W. Baker (inspector under the Petroleum Acts) and Mr. E. Kessel (collector of license duties) were again deputed to visit the Savoy on several occasions between autumn 1929 and spring 1930. Posing as bathers, they observed men having sex and were approached themselves. In April 1930 the PCC used its evidence to oppose the Savoy's licensing reapplication as "the establishment had been improperly conducted." "Indecent conduct" had taken place and, the LCC solicitor alleged, "no attempt was made to supervise or control the conduct of customers."[81]

At the public hearing the Savoy Company mounted a vigorous defense of their licence—and commercial survival—employing the highly regarded barristers Sir Henry Curtis-Bennett and Walter Frampton. Their case hinged upon two interconnected arguments. The first argument was that the Savoy was "a very large old-established business to which . . . a great number of highly reputable gentlemen go continuously." Given its undoubtedly respectable clientele it was, Curtis-Bennett suggested, inconceivable that "indecent conduct" could have occurred. Second: even if such conduct had taken place, the management and staff were unaware of it. The defense produced staff testimony, plans, models, and photographs to prove that this was indeed the case. On these grounds, Curtis-Bennett concluded, "no case had been made in opposition . . . [All] that could be said was that the staff should be instructed to take even greater care." The committee agreed. While accepting the inspectors' evidence, they remained "not entirely satisfied that the management and attendants . . . were aware of what was taking place." While "the necessity . . . of more adequate supervision . . . [was] very strongly emphasised," the licence was renewed.[82]

In October 1931 the Savoy Company faced another public hearing after Alfred Craig complained that "persons resorting to the establishment behaved improperly . . . [and that while] in bed in a cubicle . . . he was indecently assaulted."[83] This time the licence was revoked.[84] Once again the company's size, prestige, and commercial strength ensured its survival. On appeal the case came before the Marlborough Street Magistrate. The PCC again submitted that "if the servants permitted such conduct as that on the premises . . . the company are responsible and the committee are entitled to exercise their powers." Under "severe cross-examination" by Curtis-Bennett, however, the chief witness could not demonstrate the staff's connivance conclusively. Indeed, as in cross-examination at the previous hearing, Joseph Welsh, secretary of the Savoy Company, denied knowing of the previous warnings issued to the day manager by local police officers. Perhaps more importantly, the night attendant "declared that no complaint was made [by Craig] to him."[85] The magistrate was left "not in the least satisfied . . . that anything had happened which would justify him, or . . . any other court, in taking the licence away."[86]

The legal battles of 1929–31 effectively set the tone for the relationship between the large Turkish baths and the LCC, sustaining their de facto status as an impermeable sanctuary. Nominally, this relationship mirrored that between the licensing authorities and London's bars, clubs, and cafes. But it differed in two crucial respects: first, in the baths' position *outside* the Met's habitual operations, and second, in the terms upon which they were licensed. For if the owners of other commercial venues could have their licenses revoked even when they had tried to exclude queer men, the baths only risked such draconian action if it were proven that they had been "improperly *conducted*"—that they had "permitted such conduct." The General Powers Acts enshrined a particular notion of commercial responsibility that opened up a space between the sexual culture of the baths— which was rarely in doubt—and the Savoy Company's awareness of such practices. That the LCC could never prove these premises had been "conducted" as queer meeting places, coupled with the companies' strong commercial interest in retaining their licence and ability to instruct distinguished legal counsel, placed such premises almost above the law.

The power of this combination of commercial strength and an idiosyncratic licensing system becomes clear when the Savoy case is compared with the vulnerability of smaller ventures. In October 1952, for example, the PCC opposed Albert W.'s application for a renewal of his licence to carry out "toning massage, pedicure and manicure" as Pavinsky's Beauty Parlour of Belsize Park Gardens, since he was "unsuitable to hold a licence."[87] Albert— and his premises—were "suspected of homosexuality . . . because of the tone of his advert[isment]s"—displayed in Shepherd's Market and apparently directed at a queer clientele.[88] Despite the lack of supporting evidence produced by frequent inspections, these advertisements and Albert's conviction for "an act of indecency" in 1946 convinced the committee that Pavinsky's was being "improperly conducted."[89] Unable to afford legal representation, Albert testified on his own behalf against five officers of the PCC: his application was refused.[90]

That the Savoy, Harrow Road, and the Imperial were able to remain open—continuing to provide queer men with opportunities for social and sexual interactions in safety—did not mean that they were impervious to the PCC's periodic interventions. Given the formal emphasis on baths being properly conducted, management and staff remained keenly aware of the need to be *seen* to be vigilant in policing their customers' behavior. The expressions of this were twofold. There were, on the one hand, periodic clampdowns in response to external pressure. On the other, staff colluded in policing a distinctive sexual microgeography. Official surveillance never resulted in the baths' suppression—they remained affirmative, albeit exclusive, sites of sex and sociability—but it nonetheless informed their internal organization and customers' behavior.

5

A ROOM
OF ONE'S OWN

INTRODUCTION

Writing in 1931, the urban observer James Bone sought to invoke some sense of modern metropolitan culture for his readers:

All great cities have the gift of anonymity for those who seek it, but in London, where districts are so widely separated and interests so plentiful there is the added reticence of the English character and his desire to make his home his castle and the gift comes almost without seeking.[1]

For Bone—as for many contemporaries—the essential "English character" cohered upon the interconnected qualities of "reticence," privacy, and domesticity, expressed through the spatial and cultural metaphor of the home as castle. The home here represented a refuge from the perils of the public city and the pressures of professional life. This was, Bone suggested, the only space in which a man could truly be himself and do as he wish, secure in his privacy and the comfort of his family. It was, he thought, understandable that a man should maintain a distance between work and family. What Bone termed an "innocent double life" thus invoked the radical separation between public and private space that was central to dominant notions of domesticity. If this binary formula found its cultural expression in the impermeable boundary between the domestic unit and the outside world formed by the front door or garden fence it was, moreover, embodied through the institutions and conventions of the law. "The public," notes Leslie Moran, "is a realm of laws full presence . . . a space of order and decency through the law . . . This public suggests an alternative place where the law is absent—the private." The sanctity of the Englishman's "castle" was legally defined.[2]

When the journalist Michael Davidson first rented a furnished room in Gower Street in 1919, his sense of excitement was palpable. Residential space, for Davidson, held the promise of escape from the pervasive surveillance that constrained his behavior in the public city. This room was to be a sanctuary, a private space that would allow him to forge a secure urban life.

> It cost £1 a week—a third of my income, but the house had one great advantage—the primary one sought—but so uneasily found by every homosexual . . . it was free of snoopers . . . the first abode of my own in the bottomless well of wickedness.[3]

Davidson's excitement was short-lived. The dreaded knock on the door came on two occasions: he was arrested and imprisoned for something he had done in this "abode of [his] own."

As Davidson learned, the residential spaces occupied by queer men existed in an antagonistic relationship to Bone's definition of the home as castle. Indeed, in the 1950s the Law Society defined the queer as a potent challenge to normative domesticity: an attack on marriage, a barrier to demographic stability, and a threat to the nation's youth. This was an evil that the state could not tolerate. Until 1967, the prohibition of private "homosexual offences" enshrined hegemonic notions of the family home within the law. The ideological domains of residence, domesticity, and privacy were interwoven and contingent upon each other. The Law Society saw no contradiction between the criminalization of men's private sexual behavior and the legal convention that evidence should be secured without impairing the privacy and confidence of domestic life since "male persons living together do not constitute domestic life."[4] Residential space was only legally private if it were domestic space. When domesticity was defined to exclude queer men, the privileges of privacy—the freedom from official surveillance—were nominally afforded only to those who conformed to bourgeois notions of family life.

In 1952 Charles D., a thirty-year-old lab assistant, and Lawrence P., a street trader, were thus tried for gross indecency before the Tower Bridge Magistrate after being arrested in a house in Great Suffolk Street.[5] If the public revelation of such transgressive uses of the home never failed to outrage bourgeois observers, their reactions were contradictory. In part, sexual immorality was understood as a function of men's distance from the controlling influence of the ordered domestic unit. In 1934, the former army officer Cyril H. was tried for "sexual offences" with messenger boys in his

Hays Mews flat. His defense counsel attributed Cyril's actions to a "lack of moral control," the reasons for which were clear: "The real trouble here is that last year he went to live alone. He is a bachelor and his practice was to ring up for these messenger boys." In directly linking the absence of self-control to the residential experience of bachelorhood the message was simple: a man who lived outside the family could not be expected to conform to social expectations.[6]

Just as often, however, this outrage focused upon the proximity between transgressive homosex and the bourgeois home. Queer men's use of residential space disrupted the sanctified domestic unit in ways that many observers found intolerable. In 1927 several men were tried at the Old Bailey after a series of parties in a Fitzroy Square flat. For the court recorder this was a "hornets' nest of degenerates" in the public midst that had to be "smoked out." Notions of disease and purification violently distanced the flat from the health and goodness of normative domesticity.[7] The threat such spaces posed to the idealized English home was sufficient rationale to sustain the continued criminalization of private "sexual offences."

Despite this, the de jure prohibition of queer men's right to privacy coexisted uneasily with the spatial constraints placed upon official surveillance. The policeman's habitual public beat did not take in the rooming house or apartment block. As a result, it was almost impossible for officers to detect "sexual offences" that occurred in such interior spaces, and men were rarely arrested for having sex in the home. In a sample of nine years at five-year intervals between 1917 and 1957, 2,467 queer incidents resulted in proceedings before metropolitan magistrates or City of London justices. Thirty-three of these incidents occurred in locations identifiable as private dwellings, twenty-six of which followed complaints from nonconsensual partners—usually a boy or youth. In these nine years magistrates tried only seven incidents involving consenting adults in private residences.[8] The municipal authorities found it impossible to exclude queer men from the enabling resources of domestic life: in operational terms residential space *was* private space.

It was within this context that a complex and distinctive queer world took shape in London's bachelor chambers, furnished rooms, and lodging houses. Just as the contradictory legal and cultural constructions of residential space opened up potentially private space, so the metropolitan housing market enabled men to access diverse residential spaces that offered the possibility of forging secure and affirmative lives. Such possibilities depended heavily on the privileges of class and the resources provided by wider queer social networks. Some men never found private residential space and were forced to seek sex and sociability in London's streets and parks. For many others, however, a room of one's own *did* open up the possibilities that Davidson had contemplated in 1919. It is to these complex residential forms that this chapter turns.

BACHELOR HOUSING

In the past decade historians working on North American cities have developed increasingly sophisticated analyses of so-called bachelor housing—the residential hotels, apartment houses, and furnished rooms that provided rented accommodation for single men.[9] For Britain, by contrast, such analyses are conspicuously absent. Ironically, historians have echoed the contemporary assumption that the normative—indeed, the only—residential unit was the self-contained family home, focusing their attention on owner occupation, suburbia, and council or philanthropic housing. The housing choices available to single men (and women) have been comprehensively ignored.[10]

Many Londoners *did,* however, live outside the family household. Each year thousands of single men came to London from provincial Britain or the empire looking for work or pleasure or simply left home to escape parental surveillance. Faced with this massive demand, a diverse market in rented housing developed to accommodate their needs. Whether they lived in exclusive apartments or eked out a precarious existence in common lodging houses, "bachelor housing" was central to young men's urban experiences, allowing them to temporarily reject the responsibilities of the male breadwinner and forge autonomous lives in the big city. If contemporaries found considerable cause for concern in the presence of so many young men outside the constraining realm of the family, they implicitly recognized the opportunities for an unfettered social life that such spaces promised. As Robert Sinclair noted in 1937, "the irresponsible youngsters . . . are the only people who are not burdened with the cares of a home . . . liv[ing] in lodgings . . . their attention is divided between next weekend and an idealised future."[11]

It was within this dual context that queer men were able to carve out a space for themselves within London's residential neighborhoods, drawing upon the conventions of masculine independence and the opportunities afforded by the metropolitan housing market. If the choices available to them were limited by their financial means, many found opportunities to socialize or have sex safely in bachelor chambers, furnished rooms, lodging houses, and hotels. As well as being central to individual lives, moreover, these residential spaces sustained the formation of wider social networks.

Certain lodging houses became places where men could participate in a unique sexual culture; distinctive residential enclaves emerged in hotel and rooming districts.

Writing in 1960, sociologist Michael Schofield thus noted a "tendency for homosexuals to congregate in certain areas," seeing this as "a typical minority group reaction" to social marginalization.[12] By emphasizing individual decision making, however, Schofield ignored the restrictive effect of the market economy. As Hamnett and Randolph suggest, men's residential choices were "not the product of unconstrained preference" but were organized within "the opportunities and constraints afforded by the nature and distribution of the housing stock, the operation of the housing market and the differential structure of . . . [an individual's] purchasing power."[13] London's housing market divided men profoundly along lines of class and place, but it also brought them together.

CHAMBERS AND APARTMENTS. Elite masculine privileges had sustained a highly developed housing market for wealthy men since the eighteenth century. Letting rooms in bachelor chambers in prestigious residential districts like Mayfair or St. James—places like the Albany, built off Piccadilly in 1770—they forged independent urban lives before marriage.[14] From the early nineteenth century such accommodation was supplemented by the development of apartment houses and residential hotels, particularly in the streets running north from Piccadilly: Dover, Clarges, Half Moon, Duke, and Sackville. Initially built as individual family properties, middle-class men's demand for respectable accommodation meant the large terraced houses were quickly subdivided.[15] By 1931 the "private apartments and bachelor apartments" in Half Moon Street, for example, formed what one LCC official described as "a quiet and select neighbourhood," removed from the traffic and crowds of the West End.[16]

Muirhead's *Blue Guide* described these as "the most luxurious and expensive quarters" for single men, providing "flats or suites of furnished apartments" for between two and three pounds a week.[17] If they were highly exclusive, these apartments—and the traditions of urban bachelorhood within which they were embedded—nonetheless offered the richest queer men a respectable and secure residential space within which to forge lives insulated from the dangerous public city. In 1929, for example, the American schoolteacher Philip E. took a ground-floor suite in Anne Gannon's apartment house at 14 Half Moon Street. The physical and cultural organization of the house afforded him considerable privacy. His sitting room, two bedrooms, and bathroom were a self-contained unit, physically separated from other apartments within the premises and with an individual entrance. Moreover, while Mrs. Gannon lived on site and a maid cleaned his rooms every day, a culture of respect for the tenant's privacy made him sufficiently at ease to bring partners home.[18] This combination of location and distinctive residential forms meant Half Moon Street became a remarkable queer enclave, attracting men like the writer Hugh Walpole and dress designer Reggie de Veulle. Robbie Ross, Wilde's literary executor, had rooms at number 40, where he regularly entertained friends.[19] Joe Ackerley rented rooms at number 11 during the 1920s after hearing of the opportunities it offered. He described a "discreet establishment" where he took "street prowlers and male prostitutes."[20] The Albany was a similar enclave, at various times home to George Ives, Norman Douglas, and Terence Rattigan.[21]

From the late nineteenth century the transformation of London's housing market increased the availability of such accommodation as speculative property developers responded to the increased demand upon central residential districts created by population growth and the expansion of white-collar employment. The result, particularly in the 1880s and between the wars, was a massive boom in the construction of luxury apartment blocks, evident in the redevelopment of the Grosvenor Estate in Mount Street, which transformed the residential structure of central London.[22] For wealthy queer men these characteristically "modern" developments opened up new opportunities to find secure residential space, combining the flexibility of renting and a fashionable and convenient location with a choice of differentially sized and priced flats. In 1948, for example, Angus Wilson and Tony Garrett moved into a one-bedroom flat in Dolphin Square, an art deco apartment block built in Pimlico in 1937 that contained shops, a private garden, and restaurant. The flat cost £112 each year, but quickly became the focus of the couple's social life.[23] In the 1930s, Gerald Heard and Chris Wood similarly shared an apartment in a block off Oxford Street.[24] In choosing where to live, wealthy queer men were profoundly influenced by the wider organization of the housing market. They lived in the same neighborhoods and the same kinds of housing as other men and women of their class.

FURNISHED ROOMS. Self-contained apartments were both expensive and exclusive. Most middle- and working-class men instead found cheaper accommodation, renting a single furnished room in a large subdivided house from a private landlord. The availability of such housing was closely tied to particular districts. In outer London or suburbia, for example, the housing stock—primarily semidetached or terraced family residences—left single men with very few options. They were forced to move to central London areas where furnished rooms were the dominant residential unit: Pimlico, Bayswater, Paddington, Notting Hill, Maida Vale, Marylebone, and Bloomsbury.

Like all these districts Pimlico, for example, was initially a nineteenth-century development, composed of single-unit terraced family houses built for white-collar workers. From the 1890s, as market fashions and the demands of respectability shifted, this settled population moved further west or to the developing suburbs. Bought up by speculative investors and landlords, the terraces were subdivided and converted into multiple-dwelling houses composed of individual furnished rooms designed to profit from the massive demand for central accommodation. In 1923 Sidney Felstead thus described a "gloomy uninviting place," full of "woefully shabby houses."[25] It became a characteristic rooming district, offering cheap rooms on weekly leases to a transient population of single men and women, working-class families, and recent migrants. Pimlico, observed Felstead, is "tenanted by all that flotsam of a great city which ekes out a precarious existence living in cheap rooms and passing out of life unheeded."[26]

It was within this milieu that queer men most often found accommodation. Furnished rooms were affordable, appropriate, and close to central London. If most men occupied furnished rooms only temporarily, before marrying, they allowed queer men to find a more permanent home. In Pimlico, for example, workingmen like the decorator George P. rented cheap rooms in the poorer streets around Victoria Station—Tachbrook or Hugh Street.[27] Middle-class men, particularly those that had recently migrated to London seeking to establish a professional position, also utilized cheaper accommodation until they could afford to move to more prestigious apartments and areas. This convergence of classes was, in itself, remarkable, but often resulted in marked differences between adjoining streets, a complex microgeography of queer residential life. Many wealthier men rented flats and furnished rooms in the more respectable streets towards Pimlico's northern edge. Between the wars Ebury Street, for example, was home to Noel Coward, Robert Hutton, Frank Oliver, Bernard, and Emlyn Williams.[28]

Pimlico exemplified the cultural and economic processes that enabled men to find accommodation and structured the character of these residential districts, suggesting how the location of "bachelor housing" drew men to particular areas in large numbers. Men's presence was most marked within the area bounded on the east by Baker Street, south on the line of Hyde Park and Kensington Gardens, west by Ladbroke Grove, and north along Harrow Road, taking in rooming districts like Marylebone, Bayswater, Paddington, and Notting Hill. By 1955 they were sufficiently visible for Laurence Dunne, the chief metropolitan magistrate, to observe that "a large number of practising homosexuals live in the George Street, Seymour Street, Bryanston Street and Paddington area." As Dunne realized, London's housing market sustained distinctive queer residential enclaves.[29]

The protean character of these districts closely mirrored that of Pimlico and reflected their wider social composition: working and middle-class queer men living alongside recent immigrants, poorer families, and "normal" single men. Since they were close to the West End and offices in central London they were particularly popular amongst clerks or men employed in the service and entertainment sectors. In the 1930s, for example, Leslie K., and Richard D.—both waiters—lived in Westbourne Grove and Nuttfield Place, respectively, the chorus boy Jack Hewitt in Oxford Terrace.[30] There were also many men working in semiskilled or unskilled jobs in the nearby markets and industries.[31] Alongside this mainly working-class population, many businessmen, professionals, and members of the metropolitan literati found rooms in more respectable streets, attracted by the same combination of housing, location, and affordability. William Plomer moved between rented rooms in Bayswater and Notting Hill throughout his life, living at various times in Pembridge Villas, Norfolk Square, Linden Gardens, and Monmouth Place.[32]

There were similar—albeit smaller—clusters in other rooming districts. In the 1930s Virginia Woolf observed Stephen Spender, Wystan Audan, Joe Ackerley, Plomer, and Leo Charlton and Tom Wichelo "set[ting] up a new quarter in Maida Vale," ironically labeling them "the lilies of the valley."[33] This was more than a literary bohemia, reflecting the wider cultural trajectory exemplified by the number of working-class men also renting rooms nearby. The motor engineer Alfred S., for example, lived in Clifton Gardens.[34] Furnished rooms in Bloomsbury and Soho were home to a similarly diverse queer population, the latter particularly popular amongst those working in West End theaters or commercial venues.[35]

If men's presence in these rooming districts was initially determined by the nature of the housing stock, this process was enhanced by more informal social ties and information networks. Men often told friends of the accommodation such areas offered or alerted them when rooms came free nearby. John Alcock and his partner Hughie struggled to find somewhere to live when they first moved to London in the late 1940s. Walking the streets they passed a man whom Alcock thought "looked gay." He approached him, asking "if he could help us to find a room somewhere." The man, Danny Carrol (later the drag entertainer Danny La Rue) could not, since he was in the same position, though Alcock quickly found a room in Maida Vale. Carrol stayed with the couple until they found him a room nearby.[36] Interactions like this—constantly repeated—created migratory chains that sustained the formation of queer residential enclaves.

Whilst west London remained the most common site of accommodation, the precise location of these enclaves shifted constantly in response to neighborhoods' changing housing stock and general character. By the 1950s their focus was shifting south and west, as Notting Hill Gate and Earls Court became the best-known rooming districts among queer men. This chronological shift was, in part, determined by the marked deterioration of housing in Paddington and Bayswater and their increasing notoriety as slum districts. For many, particularly middle-class men, this made them far less desirable. Yet it also reflected the gradual geographical extension of subdivided housing. Like Bayswater, Earls Court was initially composed of single-unit terraced houses occupied by middle and upper-working-class families. Since it was located further west, however, the district retained this character for longer and the flight to suburbia occurred substantially later. It was only in the 1930s—and particularly after the Second World War—that terraced houses were converted into bedsits and furnished rooms, Earls Court became a predominantly working-class residential district, and queer men began to move there.[37]

The intersection between the housing market and informal social ties that shaped the emergence, location, and character of these queer neighborhoods closely paralleled the formation of residential enclaves among other ethnic and social groups. The movement of Irish migrants to Paddington in the 1930s or West Indians to Notting Hill and Brixton in the 1950s, for example, was similarly structured by the location of cheap accommodation and information passed between friends or acquaintances. In 1932, Thomas Burke thus identified distinct Italian, French, and Russian quarters in Clerkenwell, Old Compton Street, and Spitalfields, respectively, with their own social centers, religious and cultural institutions, shops, cafés, and restaurants. Each, he argued, "builds a country around itself."[38]

If the visibility, cultural organization, and institutionalization of queer neighborhoods was never comparable, men's accumulated individual movements nonetheless meant that districts like Pimlico and Bayswater—and later Notting Hill Gate and Earls Court—played a similar role in fostering a broader, if nebulous, sense of community. Men living close by forged informal social networks meeting in each other's rooms. Their sheer prevalence, moreover, sustained more public institutions around which queer neighborhood life took shape. Pubs like the Champion in Notting Hill Gate or the

Coleherne and Bolton's in Earls Court, for example, became known meeting places where local men found opportunities for social and sexual interaction. The Bayswater Road or west London urinals became sites of public cruising. As these neighborhoods grew in complexity, vitality, and scale—and thereby reputation—they became increasingly attractive to those moving to or within London.

In 1960 one man thus described

> a huge homosexual kingdom just below the surface of ordinary life with its own morals and codes of behaviour. In Notting Hill Gate this . . . seems to have come to the surface. *That's why I live there.* You would understand better if you went to a homosexual party. You find there certain things that were done and others not. It is an entirely different code of behaviour to normal life. When I walk through Notting Hill Gate I feel I'm at a gigantic homosexual party.[39]

For this man—as for many others—the home he found in London's rooming districts was not confined within the walls of his furnished room and meant more than the basis for a fulfilling private social and sexual life. Certainly by the 1950s, queer residential spaces were spilling over the putative public-private boundary, shaping the character, ambience, and possibilities of public life in particular neighborhoods. If the man exaggerated in identifying an "entirely different code of behaviour" in Notting Hill Gate, he highlighted a very real sense of locale and belonging.

LODGING HOUSES AND HOSTELS. For many unemployed men or recent migrants from the industrial north, Ireland, or the empire, or for those working in casual and poorly paid unskilled trades, furnished rooms were unaffordable. Occupying a marginal and precarious position within the labor market, such men entered the transient population residing in London's privately run common lodging houses. Between 7d and 1s 1d bought a bed for the night in a dormitory with as many as twenty other men. Often overcrowded, these "squalid dens," George Orwell noted, were redeemed by "their laissez faire . . . and . . . warm home-like atmosphere."[40] They were concentrated in the centers of casual employment—around the Covent Garden or Borough markets, the Kings Cross building trade, or the industrial districts south of the Thames. Those around the docks in Whitechapel, Stepney, and Limehouse, for example, housed an ever-changing ethnically diverse population of navvies, dock laborers, and seamen.[41] Their number and population declined from the First World War onwards, and they all but vanished in the 1940s, as the welfare state and economic changes made furnished rooms more accessible. Yet lodging houses remained central to unskilled working-class male life between the wars. A 1928 survey estimated the number of men staying in lodging houses as 16,736.[42]

The presence of so many men—often young and single—outside the civilizing domestic realm meant lodging houses generated considerable anxieties. For many bourgeois observers they were an atavistic blot on the ordered urban landscape, represented through the tropes of dirt, disorder, and disease and associated with vice and criminality. His months "down and out" led Orwell, for example, to characterize men's distance from women and marriage as "degrading" and "demoralising": "It is obvious what the results of this may be: homosexuality . . . and the occasional rape case."[43] From the 1880s the LCC responded to these generalized concerns by expanding their regulatory operations.[44] In this they were aided by the efforts of charitable organizations like the Salvation Army, Church Army, and YMCA to provide cheap, respectable and closely supervised accommodation that protected working men from vice.[45] In the 1890s, for example, Lord Rowton opened his "poor man's hotels" in Vauxhall, Kings Cross, Whitechapel, and Elephant and Castle. Rowton Houses—"for men only"—offered single beds in private rooms or cubicles together with leisure facilities for between 6d and 1s a night.[46]

These anxieties coalesced upon lodging houses' position within a rough masculine homosocial culture that transgressed norms of bourgeois respectability. As such they occupied a central place within the lives of workingmen who engaged in homosex, providing cheap accommodation, moments of privacy, and opportunities for sexual encounters. In the late 1920s, many of the workingmen who gathered around Hyde Park, socializing and picking up middle-class men, lived in nearby houses. William O., for example, met many other men while working in the Palladium Bar, several of whom he lodged with in the Soldier's Home in Buckingham Gate. Through them he met the former guardsmen Philip B. and James M., who slept at the Church Army hostel in Strutton Ground. Another acquaintance—the unemployed miner Charles P.—slept at Tommy Farmer's Lodging House in Shorts Gardens.[47]

As this suggests, many of the workingmen who looked for homosex in London's public spaces depended upon lodging houses. Gordon W., a ship steward, resided at the Sailor's Home in Wells Street, Stepney.[48] Harold H., staying at the King's Cross Rowton House, was found to have a string of convictions for "offences of an immoral character" when arrested for theft in 1932.[49] Yet men could often also find moments of privacy within many houses, particularly if they could afford a cubicle. In 1940, for example, John G. met another merchant sailor in the West End and was invited to the Aldgate Seaman's Hostel.[50] The Strutton Ground house was also known for such opportunities: in 1922 James M.—a forty-three-year-old gardener—picked up a fourteen-year-old youth at a Harlesden coffee stall, offering him "a good bed and plenty of money."[51]

Such practices suggest the existence of a remarkably open casual sexual culture within many lodging houses and hostels. Indeed, both individual cubicles *and* larger dormitories often became places where men could have sex with those they slept alongside. Orwell shared a cell in the Romton spike with a fitter who made sexual approaches. Court records support his suggestion that such incidents were common.[52] Since cases only arose when someone resented an unwanted advance, they represent only a minute proportion of the encounters that occurred. In 1927, Patrick C. was thus charged with indecently assaulting Albert B. in the Receiving Ward at Plumstead.[53] Other cases involved a thirty-six-year-old gardener in a cubicle at the Kings Cross Rowton House in 1937 and a sailor at the Seaman's Hotel in Commercial Road in 1922.[54]

Yet men always struggled to find privacy, their ability to do so depending on the house's physical layout, the vagaries of supervision, and the character of those with whom they shared a dormitory. Given this, it was often impossible to have sex, and men had to seek privacy elsewhere. In 1927, for example, Philip C.—a twenty-year-old sweep, staying at the 92 Westminster Bridge Road lodging house—was arrested in a urinal in Commercial Buildings. Having appraised the opportunities available to him, Philip was arrested at one of the most dangerous public sites.[55] Yet the alternative could be equally dangerous. A decade later, in the same house, James C.—a fifty-two-year-old tailor—was arrested for indecent assault after placing his penis between an unwilling fellow lodger's legs.[56] Here any privacy that men found was decidedly tenuous.

Despite this, certain establishments became known as places for queer men to stay or have sex. Orwell, for example, went to one off the Strand. It was, he noted,

> a dark, evil smelling place and a notorious haunt of the "Nancy Boys" . . . in the murky kitchen, three ambiguous looking youths in smartish blue suits were sitting on a bench apart, ignored by the other lodgers. I suppose they were "Nancy Boys."[57]

Late that night a "fashionably dressed" older man entered the dorm: "He could not have been seriously hard up. Perhaps he frequented common lodg-

Figure 10. Photograph, The Union Jack Club, Waterloo Road. Photographer unknown. The National Archives of the UK (PRO), ref. no AIR 20/9601.

ing houses in search of the 'Nancy boys.'"[58] Slightly more respectable was the Great Russell Street YMCA. Tony Garrett moved there in the 1940s, living with many other queer men and learning "something of what the homosexual world was like."[59]

Servicemen on leave relied upon charitable hostels like the Red Shield.[60] Best known of these was the Union Jack Club in Waterloo Road (fig. 10). Opened in 1907 and funded by the armed services, the club provided sleeping cubicles, dining rooms, a billiard room, and library, deliberately seeking to protect servicemen from temptation and vice.[61] The reality was very different. The club was located in a notorious red-light district. Moreover, the presence of so many soldiers and sailors attracted young women, prostitutes, and queer men alike to the neighborhood's streets and pubs. It was within this context that, by the early 1920s, the club itself became known for the sexual opportunities it offered. Since they slept in partitioned cubicles it was relatively easy for servicemen like John Beardmore to have sex with men they had met in Waterloo Road or the West End.[62]

As the Second World War and National Service increased the number of men using the Union Jack Club, its notoriety rose exponentially. After the 1940s it was known as *both* a safe place to take partners *and* somewhere to find casual sexual encounters. In 1952, for example, police were called when

staff found a thirty-year-old able seaman in a cubicle with a storeman.[63]
Throughout the 1950s such incidents caused the military authorities considerable concern. They considered placing the premises under military
police surveillance and, as Major Walker noted at a 1953 meeting, "every
precaution was taken . . . to prevent occurrences of this nature . . . close
watch was kept . . . by the staff."[64] Despite this, very few cases were ever
detected. Although the naval authorities were pleased that only fourteen
cases of "indecency" occurred between November 1951 and April 1953,
during which time 250,000 beds were let, in practice it seems like surveillance foundered at the cubicle wall and staff's unwillingness to police sexual
morality.[65] The club became almost legendary. As John Alcock recalled,
"You went there because it was like Everard's Bath in New York—you just
left your door open and somebody would come in and spend a couple of
hours with you."[66]

HOTELS. Those men who lacked privacy at home because they were married or lived in close proximity to family, friends, or other lodgers could
often find a safer place to take pickups or affairs by renting a room for the
night in one of London's hotels. In 1936, for example, the artist Edward S.
took a young man he had met in the Café Royal to the Tuscan Hotel, a "first
class" establishment in Shaftsbury Avenue. The men met regularly whenever
Edward was in London, always taking a single room and signing the visitors' book in their own names.[67] In so doing they exploited an ambiguous
mixture of cultural blindness and commercial laissez faire that pervaded
the hotel sector. Staff seeking to uphold their establishments' respectability focused overwhelmingly on excluding unmarried heterosexual couples.
This, and the established practice of sharing rooms to save money, meant
two men attracted little, if any, attention. They could often rent rooms in
the most prestigious of venues, including Claridge's, the Savoy and the
Regent's Palace (Glasshouse Street).[68] While men were always careful to
avoid being unduly conspicuous, in a hotel room, behind a locked door,
within a culture of respect towards guests, and knowing that they were outside police surveillance, they temporarily found the security to have sex.
Wherever they were, men remained confident that they could find a room.
When Michael R. met John G. in Whitechapel in 1940, he immediately
invited him to a hotel.[69]

In using London's hotels, men were aided by managers' willingness to
ignore propriety in order to maintain a steady income. Taking advantage of
men and women's desire for privacy, cheaper hotels often knowingly let
rooms for the night—or even for the hour—to unmarried couples or

prostitutes and their clients. Throughout the 1920s, *John Bull* conducted a sustained campaign against what it called "bogus hotels" or "assignation houses"—"mere haunts of evil" that disrupted the respectable domesticity upon which Britain's stability depended.[70] In 1925–26, for example, they drew attention to "undesirable dens" in Marylebone, Bloomsbury, Maida Vale, and Edgware Road.[71]

Such establishments were concentrated in certain neighborhoods, particularly where terraced houses had been subdivided, sustaining diverse residential spaces occupied by men and women living outside family life and often characterized as red-light districts. *John Bull* focused much of its ire on the district around Charing Cross, identifying "six notorious places" in 1925.[72] Alec Small, for example, ran both the Hotel de France (Villiers Street) and Aplin's (Craven Street), described as "houses of ill-fame . . . [where] no genuine hotel business seemed to be done."[73] It was within this transient realm of illicit sexual encounters that men most regularly found rooms for the night. Within a wider group of men and women passing through they attracted little attention. Like everyone else they were paying customers. Pat, for example, remembered one hotel manager who "didn't mind . . . he'd look at us and say oh yes I know what you are and he used to charge a bit more and you could get a room."[74]

If this was true of districts like Paddington, Bloomsbury, or Marylebone—where men used establishments like the Great Western or the Marylebone Railway hotels—their presence was particularly marked around Charing Cross.[75] This was at the center of queer life for much of the early twentieth century: pubs and commercial venues on the Strand were hugely popular; the Adelphi, Embankment, and the Charing Cross arches and station concourse were notorious cruising sites. Queer men were thus regular customers at hotels in the surrounding streets, finding a moment of privacy with partners they had met elsewhere. In 1917, for example, John H.—a private in the Canadian Army—and John J.—a British sailor—rented a room in the Shaftsbury Hotel in St. Andrew Street.[76] Five years later, the army officer John B. took a room at Aplin's with an enlisted man he had met on the Strand.[77] At different times Dannant's in George Street, the Charing Cross Hotel above the station, and Faulkner's—again in Villiers Street—were all known within queer networks.[78] These opportunities persisted into the 1950s, when Pat recalled "a couple of . . . very old lesbians who had a place in Villiers Street . . . [who] used to let the room out for a couple of hours . . . they were hand in glove with most of the rent boys in Piccadilly."[79]

The only comparable district was that around Waterloo Station. Local hotels had been notorious "assignation houses" since the 1890s. "It was," recalled the magistrate Cecil Chapman, "a very bad district in this sense . . . contain[ing] one or two streets in which it was difficult to find any house which was not used for immoral purposes."[80] In the three decades after 1894, these "horrors" became the target of a sustained "crusade" conducted by the Central South London Free Church Council, under the aegis of its secretary, J. D. Bairstow, and director, the Reverend Meyer. The council was particularly exercised by the "corruption" of servicemen staying at the Union Jack Club, who were often observed taking hotel rooms with young women they had met nearby. As Meyer wrote in 1923, "the splendid boys who . . . [fought] for King and Empire were . . . exposed in this neighbourhood to terrible temptations."[81] In removing these "temptations" Meyer and Bairstow regularly brought charges against hotel proprietors and pressured local police and the Lambeth Council into action. In 1912 they claimed to have closed 1,100 "houses of ill-fame" since beginning work.[82]

Despite this continuing zeal, the area retained its notoriety well into the 1940s.[83] Like Charing Cross, it was the intersection between these wider cultures of illicit sexuality, and the district's importance within queer public and commercial networks that meant many hotels acquired a reputation for tolerating or even encouraging men's custom. In 1936, for example, Harold G. met a young man in the Haymarket funfair:

> We went to a hotel in the Waterloo Road—he appeared to be known there—and we went to a room . . . He took the room key off a hook when we entered the hotel. We were in the room for about half an hour. We masturbated each other and I left him in the hotel.[84]

The man's confidence and familiarity with both the hotel's staff and layout suggested how such practices were well established. This was particularly the case among those working as trade in the West End. In 1934, after meeting Stanley K. in Piccadilly, A. was taken to "a room in some place in the Waterloo district."[85]

These were only two of many known hotels. In 1922, for example, Lewis H. and William S. met an Australian sailor while cruising the streets and pubs around Waterloo, inviting him to a room for "a pleasant time." They went to Caroline Pratt's hotel at 74 Waterloo Road, asking for a single room. Although Pratt refused them entry in this instance, that was because the sailor was drunk, rather than the possibility of three men having sex.[86] Lewis and William had previously taken a petty officer to "a lodging house [at] 110 York Road."[87] First identified as a "resort of sodomites" by the Free Church Council in 1916, this lodging house had a lengthy history as an apparently exclusive queer establishment. Council agents had followed

"Bert," who was "constantly . . . in Trafalgar Square and Leicester Square with boys . . . [who] have homes in London but live in Lodging Houses."[88]

Despite this, hotels very rarely attracted official attention because they admitted male couples. *John Bull,* which frequently identified the districts—and even individual establishments—frequented by queer men, focused entirely upon illicit heterosex. In this they were closely aligned with the operations of the Met, local borough councils, and moral purity organizations. Even the Free Church Council's interest in 110 York Road was only momentary, quickly forgotten in their "crusade." Hidden underneath what was deemed a more pressing danger, queer men remained invisible. This was, moreover, embodied in the law itself, particularly through the provisions of the 1885 Criminal Law Amendment Act, which explicitly targeted hotels used for *female* prostitution. While Aplin's, for example, was under observation by police throughout the 1920s and the manager was fined in 1923 and 1926 for permitting its use for an "improper purpose," there is no evidence that queer men's regular presence in the hotel ever drew official attention. No hotel was ever prosecuted for permitting impropriety between male customers.[89]

The relative safety that men found in hotel rooms was clearest in the remarkably small number of incidents that came before London's magistrates. Crucially, such cases appear to have arisen only after one of the men involved complained to the police. In 1937, for example, Alfred H. appeared at Bow Street charged with indecently assaulting two youths at Dannant's. If he had erred in his choice of partners, he had nonetheless found somewhere to take a room and had not been arrested after observation by police or hotel staff.[90] Judges reacted angrily to such rare instances, focusing upon the threat commercial laissez faire posed to attempts to exclude men from private space. In 1930 Ernest Wild thus summed up after a case in which a youth had been "taken to hotels by well-dressed men whom he met casually in the streets": "If it is true that there is any hotel in London where a man can take a boy for certain purposes," he snapped, "all I can say is the sooner the police see that the licence is taken away the better."[91] Such establishments enabled the taboo expression of queer desire, affording space for a moral evil that the state could not tolerate.

PRIVATIZING RESIDENTIAL SPACE

Within a stratified housing and labor market, queer men's residential arrangements were radically fractured along lines of class and wealth. The spaces they occupied, moreover, related to their external environment—the dangerous public city—very differently. As Martin Daunton suggests, "the threshold between private and public space [is] drawn at different points and with more or less emphasis."[92] For those living in self-contained apartments the boundary was abrupt and impermeable, the walls creating a physically inviolate space that almost guaranteed their privacy. In common lodging houses, by contrast, there was no such boundary: men were always potentially subject to surveillance, and their grasp on privacy was tenuous. Somewhere to live did not mean somewhere safe to have sex. Men living in multiple-dwelling houses and furnished rooms existed somewhere between these poles, their position on the public-private boundary ambiguous and constantly shifting.

Often such men found their presence and movements went unnoticed or unremarked upon within the transient population and distinctly louche character of many rooming houses. Reggie, for example, described his room off Pimlico Road as "quite handy for taking people back to . . . [since] the neighbours weren't the sort to complain."[93] Despite this, they had constantly to negotiate the tacit notions of proper domestic arrangements and conduct that informed neighborhood life. Landlords, fellow lodgers, and neighbors were all highly sensitive to transgressions of these parameters, maintaining a pervasive surveillance over each other's behavior. If this resulted mostly in confrontations about excessive noise or gossip about illegitimate children, it had a profound—and often disastrous—effect on queer men's lives and behavior. In 1935, for example, an anonymous caller told police "a private flat 8 Torrington Mews Edgware Road [was] the resort of sodomites."[94] If it was rare for such suspicions to result in arrests, the risk was always there, and men often feared losing their home or job should neighbors discover their sexual practices.

The danger of drawing unwanted attention was particularly marked amidst the crowded and close conditions of furnished room life. Common entrances and stairs, shared bathrooms and kitchens, and thin partition walls meant men struggled to find the security to bring friends or pickups home. It was this that led Emlyn Williams to characterize rooming houses as "strangers deprived of privacy" through their proximity.[95] Frank Birkhill, for example, once forgot to lock his door when he brought home a pickup. While they were in bed a housemate "came up to announce a telephone call and didn't knock . . . but just put his head through." The housemate wrote Birkhill a "filthy note" threatening to tell his friends about "my depraved habits."[96] Landlords also watched their lodgers' behavior closely. When Patrick Q. and a partner were undressing in his Pimlico room in 1930, the landlady arrived with a policeman, asking them to leave since "she had never seen such goings on in her house."[97] While some were more understanding or simply ignored comings and goings to make a profit, the risk was always there.

In lodging houses it could be impossible to overcome these constraints. Those living in furnished rooms, however, were remarkably successful in creating the space in which to live their lives fully and safely—a space in which they could have sex with pickups, live with partners, and entertain friends. They utilized tactics that, in effect, rendered them and their residential arrangements invisible. Actions as simple as locking the door, closing curtains, avoiding excessive noise, and taking care when entering or leaving were all intended to construct an impermeable—if precarious—physical boundary between a furnished room and the outside world. As such, men negotiated their ambiguous position on the public-private boundary to create a functionally private space. John Alcock, for example, was always particularly circumspect on his own street. While he always wore his overcoat over his shoulders in the West End—"it was camp and a risqué thing to do"—his arms went in his sleeves when he got close to home.[98]

While such tactics coalesced upon the articulation of *physical* boundaries, men also sought to reconfigure the *cultural* underpinnings of the public-private boundary. If there was no alternative to sharing accommodations and if that could be both restrictive and dangerous, why not live with other queer men? Not only did that allow men to forge affective and affirmative social ties, it also enabled them to relax and drop the masks they wore constantly in public. As one noted in the 1950s, "I attach great importance to living with another homosexual . . . it's such a relief not to be on my guard all the time."[99]

Crucially, this process depended upon men being part of wider social networks. As such it was simply impossible for those who remained isolated from queer life or who did not see themselves as queer. This is clear from Emlyn Williams's changing experiences in the late 1920s. Knowing nobody when he first moved to London, Emlyn lived alone in a room in Mecklenburg Street. Having begun to move in queer circles he moved into a Chelsea studio for a few months with Pierre, whom he had met through friends in the Criterion, but this quickly failed and Emlyn moved to Pimlico, again on his own. Wanting to be closer to the West End and to save money he took a double flat in St. Martin's Lane, initially with a "normal" actor. Uneasy at the constraints this placed upon his social life, when the actor left Emlyn was introduced to Miss Curtis, a male shop assistant, who was looking for accommodation. Later he lived with his partner, Bill Cronin-Wilson, in Greycoats Place. When the couple separated in 1932,

Emlyn moved into a room in a couple's three-story building in Ebury Street. They shared breakfast "and if Freddie was giving a bottle party I often took up drink and stayed."[100] Many men were not as lucky as Emlyn.

As this suggests, within the constraints imposed by the housing market, their purchasing power, and social ties, men's residential choices and movements were constantly informed by the wish to find somewhere secure to live. Men alerted friends or acquaintances when rooms came free in their house or looked for somewhere to live as a group, creating an extensive network of queer residential units. A couple or friends shared furnished rooms—like William D., a shop assistant, and Frank S., a printer, did in Millman Street—or a large number of men occupied every room in a single property—like the "resort of sodomites" in Torrington Mews.[101] Queer landlords like James H., who kept an apartment house at 52 Red Lion Street in Bloomsbury, were also careful to let their rooms to other queer men.[102] In the 1950s one landlord let all twelve rooms in his house to queer men.[103]

Men's reliance on these informal connections was evident in Tony K.'s experiences during 1955. Thrown out of his parents' home at the start of the year, Tony was introduced to Mark, whose house in Victoria had an empty room, by a waitress at the Little Hut Café in Greek Street, a popular meeting place.[104] After living with an older man in Jameson Street in Kensington for three months, he became homeless again when the man dumped him. Tony again drew upon his circle within Soho's commercial venues, staying first with a friend and then a pickup before being offered a room in a large subdivided house in Penywern Road in Earls Court shared by queer friends and female prostitutes.[105] When police raided the house and the tenants were given notice to vacate, Tony moved again, taking a flat in Lilford Road, Brixton, with a former housemate.[106]

The only contemporary analysis of the distinctions between residency and privacy was conducted by Schofield in *Sociological Aspects of Homosexuality*. Schofield questioned three sample groups about their living arrangements and opportunities to bring men home: those convicted of homosexual offences (HC), those seeking medical advice (HP), and those contacted informally (HO). Twenty-four of the HC group, who lived with parents, wives, or "normal" housemates, found it impossible to bring men home, while 26 found it possible.[107] For the HP group it was impossible for 31, difficult for 14, and possible for 5.[108] The sexual and social lives of both groups were thus oriented primarily around public spaces. Unlike the HC and HP groups, Schofield's HO group was primarily middle-class. Only eight of them found it impossible to bring home partners: "84% had arranged their lives so that homosexual activities in their home was a possibility": 18 by living alone in self-contained flats and 26 by living with queer friends or partners.[109] If the status of queer residential space was ambiguous, the privileges of class and social connection were key resources in enabling men to find privacy.

IT'S WHAT YOU DO WITH IT

Access to residential space could—with money, connections, or simply luck—enable men to forge fulfilling urban lives. Some, particularly middle-class men, challenged their nominal exclusion from domestic life. In 1952 Schofield described the case of D., a businessman, and H., a newspaper editor, both in their early thirties:

> Except in working hours they are seldom apart . . . they are extremely proud of their home and devote their attention on it like young newly weds. There is a certain amount of physical love between them but the most striking thing is their complete emotional harmony and the way they rejoice in each other's company . . . They occasionally visit one of the London clubs together but most evenings they are content to stay at home or entertain friends.[110]

This loving relationship constituted a queer domestic unit that mirrored marital life. In focusing their social lives on their home and devoting considerable "attention" to its appearance, D. and H. echoed the idealization of domestic space as "a place of peace, seclusion and refuge" from the dangerous public city.[111] The home both symbolized their relationship and the social value invested in domesticity *and* provided the space in which to be safe. Moreover, as the evenings on which the couple entertained friends suggest, such spaces allowed them—and others like them—to sustain wider friendship circles. Such informal evenings were regular, as for the circle socializing in Binkie Beaumont and John Perry's Lord North Street apartment.[112] Here, secure in their privacy and able to talk through everyday worries, men found a powerful site of affirmation and respectability.

If lives like this reflected the ideal of the home as an impermeable "fortress," many men simultaneously transformed their rooms into fluid spaces that dissolved rather than confirmed the boundary between public and private. Schofield's couple would have been vaguely recognizable to bourgeois observers; the ways in which many other men used residential space would certainly have not. Given the right circumstances, lodging houses, furnished rooms, and bachelor chambers all afforded opportunities for homosex—to "troll . . . or lumber [a pickup] home," as John Alcock put it.[113]

These opportunities hinged upon men's ability to cross and recross the public-private boundary, their movements—to paraphrase Sharon Marcus—making "urban and domestic spaces continuous."[114] Traversing London's streets or bars, they found partners in a realm coded as disorderly and dangerous: as one man said to a sailor in the Running Horse, "Come on darling, let's go to my place."[115] Such interactions brought the city into the home, collapsing nominally distinct spatial realms. Crucially, however, the home was then reconstituted as an inviolate private space as the door was closed and locked. In those lodging houses where men found sexual encounters, the boundary between public and private space was even less distinct. Residential spaces came to hold possibilities normally associated with the streets—for sexual exchange, observation, and chance encounters. Men's reliance upon rooms or flats thus did not isolate them from each other or public queer networks. Moving freely across spatial domains, their myriad individual trajectories created complex queer cultures at the interstices of the boundary between public and private space.

If this habitual mobility was a key resource in forging fulfilling yet safe lives, it was also a source of very real danger. To put it simply, men were never quite sure whom they were bringing home. Once inside a room, moreover, the very separation from the outside world that enabled them to have sex also left them vulnerable to assault, blackmail, or robbery. In 1929, for example, Philip E. met the ex-guardsman Roland B. on Piccadilly and invited him to his apartment in Half Moon Street. When Roland called on Philip the following evening, he beat him "into insensibility" before stealing many of his possessions.[116] The disorderly public city intruded into the supposedly sacrosanct space of the home to brutal effect.

Newspapers frequently reported incidents like this.[117] Indeed, cases of blackmail, assault, or theft generated the largest public discussion of queer life until the 1950s. This in itself is highly suggestive. Together with the remarkably small number of prosecutions for private sexual offences, it points towards men's success in constructing a secure place for themselves within London's furnished rooms and apartments, predicated upon dismantling and then reconstructing the boundary between public and private space. Yet the desire to maintain that boundary was easily exploited by blackmailers: "Money or Exposure" read one *News of the World* headline. Men often parted with huge sums to avoid "exposure" and protect their privacy.[118]

For bourgeois observers this fluidity represented a potent challenge to the order and stability of urban life. Defining these "multiple and porous spaces" as immoral, disorderly, diseased, dangerous, and promiscuous, they sought to maintain the symbolic integrity of the domestic unit and reestablish an impermeable discursive boundary between the home and the city.[119] This process was evident throughout Roland B.'s trial for robbing Philip E. In cross-examination, counsel could simply not comprehend Philip's transgression of the public-private boundary—bringing home a man he had met on the streets. Such actions, he suggested, could only point to immoral desires. Philip was questioned insistently: why had he gone for a late-night walk on Piccadilly? "His only object . . . was to take the air." Was he "prepared to take home . . . the first man [he] met?" Had he done this before? Although Philip rejected this line of questioning, his actions retained their aura of suspicion. As the court recorder surmised: "If a man were 'mug' enough to take a stranger home . . . they must not say 'serve him right.' He might be a fool, but he need not be a bestial fool."[120] While Philip's immorality had not been proven conclusively, opening his home to the unknown dangers of the streets remained "foolish."

That queer residential space collapsed the conceptual separation of public and private spheres was most evident in the role rooms or apartments played in forging wider social networks. For many, these spaces not only enabled a private sexual or social life but also sustained their ties to other queer men. Taylor Croft's *The Cloven Hoof* (1932) noted how the

> commonest medium of urning entertainment is that peculiarly modern thing—a "party" . . . there are homosexual parties in one part or another of London every evening and some of them are extremely large. Occasionally when women are invited a pretence of normality is made, but others become a mere orgy and sexual excesses are freely, even publicly indulged in. Urnings are fond of dancing together at these parties and many are dressed . . . in effeminate fancy dress of some sort.[121]

Croft anxiously sensed how residential spaces offered queer men opportunities for unfettered interaction that belied their nominal exclusion from the city. If men could never interact with complete safety in cafés, pubs, parks, and streets—could not kiss, hold hands, dress up, or dance—at parties, concealed from a potentially hostile outside world, they found a place where they could feel at home. Here they could make friends, meet partners, socialize, and relax. The sense of release was tangible: as John Alcock recalled, "When we arrived at somebody's house it was like an explosion going off . . . you shed all your secrecy and your caution that you'd had during your working day . . . let [your] hair down and became unnecessarily noisy and camp."[122]

Over the winter of 1926–27, for example, the chorus boy Bobby B. held several parties in his basement flat in Fitzroy Square, attended by up to

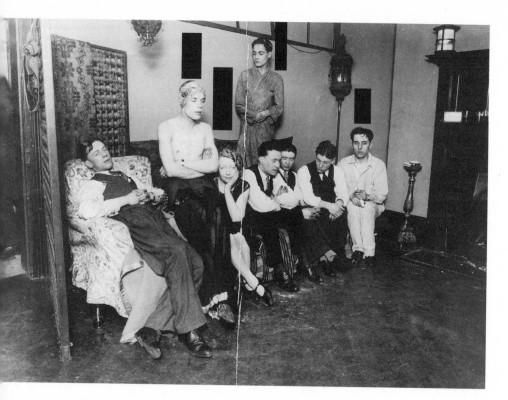

Figure 11. Photograph, Bobby B. and friends at a party at 25 Fitzroy Square, 1920s. Photographer unknown. The National Archives of the UK (PRO), ref. no. CRIM 1/387.

fifteen working-class friends and acquaintances (fig. 11).[123] The men danced together and sang along to gramophone records. They kissed and embraced and occasionally went to the bedroom to have sex. They were flamboyantly open about their sexual character: one "dressed in a black ladies dress," another "wore only a skirt and a pair of light shoes."[124] Bobby performed a "Salome dance," wearing a black transparent shirt with gilt trimming, a red sash around his waist, women's stockings and shoes and a red headdress.[125] This was, for the Met, a dangerous "resort of . . . 'nancy boys,'" which they duly raided, arresting all those present.[126]

Metropolitan queer life, as Pat recalled, "devolve[d] . . . on these sort of parties."[127] Their importance, moreover, lay in the fact that they were never closed events but were open to distant acquaintances or complete strangers, bringing overlapping social networks together and blurring the putative boundary between public and private. Parties were often announced at closing time in commercial venues: in 1925 *John Bull* thus noted "many of the effeminate looking people" from the Criterion going to a "flat in Jermyn Street where parties are held about which details cannot be given."[128] Similarly in 1937, a plainclothes officer inside a nightclub was invited to "one of our parties" by a complete stranger, who told him "they are camp."[129]

The permeability of residential space and queer social circles was manifest in Bobby B.'s Fitzroy Square parties, which interwove an amorphous and loosely connected network of friends, acquaintances, and strangers. "Some of the men I have known for a long time," Bobby noted, "they bring their friends if they care to do so." Bert L., his nephew, was living with him. Harold B., Leonard M., and Alec B. were all close friends, meeting regularly in each other's houses and places like the Adelphi Rooms on Edgware Road.[130] William C., brought to the party by Leonard, had first met Bobby at a dance in East Ham. James A. and Harold W. had also met Bobby at a dance and were "introduced by M. at our club." Neither Edwin B. nor Charles C. knew Bobby or had visited the house prior to the evening of the raid; both came along with friends or colleagues.[131] On several evenings in 1926–27 distinct geographies and social circles intersected temporarily in this basement flat.

Prior to hearing the case at the Old Bailey, the recorder Ernest Wild and the counsel involved struggled to comprehend this dangerous ambiguity; their confusion focused upon the vexed question of which statutes to proceed under. Although Wild remained convinced that "disgusting practices" had occurred in the house, there was no direct evidence: a prosecution for private sexual offences—buggery or gross indecency—was impossible. Yet acting against it as a "disorderly house" was equally problematic, since that required defining the flat as a site of public sociability. For the defense counsel, Mr. Howard, this too was impossible, since the flat was not open to the public "beyond the mere private circle of the person holding the house." Wild himself framed the case within the terms normally applied to "heterosexual" brothels. In labeling the men involved as "male prostitutes," he positioned them firmly within the disorderly public realm of the streets. There was, he concluded, "ample evidence" that this was "much more than just a private flat—[since it was] open to anyone who chose to come or who was brought by a friend."[132]

CONCLUSION

If this chapter has highlighted the social and sexual opportunities queer men found through the metropolitan housing market it has, nonetheless, shown how such opportunities were heavily contingent upon class, age, and social connections. Some men found it simply impossible to find privacy within the residential spaces they occupied. Those who were married or were unable to leave home because of poverty or youth could rarely bring a partner home. Living-in domestic servants faced similar restrictions, as Sir Ian Malcolm's valet found in 1932—forced into an uncomfortable confrontation with the police when colleagues saw him bring home a friend who "had the appearance of a male prostitute."[133] Even for those living independently in London's diverse residential neighborhoods, privacy was by no means guaranteed. If they were not to remain isolated and lonely, such men had little alternative to seeking sex and sociability in the most dangerous public spaces. Every week for two years Jeffrey J., a valet living with employers in Endell Street, met his partner in Hyde Park.[134]

Yet such experiences were by no means universal, and many men were able to find a home in the city. Utilizing the conventions of James Bone's "innocent double life," they forged a place where they could discard their public masks, somewhere they could feel safe and comfortable. It would, moreover, be wrong to view these spaces as a series of atomized residential units that isolated men from each other. Queer men created a tangled matrix of overlapping residential spaces, blurring the putative boundaries between public and private. The extent to which individual and, more importantly, collective queer lives devolved upon such spaces cannot be underestimated. Always precarious, always profoundly divided along lines of class, this was, nonetheless, a vibrant world that belied queer men's nominal exclusion from private space. If its cultural and geographical organization shifted constantly, a room of one's own remained the dominant institution of queer urban life throughout the period. It did so because it was safe—because it was, to a remarkable extent, invisible. Thus Rodney Garland's *The Heart in Exile* (1953) observed:

> The majority of the underground do not go to queer pubs, clubs or even parties, do not linger round public lavatories, railway stations or other recognised or obvious places. There are thousands of young inverts among the millions of normal young men who live with their friends in boarding houses, small flats, hostels, clubs, associations, sometimes under the roof of . . . parents . . . Secrecy is complete and scandals rare. The underground is everywhere.[135]

PART 3

PEOPLE

"Are you queer, dear?" a plainclothes policeman was asked in Billie's Club in 1937.[1] The detective's answer may have gone unrecorded, but the question was, in itself, suggestive. What did his interrogator mean? Following Steven Maynard's injunction to explore historically, culturally, and geographically specific "ways of knowing," how was "queer" used as a category of self-understanding and practice in the first half of the twentieth century?[2]

In part, the term embodied the contradictions of queer urban culture. Deployed in London's streets and bars, "queer" functioned as a tactic through which men negotiated everyday life in a city where the public expression of character could draw arrest, abuse, or assault. The term itself was initially innocuous and commonplace, suggesting little more than difference or strangeness in popular usage and hinting at deception in "underworld" slang. Appropriated as an identifying label by certain men around 1915, "queer" acquired a covert meaning. It was a double entendre, which could pass unremarked by "normal" observers in conversation, while signaling a man's sexual character to those in the know.[3] Writing in 1960, Michael Schofield thus described how

> many homosexual advances are not recognised as such by persons unaware of the signs and of the language. When two men are both trying to find out if the other is homosexual, certain words and phrases which would go unnoticed in another context are used almost as if they are code words.[4]

Like the other "code words," "to be had" or "so" and, after the Second World War, "gay," "queer" allowed men to negotiate a constant tension between secrecy and disclosure. As such, it denoted a particular problematic engagement with the city, an urban culture that existed on the precarious and mobile boundary between public and private. Men were neither there nor absent, neither visible nor invisible, and modern urban life was neither unequivocally affirmative nor negative. In its tactical usage, "queer" highlights the themes traced through the first half of this book.[5]

That the term "queer" possessed this tactical function, however, depended upon the cultural meanings it carried, particularly its association with difference and its use *both* as a mode of self-understanding—I'm queer—*and* external labeling—he's queer. In this sense, "queer" defined an apparently unified and stable subject in opposition to the "normal," whether that difference was valorized or stigmatized.[6] Yet if queer meant being different, then what exactly constituted that difference, and what was the "normality" against which it was defined? As I suggest below, the meanings of these categories were problematic, unstable, and contested, and discrete frameworks for interpreting male sexual practices coexisted and overlapped. For the policeman's interrogator, a queer man would respond to his advances positively—would have sex with him. And yet, for other men, engaging in homosex or ongoing same-sex relationships could be an accepted part of "normal" male lives. Shaped by broader differences of class, gender, age, ethnicity, and place, men understood and organized their desires and their participation in queer urban culture very differently to each other and to contemporary categories of "homo" and "heterosexuality." It is to these historical meanings of sexual difference and "normality" that this book now turns.

6

THE DILLY BOYS' STORY

Over several nights in the winter of 1927, plainclothes police surveilled a basement flat in Fitzroy Square. One evening officers followed two men from the flat to Tottenham Court Road, and then on a bus to New Oxford Street. Their reports outlined the basis of their suspicion: "They were," one officer observed, "undoubtedly of the Nancy type." His colleague elaborated: "They were both powdered and painted . . . they smelt strongly of perfume and spoke very effeminately. By their behaviour and appearance I believe them to be 'West End Poofs.'" In locating the men's assumed deviance—that which made them stand out from the crowd—the officers scrutinized the male body's "behaviour and appearance." Sight, smell, and hearing focused upon a cluster of discernible characteristics coded as "effeminate"—"powder and paint," "perfume," and speech. In the eyes of the officers, these signs labeled the men as "the Nancy type" or "Poofs."[1]

These bodily characteristics were easily—almost axiomatically—mapped onto a particular urban place, for the casual epithet "West End Poof" highlights the most widely recognized aspect of queer urban culture between the wars. In 1927, the lawyer Travers Humphreys described

a class of male creature—one did not like to call them men—who infested the streets of . . . the West End . . . Some of them were dressed as men and others as women. They were painted and powdered and wore earrings and low-necked dresses and called each other by feminine names.[2]

The West End was the heart of metropolitan commerce, tourism, and grandeur. And yet, Humphreys worried, anyone who walked the streets or frequented its commercial venues could not but witness the sight of "painted and powdered" "creatures." Such geographical knowledge of sexual transgression coalesced in the slang term "Dilly Boys" for the men *John Bull* described variously as "effeminate looking people," "painted and scented boys," and "West End pests."[3] In the popular imagination the flamboyant Dilly Boy was an arrestingly familiar figure, the embodiment of sexual difference.

The salience of a discernibly "effeminate" character that defined men as a "Poof" or quean suggests an understanding of sexual difference that cannot be mapped straightforwardly onto the modern categories "gay" or "homosexual." What, then, can the patterns of "behaviour and appearance" ascribed to the Dilly Boy tell us about the understanding, organization, and experience of same-sex desire in the first half of the twentieth century? What can men's use of makeup tell us about their own sense of self? For Judith Butler, such practices are a playful subversion of normative gender roles. Her reading of the body as an ahistorical text, while intuitive, ignores what Susan Bordo calls the "body's material locatedness in history, practice, culture." We need, Bordo suggests, to interpret these forms of self-presentation within the particular context within which they took shape.[4]

The key interpretive category here is class. For if the Dilly Boy was central to the interpretive schema through which *all* contemporaries understood male sexual practices, the men who were labeled queans were overwhelmingly working-class. Most of those arrested in the West End wearing cosmetics were employed in working-class occupations, particularly the service sector. "The working-class boys," John Alcock recalled, "the shop assistants and people like that had a tendency not to be closeted. They were quite open and in fact outrageous."[5] Wealthier men, by contrast, tended to more discreet. Workingmen's relative "outrageousness" suggests that the understandings of gender, character, and sexual practice within which same-sex desire was conceptualized as womanlike were profoundly shaped by differences of class.

This chapter thus asks what it meant to be a quean. Focusing upon the lives of men like Alcock, it explores how they understood, organized, and talked about their sexual desires and practices. It analyses their experience of the city. It interrogates their position within modern urban culture and the ways that they interacted with the individuals and groups they encountered. As such, it explores the complex meanings of sexual difference in early twentieth-century London. To explore what it meant to be queer is, moreover, also to explore what it meant to be "normal." For any analysis of the "West End Poof" has much to tell us about hegemonic understandings of gender, sexuality, and character within working-class culture. Only within that landscape were queer men able to make sense of their own desires. Only those broader understandings of masculinity and femininity invested their desires, bodies, and sexual practices with meaning. The Dilly Boys were embedded in the cultural relations of everyday life in working-class neighborhoods, shaping the contours of that world just as they were themselves shaped by it.

QUEANS AND MEN

John Alcock was called up for national service in 1945. As his platoon moved into their barracks, another soldier called out "queans this end, men the other." Alcock himself went straight up to "this end." In so doing, he positioned himself within a map of male sexual practices in which difference and "normality" were embodied in the distinction between "queans" and "men."[6] That this distinction was, apparently, readily understood by all of Alcock's platoon suggests, moreover, its broader resonance within working-class culture, both as a mode of self-understanding and as a way of interpreting other men's behavior and character. Indeed, the sexual microgeography of Alcock's barracks correlates with the terrain described by Quentin Crisp. In the 1920s, Crisp recalled:

> The same exaggerated and over-simplified distinction that separated men from women . . . ran like a wall straight and impassable between . . . roughs and . . . bitches.[7]

The language of "queans" and "bitches" evoked a commonplace equivalence between sexual difference and effeminacy. Crisp "was over thirty before I heard someone say . . . that he did not think of himself as masculine or feminine but simply as a person attracted to other people with male sexual organs."[8]

Such memories suggest an interpretive framework predicated upon the idea of what Susanne Davis calls "dichotomously sexed bodies."[9] Sexual desires and practices, in this schema, were understood as an inherent attribute of gender, underpinned by an innate physiology or psychology. Set against an "exaggerated" and rigid distinction between men and women, male and female bodies were assumed to be "sexed" in particular ways. The desire for a woman was considered inherently masculine. The desire for a man was a priori womanlike. It was within this context that sexual difference and "normality" were mapped onto the gendered opposition between quean and man, feminine and masculine. Men neither understood themselves, nor were labeled by others, through their choice of sexual partner.

This gendering of desire underpinned the ways that all contemporaries interpreted same-sex practices. It was, for example, codified through medical etiologies of sexual difference. Anomaly's *The Invert and His Social Adjustment* (1927) located men's "homosexual" desires in their essentially feminine physiological constitution—a constitution that contradicted the external signs of biological sex. In the "invert," he argued, "the balance of male and female elements is such that the element which determines sex impulse is at variance with the sex structure."[10] In this sense, what J. Chester termed "these man-woman characters" were neither and both.[11]

Yet this imaginative landscape was most important in structuring the self-understanding and lives of working-class men. "We were queer," John Alcock recalled, "so we were much more like women than we were like men."[12] For Alcock, as for many others, the idea that his desires reflected his womanlike nature invested those desires with meaning. In constituting a particular understanding of selfhood, such mentalities shaped *both* the ways that Alcock talked about himself *and* the erotic, affective, and social life he forged. Such understandings of character were, in part, signaled by men's adoption of "feminine Christian names" amongst friends.[13] Some feminized their own name: Fred-Freda. Others identified their ties to a particular place—Coventry Street Emma or Bermondsey Lizzie. Men like the Duchess, Lady Austin, and Henrietta deliberately associated themselves with glamorous and aristocratic icons of femininity.[14]

The salience of these assumptions to men's understanding of selfhood and sexual practice was evident in a remarkable series of letters written in the mid-1920s. At some point around 1923, F. E. M.—who described himself as "a poor hard-working harlot from the streets of London"—met a wealthy American "man." Their relationship developed. Soon F. E. was "married to a pet husband" and taken on a "honeymoon" that took in an Atlantic crossing and a lengthy spell traveling in North America.[15] He remained in touch with his friend Bobby B., describing his adventures in writing and sending Bobby—a chorus boy—copies of the latest American dance music. The men clearly understood their character as womanlike and modeled their relationship on female kinship. They described each other as "she" and "girls." F. E. addressed Bobby as "my dearest camping Bessie" or as "dear sister" and portrayed himself as "Old Aunt Aggy."[16]

F. E.'s use of the terms "husband" and "marriage" throughout these letters further reflected his gendered understanding of his relationship. If he was a quean, his partner was unequivocally manly. Such assumptions shaped the ways in which men organized their relationships. John Alcock met his partner Hughie in the late 1940s. The couple soon began to live together in

Maida Vale. Alcock was always careful to remain sexually passive, since he assumed that was the feminine role appropriate to his character. This gendering of the couple's relationship extended to the division of domestic labor: Alcock did all the cooking, housework, and shopping. "That's the way I wanted it to be," he remembered; "I wanted to play the female part in everything in our lives . . . he wanted to play the male part." The men's everyday social practices reflected and reproduced the gendered opposition between man and quean.[17]

That homosexual desire was thus conceptualized as contingent upon a broader deviation from normative masculinities meant that the basis for labeling someone a quean—or identifying as such—was thus not who a man had sex with but his gendered character. As Sam remembered, people "might call you queer, but . . . only because of the way you talked . . . because they thought you was a bit girlish . . . not because of the sexual act."[18] These assumptions were reproduced through the language within which sexual difference was mapped. Rather than sexual practice, terms like "pansy," "Nancy-boy," "cissy" and "Poof" denoted particular gendered patterns of appearance and behavior. They were, in the first instance, used to describe those who failed to do what was expected of a man at work, on the streets, or at play. Self-presentation was but one part of this array of expectations. In the opening scene in James Curtis's novel *What Immortal Hand* (1939), a race between working-class youths begins with the cry, "Last one there's a sissy." Tom Morgan, the slightest of the group, is determined not to lose: "His heart was thumping and his lungs were going to burst, but all the same he wasn't going to stand for the other boys calling him a collar and cuff." The loss of status which Tom so feared was, in this instance, rooted in his body's physical fragility. In losing—and thereby failing to meet tacit standards of toughness—Tom displayed a comparative weakness which was easily defined as effeminate.[19]

While, as this example suggests, men were labeled as different because their behavior approximated to practices culturally ascribed to women, the effeminized male body was automatically thought to be sexed in specific ways. In 1922 the hot blocker William S. was arrested for importuning on Waterloo Road. Seeking information about the background to his offence, police visited his workplace in Hoxton. As workmates tried to understand why William had gone looking for homosex, his apparent failure to meet the prescriptive demands of working-class masculinity acquired a deeper significance. He was, they noted, "rather womanish in habits." Set against hegemonic masculinities, it seemed, the man whose "habits" were "womanish" could not but desire men.[20]

These assumptions exercised a profound influence over both popular and official responses to men like William. In 1933 the *Morning Advertiser* reported the trial of sixty men arrested at a Holland Park Avenue drag ball under the headline "MEN DRESSED AS WOMEN."[21] Yet reports of the case, particularly the comments of the court recorder, Ernest Wild, evinced a pervasive assumption that the men's transgression went far beyond cross-dressing. Wild's summation established an easy causal link between appearance and sexual character, praising the police for bringing this "nest of sodomitical haunts" to light. A category defined by its disruption of gender norms—the quean—was inscribed onto a category defined by the behavior of the sexualized male body—the sodomite. In conceptualizing male gender inversion as a sign of sodomy, contemporaries clearly assumed that transgressive sexual desires could be read off the male body or, to put it another way, that a man's gendered character constituted those desires.[22]

IT'S NOT MAKEUP—IT'S AMMUNITION

The gendered opposition between quean and man is the key to understanding the patterns of behavior and appearance ascribed to the Dilly Boy. For it was within that interpretive schema that men's desires acquired a particular cultural meaning, as symptomatic of a womanlike physiology or psychology, and thereby constituted a particular sense of selfhood. Those practices coded as "effeminacy" thus represent the process through which men drew upon the gender culture in which they were socialized to make their bodies publicly intelligible within it. Drawn into an ongoing engagement with consumer goods and styles, men manipulated their very physicality. Clothing, cosmetics, posture—these were literally the embodiments of what men understood as their essential nature. "It was natural . . . ," insisted Alex Purdie: "The voice, the face . . . I've developed nothing . . . God gave me these attributes."[23] The Dilly Boys' flamboyant appearance rendered individual selfhood and the organization of sexual difference undeniably visible.

The most spectacular manifestation of this process was the drag quean, who emulated styles of fashionable femininity to create a complete and convincing illusion of womanhood. Particularly between the wars, there were a number of dancehalls frequented by workingmen in drag. In 1932, entering a Holland Park Avenue ballroom, Police Constable Haylock observed how "at first glance it looked as if the men dressed as women were women."[24] Albert A. was powdered and rouged, wearing a wig and plumed feather headdress with a "low front flower pattern dance frock with a small coatee," dancing with a conventionally masculine partner.[25] Joseph C. was similarly wearing a lady's dark coloured evening dress which was cut extremely low at the back and was wearing earrings, necklace . . . jewellery on both hands and . . . carrying a lady's handbag and a fur coatee. His hair was very wavy.[26]

While drag was emblematic of hegemonic notions of sexual difference, however, its importance should not be overestimated. Wearing drag in public was simply too dangerous—most of those attending balls changed at the venue.[27] That drag's everyday appeal was limited suggests an important distinction: queans saw themselves as womanlike, *not* as women. The drag ball was always a transient occasion where convention was playfully discarded.

If men rarely wore women's clothes, they nonetheless adopted styles of dress that created a public persona consistent with their nature—that made their difference legible. Just as many lesbians adopted the masculine styles encapsulated in the phrase "collar and tie," so queans managed their appearance to give the deliberate impression of femininity. Writing in 1932, Taylor Croft delineated the characteristic features of what he understood as a distinctive urban type—the "urning," an early-twentieth-century medical category for queerness:

He will dress with the most elaborate care . . . with taste of a somewhat too noticeable nature . . . fond of colour as his shirts and ties testify, while any new fashion, particularly if it is a little effeminate, will appeal to him. Wide trousers, suede shoes, pale green shirts, two-coloured shoes, black or eccentric pullovers were immediately appropriated on their appearance in outfitters' shops for the special use of these people . . . an extremely conscious and highly-coloured attire frequently denotes an invert.[28]

Croft described a style defined by its visibility—men's tastes were "somewhat too noticeable," their attire "highly-coloured." Yet the items that rendered a man "noticeable" suggest the narrow limits of color, cut, and composition within which acceptable male dress was constrained. A deviation as minute as "wide trousers" or a coloured shirt was sufficiently unconventional to signify a man's sexual character—both in his own mind and, often, to those he encountered. Signs like this were often enough for men's dress to be labeled "loud and effeminate" or "outlandish."[29]

The notion of visibility inherent to the language of "loud" and "outlandish," together with Croft's comments on men's "highly conscious" attire and the "outfitters' shops" where they bought their clothes, suggests the terms on which this urban type emerged. Amidst the flux and anonymity that characterized the modern city, as Christopher Breward suggests, clothing acquired growing importance as a public sign of masculine identity.

From the black suit of the city gent to the workman's flat cap, the "acquisition of fashion goods . . . entailed negotiation with a variety of cultural images [and was] deeply implicated in competing constructions of class," as well as gender and sexuality. The process of creating a public self thus drew queans, like all men, into an intimate engagement with consumer markets and fashions. Within that broader landscape that invested gendered or cultural meanings in clothing, men deliberately—"consciously"—made individual purchase choices to create an appropriate persona.[30] Throughout 1932, for example, the film extra Sydney C. recorded in his diary every item of clothing he bought. In May he "had new flannel suit." In August he recorded a "fitting for fur coat," which he collected a month later. Both these items were readily available in men's shops. If they were thus not unambiguously womanlike, in being considered unconventional or fashionable they still carried the taint of femininity. As such, both items were appropriated by men like Sydney as gendered signs of character.[31]

Sydney's purchases suggest that creating a queer public persona was predicated upon reworking rather than rejecting conventional masculine styles. Instead of dark suits, men wore light gray or white. If they wore a dark suit they adorned it with "feminine" accessories—jewelry and scarves.[32] These subtle modifications were emblematized by queans' adoption of the red tie from the 1920s, apparently influenced by New York fashions. If wearing the red tie was a minute sartorial departure, it was often interpreted as the ultimate sign of sexual difference. Police in Billie's Club in 1937 interpreted men's "brilliant ties" and "red and white spotted scar[ves]" as evidence of immorality. And when Angus Rae told Emlyn Williams, "I'm liberated!" he immediately qualified this: "I do everything short of wearing a red tie!"[33] The result was a hybrid style, blending conventional forms of male dress with articles that were unconventional in cut or color but still, nonetheless, rendering men visibly different.

That difference was often articulated through an engagement with images of fashionable or bohemian masculinity derived from the arts, theatre, or film. Noel Coward "took to wearing coloured turtle-necked jerseys" around 1930. Soon after,

> I was informed by my evening paper that I had started a fashion . . . During the ensuing months I noticed more and more of our seedier West End chorus boys parading around London in them.[34]

Coward's assertion of his iconic cultural status might be dismissed as self-promotion, were it not born out by other observers: in 1932 Taylor Croft observed a number of "urnings" wearing "coloured sweaters rolled to their necks." For ordinary men, it seems, men like Coward were a stylistic ideal they aspired to.[35]

The sartorial minutiae that rendered men visible, and their reliance upon mainstream retailers, meant there was never a singular and self-evident style that set queans wholly apart from the crowd. The meaning of clothing was complex and contradictory, varying across classes, ages, and era. When Stephen Spender started wearing a red tie, for example, it signified his Communist sympathies.[36] Reading a man's character from his clothes was, in this context, always difficult, particularly with the emergence of spectacular working-class youth cultures. Michael Schofield thus noted "a marked change in men's clothing, especially in the lower social groups," in the decades after the Second World War.

> Young men . . . wear informal clothes that accentuate the form of the male body . . . this has made it more . . . difficult for one homosexual to recognise another . . . today a man whose mode of dress might have been considered ostentatious ten years ago would be horrified if it were suggested that he was "dressed up like a pansy."[37]

Set against broader changes in fashionable masculinity, the styles coded as queer were constantly evolving.[38]

Croft followed his dissection of "urning" fashion with the observation that "in these most extreme cases the use of cosmetics has become general."[39] As he recognized, in constructing a public persona many men bought into consumer cultures of femininity, appropriating those ubiquitous commodities available within the mass market in cosmetics. In the East End between the wars, Terry Gardener

> went to Woolworth's for a stick of make-up . . . threepence . . . If you were posh you bought Leichner powder . . . A threepenny stick of make-up . . . a sixpenny box of powder and I was equipped for anything.[40]

Alex Purdie similarly

> was a swine for make up . . . my perfume was called Soir de Paris . . . if I could scrounge together half a crown to have a bottle of this . . . my day was made. And we used to have a velouti on the ecaf . . . one of those pancake things . . . we used to put powder on . . . thought we looked absolutely marvellous . . . the eyebrows were plucked to hell . . . all shaped . . .[41]

Men like Purdie and Gardener plucked and penciled their eyebrows; they wore lipstick, eye shadow, rouge, and powder; they painted their fingernails; they wore scent.[42] They grew and styled their hair in ways coded as feminine. Waving was most common, but some also used colors—Quentin Crisp's henna or the peroxide that gave one man his nickname, the "Platinum Blonde."[43] Drawing upon the material culture of femininity, they manipulated their bodies' physicality to create an arrestingly colorful persona, a striking and often undeniable urban presence.

In a deeply gendered consumer market, the use of cosmetics was unambiguously coded as womanlike. It was his makeup that most obviously distinguished the quean from "normal" men—that rendered his difference most visible. Common phrases like "painted boys" or "men of the powder and paint calibre" suggest the importance invested in the condition of men's face in defining their transgression.[44] In the 1920s, in particular, these visual signs echoed those in which commentators located women's sexual immorality. "Bad girls," flappers, and prostitutes comprised what Sydney Moseley called "women of the painted class."[45] Like the quean, they carefully managed their bodies to enhance their visibility and desirability to potential suitors. Like the quean, their makeup was thought to symbolize a dangerous excess of femininity and unruly sexuality.

These material tactics cohered in the demeanor and comportment of the male body itself—what Quentin Crisp called the "set of stylisations . . . known as camp." As Crisp commented, "a passer-by would have to be very innocent indeed not to catch the meaning of the mannequin walk and the stance in which the hip was only prevented from total dislocation by the hand placed upon it."[46] Through walk, posture, voice—even style of smoking—men carefully mirrored those bodily practices conceptualized as womanlike. In contemporary sources queans' voices are "girlish," "lisping," or "simpering;" their walk is "mincing;" they have an "exaggerated gait" and an "effeminate" or "affected" manner.[47] In 1922, Thomas Burke described "male dancers who walk like fugitives from the City of the Plain."[48] To a remarkable extent, the quean's sense of self saturated his body.

The commonplace association between patterns of self-presentation coded as effeminate and sexual difference exercised a powerful influence over all men. That being called a pansy was a considerable blow to a man's status meant that men policed their appearance and behavior carefully. In the 1920s, Quentin Crisp recalled, men

> searched themselves for vestiges of effeminacy as they searched themselves for lice. They did not worry about their characters but about their hair and their clothes . . . The sexual meaning of behaviour was only sketchily understood but the symbolism of clothes was understood by everyone.[49]

As Crisp recognized, the image of the quean constituted a disparaged other against which a "normal" masculine persona was articulated, inscribing the male body within a constant anxious surveillance. The quean's prominence in contemporary urban culture shaped the behavior of *all* men, constraining the clothes they wore, the hairstyles they adopted, and the way they moved.

THE AMBIGUITIES OF DIFFERENCE

Between the wars, the waiter William L. regularly frequented the West End and Waterloo Road. His dress, voice, and mannerisms were visibly "effeminate." He was "highly-powdered." He had two tattoos—a beauty spot on his cheek and his camp name—Gertie—on his arm. Character and identity were indelibly marked on and through his body.[50] Such practices addressed a dual audience. In part, assuming styles of self-presentation thought queer embodied men's understanding of their own ineffable character. Set against hegemonic understandings of gender and sexuality, it allowed them to make sense of who they were. At the same time, however, those styles allowed men to display their sense of self to the world. John Alcock "loved being camp . . . it was defiance . . . I wasn't going to be the same as everyone else. I wanted to be different as I was different." Displaying this difference was, for him, a direct challenge to experienced social exclusion: "You won't accept me . . . so I'll just let you know that I'm there." Alcock's "defiance" emblematized a tangible pride in who he was.[51] That so many men refused to wear a public mask—that they were prepared to stand out from the crowd—is powerful testament to their everyday courage and the strength of will afforded by moving within wider queer social networks. Arrested in a nightclub in 1937, the twenty-one-year-old van-boy Charles C. defiantly asserted his difference: "They call me cissie boy," he told police.[52]

For all these men, being different coalesced in the complex set of cultural practices understood as camp. Camp encapsulated the generalized aesthetics of being a quean—the dramatically enhanced and flamboyant style of demeanor, dress, and display. In 1960, Schofield thus located the term's origins in the Italian phrase *campeggiare*—"to stand out from a background."[53] If camp was about enacting difference—"standing out"—it also denoted the values and ways of being that constituted that difference. In 1934, one plainclothesman thus overheard a conversation about "camp love" in a West End club. "Camp love" here signified an alternative world beyond the constraints and conventions of "normal" urban life.[54] Indeed, many historians have conceptualized camp as a critique of the very idea of "normality," a set of theatrical performances that highlighted the artificiality of sociosexual roles through burlesque and parody. Certainly, the adoption of the nickname "Cochran's young ladies"—the most glamorous interwar revue troupe—by five friends suggests a keen sense of tongue-in-cheek irony.[55]

Camp's functions were, however, more ubiquitous and prosaic than this analysis allows. Most men understood camp as the tactics through which they negotiated everyday challenges and dangers. If being camp risked attracting unwanted attention, it was also what Alex Purdie called his "safeguard:"

> I don't wait for other people to lift me because I know they're going to sooner or later . . . In a pub you get the [kiss sound] and all this lark . . . So I lift myself first. They stand no chance cos I'm star. And I won't have it any other way . . . You've got to be the first in . . . be aggressive . . . get up the front. Give them a mouthful.[56]

Purdie responded to being "lifted" with an "aggressive" performance that deliberately played up his assumed womanlike character. In "getting up the front," he confounded commonplace associations between effeminacy, weakness, and passivity, subverting his antagonist's masculine status. Like the young working women described by Peter Gurney, Purdie deployed a "highly sexualised discourse and deportment to confer social power and undermine the status of [a] stranger."[57] To outsiders, this kind of response was unnerving, simply because it was so unintelligible. In 1937, drinking in the Running Horse, one young quean was slapped on the arse. He went on the offensive: "You bloody bitch. Leave my bottom alone." The drunk replied—"You bloody nannies give me a pain in the neck." Again he responded, "As long as it doesn't give you a pain in the arse why should you worry?" Through aggression, incongruity, and humor this anonymous quean, like many others, asserted his right to be in a commercial venue, challenging the terms of his exclusion from urban life.[58]

Yet simply reading the practices associated with camp as the unproblematic assertion of difference, and therefore as forms of empowerment and communality, ignores the ambiguities of men's everyday lives. For, while men may have assumed an underlying gendered character, they managed their bodies with considerable deliberation. Constantly aware of the need to protect themselves, their livelihoods, and meeting places, they tailored their self-presentation to the spaces and times through which they moved. They may have gloried in being different in certain commercial venues or when with friends, but at work or when alone on the streets most were reluctant to stand out. When Emlyn Williams gave his outrageous friend Freddie Mell a job stage-managing one of his plays, his misgivings were confounded as Freddie arrived "unrecognisable in his best business suit and manner; subdued, efficient." At work and in public, men like Freddie carefully regendered their bodies—"putting their hair up"—utilizing their privileged status as *men* to move through the city unnoticed. Amongst friends they could scream. In the Lilypond Freddie told Emlyn, "Oh it *is* a relief to let me 'air down!" More than just a repressive constraint, the conventions of masculine "normality" could be a powerful resource in queer lives.[59]

It was, perhaps, within this context that makeup became so significant. It was, after all, a transitory and—in certain circumstances—minute bodily manipulation. For men who needed to "pass" or appear respectable at work, with family, or in public, semipermanent alterations like dying or waving hair were risky. Cosmetics allowed them to manage a double life, tailoring their bodies to different spaces and times. Going to work looking conventionally masculine, a man could return home to put on makeup before meeting friends in the West End. Cosmetics could be also used carefully, the invocation of sexual difference subtle and near indiscernible. Alex Purdie, for example, used Lipsyl—"that colourless stuff you put on when you got sore lips"—rather than lipstick because "you couldn't have it too dark." The result was that his lips "used to glisten."[60] Before going out, he and his friends carefully monitored each other's appearance.

> If you had too much slap on when you went out . . . your mates say too much slap on your ecaf. Yeah. Oh really girl? Yes . . . Go in the lavs here and have a look. And they would look in the mirror, take some off. Or put some on sometimes . . .[61]

Through such tactics, Purdie and his friends carefully negotiated the city, forging queer lives while remaining alert to the contingencies of the messages inscribed upon their bodies. Subjectivity here was never stable, but complex and fractured, negotiated in reference to a variety of social spaces and times through a persistent engagement with wider cultural resources and experiences of the city's perils and possibilities. Difference and "normality" existed in precarious tension, the boundaries between them ambiguous and often indiscernible. At least one policeman implicitly recognized this when, in 1936, he described a group of men whose "faces . . . had been skilfully made up and was not easy to detect."[62]

That sexual difference was never necessarily unequivocal or self-evident meant the world of the West End Poof existed on an unstable boundary between visibility and invisibility, spectacle and concealment, public and private. The practices associated with camp mediated across these boundaries, providing men with the resources *both* to assert a visible queer presence *and* negotiate the dangers they might experience. Simultaneously a theatrical way of being that constituted a particular queer subjectivity, a set of gendered performances that burlesqued the "normal" world, and the everyday practices through which men forged a place in the modern metropolis, camp held display and concealment in persistent tension.[63]

These tensions were embodied in the vernacular language used by queans—polari. Derived from a mixture of lingua franca, Italian, Romany, and backslang originally associated with eighteenth-century theatrical troupes, by the twentieth-century polari was part of that amorphous "underworld" slang current amongst dockside laborers, seamen, prostitutes, and tramps. By the 1920s it had clearly entered common usage within queer urban life.[64] Although certain words—camp, drag, or cottage—were generally recognized, polari was, as John acknowledged, "common only among a certain class . . . the common end of the structure."[65] John himself learnt polari through the theatre. Others, particularly around the docks, acquired their knowledge from the working-class milieu in which they moved or from older queans.[66]

As a hypertheatrical singsong mode of expression, polari was a constituent element of camp as a cultural style, a vocal embodiment of sexual character consistent with men's womanlike "nature." Richard May remembered,

> We always said Girl at the end of a sentence . . . You'd say something like "you all right girl" or "fancy a drink girl" . . . "ooh will you just vada the bona filiomi ajax" . . . It was all camp and rather silly.[67]

If, as May suggests, polari was a linguistic practice through which men enacted their difference, it was simultaneously a tactic of concealment, evasion, and invisibility. In 1925 *John Bull* observed that the Dilly Boys "have special words of their own . . . in order to discuss their affairs and conceal the real effect from people sitting near them."[68] Whatever their degree of fluency, these "special words" allowed men to hide their character and conversation from all but those in the know. Alex Purdie quickly learnt that it afforded him transient moments of privacy in the public city:

> Heterosexual people didn't know what we were talking about—thought it was Chinese or something . . . we didn't want people to know. Didn't want to say there's a copper coming in the bar do you? You just say there's a sharping omi . . . And if you spotted a pretty boy . . . you say vada di omi-oh bona omi . . .[69]

Polari, in this sense, was a way of creating the space in which to be queer.

Purdie's examples highlight polari's crucial role in constituting a broader, albeit nebulous, sense of commonality amongst queans. Implicit in the language of a "sharping omi" or "bona omi" is a vocabulary appropriate to the demands urban life placed upon queer men. The need to avoid undue attention and the desire for a "pretty boy" were only part of this. In 1932, Taylor Croft described London's "urning's" "very large vocabulary":

> So long has the vice flourished in a more or less subterranean form . . . that it is not surprising to find that it has its own words for the things most usually discussed in its sex-obsessed talk.[70]

For Croft, polari symbolized a dangerous "subterranean" community. Implicitly, he recognized how, in mapping the cultural organization of queer urban life—"the things most usually discussed"—this "vocabulary" allowed queans to talk about a world that was "their own." Terms like *butch, bitch, swish, trade, seaweed* (a sailor), and *naff* (normal as fuck/not available for fucking) mapped gendered conceptions of sexual difference and "normality" and denoted instantly recognizable urban types. Words like *ecaf* (face), *slap* (makeup), and *riah* (hair) underscored the crucial function of careful body management in men's lives. As a shared language appropriate to a peculiarly queer way of being, polari—like the broader practices that cohered in camp—constituted a complex sense of subjectivity, belonging, and affirmation and embodied the ambiguous understanding, organization, and experience of sexual difference in the first half of the twentieth century.[71]

ON THE DILLY

It was in the district surrounding Piccadilly that Londoners encountered "painted boys" most often—either directly or through the pages of popular newspapers. Certainly, queans did not confine their social lives to the Dilly, and the neighborhood attracted many more discreet men. But the Dilly Boys provided *the* dominant image of sexual difference, and the world they forged at London's glittering heart highlights the social and cultural organization of queer urban life. The Dilly's alluring reputation as a site of sexual and social opportunity for flamboyantly camp men was clearly well established by the late nineteenth century. By the 1920s, men were reproducing accumulated traditions of public sociability; they went up west because that was where they could find other men like them. The neighborhood's importance to such men thus echoed its broader position within metropolitan cultural life. Symbolically and spatially, Piccadilly Circus was the centre of West End consumerism, entertainment, and leisure. Here there were things

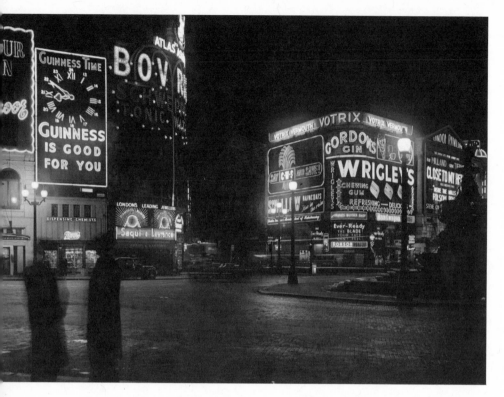

Figure 12. Photograph, Piccadilly Circus at night, 1930s. Photographer unknown. Getty Images.

to see, places to go, people to meet. Queer men, moreover, found further opportunities in the circulating crowds that legitimized and partially concealed their presence on the streets. The colorful mingling of urban types, races, styles, classes, and fashions that constituted this cosmopolitan milieu provided the context in which the quean could, in certain circumstances, openly display the physical signs of character. Here they stood out far less than in the suburbs (fig. 12).

Like the female prostitutes who also walked the bustling streets, many queans actively looked for commercial sexual opportunities. Cruising the streets and commercial venues around Piccadilly, they either solicited "normal" men or were approached by those who had no other idea of how to find a partner other than to approach an obvious "screamer." In 1936, for example, "Gertie" was seen outside the gates to the Royal Academy, "look[ing] at

[the] faces of [the] men who passed him and smil[ing]" and saying "in an effeminate way, 'Hello.'"[72] To focus—as did most contemporaries—upon this public cruising, however, is to ignore the fundamental social ties that underpinned men's participation in this world. Certainly, many men were casually involved in "trade"—and often blackmailed or robbed pickups— but the Dilly offered them far more than a quick fuck and seven shillings and sixpence.[73]

For young working-class queans, in particular, the Dilly was a crucial site of sociability. Poverty was a powerful obstacle to privacy. Informal surveillance often made men unwilling to draw attention in their own neighborhood. In this context, the public spaces of the West End were one of the few places that some men could make or meet friends and visibly be themselves, a point of connection to queer urban life. After work, young men thus met on Piccadilly corners, around the Circus subway and in Soho's narrow streets and alleys. These social ties centered upon the area under the County Fire Office Arches, on the north side of Piccadilly Circus. Central, partially concealed from casual observers, and sheltered from the elements, the Arches were a widely recognized meeting place between the 1930s and 1950s. Here what Harry Daley called "the screaming bitch type" gathered, talked with friends, and looked for pickups night after night.[74] Moreover, these social networks also took hold in the backstreet pubs and all-night cafés that clustered in the streets around the Circus. If they remained forever alert to the demands of the spaces though which they moved, to a remarkable extent, the Dilly Boys lived their social lives in full view of the metropolitan public.

It was these public social possibilities that made the Dilly so important. Indeed, many contemporary observers often implicitly recognized how "painted boys" found friendship, affirmation, and sex in central London. In 1925, for example, *John Bull* characterized the "rouged rogues" that had attracted its ire as a *"gang"* of the "powder and paint calibre."[75] In 1926, similarly, a policeman identified Gertie as "one of a *gang* of despicable male persons." In part, the language of "gangs" mirrored the generic conventions of crime reportage. Yet it also embodied nagging fears about the very real social ties that men forged. If Gertie was only *"one of* a gang," it was impossible to define him as an isolated, marginal, or aberrant individual. Like the term *Dilly Boys* itself, in gesturing towards that shadowy social world through which men moved, such reports raised the chilling specter of a visible, vibrant, and extensive subculture of sexual "deviants" at London's center.[76]

The world of the "West End Poof" always overlapped with that working-class and immigrant "underworld" that also took shape around the Dilly—as polari's currency amongst queans, prostitutes, and "criminals" alike indicates. Indeed, these spatial and cultural commonalities suggest how queans regularly found acceptance from the men and women they encountered each night. Quentin Crisp, for example, talked nostalgically about the "thieves, prostitutes and other social outcasts who were my friends."[77] Such a casual tolerance was particularly marked amongst the female prostitutes who walked the same streets and with whom men forged remarkably strong friendships. In 1936, for example, a plainclothesman watched a group of young women and "male importuners" in the Running Horse laughing and comparing notes on the state of London's sexual economy:

> One of the women said to the man, "You're a bloody pirate. I haven't had a man for two fucking days." This man said "you ought to cross your fingers on both hands then dear." The woman shouted, "God dearie let me cross all my fingers. I want a few men bloody bad. My rent hasn't been paid for two weeks." Another man . . . said . . ."Don't you believe it dearie, I walked all the way down Piccadilly last night with my fingers crossed and didn't even get a kind smile from any of the old bastards."[78]

Norwood East and Hubert's *Report on the Psychological Treatment of Crime* (1939) identified the deep social ties between these "asocial or antisocial" figures as characteristic of London's "underworld," rooted in the shared experience of social exclusion. Queer men, they argued, "are a persecuted class and therefore tend to become associated with others who are condemned for other reasons."[79] Certainly, queans, prostitutes, recent immigrants, and criminal "gangs" may have shared a nebulous sense of "persecution." But the casual interactions between these diverse groups had a more fundamental basis. In part, they were simply a function of proximity—they met each other regularly and repeatedly. More important, however, was the working-class character of this protean milieu. Set against hegemonic understandings of masculinity and character, the quean's public persona was both intelligible and acceptable.

Queans had a more ambiguous relationship with the other group that inhabited the streets around the Dilly: local policemen. Through their habitual patrols, C Division's officers became increasingly familiar with the people and places that constituted their "ground." Just as they met the same prostitutes, petty criminals, and café owners night after night, so they also regularly encountered the queans who gathered in the neighborhood. Experienced officers knew many of the men they saw by sight, name, or

criminal record—often even knowing their camp name.[80] Police and policed
engaged in an ongoing interaction that went far beyond the formal enforcement of the law. Indeed, given the everyday nature of these encounters,
arrests were comparatively rare. The police may have seen queans around the
Dilly every night, but they were as likely to move them on, have a quiet
word, engage in good-humored banter, or ignore them as they were to take
them into custody. In Piccadilly Circus, Michael S. remembered, the "police
used to come and the . . . [queans] used to run away—they weren't too both-
ered about it."[81]

For the Dilly Boys this everyday familiarity was, nonetheless, always
braced by the risk of arrest. They were individually "known" to local officers. They relied upon public space for sociability. They embodied the Met's
working definition of the "male importuning type." As a result, Frank
Birkhill observed, "The screamers had a hell of a time with the police."[82]
Gertie, for example, was arrested in Piccadilly in 1926 at the age of twenty-
six. He already had a long criminal record. "Since 1922," Detective Pearse
observed, "for similar offences in the West End and south London he has
been ordered five terms each of 6 months." On this occasion he was imprisoned for eighteen months. He was convicted six more times for importuning and "being a suspected person." His last arrest came in 1938, when PC
Hooper followed him from Piccadilly into Jermyn Street. Hooper knew
Gertie well—he had arrested him six years earlier. Gertie was convicted
fourteen times in sixteen years. He spent over eight years in prison.[83]

Such experiences suggest the uneasy symbiosis within which the Dilly
Boys and local police existed. Men like Gertie constantly negotiated the
tacit boundaries constructed around their visibility. When their behavior or
appearance became too obvious, they were arrested or told to move on.
Crucially, however, these interactions were shaped by an implicit microgeography of the West End. North of Piccadilly Circus, in Soho, arrests for
sexual offences on the streets were rare. In operational terms, this was a tolerated "red-light district." Such practices were underpinned by a dual logic.
Here men were physically removed from the crowds that thronged the West
End proper. Given the district's cosmopolitan character, they were also less
culturally visible—their appearance could easily go unnoticed or unremarked upon. Where the Dilly Boys were less visible, there was less reason
to police them vigorously. Yet this toleration was always geographically contingent. When men moved outside of this area—onto Piccadilly or into the
Circus—their public presence represented an intolerable incursion into
the sites of tourism, leisure, and consumption. In concentrating their patrols
on this main thoroughfare, officers attempted to articulate a rigid boundary

around the spaces within which sexual difference could be expressed. The Dilly represented the focus of an ongoing struggle over the terms on which queer urban life could take shape.[84]

If the Dilly was the most widely recognized site of quean sociability, it was by no means the only one. The risks attendant on attracting undue attention at work, in particular, meant many men gravitated towards jobs where there was less pressure to hide their character—where they could "let their hair down." The most renowned of these was the hotel and service sector, which sustained extensive overlapping queer social networks. Most of the men arrested in the Holland Park Avenue ballroom were chefs, barmen, or waiters. Indeed, for Ernest Wild, "one of the most disquieting features of this case [was] the fact that most of you are connected with hotels, boarding establishments and restaurants, showing that these form a nucleus for this foul vice." The balls had been advertised as "Hotel Staff dances." Whether waiting on tables, serving behind a bar, or working as a porter in a central London bar, restaurant, or hotel, men were often able to *both* be flamboyantly camp *and* meet other queer men. Most queans were not that lucky.[85]

A PLACE IN THE CITY

Tabloid newspapers or judicial pronouncements give the impression that the quean occupied the disparaged margins of metropolitan society. Castigated as a threat to Britain's manhood, he seems to have been a perpetual victim of arrest, assault, or abuse. We are, indeed, told that this was so, by someone who was there. Quentin Crisp's memoirs are a moving litany of the experience of exclusion and violence.

> If I was compelled to stand still in the street . . . to wait for a bus or on the platform of an Underground . . . station people would turn without a word and slap my face, if I was wearing sandals passersby took care to stamp on my toes . . . Housewives hissed and workmen spat on the ground.[86]

For a contemporary reader, *The Naked Civil Servant* is a powerful testament of a less tolerant time.

I don't want to deny the actuality of Crisp's experiences, rather to suggest that the quean's position within metropolitan culture was more ambiguous than they might suggest. Certainly, men often drew the ire of passersby in pubs or on the streets. But just as often the attention their bodies attracted was underpinned by amusement, not anger, fascination, not revulsion. Certainly, newspapers and officials reached extremes of vitriol in their condemnation of "painted boys." But popular attitudes cannot easily be mapped onto such pronouncements. Ambivalence—even ignorance—rather than anger, probably best characterizes popular attitudes towards the quean. Indeed, for many Londoners, such men were an integral part of the kaleidoscopic mixing of urban types that underpinned the West End's cosmopolitan reputation. By becoming part of this spectacle, queans acquired a precarious social acceptability as a theatrical source of color, entertainment, and fun.

Places like the Running Horse in Shepherd's Market, for example, often attracted those seeking a taste of London's bohemian nightlife. Casual customers occasionally reacted angrily to the sight of camp men joking and flirting. In February 1937, one man left shouting, "They're all fucking poufs in here."[87] Yet such reactions were rare. A month later a plainclothesman spoke to "two elderly ladies" who "visited the house for the purpose of seeing the 'puffy boys' playing about" and were, he noted, delighting in the spectacle.[88] They were certainly not alone in enjoying the sights of queer London, but were part of a "great number of people" who, a policeman observed of Billie Joice's Little Denmark Street establishment, "visit this type of club out of curiosity."[89]

In the West End this kind of contingent tolerance, embedded in broader traditions of cosmopolitan sociability, coexisted uneasily with the persistent risk of arrest and the greater danger of assault or verbal abuse. It was, by contrast, in the working-class neighborhoods of east and south London that queans were most firmly integrated into everyday life. Alex Purdie was born in Deptford in 1913. From an early age his flamboyantly camp persona was accepted by family, friends, and neighbors. He "always had a boyfriend." When he worked on his parents' market stall "the customers loved me . . . I gave them a first class performance . . . all the laughs and—'oh Al you are funny.' That's all I used to get." Purdie never wore a public mask—he didn't need to: "It was," he remembered, "my world." Like many other queans, Purdie was not only accepted but treated with real warmth by his local community. His waved hair, makeup, and manners were easily intelligible within working-class conceptions of manliness, sexuality, and character. Moreover, as the ease with which Purdie found "boyfriends" suggests, workingmen's conception of masculine sexual normality structured their intimate relationship with the queans they encountered. Queans and "men" socialized freely, engaging in sexual encounters or ongoing emotional relationships.[90]

This acceptance was, however, always equivocal. It was underpinned by a significant tension, an ambiguity that goes some way to explaining the contradictory responses the quean elicited. Queans could forge a place within neighborhood life precisely *because* they had forfeited their status as men—because they were thought womanlike. If this could readily be attributed to their ineffable nature, it placed them firmly at the subordinate pole within the tacit hierarchies of manliness that structured men's social interactions. As such, queans were an easy target for the jokes, catcalls, and rough treatment through which "normal" workingmen enacted their masculinity. Purdie and queans like him regularly engaged in this kind of verbal confrontation as they defended their presence in public or commercial space. Here the boundaries between acceptance and abuse were uncertain. In certain contexts, affectionate teasing could shade into violent disdain, a passing joke into a physical assault.

Despite these tensions, men like Purdie were, nonetheless, a familiar presence in working-class neighborhoods—acknowledged, precariously accepted, and often welcomed. Indeed, the reputation of the district around the docks for tolerance, friendliness, and sexual possibility was sufficiently pronounced that local nightspots attracted queans from across London. In the 1930s, John remembered:

> Homosexuality in the East End had always been absolutely accepted . . . we used to go . . . to one of the pubs where the mums and dads used to go . . . they used to refer to the boys by their camp name, "Hello Lola love, how are you dear? You going to give us a song?"[91]

The ready request for "a song"—drawing upon a commonplace equation between effeminacy and entertainment—suggests a further manifestation of the cultural mentalities explored above: the popularity of the drag quean and pansy entertainer.

Such figures were ubiquitous within the cultural life of east and south London neighborhoods. In 1926, for example, as "No. 6" in their "London Clubs and Cabaret" series, the Pathé film company produced a short actuality film on the "Anchor Cabaret." Their footage of a typical "working man's cabaret"—reproduced for British cinemagoers—is remarkable in that it apparently includes *two* queer acts. The camp and made-up George Young and Jack Esmonde perform a "prancing" dance routine—"they have their bit of fun too," a caption observes. They are followed by almost a minute's footage of a shameless drag act, introduced by the knowingly ironic caption "We'd never seen or heard the 'Dancing Lesson' sung quite like Kitty Keys sang it." Amidst a smiling crowd that includes families and workingmen of all ages, Kitty—an undeniably "manly" matron—dances and sings. At one point she pulls a powder puff out of her décolletage, vanishing amidst a white cloud in using it to the utmost comic effect (fig. 13).[92]

Figure 13. "We'd never seen or heard the 'Dancing Lesson' sung quite like Kitty Keys sang it." Film still of "Kitty Keys" singing, ca. 1926. ITN Archive.

As the Pathé film suggests, acts like Kitty Keys's were immensely popular amongst working-class audiences. Drag was integral to traditional forms of popular entertainment, possessing sufficient box office appeal that it endured well into the 1980s. Between the wars, street troupes performed in districts like the Elephant and Castle. In the 1940s and 1950s the big revues like "Soldiers in Skirts" or "Morning Girls, Good Evening Boys" attracted sellout crowds to theatres like the Queen's in Poplar. And throughout the period many local pubs staged weekly drag acts for their customers' entertainment. The Duke of Cambridge in Islington, for example, did so throughout 1954. Their act included a rendition of "Diamonds Are a Girl's Best Friend" that left "most of the customers . . . amused."[93]

The popularity of drag acts within working-class neighborhoods represented a broader comprehension and tolerance of gender inversion. This tolerance was, moreover, not confined to the sites of public entertainment but instead permeated the ubiquitous spaces of everyday life. In moving through particular locales, the quean drew an ambiguous mix of desire, curiosity, amusement, or affection from working-class observers. Far from an apocalyptic threat, the apparent disruption of gender identities he embodied was part of the rich spectacle of everyday life, confirming rather than challenging local understandings of masculinity and femininity. If this ambiguity could shade into disdainful catcalls, it just as easily—and just as often—allowed him to forge a place of his own in the modern metropolis.[94]

In 1934, the arrival at court of the men arrested in the Caravan Club thus attracted a "great crowd" of porters from Covent Garden market.

> News of the raid and hints of the nature of the summons spread throughout the West End . . . long before the court opened Bow Street itself was filled . . . So great was the crowd that constables had to be sent out of the station to clear the thoroughfare for traffic.[95]

At the third hearing

> several of the defendants had to force their way through [the crowd] to get to the court and were the objects of much laughter and derision . . . cries raised of "hello darling" and "come on Tilly."[96]

The Caravan defendants attracted a massive degree of popular intrigue, their assumed effeminacy making them an easy target for the crowd's "laughter" and catcalls. Yet the porters' response was more ambiguous than the invocation of their "derision" suggests. Throughout, their mood remained good-humored. They showed none of the hostility the defendants attracted *inside* the courtroom, where they were subjected to the disdainful comments of the magistrate and prosecuting counsel. Even the *News of the World* could not decide if the porters "cheered or jeered."[97]

THE DILLY BOYS' STORY

So what happened to the Dilly Boys? "Dilly Boys" was used in 1973 as the title for Mervyn Harris's study of "male prostitution in London." Yet the Dilly Boys Harris described were not the "painted and scented" men who had so exercised *John Bull* in the 1920s. They were aggressively masculine and "straight" identified, "hustling" queers in the West End. As a cultural label the Dilly Boy had been so profoundly reconfigured that by 1973 it was applied to a set of practices that in the 1920s were conceptualized as its very antithesis: from "screaming" to "straight" in fifty years. This shift, moreover, reflected the changing organization of public queer life itself. If obviously camp men had been an undeniable presence in Piccadilly Circus between the wars, by the 1970s they had all but disappeared.[98]

The waiter and merchant seaman John Alcock lived through these changes after he moved to London in the 1940s. Looking back, he observed:

> People aren't as camp now as they used to be . . . When I was young camp was overt . . . very pronounced . . . as the years have gone by I see that now . . . you cannot pick out an obvious gay person . . . outrageous gayness . . . really doesn't exist any more.[99]

Alcock mapped a movement from "overt" to covert, "outrageousness" to visual conformity. By the 1980s, he suggested, the "obvious" quean had given way to the invisible "homosexual." This external chronology was, moreover, mirrored by an implicit evolution in Alcock's own understanding of selfhood, desire, and difference. In the 1940s he conceptualized his desires within the gendered opposition between man and quean. In the 1950s, by contrast, Alcock began to talk of himself as "homosexual," articulating a subjectivity defined by his partner's biological sex. Still, however, he continued to acknowledge his own campness. Crucially, he did not interpret this as the embodiment of a "womanlike" nature, but as a "homosexual" style of self-presentation. Interviewed in the 1980s, he defined himself as a "gay man."[100]

Taken together, these fragmentary narratives suggest a significant change in hegemonic understandings of sexual difference over the first seven decades of the twentieth century. Within working-class culture in particular, the boundaries between difference and "normality" were remapped, eroding the salience of the quean-man schema to the ways that men interpreted their desires and the lives they led. The disappearance of the Dilly Boys and the declining visibility of camp after the Second World War suggest that it was possible for workingmen to separate sexuality from gender as a component of personhood, to have sex with men while seeing themselves as masculine. If homosexual desire was no longer automatically conceptualized as womanlike, the quean was no longer the embodiment of sexual difference, and camp as a cultural style lost much of its resonance.

The reasons for this change are obscure. In part, the change suggests that the rigid distinction between men and women was being undermined by broader shifts in the social and cultural organization of work, leisure, and family life within working-class neighborhoods. If masculinity and femininity were no longer conceptualized as antagonistic and mutually exclusive entities, then the explanatory power of the quean-man axis was considerably attenuated. In part, it suggests that workingmen had more invested in meeting the prescriptive demands of masculine respectability and refused to accept the loss of status associated with being a quean. In part, it reflects the growing marginalization of visible gender transgression within queer urban life. From the 1930s onwards, facing increasingly active policing, the proprietors of commercial venues—and, indeed, many other queer men—were less willing than ever to accept the risks attendant upon accepting the custom of flamboyantly camp men.

In the decades after the Second World War, these trajectories were, moreover, reinforced by the increasing public prominence of "modern" medical etiologies of sexual difference. In the 1950s, in particular, newspapers began to frame their exposés of queer urban life within the binary opposition between "homo" and "heterosexual." Rather than a womanlike character, the "homosexual's" difference was located in his choice of a male sexual partner. At the same time as a gendered interpretive schema was losing its explanatory power, alternative and, it seems, more compelling conceptions of same-sex desire became current. In this context, many men still understood themselves as queans—and organized their sexual practices and self-presentation accordingly—but they were a declining minority.

If camp's declining significance as a visual embodiment of sexual difference was one manifestation of the shifting relationship between gender appearance and sexual practice, that process was echoed by a significant reconfiguration of medical interpretations of cross-dressing. The critical moment here was Augustine Hull's 1931 trial for gross indecency. Arrested after being discovered posing as a woman, campaigning sex reform groups attempted to shield Hull from imprisonment by portraying him as an asexual transvestite whose conduct was natural and innate. Rather than a sexual deviant, he was, in effect, defined as female in all but his physicality. From the 1930s onwards, influenced by the growing public salience of medical categories of transvestitism after the Hull case, doctors were reluctant to read "masquerading" as an a priori sign of homosexual desire.[101]

These shifts in medical etiologies of gender inversion shaped both the self-understanding of and external responses to cross-dressing men. If queans occasionally wore full drag, they only did so in particular times and places, living their everyday lives as men. From the early 1950s, by contrast, newspapers reported a growing number of cases in which men permanently lived as women. In 1957 the *News of the World* described the "eerie half-world" inhabited by twenty-four-year-old Maurice F:

> He wears women's clothes. His blond hair is long. His fingernails are painted red. His insurance cards are in the name of Mary B. Yet he is a man whose sole desire is to change his sex if only it were possible.

Arrested on Denman Street, Maurice/Mary was wearing a red coat, a black-and-white blouse, nylon stockings, and high heels. Unlike the Dilly Boys, this was a deliberate and complete illusion of femininity. In "desir[ing] to change his sex," it is clear that Maurice/Mary saw himself as a woman. Indeed, he portrayed this as "more natural and . . . normal" to him than living as a man, pointing towards a medical diagnosis of transvestism. This self-understanding was reinforced by the emergence of surgical and hormonal techniques for sexual reassignment after the Second World War. Maurice/Mary was attending the Marylebone Clinic for that purpose.[102]

Yet the Dilly Boys' story is more complicated than the linear transition between a world in which sexual difference was articulated around the opposition between man and quean to one in which it was mapped onto categories of "straight" and "gay." Established conceptions of gender inversion continued to overlay *both* popular and medical categories of sexual difference *and* many queer men's self-understanding long after the 1950s. Camp, as Alcock's memories suggest, persisted as a cultural style that, however watered down, still informs many men's public persona. The "West End Poof" has had a long afterlife. Despite this, however much we may see the contemporary traces of "painted boys," camp's significance has been profoundly reworked. Rather than the physical embodiment of a womanlike character, it reflects enduring cultural constructions of gayness, style, and fashionability.

The quean's enduring cultural legacy was further manifested in the categories of sexual difference deployed by legal and medical experts. In the late 1930s, for example, some police divisions began to identify "homosexuals" in their reports. The descriptions attached to these labels, however, suggest that they were overdetermined by older notions of the effeminate "male importuning type."[103] Similarly, conceptions of gender inversion left residual traces on the most self-consciously modern etiologies of sexual difference. In 1957, writing in the *Daily Telegraph*, Clifford Allen drew upon Freudian ideas to characterize "homosexuality" as a "psychological disease." At the same time, however, this "disease" was articulated in explicitly gendered terms. Allen's "homosexual" lacked any identification with a father figure, meaning he also lacked "those reactions which make him masculine in behaviour." If the "homosexual" was no longer necessarily visibly effeminate, the trained doctor could still discern the ineffably womanlike psychological constitution behind the mask.[104]

Despite this, and however much popular associations between queerness and effeminacy persist, it is clear that the world of the "West End Poof" is long gone. The declining visibility of camp, the disappearance of the Dilly

Boys, and the public emergence of the transsexual denoted broader changes in the understanding, organization, and experience of sexual difference in working-class culture in mid-twentieth-century London. And if the meanings of sexual difference were reworked then so too were the demands of masculine sexual normality.

7

~~~~~~~~~~~~~~~~~~~~~

"LONDON'S BAD BOYS": HOMOSEX, MANLINESS, AND MONEY IN WORKING-CLASS CULTURE

JOHN'S STORY

Growing up in the working-class neighborhood of Finsbury between the wars, John Binns and his mates regularly gathered on local street corners in the evening. Occasionally, Binns recalled, they encountered men he identified retrospectively as "gay."

> We treated them as a joke. We had various names for them, not very nice names . . . we would say "he's pushing shit up a hill" . . . "pansies" . . . "brown hatters" . . . that summed it all up . . . I used to class it as buggery . . . couldn't stand it.

Subjected to hostile catcalls and disdainful gossip as they passed, these "pansies" were "a joke," a disparaged and inferior other that confirmed Binns's sense of his own manliness. Yet his sexual mores and practices were more ambiguous than the assertion that he "couldn't stand it" might suggest. In the gallery of the Islington Music Hall, standing amongst a crowd of men, "someone undone me . . . flies and started pulling me out . . . I let them do it for a couple of minutes before I buzzed off."[1] The two instances jar. How could Binns pejoratively label other men "pansies" or "brown hatters" while having sex with men and not considering himself anything other than a "normal" man?

A second sketch: in the 1940s, John Beardmore and his mates from the Navy would come to London on leave, staying at the Union Jack Club in Waterloo Road. They would "go dancing and try to get off with girls, usually unsuccessfully, so we'd return to the . . . Club and end up in the same bed together." They picked men up in nearby pubs, boasting of their encounters: "When . . . you met somebody who took you home for five bob or so many pints of beer you would say 'I went with a brown hatter last night.'"[2] Beardmore's willingness to move between male and female partners was widely echoed in the neighborhood's streets and commercial venues. Here workmen, sailors, and servicemen socialized and interacted with young women, prostitutes, queans, and middle-class queer men. Policemen regularly observed women and men approaching the same serviceman, both clearly believing that their invitations could be accepted. On leave from HMS *Tyrian* in 1927, for example, Robert M. spent several days enjoying the district's vibrant nightlife. He passed one evening with a young woman. He met her again the following night and chatted for a while, but then left to talk to Reginald S. They passed half an hour together, before Reginald offered Robert a bed for the night.[3]

Taken together, the experiences of men like Binns, Beardmore, and Robert highlight the central difference between the sexual landscape of interwar London and the present day. Young workingmen were not labeled queer or "pansies" because they had sex with men. Engaging in homosex or an intimate relationship with another man was not incompatible with definitions of masculine "normality." Such encounters were, indeed, sufficiently accepted that men could openly look for, enjoy, and talk about male partners without worrying about any potential repercussions. Homosex and intimacy were, as Beardmore indicates, integrated within erotic and affective lives that encompassed male *and* female partners. Just as the "West End Poof" embodied an understanding of sexual difference that cannot be mapped straightforwardly onto the modern categories "gay" or "homosexual," so the boundaries of sexual "normality" were not simply coterminous with "heterosexuality."

This chapter thus explores the world within which such practices took shape, asking what it meant to be a man and how understandings of "normal" masculinities allowed men to move between male and female partners. It focuses upon the lives that young single workingmen forged in London's streets, lodging houses, pubs and cafés. Whether working or relaxing on local streets or in the West End, such men were an arresting public presence. The demand for casual labor in industry, commerce, and shipping was massive, employing thousands of Londoners and drawing migrants from provincial Britain and beyond. As a bustling port London attracted seamen from across the world. It was, moreover, a major military center, permanent home to the Brigade of Guards and a magnet for all servicemen on leave. This was an amorphous bachelor culture, linked by age, economic marginality, and lives lived within all-male spaces. And here sexual and emotional relationships between men were deeply embedded within the contours of everyday life.

Yet this world has vanished. In a culture permeated by the opposition between "homosexual" and "heterosexual," it is difficult to comprehend how working-class understandings of "normality" could encompass encounters with men and/or women. When John Binns was interviewed in the 1980s, times had changed. His sexual past contradicted contemporary expectations of manliness. His framework for interpreting sexual behavior had itself changed since the 1930s. Those he had identified as "pansies" were now anachronistically labeled "gay." This tension between past and present pervaded Binns's narrative. When the opportunity for casual sexual pleasure presented itself in the Islington Music Hall he accepted, and enjoyed the encounter for "a couple of minutes." Looking back, however, Binns struggled to reconcile this with the demands of masculine normality. In protecting his "heterosexual" status, Binns composed a narrative that persistently distanced him from this encounter. His willing participation in homosex was "much to my discredit." It was only a short time before he "buzzed off." It was, moreover, the "biggest shock of my life."[4]

In part, this is one man's attempt to come to terms with an uncomfortable incident in his past. Yet in its internal tensions Binns's narrative has a far wider significance for historical analyses of working-class masculinities in general and men's sexual practices in particular. It highlights the massive distance between the meanings of sexual "normality" and difference in early twentieth-century London and the cultural landscape we inhabit today. The evasions and dissonances within Binns's narrative signaled a broader chronological shift in what it meant to be a man within working-class culture. It is to the lost world towards which Binns gestured and to the manner of its passing that this chapter turns.

ALWAYS A "NORMAL" MAN

In his 1950s VD clinic, Dr. F. G. Jefferies was "told often by homosexuals that there are many men, tough manual workers and others not homosexuals, who seek them out and have intercourse with them." Despite having "intercourse" with men, these "tough manual workers" neither thought of themselves, nor were thought of by others, as anything other than "normal." They were "not homosexuals."[5] Men like this had been identified as a specific category within metropolitan queer life since the late nineteenth century—labeled "renters," to be had or, most commonly, "trade." As the terms themselves suggest, "trade" conceptualized workingmen's participation in homosex in a particular way, delineated in one 1929 encounter. At Hyde Park Corner the guardsman Herbert W. approached Mr. L. After asking, "Would you like a nice man?" and naming his price—"7/6 or 5/6"—they entered the park. Their interaction was replicated at countless sites across London where working-class men were to be found, seeking—and being sought by—older, wealthier men.[6] Trade, in the first instance, denoted precisely this kind of commercial sexual transaction. Combined with the adjective "rough," "trade" described men like Herbert—working-class, "normal" yet available, and unequivocally manly. So commonplace were such encounters that by the 1930s "trade" simply meant sex.[7]

The desires that drew workingmen to these sites and their interactions with other men were, however, more complex than the term "trade" suggests. Certainly, the common organization of workingmen's sexual encounters as a commercial transaction could represent a contingent response to social inequality. Yet to foreground economic motives is both misleading and unproductive, for this was, in one sense, paradoxical. While cash or gifts could be accepted from middle-class men, taking drinks from mates undermined a man's status.[8] This paradox highlights the limitations of analytic categories of "prostitution" in understanding men's sexual practices, suggesting the need to move beyond seeing homosex as an instrumental response to poverty to explore understandings of sex and masculinity within working-class culture.[9]

That this is the case is evident from the very different forms such encounters could assume. In 1960 one lance-sergeant from the Brigade of Guards recalled that

> some of us get quite fond of the blokes we see regularly . . . they're nice fellows . . . and interesting to listen to. As for the sex . . . some of the younger ones aren't bad looking . . . I've had some real thrills off them.[10]

This man talked not about commercial reward, though he was certainly receiving money from his "bloke" and appreciated the opportunity to access otherwise unavailable consumer pleasures. Rather, the language is of emotional intimacy—of "fondness" and mutual "interest"—and of sexual desire and "thrills." John Lehmann similarly described his "friendship" with Jim, who "treat[ed] my flat as another home and relaxed happily on the sofa." Jim wrote to Lehmann just after *he* had married and ended their relationship.

> I wish I was still seeing you Jack as you were the best friend I ever had . . . you were always such a good friend to me we had good times together Jack and I hope I shall see you some time.[11]

That casual sex shaded into an ongoing relationship suggests the erotic and affective possibilities of working-class masculinities and the complexities of men's desires.[12] Arrested cruising Waterloo Road in 1927, Joseph P. articulated his desires in terms that moved easily between sexual pleasure and emotional intimacy: "He is better than sleeping with some filthy woman. I want love and affection."[13]

Before they married many workingmen thus entered into diverse relationships with other men, often while they had steady girlfriends. Such patterns suggest that homosex and male intimacy were accepted aspects of masculine sexual "normality," that, in George Chauncey's terms, "male identities and reputations did not depend on a sexuality defined by the anatomical sex of their sexual partners."[14] Rather, identities were constituted through men's gendered character—their relational status as physically tough, manly, and dominant. Although working-class masculinities coalesced upon the ideal of the breadwinner, this was less compelling for young men. Unable and unwilling to accept domestic responsibilities, they forged independent lives outside the family, centered upon the all-male spaces of work, pub, street, and lodgings. As Andy Davies suggests, this world was permeated by the "connection between hardness and masculine status." Identities and reputations were invested in the physical body, to be gained through repeated performances and enacted *against* other men.[15]

The correlation between manliness and dominance was reflected in men's interactions with women. Promiscuity, public sex, and "conquests" all enhanced a man's reputation. These mentalities crystallized in the "peculiar self-asserting bullying manner" towards women S. F. Hatton observed in 1931.[16] Assertiveness shaded into aggression and violence, with women considered little more than a passive vehicle for male "relief." The key audience for these displays was male. Sexual prowess, like the ability to drink or fight, allowed men to establish their place within a hierarchy of masculinity.[17] Men's interactions with women were, however, often limited, particularly if they occupied all-male residential, labor, or leisure spaces. Unemployed or casual laborers rarely met women and could certainly not treat them. Others deliberately rejected female company, preferring close male friendships. There were, moreover, powerful cultural constraints upon sexual behavior, particularly the stigma attached to premarital sex. A girl's reputation depended upon "playing hard to get," resisting men's advances until marriage or engagement.[18]

That women were often unavailable partners, and "normality" was not equivalent to "heterosexuality," meant there was nothing to stop men finding sexual pleasure and intimacy with other men. The notion of the male body as a site of domination and interiority meant men could enact their masculinity against female *and* male sexual partners, and through casual encounters *and* ongoing relationships. These mentalities were embodied in the ways that workingmen organized their homosexual encounters. For— notionally—these encounters were constrained within particularly narrow limits. In oral or anal sex, men were often unwilling to be sexually passive— to "take it"—since that would require their submission to another man— interpreted as effeminizing—and risk being labeled "girlish" or "queer."[19] Active and penetrative sexual practices, and the demand for "relief," by contrast, embodied the domination of a lesser man that rendered them unequivocally masculine. Buggery, Emlyn Williams heard, "doesn't have to mean you're *un peu* Marjorie, I know a Guardsman who's just crazy 'bout it."[20]

The salience of this interpretive schema was clearest in the way men talked about homosex publicly. In 1953, 1,069 men in prison for sexual offences were questioned by representatives of the Prison Commission. Eighty percent of this sample was working-class. When asked about their preferred sexual role, 71.9 percent said they took the "active" part in oral or anal sex. Only 19.1 percent, by contrast, admitted being "passive," with 6.1 percent taking both roles. Faced with a be-suited stranger asking intimate questions, men's immediate response was to claim to be unequivocally dominant.[21]

Yet rather than a fixed rule, this valorization of penetration was a mode of publicly and legitimately representing homosex, suggesting the importance of performativity to notions of manliness. Most "large masculine men," one man observed in 1960, "insist on being . . . active . . . but some of them can be persuaded to be passive provided they feel sure you will keep it secret."[22] As long as their practices never become known amongst mates— thereby compromising their masculinity—many men were prepared to be more flexible—as Herbert told L., "You can bum me."[23]

Many, moreover, found other ways to negotiate these prescriptions while still finding sexual "relief." Men met in public, participating in encounters in which *both* strictly limited their behavior. In summer 1933 a trunk maker, leather worker, shop assistant, and ship's steward were arrested separately in a Fair Street urinal. Rather than penetrative sex, all had engaged in mutual masturbation—an encounter between *equal* male bodies and by far the most common form of public sex.[24] When Waldemar C. entered a York Road urinal, "This man . . . caught hold of my person and like a fool I messed about." In taking this opportunity almost without thinking, Waldemar's actions highlight the casual acceptance of certain forms of homosex. A quick wank offered sexual pleasure, without the danger of being labeled queer but also without the opportunity to demonstrate toughness.[25]

The correlation between identity, reputation, and dominance also shaped the boundaries between acceptable and unacceptable forms of male emotionality. Although many men entered ongoing relationships, they carefully limited their role, manner, and forms of expression. Albert Burton's friendship with Joe Ackerley is instructive. Burton, a sailor, exhibited a "manly respectability" and distance that frustrated Ackerley's idealized romance.[26] Asked for advice, E. M. Forster emphasized the disruptive influence of class differences: "Standards which are so obvious to you are very remote to him and his class . . . not only conventions but methods of feeling." As for many other men, Burton found the expression of sentiments culturally ascribed to women anathema, threatening to undermine his masculinity. However strong men's feelings were, their words and comportment had always to meet dominant ideas of manliness.[27]

In the cross-class relationships men forged with wealthier queers, these tensions were exacerbated by the intersection between gender and money. Dickie Flower told Peter Wildeblood:

> One meets a boy . . . and . . . one is much richer than he is so naturally one starts giving him things . . . the more you give him the more he seems to resent it . . . men . . . don't want to be dependent; they're too masculine for that.[28]

As Flower recognized, middle-class expectations of intimacy, particularly *their* role as provider or "husband," contradicted workingmen's understandings of manliness. Toughness was a refusal to be subordinated to any man. That being "kept" could be experienced as effeminizing and emasculating was evident in Tony Hyndman and Stephen Spender's relationship, who moved in together in 1933. Although they tried to negotiate these contradictions—Hyndman was ostensibly Spender's "secretary"—their relationship ended in 1935. Hyndman believed Spender

> began to be jealous as I made friends on my own . . . he . . . felt that I only ought to know [other people] through him . . . he wanted to own me. I was to be . . . his wife . . . his, altogether . . . it was jealousy of me being someone in my own right . . . it's against my dignity.[29]

Spender wanted his man also to be a "wife," a role Hyndman could not and would not perform. If masculine sexual "normality" could encompass diverse encounters between men, those encounters were thus never unconstrained. The demands of manliness were powerful and prescriptive. They were, nonetheless, not the same as those of "heterosexuality."

MAPPING HOMOSEX

Workingmen's desires for other men were thus actuated, legitimated, and constrained by the gendered differences *between* men. They could have sex or forge intimate relationships with men because their partners were understood and deliberately positioned as less manly. The clearest manifestation of this relationship of domination and subordination was men's interactions with queans—who understood their *own* desires as womanlike. His partners, Sam remembered, "made love to you . . . because they saw you as a woman."[30] In 1940, the sailor John G. thus met the hairdresser Michael R. on Whitechapel High Street. They walked to an alleyway, where John undid his trousers, telling Michael to turn round and bend over. Michael did so. In automatically assuming reciprocal sexual roles, both men demonstrated a shared understanding of the encounter and their role in it.[31] Whether expressed through casual homosex or domestic roles, such patterns reflected the understanding of this as, in Quentin Crisp's terms, a "pseudo-normal" relationship between "rough" and "bitch."[32]

If the opposition between "rough" and "bitch" highlights the gendered organization of working-class sexual practices, it was not the most common pattern of behavior. Differences of class and age were similarly gendered, structuring a hierarchy of masculinities that opened up further erotic and emotional possibilities. Age differences, for example, were mapped onto the opposition between masculine and feminine, dominant and subordinate. In working-class neighborhoods, one man recalled, "opinion . . . was that homosexuality consisted of older men taking young boys as female substitutes . . . I don't think that people regarded it as a homosexual act. It was a homosexual situation satisfying a heterosexual need."[33]

This easy equivalence between youth and femininity was played out in everyday encounters in London's streets, parks, and lodging houses. In 1927, passing Commercial Buildings in Lambeth, thirteen-year-old J. M. L. was approached by the older Walter S.:

> He got hold of me and dragged me down the alley said, "come along with me how would you like had with a lady—how would you like [to be] my wife?" He said the other two blokes had a girl.

In inviting J. M. to be his "wife," Walter clearly equated him with the "girl" his friends had picked up. Defining the desirable younger man as subordinate—thereby womanlike—made him a legitimate sexual partner. In the physically aggressive manner of his approach Walter enacted his own manliness. Above all, his willingness to approach J. M. L. around the "two other blokes" suggests an easy acceptance of his actions.[34]

Such interactions were particularly associated with the lodging houses and public spaces occupied by tramps, casual laborers, and the unemployed. Within this itinerant milieu, Orwell heard that "homosexuality is general."[35] In part, this "homosexuality" took the form of casual mutual masturbation. But it also included more enduring relationships between older and younger men. In his "Homosexuality among Tramps" (1897) Josiah Flynt thus described "a number of male tramps who had no hesitation in declaring their preference for their own sex . . . particularly for boys." They were "abnormally masculine . . . always tak[ing] the active part."[36]

It was this imaginative landscape of manliness that underpinned the cross-class encounters associated with trade. Workingmen could accept money from middle-class queers partly because this was a reciprocal exchange but also because differences of class were interpreted as making their partners less manly. Sedentary white-collar occupations were womanlike compared with physical labor. And if the bourgeois body did not measure up to prescriptions of hardness, differences in self-presentation also seemed effeminate. Trade, in this context, did not compromise a man's reputation.

The organization of trade was, however, always shaped by the material conditions experienced by men on the margins of metropolitan life, particularly low wages, unemployment, poverty, and destitution. For men "left lounging on street corners," S. F. Hatton observed, "the temptation to petty theft and crime is obvious." As Hatton recognized, such men drew upon diverse informal economies to manage a peripatetic public existence, casual criminality meshing with ad hoc labor, singing on the street, and begging.[37] Exchanging sex for money and food was thus consistent with ideas of manliness and an appropriate response to hardship. John S. was arrested with another man in Archbishop's Park in 1928. He described himself as "down and out": "I was hungry and I wanted money. That is why I did it."[38] The previous convictions of men arrested for sexual offences underscore the connection between trade and other survival tactics. Philip T. was an unemployed sweep, convicted twice for larceny. He met the Reverend Thomas R. in 1924, entering an enduring relationship during which Thomas "at times assisted him with a little money." They were arrested in Lambeth in 1927 when Thomas was "taking [Philip] to a coffee stall to have refreshments."[39]

The Depression exacerbated these cruel realities. The number of men spending their days in the streets, sleeping on the streets or applying to the LCC Welfare Office or charitable agencies for assistance increased dramatically. Men's movement from the decimated industrial north and South Wales to London in search of work further widened the experience of metropolitan destitution.[40] Against this background, many observers began to discern growing numbers of workingmen involved in "sexual offences." "Since the war," Mrs. Neville-Rolfe observed in 1935,

> those concerned with social work among men and boys have gained the impression that the practice [of trade] has increased . . . The Church Army . . . are constantly having cases brought to their notice . . . some youths and young men refuse other work as they can earn more "by this despicable trade."[41]

Church Army officers were particularly prominent in confronting what Captain Hanmore called the "curse of the embankment": "How quickly in Difficulty Street are evil ways learned," he commented; "when hungry and destitute the temptation to earn bed, board and pocket money easily has a great appeal." Like many others, Hanmore established an easy equation between "hunger and destitution" and homosex, mapping the geography of trade onto that of metropolitan poverty—the Embankment, the Mall, and Trafalgar Square.[42] Norwood East similarly identified the "young Welsh boys and others from distressed areas who came to London . . . and prostituted themselves . . . in Piccadilly."[43]

Destitution, in this schema, was a site of sexual danger, leaving workingmen vulnerable to the exploitative advances of predatory queers with money to burn. Certainly, many wealthy men did see the Depression as an unrivalled period of sexual opportunity when, in Michael Davidson's words, "picking up was easy."[44] In 1927, police observed over sixty unemployed men enter Robert M.'s Gloucester Terrace flat in three months. Meeting "casually in the street," Robert enticed the men to his flat with the promise of work. Once there he made sexual approaches towards them.[45]

Workingmen were not just passive victims of economic crisis, however. In most cases, they actively *looked* for such encounters. Trade was, moreover, understood as a source of considerable status. "Tapping" wealthier men demonstrated the streetwise intelligence, resourcefulness, and toughness that marked a real man. Homosex itself enacted manliness. The extent to which workingmen were active participants in queer urban culture thus made districts like Piccadilly and Trafalgar Square notorious haunts of rough trade. In the mid-1930s, for example, unemployed youths socialized and cruised in the Haymarket Funfair. Jim was eighteen and "not too prosperously dressed." In 1936 *he* approached the older Theatrical Agent Harold G., commenting on the machines. After chatting, *he* invited him to a Waterloo Road hotel. They had sex and Harold gave him a pound. Jim told him he was usually in the funfair. He met the older man several times over the following months. They had sex regularly, and Jim always received a few shillings. Jim may have been "hard up," but he remained fully in control throughout these encounters, using his wits to successfully negotiate the harsh realities of social exclusion and, in the process, securing his identity as a man.[46]

Commercial homosex could thus be a source of considerable power, allowing men to exploit their desirability for material reward. In 1952, sociologist Michael Schofield described how

> Young men from the poorest sections of the community . . . find they can drink in the best bars, sit in the most expensive seats in the Theatre and . . . enjoy a mode of experience that would otherwise be denied to them.[47]

As Schofield realized, as well as offering sexual pleasure and emotional intimacy, trade opened up an alluring world of consumerist pleasures, attracting men who were far from destitute. This was certainly true of servicemen, "many of [whom]," Taylor Croft noted, "will countenance urnings for monetary motives."[48] Guardsmen and sailors were a particularly striking metropolitan presence. In part, their visibility was derived from their distinctive uniforms. But it also reflected the frequency with which they participated in queer urban life and their willingness to enter into diverse relationships with other men. Sailors on leave regularly frequented commercial and public spaces in the West End, Victoria, and Waterloo. Guardsmen stationed in London looked for wealthy pickups in the streets around Hyde Park and commercial venues around the Knightsbridge and Edgware Road barracks. They participated in what was, in effect, an institutionalized erotic trade.[49]

"POOF RORTING"

Paradoxically, the strongest evidence of the sexual and emotional possibilities actuated by these mentalities rests in practices that apparently contradicted workingmen's involvement in homosex and intimate relationships. For many men interacted very differently with the queers or queans they encountered in London's public and commercial spaces. Utilizing knowledge of London's sexual geography and of their own desirability, they "picked up" men whom they later robbed, assaulted, or blackmailed—often *after* sex, or within an ongoing relationship. Considered effeminate and weak, outside the law's protection, and often in public spaces alone late at night, queer men could be considered an easy target by young workingmen. So common were such encounters that, by the 1920s, they had permeated everyday slang within working-class neighborhoods. "Poof rorting," Eric Partridge noted, described the "robbery with violence of male harlots by a particularly brutal type of criminal."[50]

In part, robbery and blackmail were alternative responses to poverty. Threatening to falsely accuse a man of "indecency" and naming the price of silence, for example, could be easy money. Most instances of blackmail, however, happened *after* men had had sex. For the tabloids, blackmail was typically a lucrative criminal "racket," elided with drug trafficking, prostitution, and organized "vice." The *News of the World,* in particular, regularly produced sensationalist narratives in which flamboyant underworld characters like the "Squint Eyed Sheikh" exploited workingmen's bodies and the queer's aberrant desires to the tune of £30,000.[51] The reality was usually more prosaic, ad hoc, and opportunistic—and less profitable. Blackmail allowed workingmen to negotiate trade's inherent inequalities and extract more from their partners. In 1925, the "hard-up" Frank G. went to a pickup's room after meeting at Hyde Park Corner. He was fed, they had sex, and he received a pound. Frank then demanded more money, threatening to call the police. In a commercial transaction the line between paying for sex and blackmail was extremely fine.[52]

At the same time, blackmail, robbery, and assault were critical operations in enacting masculinity *against* other men. The ex-guardsman Roland B. regularly frequented Hyde Park looking for trade. In 1929, he met an American schoolteacher. He later told a friend he was "broke . . . but I won't be . . . tomorrow morning. I met an American . . . He's rolling in money and I've got to meet him at . . . his flat . . . When I get the money off the mug I intend going home."[53] Entering the flat, Roland beat the man "into insensibility" with his fists and a chair leg, leaving with a suitcase full of money, jewelry, and clothing.[54] He went to the Hyde Park Corner coffee stall, treating other guardsmen to drinks and boasting of having "done a mug." In lingering detail he described the source of his wealth. "I bumped a chap . . . for it . . . when I hit him I didn't lay him out the first time . . . as he looked like kicking up a noise I had to hit him a few times more. I just about half-killed him."[55] The violent enactment—and public reenactment—of his domination embodied Roland as unequivocally masculine.

In sliding between intimate friendship and brutal assault, workingmen's encounters with the queer transcend contemporary understandings of "homosexuality" *or* "homophobia." Intimacy, sex, blackmail, theft, and assault constituted a continuum within the *same* cultural terrain, underpinned by dominant conceptions of masculinity as toughness and resourcefulness. Within this milieu, sex or intimacy, as much as verbal abuse or assault, confirmed understandings of the male body as a site of interiority. Quentin Crisp, for one, understood this all too well. Crisp was so regularly attacked by youths around his Clerkenwell room that the journey home became a nightmare. Yet many of them were the same "roughs" who readily had sex with him. All these encounters, Crisp suggested, were "consistent with their heavily guarded ideas of manliness." The "roughs"

> Must never admit to themselves or to god or to one another that they even liked the company of homosexuals, let alone that trade . . . was a pleasurable pastime. Any attention that they paid to us had to be put in the form of an affliction. Such gestures as running their fingers through our hair were accompanied by insults about what a bloody awful mop it was . . . more definite sexual advances . . . must be ruthlessly stripped of any quality of indulgence.[56]

The ambiguous boundaries between intimacy and brutality are clear in Crisp's experiences of the prescriptive demands of masculine comportment. Men played roles that reproduced a *difference* from their sexual partners, articulating a toughness that asserted their physical and moral superiority.

These elisions were crystallized through the everyday public languages within which workingmen inscribed the queer and their encounters with him. When masculinity and femininity were understood as diametrical opposites, the obvious quean's or middle-class man's transgression of working-class masculinities was easily reduced under the stigmatic category of "effeminacy." "Poof"—or the rhyming slang equivalent "iron" (from "iron hoof")—"Nancy-boy," "sissy," "Mary-Ann," or "twank" positioned the queer as a lesser—womanlike—man. Through a second order of terms men inscribed themselves within the valorized qualities of domination. Queers were "mugs," "steamers," or "twisters," terms that usually denoted the hapless victim of crime, but here implied the simplicity allowing a strong man to exploit a weaker victim.[57]

As catcalls hurled at passing men on the street or in conversation in the barracks, workplace, or street, the language of "poofs" and "mugs" reproduced hegemonic understandings of masculinity. Persistently reiterated, these pejorative labels constituted a male subject *against* the emasculated body of the queer, defining the boundaries between self and other, masculine and effeminate, "normal" and queer. Such labels, Judith Butler suggests,

> operate . . . as [a] linguistic practice whose purpose has been the shaming of the subject it names, or, rather, the producing of a subject *through* that shaming interpellation . . . This is an invocation by which a social bond among homophobic communities is formed.[58]

Butler's conceptualization of language's productive power is convincing. Yet her reading of the *effects* of this operation is overly narrow, particularly in the historically and culturally blind category of "homophobia." Certainly, the deployment of these terms established "social bonds" between workingmen. Yet they also enabled encounters with that "shamed" object that transcended that category.

Throughout 1923, for example, the teenage messenger boys at Spring Street Post Office in Paddington regularly gossiped about their experiences delivering to Robert M.'s Gloucester Terrace flat. When Robert was "unduly familiar," Thomas B. asked the other messengers about him. Robert, he learnt, was notorious in the office, had made similar advances towards many of them, and was known as a "bummer" or the "bum Major." In distancing themselves from Robert, this gossip affirmed the messengers' sense of their own manliness. Disdainfully labeling him the "bum Major" and boasting that "I'll hit him if he said anything to me" was, moreover, another way of proving their toughness to workmates. Nonetheless, Cyril M. *did* have sex with Robert. As Cecil H. recalled,

> one boy used to visit M.'s house and . . . go inside and . . . get money from Major M. . . . I was told that [Cyril] undressed and let M. lie with him. I have heard [Cyril] say that he had been into M.'s house and . . . let them do what they liked . . . the other boys . . . told me that [Cyril] told them that he had let the men "toss him off."

There was no indication that Cyril himself became the subject of hostile gossip and name-calling. Indeed, that he was prepared to talk openly about his encounters in the office suggests that, rather than undermining his masculinity, they bestowed considerable status.[59]

The oppositional positioning of man and queer as *different* thus structured all their divergent encounters. Imagining the queer as effeminate or subordinate simultaneously actuated the desire for homosex and emotional intimacy—providing a way of publicly and legitimately representing those desires—and rendered him an object to be targeted in other ways. These hierarchical understandings of masculinity coalesced in the notion of "playing the queers"—the idea that workingmen were exploiting their partners for sexual pleasure and commercial reward. Such mentalities allowed workingmen to have sex with other men precisely because of the distance it established between them. If this distance were eroded, the consequences for a man's status were potentially disastrous. In the 1950s, one man was introduced to a known bar by a friend:

He told me I could make good money by playing around with queers. I was picked-up the first night by a man and went back with him but I didn't ask for money. I . . . went back with many people but I never asked for anything. Then my mate found out I wasn't taking the money and he let on to my other friends and said I must be queer.[60]

When his behavior became public knowledge, the difference between queer and "normal" collapsed. Crucially, however, it was not his participation in homosex that meant he "must be queer," but his failure to take money. Unable to claim to be "playing the queers," he came into dangerous proximity to this disparaged figure, and his own manliness was called into question. The boundaries between "normality" and difference were elastic and unstable, and men had to police their behavior with care.

As such experiences suggest, labeling someone "queer" or a "pouf" enabled acts of sex, intimacy, or aggression, just as those practices demonstrated one's masculinity against another male body. Significantly, assault, blackmail, and pickups were all inscribed within the same terms. "Catching a mug" denoted complex cultural possibilities, consistently positioned within the gendered relationship between man and queer. The line between emotional friendship, casual fuck, and predatory assault was never clear, and the queer was both desired and disparaged.[61]

In tracing the possibilities of masculine "normality," I do not want to suggest that *all* young single working-class men participated in homosex or entered into ongoing relationships with other men. But they certainly all *could,* and their practices would be readily understood and accepted amongst mates. As the Spring Street messengers indicate, they could thus talk publicly about their encounters without worrying about attracting any hostile comment. The men they had sex with might have been subjected to vitriolic condemnation, but providing they themselves articulated their desires and conduct within dominant understandings of manliness young workingmen could move easily, albeit carefully, between male and female partners.

When Cecil E. joined the Welsh Guards in the 1920s, he thus quickly found that same-sex encounters were "talked of in the barrack room." Immersed in this milieu, Cecil was socialized into dominant forms of masculinity and sexual and cultural practice. Shortly after enlisting "another Guardsman took him to London and introduced him to some people he called 'soldier's friends.'" Cecil learned of the possibilities of homosex; blackmail and theft; the sexual, social, and commercial pleasures; and masculine status that it offered. Introduced to the sites where those opportunities could be found, he began to frequent Hyde Park regularly, often with other guardsmen, looking for queers. He received guidance in the conventions that should structure his interactions with other men: what he should—and should not—do, where and how he should do it. There was, he learned, an informal "list of charges for the various grades of offence"—seven shillings for a casual encounter. Throughout, his investment in these practices was complex. He formed a relationship with a clerk that lasted for two years, ending when Cecil blackmailed his partner, seeking the money to buy himself out. The older soldiers who "taught him these practices" thus represented accumulated experience and knowledge, permeating the regiment through these ad hoc networks of connection. Constantly reproduced in this way, homosexual encounters were both institutionalized and highly regulated. Never isolated, marginal, or secretive, they were widely experienced and generally accepted.[62]

The guards were, in many ways, unique. Yet their diverse encounters with other men exemplified broader understandings of masculine normality within working-class culture. In his exploration of workingmen's involvement in trade, Jeffrey Weeks argues that "unlike female prostitution, no subculture developed among male prostitutes."[63] In searching for a "subculture" organized around the category of "prostitution," however, Weeks remains profoundly insensitive to the historically specific organization of homosex and the social institutionalization of the patterns he explores. Workingmen's desires were more complex than the term "prostitution" allows. As an integral part of what it meant to be a man they were, moreover, embedded within everyday life within a sprawling metropolitan bachelor "subculture."

THE AMBIGUITIES OF INTERGENERATIONAL SEX

When contemporaries described the interclass encounters associated with trade, they often identified the working-class participants as "lads" or "boys." In part, positioning one man at the subordinate pole of class and age hierarchies was simply an established narrative trope, counterposing the predatory queer with his vulnerable victims. The terms were, moreover, an imprecise guide to men's actual age. Certainly between the wars, a "lad" referred to a married man in his twenties as often as a young teenager. Yet if the language is misleading, sexual encounters between older men and boys well under what is now the "age of consent" were, nonetheless, common.

Such encounters were embedded in—and shaped by—the everyday spaces inhabited by those growing up in working-class neighborhoods. Outside of school, overcrowded housing and the desire to escape parental supervision meant boys' social interactions and play focused on the street or park. Public space was also an important economic resource, where fallen fruit could be picked up from passing vans, errands run for local tradesmen, or shopkeepers subjected to petty thefts. Street life offered excitement, allowed boys to contribute to the family economy, and opened up the possibility of accessing further commercial pleasures. The cultural geography of boy life was reinforced by the unskilled labor market, which absorbed fourteen-year-old school leavers into an array of delivery jobs.[64] Working-class boys thus encountered adult men constantly, their interactions constituting age as a category of gendered and social inequality. Youth could mean relative poverty, physical subordination, and vulnerability. Youth could also mean desirability, and therefore the power to exploit an elder. In such encounters, danger and possibility existed in an ambiguous, perhaps irreconcilable, tension.[65]

Those who were older, and so able to physically defend themselves, transformed their desirability into a source of commercial and physical reward, echoing the activities of the men discussed above. In the 1920s, Henry P. and Albert T. lived in Harlesden, a poor working-class neighborhood. Both had left school but had no regular work. During the daytime and evenings they "used to knock about the Paddington Railways Station," looking for money, food, and excitement. One afternoon Albert told Henry, "I'm going to earn some money. I am going up to the park to get some." Walking to Hyde Park, they sat by the West Carriage Road until dark. Then, Henry recalled "we met a tall gentleman . . . T. got up and said I've clicked and went after him very quickly." He spoke to the man—a colonel in the Indian army—before going under a tree with him.[66]

Albert and Henry deliberately exploited their good looks and familiarity with London's queer geography to gain a degree of erotic pleasure and commercial reward. They knew exactly what they wanted and, most importantly, where to go to get it. If the sense of control, calculation, and prior knowledge that permeates this incident is striking, their behavior was commonplace. In 1937, for example, Colin E. "picked up" two boys in Trafalgar Square and took them to his room in Austral Street. "Both," he told the policemen who later came knocking, "were of a bad type and welcomed my indecent suggestions and acts." In part, these are the desperate protestations of a man facing imprisonment. But Colin's comments also suggest that knowledge of some boys' involvement in trade permeated metropolitan culture.[67]

This confident streetwise behavior, however, coexisted with unambiguous sexual assaults in which men forced themselves on unwilling partners. In 1947, for example, a fourteen-year-old boy visited a Victoria cinema where he was "molested by a man . . . who . . . endeavoured to force the boy to interfere with him and prevented the boy from leaving." This traumatic, violent, and coercive encounter left him in "a state of distress."[68]

In many ways these encounters are polar opposites. Nonetheless, they highlight the precarious balance between danger and possibility that pervaded *every* encounter between boys and men. Such encounters took place in everyday locations—while boys were playing in parks and streets, making deliveries, working in men's homes, watching films.[69] Violent assaults in these public spaces were comparatively rare, since there were usually people around. Often, however, boys were offered money, cigarettes, sweets, and entertainment in exchange for sex. In 1936, for example, the Lambeth delivery boy Reuben E. received a letter promising him "some dinner, a wash . . . a lot of fun . . . in the afternoon tea and then the pictures . . . You and I could have a good time together and a few shillings in your pocket."[70] While Reuben rejected this approach, others seized such opportunities, captivated by the allure of fashionable consumerist pleasures like the cinema or teashop. Arrested masturbating a man on Hampstead Heath in 1932, Frederick F. responded: "He told me he would give me eighteen pence if I rubbed him off . . . I said I would because I wanted the money."[71]

Given the precarious balance between danger and possibility, such encounters could easily have ended very differently. Boys were assaulted in parks, just as they exploited their good looks for material reward there. This balance, moreover, could shift within the *same* encounter. In 1936, the errand boy William R. met Edward R. outside an Islington cinema. William told Edward his car light was broken. He was thanked with a cigarette, and then invited for a drive and something to eat. William eagerly accepted this opportunity. The two drove onto Hampstead Heath where

> he took off my coat and put it on grass. He sat down and told me to. I was afraid. I did sit down. He held me tight. He tore my jacket. He took his thing / person out. He rubbed it up and down. He took mine out and tried to put it in his mouth. I tried to get away. He held me tight. Eventually got away.[72]

What began as a moment of excitement and adventure, quickly turned into something more frightening. Implicit in William's narrative are both the opportunities opened up by his appearance—which he was willing to exploit—and the danger such decisions placed him in, given his physical size. On this occasion he escaped and informed the police, perhaps the only way to resolve tensions otherwise beyond his control.

In working-class neighborhoods, the attitudes of parents and other adults to intergenerational encounters were equally ambiguous. Certainly, physically coercive advances generated considerable anger—the lengths to which men often went to ensure boys' silence testifies to that. Many parents, moreover, turned to the police to punish such acts, even when their sons had been willing participants in ongoing sexual relationships. In 1937, for example, a schoolmaster and photographer were arrested for their encounters with a fifteen-year-old pageboy over several months. It was not the page's complaints that brought the men under police scrutiny. Rather, his mother "wanted a cigarette and hunted through her son's pockets for one [and] came across [a] letter and read it." When confronted by an angry mother, the page made a formal statement.[73]

Other parents reacted very differently. Fourteen-year-old John D. first met Charles R. in 1922 while delivering groceries to his Battersea rooms. From then he

> used to go and see [him] nearly every week . . . I used to help clean up . . . He used to be with me in the bedroom and play about with my privates. He used to undress me and used to undress himself . . . He used to put his private up my back passage.

This relationship lasted almost six years. When John was unemployed Charles gave him ten shillings on every visit, reducing this to 6/- when he was working. He loaned him £20 to buy a motorbike, and another £10 when he was unemployed. Their relationship was never hidden. John's mother Annie was well aware of his movements and his relationship with Charles, who was a familiar figure in the family home. The money generated through John's sexual practices was, moreover, integral to the household economy. When John's father was unemployed, Charles loaned Annie money and paid her to clean for him. She gave him coal and chickens during the General Strike. "There was," Annie remembered, "no secrecy . . . [Charles] has always been very kind to me and to my boys."[74]

Annie's easy acceptance of John's relationship with an older man is striking today. It suggests, in part, a very different understanding of the transition from childhood to adulthood. Having entered the labor market at fourteen, boys were clearly considered to be approaching adult status and attributed with a degree of independence, responsibility, and strength, rather than being viewed as weak and in need of protection. It suggests that the boundaries between acceptable and unacceptable intergenerational encounters were partially articulated as the difference between coercion and consent—there was no *automatic* assumption that such encounters were dangerous. It underscores the definitions of masculine "normality" discussed above. It suggests, finally, the demands that poverty placed on the family economy during the interwar period. Within this cultural landscape, sexual encounters between men and boys could elicit little or no response as often as they generated outrage.

Violent coercive assaults, enticement by cigarettes and streetwise trade, thus all occupied a similar position within the metropolitan landscape, structured by the same geography of boy life and the social and economic conditions of working-class existence. Boys responded to men's advances in various ways. Some went straight to the police or parents. Others eagerly accepted the opportunity for sexual release and easy money. The choice— even the possibility of a choice—depended upon age or relative poverty. Accumulated neighborhood traditions were equally important—gossip between boys, their experiences of older men, and the attitudes of adults around them. Michael Davidson had "known a London district . . . where within the space of five years any boy would be ready to be picked up; and in the next five years that vogue would somehow have died out."[75]

THE LIMITS OF HOMOSEX

The world explored in this chapter was constrained within very specific parameters of class, age, and ethnicity, and ideals of toughness associated with an unskilled, public all-male world. Skilled men, by contrast, tended to reject this disorderly realm, investing status and respectability in the role of breadwinner.[76] For most men, moreover, participation in this world was a transient experience, associated with a particular life-cycle phase. Some— particularly those who spent all their lives in all-male milieus at sea, work, or living on the streets—continued to enjoy sexual and emotional relationships with men. Henry P.—the Harlesden youth discussed above—seems to have cruised Hyde Park for many years.[77] Such behavior was exceptional. Most men married; and when they did, their sexual practices changed. William B.—an errand boy and clerk at the Royal Courts of Justice—was involved with his older colleague Eric R. for six years, while also having a steady girlfriend. If William clearly enjoyed their relationship, he told Eric it was over when he married in 1924 at the age of twenty.[78]

Such life-cycle shifts in sexual practice highlight the salience of masculine forms associated with a public bachelor culture to workingmen's same-sex relationships. When men married they notionally exchanged the homosocial world of the street or pub for the home, relinquishing the independence of bachelorhood for adult responsibility. In so doing, their understandings of manliness changed perceptibly. The ideal of the tough man was, in part, replaced by the ideal of the breadwinner—a more domesticated, home-centered version of manliness. Married men were thus less likely to frequent those public sites where they might encounter the queer. They occupied a milieu in which definitions of masculine normality that encompassed same-sex encounters were less compelling. Within working-class culture, moreover, *any* extramarital sexual encounters contradicted what was expected of a real man.

In 1934 the Coldstream guard Fred Turner thus ended his relationship with John Lehmann when he married his pregnant girlfriend. Fred's letter was apologetic and regretful, yet his choice was clear: "I think too much of my wife to play a double game . . . I am going to lead a straight life and play the game with her."[79] There was no suggestion here of repudiating or denying former friends or behavior. Rather Fred—like many others—saw marriage as a moment at which he simply moved on, his changing sexual practices and desires and fidelity simply a natural and inevitable part of growing older.[80] The powerful cultural pressures towards marriage often confined sexual and emotional relationships between men to a particular period in workingmen's lives.

Just as male sexual practices were shaped by class or age, so they were also structured by differences of race. If the conventions of court records and newspaper reports make the evidence problematic, particular ethnic groups were, it seems, more likely than others to inhabit the world described in this chapter.[81] What is most striking is the almost complete absence of Jewish workingmen—London's largest immigrant community—from queer urban life. In nine sampled years of the Thames and Old Street court registers— responsible for the densest areas of Jewish settlement in the East End—only eleven Jewish men were prosecuted for sexual offences.[82] In forty years the *News of the World* reported only one case: Max G., born in Russia in 1902, arrested for importuning in 1927 and described as "well-known in the West End."[83] Jewish men's absence from court and newspaper records could, in part, be a statistical artifact, since local officers never policed sexual offences with the same vigor as central divisions. Their invisibility in diaries and memoirs, however, suggests they *were* less likely to engage in homosex. Young Jewish men often occupied the same spaces and socioeconomic position as their Anglo-Irish neighbors, yet their sexual practices differed markedly.[84]

Why? In his work on New York, George Chauncey suggests that the Jewish tendency to migrate as families shaped a distinctive neighborhood culture that partially distanced young men from the rough bachelor milieu in which homosexual practices were embedded. Certainly, such men forged public lives in East End streets. Yet those everyday lives continued to revolve around the family home to a greater extent than for many Anglo cockneys; and in public men's behavior was subject to a pervasive communal surveillance. Jewish neighborhood institutions, moreover, provided a space where young men and women socialized regularly. For young Jews, masculinity, respectability, and status were as likely to be invested in the spaces of family life, heterosociability and work as in the public world of men. The comparison between London and New York is awkward; these suggestions are only tentative and Jewish men's experiences need further research. Nonetheless, it seems as if young Jews conceptualized masculinity in ways that precluded the possibility for homosex within "normal" everyday life.[85]

This again suggests the close correlation between homosex and a male world *outside* communal and domestic ties, particularly when Jewish men are compared with other ethnic groups. While Jews tended to migrate within their family, until the 1950s most other immigrants tended to be young single men from the Empire and beyond, looking for work before returning "home." Black, Indian, and Asian seamen and laborers forged a transient cosmopolitan world in lodging houses, cafés, and pubs around the docks. And in 1927 *John Bull* identified a "Black colony" with its own communal institutions, cafés, and dances in that "insalubrious neighbourhood . . . situated around Bloomsbury, Charlotte Street and the Seven Dials."[86] For many metropolitan observers, the presence of so many "foreign" bachelors provoked considerable anxieties, focused upon their interactions with white women and the dangers miscegenation posed to Britain's stability.[87]

This focus on interracial "heterosexuality" concealed such men's participation in queer urban life. Dockside streets, pubs, and lodging houses were a characteristic site of casual sexual encounters between men from diverse ethnic backgrounds.[88] Between the wars, moreover, London's "Black colony" overlapped with many sites of queer sociability. Several key figures in public narratives of a problematic black "underworld" were connected with the most notorious queer cases. Laurie F. and James R., for example, were arrested for trafficking in opium in Seven Dials in 1925. Laurie later ran a series of dances for black men and white women in the notorious Edgware Road Adelphi Rooms. And in 1937 James was arrested in Billie's Club on Little Denmark Street and found to have a previous conviction for buggery.[89]

Black men were thus a striking presence in such cosmopolitan neighborhoods, interacting socially and sexually with the men they encountered and often actively seeking homosex. In Reginald Underwood's *Flame of Freedom* (1936), Julian Ferrers waits at a bus stop in Piccadilly Circus watching "a strapping Negro . . . march up and down . . . in front of [him]." The man approached, asking for money as he was "hard-up." He then leaned closer and said, "Don't mind earning a bit, you know sir, do anything you like." If Underwood's prurient fictionalized encounter suggests an economic motive for black men's participation in "trade," the "flash of disappointment" in the man's eyes when Ferrers rejected his advance—but still gave him money—suggests that the desire that drew them to the Dilly were, again, more complex.[90]

Of all these groups, it is the sexual practices of young Irishmen that have left most trace. From the 1920s well into the 1960s queer men regularly identified "rough Irish layabouts" or "burly Irish laborers" as both objects of desire and likely to accept their advances.[91] Paddington was John Alcock's "favourite haunt" in the 1940s.

> It was my experience . . . that the Catholic Irish boys were much more prone to go home with a queer gentleman . . . for a . . . ten-shilling note . . . something to eat . . . a clean shirt . . . The rent scene was . . . very predominately Irish.[92]

Alcock's recollections suggest how profoundly urban sexual culture was shaped by ethnic difference. In linking class, ethnicity, and commercial homosex, moreover, such accounts begin to explain Irishmen's "predominance" in this world. Thousands of men left Ireland for London in the early twentieth century, drawn by the opportunities offered by the casual labor market. They forged a tough bachelor culture, living and socializing together around west London rooming districts while constantly negotiating the realities of poor wages and irregular employment.[93]

Irishmen thus participated in London's "rent scene" partly because they occupied the margins of the metropolitan economy.[94] There was, however, nothing uniquely Irish about the experience of poverty. Irishmen's apparent visibility within queer urban culture thus reflected the particular resonance of ideals of toughness for them. Irishmen were, quite simply, more likely to inhabit the cultural landscape explored in this chapter—to equate masculinity within dominance. They lived outside the constraints of communal or family life, married comparatively late—often in their thirties—and lived, worked, and forged their identities as men within an all-male world. In this context, Irishmen accepted homosex as part of everyday male life more easily. This tendency was reinforced by Catholicism's cultural taboos. The vigor with which the church defined premarital "heterosexual" encounters as sinful contrasted with a comparative silence over homosex.

CLOSING FOR TRADE

That the world explored in this chapter is almost incomprehensible today is a powerful testament to how profoundly masculine sexual practices have changed over the past century. The guardsman or sailor no longer inhabits the queer urban landscape. Young workingmen no longer move between male and female partners. We no longer have the conceptual vocabulary to comprehend how men could participate in homosex or intimate same-sex relationships while seeing themselves—and being seen by others—as "normal." The boundaries between sexual "normality" and difference have been reconfigured to preclude the possibility of sexual or emotional relationships between men being an intrinsic part of everyday life. Increasingly, in the decades since the Second World War, to be considered "normal" has demanded an exclusive sexual and emotional interest in women.

The first signs of these shifts came in the 1950s, when many queer men themselves sensed that their world was changing. If the Second World War liberated queer sexuality for many, if it had, in Rodney Garland's words, "made most members of the underground profiteers in an emotional bargain basement," the period of prosperity and rising real wages that followed destroyed much of the economic rationale for the cross-class liaisons described above. In Garland's novel *The Heart in Exile* (1953), the MP Hugh Tidpool laments trade's declining availability. The reasons seemed clear: "People like us have less money now . . . the working class no longer respects us as they did . . . Not to speak of the fact that there's now full employment." Tidpool yearns for the golden years before and during the war when young workingmen "were yours for the asking." He continues:

> Boys accepted us because we were class . . . they liked us because, unlike women, we didn't cost them money . . . we made a fuss of them, which their girls didn't . . . [T]oday they can afford women, and if they don't want women they have plenty of money for other amusements.[95]

The affluent worker was less likely to want a liaison with another man. Tidpool saw only one solution: a return to the Depression.

Tidpool's narrowly economic model cannot adequately explain why workingmen's sexual practices changed. Certainly, affluence attenuated the radical differences of wealth in which trade was embedded. But the transition from austerity to affluence was neither absolute nor universal, and the experience of poverty and homelessness persisted for many young men. For a minority, exchanging sex for money has remained a way of negotiating those problems throughout the postwar decades. In 1955 Laurence Dunne could describe the "young vagrants who arrive in London with no work or pied de terre [and] drift into the traffic."[96] Subsequent studies by Mervyn Harris (1973) and Barbara Gibson (1995) highlight the continued presence of young "straight" hustlers in central London.[97]

To see homosex as simply an instrumental response to poverty—and, as such, something that faded away as real wages rose—is, moreover, misleading. It obscures the complexities of the sexual, social, and emotional interactions between men and fails to comprehend the mentalities that made such interactions possible. To understand how this world vanished we need instead to explore the broader cultural shifts in the decades immediately before and after the Second World War, and particularly the cultural changes in working-class life associated with postwar affluence. While the answers are tentative, the questions are simple: how did ideas of what it meant to be a "normal" man change to define homosex as unacceptable? How did "homosexuality" and "heterosexuality" become defined as distinctive and mutually exclusive entities?

In part, the answer lies in the widening accessibility of new forms of heterosociability, as affluence and rising real wages reconfigured the spatial and cultural contours of working-class life. The massive expansion of metropolitan youth cultures in the 1950s—embodied most spectacularly in the figure of the Teddy Boy—reflected young workers' growing power as consumers. Increasingly, men's lives moved away from the street corner into London's commercial venues—the milk bar, coffee house, and pub—where they socialized alongside young single women.[98] When queer venues were becoming ever more exclusive, this trajectory opened up a growing physical and cultural distance between heterosocial and homosocial interaction, inscribing a difference between "normal" and queer into London's commercial geography. Whereas workingmen, workingwomen, the respectable queer, and the flamboyant quean had often rubbed shoulders in commercial venues between the wars, they were less likely to do so after the 1940s. The fluid and amorphous sexual culture evident on Waterloo Road—in which workingmen moved easily between male and female partners—simply disappeared. The movement off the streets and the growing differentiation of commercial sociability distanced the everyday spaces inhabited by young workingmen from those that constituted London's queer underworld. Men were less likely to encounter the queer, unless prepared to actively visit a known venue.

The obverse of this process was that male and female workers encountered each other more regularly in the 1950s and 1960s. They did so, moreover, within a milieu in which attitudes towards sex, relationships, and marriage were changing. The decline of old taboos and growing availability of contraceptives uncoupled the link between sex and unwanted pregnancy, reducing the stigmas and dangers attached to premarital sex. Women were, perhaps, more willing and available sexual partners. Economic change, moreover, had a profound impact on marriage itself. Workingmen married and exchanged the all-male realm of the pub or street corner for the home at an earlier point in their lives than ever before. Marital life was more affordable and—in a culture increasingly saturated with idealized images of domesticity, romantic love, and marital intimacy—fashionable. In this context the working-class family, argues Joanna Bourke, became "irresistible."[99]

To emphasize the salience of this new geography of sociability and emotion to workingmen's growing refusal of homosex is not, however, to assume a normative "heterosexual" desire that was freer to express itself in postwar Britain. Rather, these trajectories underpinned a transformation in hegemonic conceptions of what it meant to be a man. That young men married earlier, were more likely to socialize regularly with women, and benefited from increasing security in the labor market eroded the salience of a public world of men and ideals of toughness and domination to definitions of masculinity. Status, identity, and reputation were increasingly mapped onto the alternative spaces of work and home, effectively domesticating ideals of manliness. The conceptions of masculinity as physical and cultural domination that had sustained the possibilities for workingmen's homosexual interactions were undermined, losing much of their cultural resonance and explanatory power. Definitions of masculine sexual "normality" were reworked to preclude a sexual or emotional interest in men.

The shifting boundaries between sexual "normality" and difference underpinned by these drawn-out cultural changes were reinforced, in the short term, by the explosive politics of sexuality in postwar London. In the late 1940s and 1950s, the queer became a more visible and dangerous part of everyday discourse. Such "evil men" were a staple of tabloid exposés, defined as a potent threat to Britain's very existence. A constant trickle of newspaper reports saw a growing stigma in sex between men. Through such reports, moreover, medical etiologies of sexual difference that distinguished between men on the basis of who they had sex with permeated everyday life. It was increasingly difficult for workingmen to engage in homosex and see themselves as "normal." Through these intersecting processes the sexual landscape inhabited by workingmen was reconfigured over a period of decades, mapping the boundaries between "normality" and difference more firmly onto the binary distinction between "heterosexual" and "homosexual," "straight" and "gay." More than ever, to be a man within this milieu meant not having sex or intimate relationships with other men.

If the frustrations of those attracted to trade were one tangible manifestation of this process, a second came when many novelists and "experts" began to include a new figure within their typologies of queer urban life in the 1950s and 1960s. Alongside its lament for a lost world, *The Heart in Exile* maps an emerging "post-war generation of inverts" who, especially by contrast with the middle-class queer or flamboyant quean, tended to be "tougher in mind and body" knowing that "tolerable biceps and a good pair of shoulders are better selling points today than an acquaintance with books by Sartre and Maugham or cracks by Gingold or Coward."[100] Garland's avatar for this "generation" is the figure of Terry, Dr. Anthony Page's housekeeper. From a poor background in Stockton-on-Tees, Terry moved to London to work as a nurse. He was "an invert." His appearance was resolutely "cheerful and manly," and he was always "more at home in blue jeans, lumber-jackets, moccasins and loafers, windcheaters, cowboy shorts, in essentially masculine, revolutionary, anti-traditional, almost anti-capitalist garments."[101]

Garland was, perhaps, extraordinarily prescient, for such figures proliferated in sociological and literary texts in the following decades. Terry found his mirror image in the "leather boys" described by Elliot George in 1961 or the "excessively masculine" homosexuals identified in Michael Schofield's *A Minority* (1960). Like Terry, this figure possessed a distinctive physicality—a toned, hypermuscular body. Like Terry, he was associated with particular forms of self-presentation—"butch" fashionable clothes, including jeans, checked shirts, boots, and leather jackets. And, like Terry, he was situated in apparently new arenas of queer sociability and display—the gym, swimming pool, bathing pond, and the nascent leather scene taking hold in bars like the Coleherne.[102] Neither a quean nor "normal," unequivocally masculine yet exclusively queer, this was a novel figure within working-class culture.

This new urban archetype embodied more than the ebb and flow of metropolitan fashion. He represented a changing sexual landscape, a visible sign of the ways in which working-class understandings of masculine sexualities were shifting. Men who *looked* like this—who wore work clothes, who were "rough"—had participated in London's sexual landscape for decades. What changed in the postwar period was that rather than being understood as "normal" or trade, such men were increasingly thought of—and considered themselves—as "homosexual." The "excessively masculine" queer was the counterpart of the "normal" man who refused homosexual encounters. Just as many workingmen stopped having homosex, so others organized erotic and affective lives focused exclusively on men. Just as the possibilities for emotional and sexual intimacy between men were more tightly circum-scribed, so it became possible for working-class men to separate sexuality from gender as a component of personhood, to see themselves as masculine *and* queer. By the 1970s at the latest, working-class understandings of mas-culine sexualities approximated the hegemonic understanding of middle-class culture since the 1920s.

8

"THE HEART IN EXILE": RESPECTABILITY, RESTRAINT, AND THE CITY

NARRATING DIFFERENCE

If the contrasting figures of the "West End Poof" and the working-class "man" embodied a gendered conception of sexual difference and "normality," this was not the only interpretative framework within which male sexual practices and identities were understood, organized, and experienced. Certainly by the 1920s, when middle-class men identified themselves as queer, they did not locate their difference in a discernible and ineffable womanlike character. Queer, in this context, was interchangeable with the emerging medical categories "invert" or "homosexual." Positioned within a map of sexual practices in which difference and "normality" were embodied as the distinction between "homo" and "heterosexual," queer articulated a difference predicated *solely* on men's exclusive sexual and emotional attraction to other men. Just as the "West End poof" was embedded in working-class understandings of masculine sexualities, so these forms of selfhood and cultural practice took shape within peculiarly middle-class masculinities—though they came to exercise a powerful influence on the lives of all men. More than a mode of self-understanding, queer was a way of being predicated upon the values of privacy and discretion that permeated bourgeois culture in the first half of the twentieth century.

The clearest sign of this alternative conceptual framework lies in middle-class men's reactions to the public manifestations of queer urban culture. The cinema manager Dudley Cave, for example, became aware of his desires during the 1940s. In so doing, he was forced into an uncomfortable engagement with the dominant images of sexual difference—his apparent ties to the screaming quean and sites of public sex. "Queers," he thought, "tended to be broken-wristed . . . wear make-up, exaggerated in their gestures." As a "gay young man," his "big problem . . . was that I didn't realise what I was; I had no role models . . . the only people I knew who were gay were the camp transvestite[s] . . . I didn't belong to that." Never considering himself anything other than conventionally masculine, Cave refused to accept that his desires made him a man like *that*.[1] Like others of his class, he reacted similarly to the spectacle of the promiscuous queer, driven by uncontrollable lust into London's most abject spaces.[2] This meshed with a wider antagonism towards working-class sexual practices that focused on public space and encompassed encounters with men and women. Writing in 1952, the sociologist Michael Schofield thus suggested that amongst respectable "homosexuals," "bisexuals are considered immoral . . . [since] a true homosexual could not tolerate such practices and so a bisexual is one who is only concerned with sensuality—the sex of the love object being immaterial."[3]

From the late nineteenth century, these antagonisms were refracted through medical etiologies of sexual practice. The relationship between sexual science, social behavior, and individual selfhood has been subject to ongoing debate.[4] What is significant here is the congruence between medical discourse and the cultural landscape mapped above. For many doctors, the conventionally respectable men they encountered in their consulting rooms could not easily be labeled effeminate or depraved. Rather than immorality, their desires seemed to have some hidden physiological or psychological origin. Sexual difference, following this logic, was congenital and natural—what Havelock Ellis called a "biological variation."[5] By the 1920s medical opinion mirrored Anomaly's position: "Inversion is involuntary not voluntary, it is constant not inconstant and it is instead of not in addition to the normal impulse . . . The whole of [the invert's] personality is turned towards men and away from women."[6]

If such ideas legitimized homosexual desire as stable and innate, they were never unequivocally affirmative and inclusive. Positioned within a particular moral framework, the boundaries of "homosexuality" echoed and essentialized the position explored above, excluding those practices deemed disreputable or immoral. In part, this process focused on what would now be termed "bisexuality." Doctors from Ellis onwards distinguished between men whose desires were congenital and exclusive—"inverts"—and those who *chose* to engage in homosex through viciousness or immorality—"perverts."[7] Explicitly, the difference between inversion and perversion was one of class. In the mid-1950s, Dr. Sessions Hodge categorized fifty cases from his criminological practice. He labeled twenty-one men perverts. Of these, seventeen were skilled or unskilled laborers and two were clerical workers. None worked in the professions. Of twenty-nine inverts, by contrast, eleven were professionals, four clerical workers, and only six laborers.[8] Homosexual desire was not "natural" to all men, and if medical discourses legitimated middle-class practices, they simultaneously excluded and stigmatized those of working-class men. As Norwood East and Hubert's *Psychological Treatment of Crime* (1949) observed, "a certain type of personality has difficulty in developing the normal complicated heterosexual pattern . . . tend[ing] to show general, primitive sexual interests with an interest towards all forms of sexual activity."[9]

Medical discourses were permeated by such moral assumptions. The National Association for Mental Health, for example, located public sex and promiscuity in the dissociation of sex and love—"the most basic disturbance of sound emotional development in our civilisation."[10] The quean's effeminacy was interpreted in similar terms. Wolfenden himself characterized such men as "severely damaged personalities . . . flauntingly exhibitionistic . . . grossly inadequate, passive weak-willed persons . . . deeply resentful antisocial types."[11] Set against bourgeois notions of morality and respectability, particular cultural practices could easily be attributed to a sociosexual pathology.

Read together, medical discourse and middle-class men's engagement with queer urban culture evinced complex cultural antagonisms that articulated a respectable "homosexual" identity at the intersection of class, masculinity, sexuality, and place. The modern city was fixed within an anxious, categorizing gaze, a constituent element of men's self-definition. Men defined their respectability in relation to and repudiation of these all-too-visible queer spaces, in the process presupposing a stable, autonomous, and privileged male subject position. The respectable "homsexual" was attracted exclusively to men, conventionally masculine, neither a pansy nor promiscuous, neither looking nor behaving any differently from other men. Inscribing the "underground" within pejorative categories of difference thus not only defined their sense of self as a queer subject but also a sense of class position and masculine respectability. They were different from the "normal," but they were also different from other queer men.[12]

This "respectable" position crystallized around three assumptions. First, sexual desire was located within a distinct domain of personhood. Men's "homosexuality" or "inversion" was, in this sense, independent from gender identity. Second, it was innate and unchangeable—what Lionel Fielden called "[my] natural bent, born with me and inescapable."[13] Third, it did not automatically place them outside conventional social and moral codes.

As Anomaly argued, "the invert in his emotions differs but little from his normal brother . . . that his sexual reactions are inverted does not necessarily imply other deviations from the normal."[14] The boundaries between sexual difference and "normality" were simply a matter of men's choice of sexual partner.

That medical discourse and a class-specific moral position emerged as adjacent and intersecting cultural formations is clear from the ways in which middle-class men encountered the work of Ellis, Anomaly, and others. That encounter was often articulated not as the shock of something new, but as reading something strangely familiar. Frank Birkhill moved to London from Cheshire in the 1930s.

> In Notting Hill Gate on a bookshop I found Havelock Ellis's book Volume 6 *Sex Psychology* [*sic*] and that was banned at that time . . . and it revealed everything. To me it was a revelation. This is me. I really am . . . I exist . . . I have a relationship with humanity and this oddity in me is an orthodox movement . . . That book made me very very happy. I was very very happy to meet it.[15]

Birkhill remembered this illicit "meeting" in terms he might have reserved for an encounter with another man. But in his account it is often unclear exactly who that other was. In part, it was Ellis speaking through his text. In part, it was the "inverts" Ellis described. In part, as the language of "revelation" suggests, it was Birkhill himself. Reading through the scientific jargon he found something deeply personal—"this is me." For Birkhill, *Sex Psychology* simultaneously confirmed that he "existed" as a subject; invested previously unsettling desires with a scientific validity, meaning, and permanence; and, crucially, it made him realize that he was not alone. Birkhill's ensuing "relationship with humanity," in this sense, represented *both* his difference from "normal" heterosexuality *and* his commonality with certain men like that. Given this tangible self-realization, there is little wonder he was "very happy."

DOMESTICITY AND INTIMACY

The emergence of these modes of respectable "homosexuality" was underpinned by a broader structural transformation of bourgeois culture within which the domestic sphere became the central site in the formation of male sexual practices and identities. The key process here was the reconfiguration of understandings of sex, intimacy, and marriage from the late eighteenth century. Through this process, as Harry Oosterhuis and others suggest, the ideal of romantic love—the intense emotional attraction between husband and wife—acquired increasing salience as *the* basis for marriage. Decoupled from its association with procreation, sexual passion was invested with "autonomous and positive meaning . . . as an essential constituent of the emotional bond." Marriage, in this schema, was a site of profound privacy and intimacy, and achieving these romantic ideals was integral to an emotionally fulfilled life.[16]

Such understandings clearly shaped bourgeois expectations of marriage throughout the nineteenth century. It was, however, in the decades immediately before and after the First World War that ideals of companionate marriage became most compelling. The clearest sign of this process was the proliferation of popular marriage guidance texts like Marie Stopes's *Married Love* (1918). Always addressing men *and* women, writers like Stopes placed marriage and domesticity at the very center of social and cultural life. Marriage was, moreover, conceptualized as a union of equals, integrating friendship and sexual attraction. According to this logic, sexual intimacy was integral to the marital bond—a "conjugal art" through which couples embodied their companionship. Within these prescriptions, masculine identities and status were invested in the private and domestic sphere—in the emotional quality of marriage and men's ability to sexually satisfy their wives.[17]

In part, the increasing centrality of the private domain to masculine identities reflected an ongoing engagement with modern urban culture from the late nineteenth century. The transformation of work, particularly the shift to salaried white-collar professionalism, undermined the independence traditionally underpinning masculine status. That status was further challenged by working men's assertiveness—symbolized by the vociferous demands of organized labor—and women's penetration of the traditionally masculine spheres of work and public life. Middle-class men saw these changes all around them. The public city itself embodied modern life's uncertainties, bringing them into unsettling proximity to cultures they found distasteful. This was a disorderly space that questioned the very basis of gender identities.[18]

In this context, many bourgeois men retreated to the privacy of the home or the respectability of London's suburbs, ideologically and physically distancing themselves from the problematic spectacle of urban life. Suburbanization and domesticity were potent symbols of deep cultural anxieties. Particularly between the wars, the emphasis on companionate marriage and family life, the home's developing status as a site of sociability, the growth of domestic consumer cultures, and the emergence of gardening and

DIY as manly pursuits marked a profound reworking of middle-class masculinities. The home was constructed as a sanctified space of order and security, insulated from the disruptions of modern life.

If this process was underpinned by drawn-out social and economic changes, it acquired further impetus through the experience of the First World War. As Alison Light suggests, the retreat to home was a characteristic feature of interwar British culture. In part, this reflected individual men and women's desire to "reconstruct" their lives after the war, to find a private space in which they could forget and transcend their experiences. In part, it reflected a broad movement away from heroic, adventurous, and aggressive modes of masculinity after the brutal realities of industrial warfare. After the carnage of the Western Front, Britain's stability was increasingly located in the domestic, the familial, and the suburban. The retreat to home was, finally, sustained by the changing materiality of domestic life: increasing professional incomes, declining family size, a physically improving home environment. Within these shifts, James Hammerton suggests, the model of the domesticated affectionate husband "moved a little closer to the centre of idealised masculine identity" in the postwar decades.[19]

Just as the increasing salience of romantic love and domesticity to bourgeois masculinities had a profound impact on "heterosexual" relationships, so it similarly reshaped emotional, affective, and sexual relationships between men. When physical intimacy was conceptualized as the defining component of emotional attachment, established traditions of male companionship were undermined. When love, sex, and marriage were intertwined, passionate friendships between men acquired unsettling overtones. That men's "love letters" were often used in court as evidence of sexual transgression from the late nineteenth century, suggests that the boundaries of "normal" masculine intimacy were narrowing.[20]

Simultaneously, however, this cultural landscape provided the context within which men were able to forge a respectable "homosexuality" predicated upon those emotional and sexual attachments that defined romantic love. At the same time as companionate marriage became a compelling ideal within bourgeois culture, several writers thus began to express these parallel ideas publicly. Havelock Ellis, John Addington Symonds, and Edward Carpenter, in particular, articulated an affirmative model of love between men, interweaving Hellenism, spiritualism, and Whitmanite ideas of comradeship. Carpenter's *Love's Coming of Age* (1895) and *Intermediate Sex* (1908), for example, deliberately challenged the association between sex and procreation. Drawing upon circulating ideas of romantic love, Carpenter defined sex as a vehicle through which individuals expressed their spiritual unity.

He advocated "sincere attachment and warm friendship, and allow[ed] that this may have fitting expression in caress and embrace." This was a powerful moral ideal, validating love between men.[21]

In part, this deliberate equation between same-sex relationships and companionate marriage was a tactical response to hegemonic ideas of the queer's depravity, challenging the sexual offences laws. Yet the lives described in Ellis's case histories suggest that Symonds and Carpenter emblematized a broader process through which love and comradeship became the central component of a respectable "homosexuality."[22] Their writings were well received since they meshed with many men's understandings of their desires and the lives they aspired to lead. John Lehmann, for example, was "always looking for the friend who will give me the direct, warm and natural, entirely loyal relationship that I dream about . . . the only thing I care about"; not simply a platonic ideal, but an intimate fusion of the sexual and emotional.[23]

Lehmann's aspirations were shared by many men of his class. Robert Hutton's first sexual experience was an anonymous encounter at Victoria Station. Yet he knew

> there must be more to it than a rather untidy tussle in a summerhouse . . . I wanted to meet someone who would become important to me; to my emotional life and I knew that this also meant to my physical life.

For Hutton, "physical and mental fulfillment" could "only be achieved by association with a member of his own sex." Around 1918, he found such fulfillment, with a young officer, Julian Mase:

> He was a lover . . . but far more than that he was a friend and counsellor, wise[,] witty and understanding. We enjoyed the same things, laughed at the same jokes and read the same books. It was important to both of us that we should be together.[24]

Here was what Emlyn Williams characterized as "two lives joining in one salubrious stream."[25]

The emotional ties described by Hutton or Williams directly paralleled those associated with companionate marriage. Indeed, men often explicitly referred to their relationships in those terms.[26] Such practices transformed the domestic sphere into a central site in the formation of queer identities, a space of love, intimacy, and respectability that mirrored wider middle-class constructions of the home. If this private orientation did not remove men from wider queer networks, it was central to both their sense of self and their social and sexual lives. Antony Grey met his lifelong partner in the 1950s, enjoying "the enormous privilege and happiness of a settled relationship in a joint household with somebody who is absolutely a central part of my world." The couple occasionally met friends in the more discreet clubs, but socialized primarily at home—"prefer[ing] to have a few real friends than to being out and about."[27] The salience of this ideal rendered the dominant forms of middle-class queer culture invisible. As one man suggested,

> the people one sees around London are the promiscuous ones, but there are a lot of us who lead quiet lives with a chosen friend. Homosexuality is like an iceberg—one only sees a small part of the whole—the more unpleasant part.[28]

As this suggests, the prescriptions of romantic love underpinned the emergence of parallel, but mutually exclusive, forms of "heterosexual" and "homosexual" intimacy by the 1920s. The first discernible manifestation of this process was a radical shift in sexologists' attitudes towards queer men marrying. If doctors advised men to marry as a "cure" for their "abnormal" desires as late as the 1870s, within fifty years Havelock Ellis could argue that such a treatment "must be rejected, absolutely and unconditionally." That same-sex desire was innate and unchangeable meant marriage would be purposeless. To encourage men to form a relationship lacking "that intimate unreserve and emotional extravagance which are the essence of sexual love" was, moreover, immoral. Given the prescriptions of companionate marriage, it was increasingly difficult, if not impossible, for queer men to meet those demands.[29] Anomaly had thus "known only a few married men who have admitted they were inverts."[30]

This is not to say that married middle-class men did not engage in homosex; yet they were unlikely to move in private queer circles, to consider themselves—or be considered—queer. More importantly, they often experienced their practices within a tangible guilt, recognizing that they were breaking their marriage vows. This highlights the second discernible manifestation of the process explored above—the experiences of those who would now be labeled "bisexual." While workingmen moved between male and female partners with apparent ease, middle-class understandings of intimacy, fidelity, and masculinity, by contrast, were incompatible with such practices. Unable to fully meet the cultural demands attached to marriage or same-sex relationships, many men found themselves excluded from both "normal" and queer worlds. The desire for men *and* women profoundly disrupted middle-class masculinities, generating an ongoing emotional conflict.

The terms of this conflict were vividly evoked in the memoirs of the actor and playwright Emlyn Williams. After moving to London in the late 1920s

Emlyn enjoyed a series of relationships with men, including a deeply intimate affair with the actor Bill Cronin-Wilson.[31] Disturbingly, however, he
remained attracted to women. "I was standing stock still in the middle of
the road, and that's as good a way of getting run over as any."[32] This conflict
came to a head after Bill's death. After a long holiday, Emlyn returned to
London. There he fell in love with Molly and proposed to her:

> I faced the final hurdle, the high one I had been skirting, my attitude
> towards my own sex . . . though I had never been a slave to pursuit, however
> undemanding my sudden sallies I had always been free to indulge in them.
> The idea that I should be cut off from that freedom was alarming.[33]

Emlyn's "alarm" at meeting the standards of fidelity and commitment
marriage demanded was compounded by his developing relationship with
Fess, a young workingman. At one point Emlyn, Fess, and Molly were hol-
idaying in the same house.

> I looked at the door. If it opened which of the two would I hope to see? . . .
> I was waiting for him now in a torment I had not expected and if he entered
> now I would feel tormented relief. If she appeared I would be delighted by
> the sight of the person I loved.[34]

The protracted conflict between differing desires and loves, his attraction to
men and his feelings for women, threatened to tear Emlyn apart. His
anguished cry, "Is everyone two people constantly?" suggested his emotional
"torment."[35] It was only after Emlyn discovered that Fess had stolen from
him and was sleeping with women—thereby falling short of his own expectations—that this conflict was resolved. He rejected Fess and married Molly.
Although he had celebrated his relationships with men, the emotional and
cultural demands of middle-class respectability meant Emlyn simply could
not love both men and women. Unable to fully enjoy a life that was neither
queer nor "normal," oscillating unsettlingly between two poles, he could
only reconcile those pressures by forging that loving, intimate relationship
idealized by men of his class. That relationship was only incidentally "heterosexual."

DISCRETION

This idealization of intimacy, domesticity, and privacy was clearly informed
by hegemonic understandings of romantic love within bourgeois culture. In
articulating a respectable "homosexuality," men focused not just on what
made them different but also on those values they shared with men and

women of their class. Their insistent refusal to accept that their sexuality placed them outside conventional morality thus marked the salience of the dominant codes of bourgeois masculine character in framing their sense of self. As Martin Francis suggests, middle-class notions of respectability, masculinity, and class devolved upon the qualities of self-control, reserve, and discretion. The respectable gentleman exhibited a restraint of deportment, emotionality, dress, and speech—he was moderate in all things. The emphasis on self-control inherent in men's rejection of public sex and promiscuity thus echoed more pervasive cultural practices. For queer men, the intertwined qualities of restraint and discretion constituted a particular understanding of selfhood and way of being, expressed as a compelling set of behavioral codes that shaped their erotic, affective, and social lives.[36]

The external logic of these codes was a conventionally "normal" public persona. Addressing the respectable "invert" in 1927, Anomaly outlined unacceptable modes of behavior—"dictated by the needs of discretion":

> Don't masquerade . . . in women's clothes . . . or use make-up; don't be too meticulous in the matter of your own clothes, or effect extremes of colour or cut; don't wear conspicuous rings, watches or cuff-links or other jewellery; don't allow your voice or intonation to display feminine inflection . . . ; don't stand with your hand on your hip or walk mincingly; don't become identified with the groups of inverts which form in every city . . . don't become involved in marked intimacies with men who are not of your own age or set; don't let your enthusiasm for particular male friends make you conspicuous . . .[37]

Anomaly demanded painstaking self-control that encompassed "tone," "expression," and conduct. The "invert," he suggested, should strive towards a respectability of appearance appropriate to his status. He dismissed the "West End Poof's" brash flamboyance, since "conspicuous peculiarities are undesirable." The "invert" should be nothing other than respectably masculine, his difference invisible.[38]

Such assumptions were commonplace. As John Hardy commented, "Going about your ordinary day to day business you wouldn't think of wearing anything really outrageous. You tended to dress down and look like everyone else." Hardy, like many others, automatically managed his appearance in order to remain invisible.[39] The result, Donald West observed, was that "homosexuals are to be found anywhere and everywhere . . . but as most of them possess no distinguishing features . . . the unsophisticated remain in ignorance of their existence."[40]

Men described such practices as their public "mask"—that which allowed them to work and move around the city successfully and safely.[41] Stephen worked as a senior civil servant from the 1930s onwards: "One really had to be astonishingly careful . . . [since] one occupied a pretty prominent position." He went to considerable lengths to be "discreet." Aided by the distinction between home and work that permeated professional culture, Stephen maintained an absolute separation between the different parts of his life. He socialized discreetly in exclusive commercial venues with similarly respectable friends. Later he lived quietly with his partner. In presenting himself like a typical civil servant—and never talking about his sexuality at work—Stephen was able to move between these distinct spaces without ever drawing unwanted attention. This was the basis for what became a richly fulfilling life. Far from being a disavowal of his sexual character, such circumspection was a constitutive element of Stephen's self-understanding—it was who he was.[42]

This kind of deliberate compartmentalization was a characteristic feature of middle-class lives. Appearing conventionally respectable at work, in the streets, or in commercial venues, men only discarded their "mask" amongst friends or at home. Moving constantly between the queer and "normal" worlds, they constructed what was commonly called the "double life." As Peter Wildeblood put it, "I had two sets of friends; one might say two faces. At the back of my mind there was always a nagging fear that my two worlds might collide." While they may have all experienced this "nagging fear" of exposure, most men were remarkably successfully in keeping their "two worlds" apart.[43]

Given this emphasis on restraint and discretion, the visible indiscretions of queer urban culture were deeply troubling. In public, respectable men saw a realm of womanlike queans, blackmailers, rent, and workingmen driven by uncontrolled lust into the city's most abject spaces. This was far from the lives they wished to live or the person they thought they were. Public queer life embodied promiscuity, disorder, and bad taste—desires and emotions dangerously free from self-control. Paradoxically, however, this spectacle performed a productive role in the formation of middle-class queer identities, providing a reassuring sign of men's own respectability and shaping the urban lives they forged.

Most deliberately distanced themselves from public queer culture, avoiding looking for partners in bars or streets. In part, this was because they were keenly aware of its dangers. As Antony Grey remembered,

> it's perhaps difficult for people . . . to realise what [the law] meant for those of us that were "respectable" and did care about what the effects might be on our families . . . by getting into legal trouble . . . the disgrace involved was absolutely unthinkable.[44]

Grey didn't go cruising because he didn't want to be arrested. His implicit contrast between "respectability" and "disgrace," however, suggests these choices were shaped by a more nebulous geography of cultural practice. Bourgeois spatial morality, predicated upon the rigid distinction between appropriate public and private behavior, defined public sex as promiscuous, immoral, and dangerous. Grey, like many others, understood public sex as an indiscretion committed through a failure of self-control. It was "absolutely unthinkable" because it was incompatible with the behavioral codes of respectability.

Repudiating public sex was, moreover, explicitly a process of self-definition. "If the only place to meet a person is in some nasty smelling lavatory," one lawyer commented, "then really I would do without." Refracted through the language of dirt, abjection, and disdain, he produced a moral geography that articulated a discreet and respectable "homosexuality" embedded in the private sites of intimacy and love.[45] Such geographies were well established by the 1950s. Indeed, writing in 1927, Anomaly presented the city itself as an entity that disrupted stable and respectable queer identities. "If left without direction," he worried, "a young man may become a subject for police surveillance or a member of one of those furtive groups which haunt cheap eating places." A loss of "direction" endangered an individual's freedom and—as the disdain inherent in the notion of "furtively" "haunting" the shadows suggests—his reputation, character, and respectability. The modern metropolis held nothing but corruption, contagion, and dangerous temptation. The police courts and tabloid press vividly demonstrated the disasters awaiting the man "left to grope for self-knowledge in the social sewers of a city."[46]

In this sense, the formation of queer social networks was shaped by a conscious attempt to distance oneself from the city's "social sewers"—to forge a life consistent with the values of discretion, privacy, and respectability. This process was emblematized by the idealization of domestic space as "a place of peace, seclusion and refuge."[47] Whether they lived alone, with a partner, or with friends, middle-class lives devolved on the private sphere to a remarkable extent. The behavioral codes associated with respectability further shaped men's participation in queer commercial sociability. Often shunning the rougher pubs and dance halls and always remaining conventionally masculine, they met friends in exclusive restaurants and members' clubs, forging social networks that were, in effect, private and invisible. The cultural distance between somewhere like the Rockingham and the "painted boys" in backstreet Soho cafés was huge.

Many men, moreover, distanced themselves from London's "social sewers" through the realm of the imaginary, seeking out a place where queer identities were stable and unproblematic. Browsing a bookshop off St. Martin's Lane in the 1950s, John Chesterman discovered the work of Jean Genet. He remembered the moment vividly: "The whole world opened up . . . I realised that there was literature and art . . . It wasn't just hustling the streets[;] there was a whole other thing that went along with it."[48] For Chesterman, Genet's celebration of love between men was the very antithesis of the sordid "hustling" he saw on London's streets. Set against pejorative images of queer urban life, literature and art—this "whole other thing"— offered a positive image of desire as pure, fulfilling, and spiritual. In the process of working out exactly who he was, escaping from the city into this imaginative otherworld was a turning point. Simultaneously, Chesterman's reading legitimized his desires, constituted a respectable queer self and offered a guide for the kind of life he wanted to lead. This was, his memories suggest, a positive experience.

Chesterman was certainly not unique in this. Men like him read voraciously, avidly seeking out any texts rumoured to offer a sympathetic treatment of "homosexuality" in bookshops, libraries, or through friends. If, as I suggest above, they often focused upon the medical writings of men like Ellis, their reading also included a distinctively queer literary canon. Between the wars, Edward Carpenter's work was particularly important in framing a respectable "homosexual" selfhood, predicated upon his exaltation of the moral and spiritual worth of love between men in texts like *The Intermediate Sex*. For educated readers, such ideas were so powerful that Michael Davidson could describe Carpenter as having the "bright light of an evangel," and Reginald Underwood as "a seer, a saint."[49] Indeed, Carpenter inspired successive generations of writers including Leonard Green—author of *Dream Comrades* (1916) and *The Youthful Love* (1919)—and the contributors to the single-issue journal *Quorum: A Magazine of Friendship* (1920).[50]

These texts coexisted with very different literary traditions that, nonetheless, operated as a discursive space to argue and validate the existence of same-sex desire. The appropriation of models of friendship from Hellenic texts, for example, persisted well into the twentieth century. Contemporary writers often deliberately guided their readers to these texts. Anomaly, for example, included a detailed queer reading of Greek texts in his literature chapter in *The Invert* (1927), pointedly highlighting the positive constructions of same-sex desire they offered.[51] While Hellenism's influence was in abeyance in the 1950s, commercial publishers began to publish a series of realist popular novels that explicitly focused upon queer men's lives. Texts like Mary Renault's *The Charioteer* (1953), Angus Wilson's *Hemlock and After* (1952), or James Barr's *Quatrefoil* (1953) offered men an instantly recognizable engagement with the individual and everyday—with the lives of men like them. Usually narrated through a middle-class subject, they embodied the forms of respectable selfhood, conduct, and emotionality explored in this chapter.[52]

Whatever they read, the written word allowed men to forge an affirmative sense of self and established their connections to men like them—both in the past and in the present. This sense of commonality was particularly important in establishing a notion of the worthy, creative, and principled "homosexual"—the "homosexual" who had made a contribution to the society he inhabited. Taylor Croft thus leavened his persistent attacks on the disorderly public city in *The Cloven Hoof* (1932) with the recognition that "homosexual instincts among high-principled men may be an innocuous or even an inspiring thing." For Croft, individuals like Shakespeare and men's prevalence in "artistic" professions, highlighted the "urning's" unique creative talents. He noted their "extraordinarily high standard of conversation and wit . . . their gift for brilliance and laughter." Such literary and historical traditions were far removed from the dominant images of queer urban culture, contributing to the construction of an unequivocally respectable "homosexuality."[53]

THE TRIALS OF RESPECTABILITY

Given the salience of discretion and self-control to notions of masculine respectability, many observers found it simply impossible to believe that businessmen or professionals could cruise streets and cottages or drink in West End pubs. Set against these geographies of class and reputation, their movements seemed somehow out of place. Indeed, for those men who *were* arrested in public, asserting their "good character"—that nebulous admixture of moral rectitude, discretion, and respectability attributed to men of their class—was a strong defense in court. Frank Champain, for example, was arrested in an Adelphi urinal and tried at Bow Street in 1927. For Champain's defense counsel "it was inconceivable that he could be associated with the class of offence alleged." It was, indeed, inconceivable that a man of Champain's background could even have been in the Adelphi at night. While Champain was convicted, the length of his sentence was reduced— "having regard to [his] excellent character."[54]

Champain appealed to the County of London Sessions. In court Henry Curtis-Bennett cross-examined PC Handford, the arresting officer, in terms that embodied tangible class antagonism. "Your evidence is absolutely uncorroborated?" he asked Handford—"Yes." "You know Mr. Champain is a gentleman of the highest character?" Again—yes. Handford was himself now on trial for daring to arrest a "gentleman." At the same time Curtis-Bennett thus described how Champain "bore the highest possible character." He outlined his Oxford education, his cricket and rugby awards, his particination in the Gentlemen versus Players match, his public school employment, and his wartime commission.[55] He summed up:

> This is the man . . . who, because he offered a cigarette to a plainclothes officer, is brought before the magistrate and convicted . . . But cases like this do not occur with great sportsmen like Mr. Champain . . . I ask the Bench to say that this conviction cannot stand and that he still bears the highest character he has always had.[56]

Champain's "character" rendered him unequivocally respectable, masculine, and controlled—precisely the sort of man who would *not* be importuning. Implicitly, Curtis-Bennett suggested that Champain's social position precluded the actions attributed to him. The appeal succeeded: Champain's sentence was quashed, his good character affirmed, and his costs awarded.[57]

But men like Champain *were* a distinctive presence in the public spaces they frequently dismissed as immoral and disreputable. In 1937, for example, a notorious blackmail scandal exposed several "men of good standing" picking up working-class youths around the Dilly—including a retired Indian judge, a "prominent city stockbroker," and an ICI executive.[58] The values of discretion, intimacy, and privacy existed in a persistent tension with everyday social practice; respectable "homosexual" identities were unstable and problematic.

In part, public queer sites were a last resort of those men who had nowhere else to go—because they were young, lived outside London, or were married, and thereby did not see themselves as queer. Many more men, however, were inexorably drawn to London's streets, parks, pubs, and cottages in search of companionship. The idealization of romantic love failed to address one crucial question—where was the ideal friend to be found? For those who were part of informal friendship networks meeting in each other's homes or exclusive commercial venues, the answer was straightforward. For those who remained isolated from such networks, however, reconciling their affective desires with the behavioral codes of respectability was difficult. If the rigid compartmentalization of the "double life" was integral to protecting one's person and livelihood, it could often leave men isolated. Unable to meet other queer men at work or through informal introductions, many saw no way to meet partners apart from entering the disreputable public realm—that most accessible of queer spaces.

To emphasize the necessity of public space, however, underestimates its positive attractions. Cruising—like public sex—was erotic and exciting precisely because it generated the electric thrill of social and spatial transgression. The deliberate rejection of propriety and respectability was, in itself, alluring. John Lehmann remembered how William Plomer "wouldn't take somebody home if he could find a blacked-out park."[59] A sense of adventure, transgression, and danger drew men like Plomer towards public space. In 1957, writing in the *British Medical Journal,* Desmond Curran and Dennis Parr thus noted how

> some . . . [men] were extremely promiscuous and great risks were taken in making contacts in public lavatories despite the known observation kept on such places by plain-clothes police . . . the illegality of homosexual acts enhances their appeal . . . some homosexuals gain vicarious pleasure by eluding capture.[60]

This was, they suggested, a great game, a thrill-seeking flirtation with public urban culture.

Set against bourgeois notions of space, cruising was thus experienced as an erotic descent into a metropolitan underworld in which men exchanged propriety for a realm of sexual possibility and pleasure. This movement was often represented by discarding middle-class styles of dress, echoing the conventions of social investigation, and disrupting the visual cues of class. When Champain was arrested, for example, Handford did not realize he "had to deal here with a gentleman, a person of superior social position." The Street Offences Committee anxiously asked whether "did his dress or manner not indicate . . . what his class was?" Handford thought he was "working class. He did not appear to be anyone of note or a perfect gentleman . . . his dress . . . was a striped blue suit and mackintosh and a cap."[61] By manipulating his appearance Champain had taken on an alternative social identity, one more appropriate to the nocturnal spaces in which he moved. Rather than simply passing through an otherworld, he had become part of it.

As this suggests, public space was particularly alluring for those middle-class men who were attracted to trade—soldiers, sailors, and workmen.[62] Trade's desirability was evoked vividly in John Lehmann's *In the Purely Pagan Sense* (1976). Lehmann's narrative plays out his erotic fascination with the Brigade of Guards, following Jack Marlowe's meandering "safari" around London. As Marlowe encounters guardsmen, his gaze inevitably and immediately fixates upon the bodily signs of toughness. Entering a "pub near Victoria" he meets Bill, "beautifully built with full thighs, a strongly-developed torso and hairless skin." In an Edgware Road pub he "gravitate[s] . . . to[wards] one exceptionally tall and sturdily built young soldier." Marlowe's guardsmen are always "tall and dark"; "strongly built" with "beautifully developed torso[s] and large biceps"; they "[bear themselves] in a very soldierly way with a straight back and purposeful walk."[63]

These bodies were not eroticized in themselves but for the broader masculine qualities they seemed to represent. That toughness invested in the working-class body denoted a "real man," rendered closer to nature by his class.[64] Imagined as more instinctive and spontaneous than the middle class, trade became infinitely more desirable. That workingmen moved with apparent ease between male and female partners only reinforced these constructions. Lehmann thought his partners "entirely without moral qualms . . . behav[ing] as if what we did was the most natural and agreeable thing in the world. This did me the world of good." These "therapeutic" relationships were explicitly contrasted to the restraints and discretion that permeated his milieu, to an experienced sense of bourgeois self-loathing: "The *straightforward pagan coarseness* of these boys was a constant delight to me, a contact with *earthiness* which I needed very badly."[65] The language is of freedom, of simplicity: that the working-class body, by dint of its very physicality, approached some kind of "reality" from which middle-class masculinities had become distanced.[66]

This distance, articulated as the encounter with a social other, generated a powerful sexual charge. Rather than being erased by sexual desire, class difference *actuated* that desire, eroticized in almost gendered terms.[67] Of the ex-guardsman Tony Hyndman, Stephen Spender commented:

> The differences of class . . . between [us] . . . provide[d] some element of mystery, *which corresponded to a difference of sex.* I was in love . . . with his background, his soldiering, his working-class home.[68]

Spender loved the alterity Hyndman represented as much as who he was. This encounter between different and unequal male bodies, the thrill of social transgression, was a defining aspect of the workingman's desirability.

Yet this desirability was never unproblematic. In part, this followed from knowledge of trade's "tendency . . . to robbery . . . violence," or blackmail.[69] The toughness structuring workingmen's sexual practices could underpin very different encounters. The muscularity that rendered them so attractive also made them a physical threat, their desirability tainted with unease and fear. Lehmann's description of Bill moved to note how "under [his] charm and good manners lurked always a hint of danger and violence."[70]

Moreover, while the commercial organization of trade made such men accessible, many middle-class men were deeply troubled by paying for sex—a practice incompatible with ideals of romantic love. In part, the enduring relationships they often forged deflected nagging fears that this was simply "prostitution." Soldiers, noted Lehmann, "were really anxious for friendship."

> They wanted a protector who would provide a sexual outlet of . . . a completely innocent sort . . . supplement their miserable pay, and spoil them a little with good food and drink . . . and . . . [those] . . . semi-luxuries, which they coveted but could not afford . . . [this was] a warm fatherly or elderbrotherly relationship.[71]

Displacing these anxieties into an idealized "friendship" preserved the moral integrity of Lehmann's fantasy.

Yet the emphasis upon a particular power dynamic rendered this ideal inherently unstable. In the 1950s, Lehmann encountered a "wave" of "military prostitution" in which "the troopers were having a succes fou." "Their popularity had gone to their heads . . . some . . . were making . . . £40 or £50 a week . . . servicing a list of older admirers." Lehmann soon "discovered . . . a deep-seated objection in . . . being just one of the dates on their nightly list."[72] When men's "callous" and "mercenary" motives became evident, his idealized friendship became polluted and untenable. Sensing that *he* was being exploited, Lehmann reacted angrily. The "fatherly" relationship was intrinsically possessive. The queer's wealth and status was supposed to give him the upper hand. Middle-class expectations of intimacy, particularly *their* own role as provider or "husband," thus contradicted dominant scripts of manliness within working-class culture. Toughness was a refusal to be subordinated to any man.

Social distance produced further antagonisms between middle-class men and their working-class partners. In Ackerley's social circles, for example, his partners could find themselves socially isolated, disparaged as inferior, coarse, and uneducated.[73] This hostility went further. Ackerley thought Freddie Doyle's coiffed hair "a typical example of working-class vanity and ineptitude and propriety." He continued: "How irritating and unsatisfactory the . . . working classes are . . . with their irrationalities and superstitions and opinionatedness and stubborness . . . and laziness and selfishness." These were "ignorant people who think they know everything."[74]

Simultaneously, therefore, the idealized workman was a disparaged other, the two existing in persistent tension. Middle-class men's desire for sex *and* intimacy made this an unrealizable fantasy. When the ideal "friend" proved unobtainable, all that was left was the workman's apparent "venality." Objectified easily, his body could be imagined as a commodity to be bought, possessed or "given," and Ackerley could regard Doyle as, "after cigarettes, a thing I must cut down or . . . altogether abolish."[75] Rendered passive and quiescent, the workman, notionally, existed for the queer's pleasure. He was, noted Michael Davidson—using the slang that so evokes this arrogance—"to be had."[76]

It was in this context that many of those attracted to trade fell into the promiscuity evident in Joe Ackerley's encounters with "several hundred young men, mostly of the lower orders."[77] In so doing they were always equivocal and uneasy about their practices. John Lehmann, for example, "thought with bitter envy of some friends and acquaintances . . . who had been living for years with one chosen boyfriend . . . Why couldn't I achieve the same peace?"[78] "Peace," for Lehmann, meant the enduring domestic intimacy his class idealized. Ackerley, similarly, characterized his practices as a desperate search for this kind of affective relationship: "Unable . . . to reach sex through love, I started upon a long quest in pursuit of love through sex."[79]

When, decades later, Ackerley reread his 1930s diary he burned it immediately. He found "no single gleam of pleasure or happiness . . . [This was] a story of deadly monotony . . . frustration, loneliness, self-pity . . . boring finds . . . wonderful chances muffed through fear."[80] Looking back, his shame was tangible. This kind of emotional response to promiscuity and public homosex had its own chronology, underscoring the broader changes in middle-class culture explored in this chapter. In the 1910s and 1920s many men simply accepted such practices as integral to queer urban life—it was something they got on with and enjoyed. Emlyn Williams, for example, was typically nonchalant—"drawn to the alleys of Chelsea for a quick dip in the murky briny, to emerge invigorated."[81]

Yet from the 1920s onwards, the prescriptions of respectable masculinity became increasingly incompatible with public sexual practices. Certainly by the 1950s, when Schofield conducted the interviews for what became *A Minority* (1960), such practices were sufficiently invisible for him to conclude that "homosexual activities in public places are uncommon among the self-confessed homosexual." Schofield might well have rephrased this, for perhaps the difference was not what the "homosexual" did, but what he was prepared to "confess" to. Men still went cottaging, but they were increasingly unwilling to talk about it. Even those who did "confess" were forced to frame their behaviour within hegemonic ideals of intimacy. One of Schofield's interviewees described how when my work becomes difficult I get depressed and I feel I must go out. And yet I know quite well that I won't get anything from a casual pickup—after all the only worth while sex is an affirmation of yourself and another person.[82]

He talked about the emotional conflict attendant on "going out," and the negative feelings it generated. "Depression" pushed him into something inevitably futile. Acknowledging dominant expectations of romantic love, he saw the "only worthwhile sex [as] an affirmation of yourself and another person." A "casual pickup" was never going to meet this craving for "affirmation." Wracked by guilt and self-pity he still, nonetheless, felt the need to cruise London's streets. Like Barry, set against the increasingly prescriptive demands of respectable "homosexuality," "there was the thought that one really shouldn't be doing that sort of thing."[83]

For middle-class men the public city thus remained a problematic and disruptive space. Some consciously distanced themselves from queer urban life, investing their respectability in the private space of the home. Others cruised bars and toilets, their excitement balanced by the nagging unease that they were failing to do what was expected of them. Whether they relished a quick wank in a cottage or lived in intimate domesticity, however, the city remained central to all men's sense of self, simply because it embodied so many of the pejorative images they negotiated and had often been a common starting point in the process of forging a respectable "homosexuality." The city was an object of fascination that evoked an ambiguous mixture of desire and disgust. Familiar yet distant, it was connected to them but somehow other.

Throughout 1955, the Public Morality Council (PMC) was "inundated" with over a dozen "long letters" from a Mr. L. J.—a "teacher of art"—who asked for their help in dealing with Tony K., a young unemployed man he had taken into his home, who had "adopted the vile profession of a male prostitute." L. J.'s letters took the PMC on a tour of queer London, a carefully mapped set of spaces he implored them to rescue Tony from. He described the "vicious sordid all-night cafés which cater almost exclusively for ponces, prostitutes of both sexes, procurers and parasites." He identified pubs like the White Horse in Brixton and cruising grounds like "Orator's Corner." He described their character and clientele. He overheard "so-called males" in the Little Hut who were "openly called . . . by girls' names," and "discuss[ing] the fact they are male prostitutes." He visited a series of queer "brothels" around Earls Court, watching the "clients" and "prostitutes" and questioning local taxi drivers. He carefully distanced himself from this "vile" or "pernicious" world inhabited by "loathsome depraved degenerates"—thereby asserting his own respectability. Yet he remained obsessively fascinated, describing the "strain and anxiety" infusing his habitual patrols. As the PMC itself concluded, "his interest in this young man is not a healthy one and amounted almost to infatuation." Like many other middle-class men, L. J. tried to distance himself from queer urban life, yet could never fully tear his gaze away.[84]

CONCLUSION

In 1953, W. H. Allen published *The Heart in Exile*, a novel by the Hungarian émigré Adam de Hegedus, writing under the pseudonym of Rodney Garland. The novel maps the progress of its narrator, the psychiatrist Anthony Page, as he investigates the mysterious death of Julian Leclerc, a former lover. Page is drawn into the queer "underground" of 1950s London. His investigations take him from West End pubs and nightclubs to the seedier enclaves of a still-derelict Islington, from the informal circles of clubland to London's cruising grounds. Throughout the novel he maps, in minute detail, the characteristic structures of queer life: the urban spaces inhabited by the postwar queer, the operations of class in the queer world, the attractions of rough trade, the practice of blackmail, and the constant presence of suicide. Page is Garland's cartographer of queer London.[85]

Page depicts these movements as a return to a past world, a life he had left behind after the Second World War, exchanging apparent promiscuity for the respectable spaces of home and work. He was now "something like an outsider . . . at least in Soho pubs with a reputation," who needed to approach an acquaintance for "guidance in the underground" (45). As an expert witness—therefore objective—he is distanced from what he sees. In conforming to the public sartorial and behavioral demands of masculine respectability he is, moreover, invisible, never looking like anything other than a conventional—"normal"—middle-class man.

This distance means that Page is always the man standing alone in the corner of the pub, observing and categorizing rather than participating, minutely describing the process of picking up while never doing so himself. As he first enters the Lord Barrymore, for example, he carefully holds himself at one remove from the interactions therein: "My technique was a gentlemanly disregard of the stares, open and concealed" (60). After buying a drink he realizes that he has no matches on him: "It was out of the question to ask for a light unless one knew somebody. The legitimate phrase, 'could you give me a light please?' was, in these surroundings, a recognised approach and a too obvious one at that" (60–61). He goes to the bar for a box of matches. Simultaneously, Page exists within and without the queer city, venturing forth but always returning to the safe enclave of his flat in a "quiet street" in Kensington. The novel's title, denoting as it does a tension between love and the city, desire and distance—somehow this "heart" is in "exile" in London—encodes these problematic experiences of the urban landscape. It suggests a feeling of unease, ambiguity, dislocation, and anomie, of never fully being a part of this world.

Yet Page's forays into the "underground" belie all attempts to maintain this distance, forcing him into an uncomfortable engagement with queer urban culture. In its public and commercial spaces he sees a realm of womanlike "pansies," blackmailers, and rent, men inhabiting the city's most degenerate spaces. He finds "the parties dull and strained and the pubs sordid and uninteresting" (42). He "shudders away" from the "pathetic" pansies and finds the prospect of going to the Aldebaran "depressing." Repelled and yet fascinated by what he sees, Page fixates upon the workingmen he encounters but turns away with disdain. His gaze focuses upon the "coarse and rugged attractiveness" of the street corner gangs in Islington before he attempts to avoid them "for fear of the danger" (229–30). The "underground" is mapped as a realm of promiscuity and disorder, a potent site of transgression and danger that generates all the symptoms of physical repulsion. It is a realm far from the life Page wishes to live or the person he thinks he is.

This is an experience that profoundly unsettles Page's sense of self. Reflecting on his observations in the Lord Barrymore, he begins to articulate the ways in which urban life disrupted the middle-class queer subject:

> All this was sordid from beginning to end. There had never really been a time when I had not regarded places like this as sordid, but in the past there had been a sense of curiosity, a sense of adventure, some cynical amusement and intermittent desire. Now it was merely repellent. It ought not to have been, if I had been normal, because a psychiatrist is a man who deals with more dirty linen than most other people, and he is detached. But I was not normal and not in the least detached. I thought I had said goodbye to these places, but I was wrong. (64)

Page is neither "normal" nor "detached." As such, and in unwillingly having been drawn yet again into this sordid "sink," he is forced into an uncomfortable confrontation with people and places he has already repudiated as abject—forced, in effect, to recognize his connections to them. In London's queer "underground," Page recognizes, and is profoundly disturbed by, his own unconscious desires, desires to which he thought he had "said goodbye," desires repressed and denied in the process of forging a respectable queer self.

For Page, the "case" thus generates uncertainties that prompt repeated moments of angst: if he is not a screaming "pansy," if he is not a promiscuous cruiser desperately chasing after rough trade, if he is not a disreputable queer—then who is he? If he cannot inhabit the disorderly spaces of the West End pub or the abject realm of the cottage or street corner—then where does he actually belong? Page's movement through the diffuse sites of queer urban culture forces him to examine his own moral code. He realizes that he was uneasy having sex with someone he didn't love and that he was "against corrupting someone who was normal, especially if he were young" (104). Despite this, there was the nagging awareness that his "life lacked something, and that something wasn't sex" (187). He goes walking, alone, in Hyde Park and contemplates the freedom that he previously enjoyed in his relationships with men:

> But that lack of permanence became tiresome after the sensation of novelty had worn off, and coupled with a few other factors, was instrumental in my retirement. There was the moral issue. The battle in my conscience had caused me to decide that freedom had to be sacrificed for virtue; my new moral code said that it was immoral and foul to have sex without love. (201)

Seeing a bleak and dystopian vision of his future—"the prospect of a seedy, old homosexual doctor haunting the twilight"—Page panics: "One had seen almost too many elderly inverts whom the passage of time merely drove into satyriasis" (201).

Page negotiates these disruptive tensions by representing his journey through this disreputable realm—both as a life-cycle process and in his careful investigation into Julian's death—as necessary for his moral progress. It is a journey to self-realization and happiness that can only be achieved by once again experiencing and repudiating the queer city, by immersing himself in the "sinks" of the "underground" and rejecting them in favor of something altogether more pure and fulfilling. His return to London's queer world is thus a necessary return to a state of immaturity prior to his achievement of full maturity at the novel's conclusion. He solves the case, learning of the circumstances in which Julian committed suicide.

Yet Page's mood of dislocation and anxiety is only fully overcome when he admits his own love for Terry, his enigmatic live-in housekeeper. If, in revisiting the "underground," Page has learnt much about postwar queer life, his most important lesson has been personal: his adventures progress towards a moment of self-realization—of what he wants and of the kind of man he really is. Page, in effect, realizes that his "moral code" can be integrated with his desire for intimacy, that he can ultimately find a place in which to be happy and fulfilled:

> I now knew that I was in love with Terry. . . . Each of us waits for the miracle which will change his life. Sometimes it comes late. For me, this was it, and it had come mercifully early, just when I felt it was time for me to come to a decision and to settle down. . . . Love makes some people young and irresponsible, but I knew that I would mature under its influence. I should not be restless. I should no longer have that mad craving for excitement. (288–89)

The Heart in Exile concludes with a symbolic commitment: Page leaves London and takes Terry on holiday with him to France. In physically distancing himself from the metropolis, Page mapped the contours of his respectable subjectivity onto a precise spatial trajectory. He rejects London's seamy "underground"—initially for another country, then subsequently for the privacy, love, fidelity, and intimacy of the queer domestic unit. This afforded him the composure and security for which he had been searching: the "case was finished" (289).

What do we make of this? Writing in the forward to the 1995 edition of *The Heart in Exile* the novelist and critic Neil Bartlett asks

> why is it that in Dr. Page, the figure of the virtuous homosexual, the homosexual who isn't a quean, the homosexual who knows about such things but doesn't do them himself, the homosexual who never has to fight for his life or living, the homosexual who doesn't make a fuss in public, the homosexual who in fact isn't a homosexual is still 40 years on entirely recognizable?

Bartlett's characterization of the behavioral codes of "virtuous homosexuality" is perceptive, highlighting the complex interplay between class, gender, and sexuality that shapes Page's engagement with 1950s London. Yet in moving from this to suggest that Page "in fact isn't a homosexual," Bartlett remains profoundly insensitive to the historical meanings of sexual difference and "normality." Conventionally masculine, private, moral, and discreet, his difference articulated purely as a matter of his choice of sexual partner, yet persistently beset by nagging anxieties and desires, Page is perhaps the *quintessential* homosexual. His unstable character encapsulates the contradictions at the heart of respectable "homosexuality" in the mid-twentieth century.

PART 4

POLITICS

9

SEXUAL DIFFERENCE AND BRITISHNESS

KARL'S STORY

In June 1937 the Danish milliner Karl B. left Paris for London. At Croydon Airport he was met by an immigration officer and turned back. This was not the first time Karl had been refused entry to Britain. Initially barred in 1933, he was denied permission to land at Harwich in 1934 and had an application to return declined in 1936. "He is a sex pervert," noted an official from the Home Office Immigration Branch, "he should not be allowed to land in the United Kingdom."[1] While there was no suggestion that Karl had been prosecuted for a sexual offence, in 1933 officers found the addresses of several Government officials on him and suspected that his "visit was for the purpose of blackmail." He was, further, "in possession of a considerable number of letters written by [Arthur P., his business partner] couched in affectionate terms which left little doubt that both persons were moral perverts." Arthur visited the Harwich Immigration Office and Home Office, seeking permission for his partner to land. He was unsuccessful.[2]

Why was Karl B. kept out of Britain? We might widen the question, since if Karl was excluded from Britain's territorial boundaries, queer men in general were positioned beyond the imagined boundaries of Britishness. In part, this was a physical process, embodied in the criminalization of particular queer practices and the logic of imprisonment—removing a source of danger from the community. Exclusion was also a cultural process, emblematized by the construction of sexual difference and queer urban culture as disturbance, immorality, and threat. These were, indeed, mutually constitutive. The sexual offences laws were underpinned by ideas of the

queer's transgressive character, which were, in turn, reinforced by the operations of those laws. Again: why were queer men legally and culturally
excluded from British society? Rather than identify an innate hostility
towards the "sexual pervert"—the ahistorical category of "homophobia"—
we need to understand the public meanings of "homosexuality" in the early
twentieth century. What negative attributes was it invested with? Why was
the sexual deviant deemed so threatening as to warrant the forms of regulation explored above?

The answers lie in the law itself. If official surveillance exercised a profound influence on the cultural and geographical organization of queer
urban life, it also exercised a similar influence on official and public knowledge of that world. While many queans flamboyantly carried their difference
into London's streets, most men sought to avoid the public gaze. It was only
through their encounters with the police that they were, reluctantly, drawn
into that gaze. Whether through the nightclub raids that initiated the spectacular "pansy cases" of the 1930s or the everyday patrols behind the stories
of errant clergymen and cottaging laborers appearing each week in the *News
of the World,* police operations were central to the process through which
queer lives were uncovered, codified, and named for popular consumption.

Policing's importance to this process was reinforced by the conventions
of newspaper reportage. In contrast to the "new journalism" of the late nineteenth century, it was exceptionally rare for any newspaper to investigate
queer London independently between the end of the First World War and
the early 1950s. While all papers regularly reported aspects of that world,
they were, with one notable exception, accounts of trials—near-verbatim
narratives based upon police depositions, witness statements, counsels' arguments, and judicial pronouncements. Unless engaged with the apparatus of
the law, queer lives remained hidden from newspaper readers. It was always
through the intermediary figure of the policeman and in the mediating
space of the courtroom that the press, public, and state encountered queer
urban culture. Newspapers often presented such cases as exposing a dangerous underworld to the purifying light of the public gaze, but they rarely
undertook that task themselves.[3]

The sites at which queer men encountered the law were what Steven
Maynard calls anchor points, or local centers of power-knowledge, constituting a public domain within which the meanings of sexual difference were
contested, produced, and consumed. In understanding those meanings we
need, Maynard suggests, "to view subcultural and discursive formations as
existing in a reciprocal relationship, both shaped by a process we might call

the dialectics of discovery."[4] Police operational procedures were thus integral to shaping what officials and the public knew about queer urban culture and what "homosexuality" actually meant. The bodies and spaces mapped through this process were, however, neither arbitrary nor representative selections: we should consider exactly what was "discovered." Surveillance was idiosyncratic and contingent, throwing certain people and places into sharp relief, just as it left others effectively invisible. The "Dilly Boy" and urinal regularly appeared in court and the news; the discreetly respectable "homosexual" and exclusive bachelor apartment did not. Policing generated a distinctive public map of queer London.

Framed within the operations of the law, sexual difference was thus indelibly marked as sexual danger, and "homosexuality" equated with criminality and vice. While the queer was thus constructed as endangering British society, this assumption masked competing narratives of the nature of that threat. Changing forms of urban culture intersected with the Met's operations to shape distinct narratives of sexual danger. In broad terms these were threefold. First: sexual difference meant effeminacy—the queer challenged the "natural" boundaries between men and women upon which Britain's stability depended. Second: sexual difference meant uncontrolled lust, promiscuity, and a predatory character—the queer transgressed the characteristically British qualities of restraint and self-control and threatened to corrupt all "normal" men. Third: sexual difference meant intergenerational desire, endangering Britain's very future—her youth—and the family, supposedly the repository of national stability.

These overlapping discourses constituted the terrain within which judges, politicians, and civil servants understood, represented, and responded to queer urban culture and exercised a significant influence on policy-making. They informed the work of diverse moral entrepreneurs—the Protestant purity lobby, the crusading moralist, and—on occasion—the campaigning journalist. In turn, the activities of these bodies reinforced particular notions of sexual difference. Each narrative, however, possessed a distinctive chronology, dominating public discussion of "homosexuality" at particular moments while fading from prominence at others. These chronologies emerged through the interactions between policing, the interventions of the state and Britain's self-appointed moral guardians, and broader social changes and cultural anxieties. It is on these interactions, and competing constructions of the queer as source of cultural danger and threat to national stability, and hence a suitable subject for the criminal law, that this chapter focuses.

THE "PAINTED BOY MENACE" NARRATIVE

The quean was the dominant image of queer urban culture, the embodiment of sexual difference. Whereas most men wore a "mask" of "normality," the Dilly Boy was a visible urban type and, as such, more likely to draw unwanted attention. The result was that such men were arrested more often than the discreet "homosexual." The enforcement of the sexual offenses laws and the regulation of commercial sociability produced a particular public map of the queer's behavior and appearance.

It was in this context that, in 1925, the journal *John Bull* suddenly turned its attention to what it depicted as a new metropolitan phenomenon. In June, writing under the pen name "A Man with a Duster," the social critic Harold Begbie wrote a lengthy article in which he called London a "Modern Gomorrah." Begbie drew his readers' attention to

> a well-known teashop and public house in Coventry Street . . . where painted and scented boys congregate every day without molestation of any kind . . . sit[ting] with their vanity bags and their high-healed shoes, calling themselves by endearing names and looking out for patrons.

This was a disturbing sight: "We . . . conquered the Germans and now in London there is an outbreak of this deadly perversion . . . which will surely rot us into ruin unless we recover our sanity and fight it to the death." Emerging scientific etiologies of "homosexuality" that "induc[ed] tolerance" and "encourag[ed] interest" only exacerbated this danger: "If the nation entrusts its moral destiny to science and does not act vigorously upon its natural instincts we shall as surely perish from moral rottenness as Sodom and Gomorrah, Greece and Rome." He demanded William Joynson-Hicks, the home secretary, order the Met to

> make a clean sweep of so monstrous an iniquity . . . encourage the public to go on charging these boys day after day in the police courts, forcing them to prove how they get their living until the streets are swept clean of them . . . make Coventry Street exceedingly unpleasant to creatures who shame the name of England and degrade the face of man.[5]

Drawing upon the associations between national identity and sexual morality that Pemberton-Billing had deployed during the 1918 "Black Book" trial, Begbie defined sexual difference as gender transgression and essentially un-British. This "German" "perversion" threatened to destroy the nation from within, where the kaiser's armies had failed from without. The "painted and scented boys" enjoying themselves in the Lilypond were an alien, foreign, and unnatural presence. Queer urban culture not only "shamed the name of England" but jeopardized its very existence.[6]

Begbie's article—elaborated in subsequent weeks—was the centerpiece of a concerted attack on what *John Bull* labeled the "Painted Boy Menace." This series of articles was the only independent exposé of queer life until the early 1950s. These "Rouged Rogues" were, he suggested, "one of the worst menaces of modern times."[7] Simultaneously, the journal posed as a privileged urban observer, and the "outraged" voice of "respectable citizens."[8] It described queer London explicitly, presenting that process as a purifying step necessary to mobilize public opinion and force the authorities into action:

> It is the policy of *John Bull* to deal frankly and fearlessly when necessity demands with all matters of public interest which, though at times disagreeable, may easily have a very dangerous effect upon the social life of the country unless adequate publicity is directed to them at the proper time.[9]

In May they offered Begbie's "dossier of information"—"an amazing document bristling with true but almost incredible stories of sordid filth and sickening shame"—to the Met, "so anxious are we to remove this blot upon the reputation of this country."[10] This was a crusade, defending the "social life of the country" against a "dangerous" and "sickening" threat.

Such fears were shaped by an assumption that London's public spaces were a sensitive indicator of the nation's moral health. Nominally an idealized realm of order, purity, and respectability, they were subject to a perpetually anxious surveillance. The visible incursion of the quean's disorderly body thus represented both a symptom of disease *within*, and potential threat *to* the social body. One observer found "painted boys" at the symbolic heart of nation and empire, commerce and culture, a clear sign that "the moral condition of London is worsening."[11] Begbie, similarly, saw a "grave . . . symptom of moral rottenness" which was potentially "destructive."[12] The problem seemed evident:

> Britain is regarded as the most moral and clean-minded nation in the world, yet in its centre is a canker which would put any nation to shame and with which those who should use the knife seem powerless to cope.[13]

The quean's public presence could only be understood within the tropes of disease, dirt, or corruption. Queer urban culture was a "canker," eating away at the national body's heart. Newspaper exposés and police operations, by contrast, were acts of cleansing, purification, or surgery, undertaken for the good of the nation at large. Begbie's pen name suggested his role in "sweeping" away the "dust" of modern life.[14]

The "Painted Boy Menace" exposé drew upon established images of sexual difference. It interwove traditional languages of racial degeneration, moral decline, and urban civilization—evident in the repeated allusions to Rome, Greece, and the Cities of the Plain, and the fears that the British empire would suffer a similar fate if this vice went unchecked.[15] The "painted boy" was, however, the "worst menace of *modern* times," becoming a figure of profound cultural disturbance in 1920s Britain because he embodied particular historical fears and anxieties related to the experience of the First World War. The war, for many observers, disrupted established gender roles. As women gained opportunities in the workplace, political power, and a degree of personal freedom, men were emasculated and feminized, a process exemplified by the hysterical victim of shell shock and the shattered body of the disabled. Set against this upheaval, as Susan Kingsley Kent suggests, postwar reconstruction consciously attempted to recreate a more ordered world, a desire "nowhere more evident than in the realm of gender identity and relations between men and women."[16]

In reconstructed Britain social stability and racial survival was thus predicated upon traditional ideas of masculinity and femininity, particularly a domestic ideal embedded in the rigid division between gender roles and public and private life. This made the "painted boys" appearing on London's streets and in the courts a terrifying threat. Writing in 1925, Freda Utley inveighed against a "languid youth"—antithetical to the strength, dominance, and physicality that defined a real man. Britain had not been destroyed by the kaiser, but "she may yet by my Bond Street friend—by the follies and vices for which he stands."[17] Such an effete figure was unfit for the communal demands of reconstruction and the responsibilities of national citizenship. Indeed, he challenged the very premise of that process. In 1920, touring London's night haunts, Sydney Moseley observed "a crowd of young men so made-up that it is not easy to guess their sex."[18] Shaken by his inability to discern these men's "sex," Moseley found the "painted boy" an unnerving reminder that masculinity was neither stable, biologically given, nor self-evident. In the 1920s, many Britons were terrified by the erosion of the boundaries between men and women. The quean's behavior and appearance embodied those terrors.

The "painted boy" was not the only subject for *John Bull's* vitriol, nor was the journal alone in anxiously scrutinizing metropolitan vice in the 1920s. Almost every week, the journal exposed instances of contemporary immorality, forging a generalized narrative of urban moral decline.[19] They were echoed by several published works in which observers like Sidney Felstead or Taylor Croft descended into London's "underworld." Such accounts traded in stock characters and settings: prostitutes, flappers, pimps, black or Chinese drug dealers, nightclubs, "bogus hotels," and opium dens—independent women and transgressive sexualized cosmopolitan spaces. For all, the spectacle of a metropolis undergoing what Douglas Goldring described as an "uninhibited fling"—a "psychological compensation" for the horrors of the Great War—emblematized a wider cultural malaise. For all, this demanded instant action since, like the quean, such practices disrupted the social and cultural boundaries on which Britain's future depended. The "painted boy" became a "menace" deserving of public condemnation and legal repression within these broader anxieties.[20]

THE PREDATORY QUEER NARRATIVE

The association between sexual danger and effeminacy persisted well into the 1950s but never acquired the same resonance as in the 1920s. Changes within British society rendered gender transgression less threatening. Changes within queer urban culture undermined the quean's salience to understandings of sexual difference. Particularly in the early 1930s, and again in the 1950s, the predatory masculine queer supplanted the "painted boy" at the center of public narratives of sexual danger. The very nature of police operations constructed a popular image of the queer as driven by inescapable, threatening lust to accost any man he encountered. The Met's focus on public urinals and use of agents provocateurs to initiate "indecent assault" cases defined the queer as an uncontrolled, promiscuous figure—displaying the antithesis of that self-control and reserve that supposedly characterized British masculinities.

This narrative was reinforced by the public prominence of the encounters between middle-class men and soldiers from the Brigade of Guards. The guardsman was *the* British soldier-hero; a potent image of the nation and its manhood, his iconic status was inscribed into the pageantry of metropolitan life through his role as guard at the royal palaces—symbolic heart of nation and empire. Given this powerful cultural investment, the evidence of the guardsman's sexual practices that regularly appeared in the courts and press was profoundly disquieting. As Graham Dawson suggests, while the guardsman's status was enshrined in national rituals, "other subversive or non-functional [masculine] forms (notably the effeminate man or the homosexual) . . . met with disapprobation and repression in explicitly national terms."[21] The guardsman-queer encounter brought together positive and negative poles in a supposedly unambiguous hierarchy of British masculinities.

In 1931, for example, the trial of the Welsh Guardsman Cecil E. sparked a series of revelations surrounding the brigade's sexual culture. During the trial, Ernest Wild, the recorder, asked Inspector Sharpe anxiously "if Guardsmen lent themselves to this sort of thing?" "I am afraid they do . . . there is an atmosphere of this kind permeating a section of the Guards."[22] Wild erupted in fury:

> If . . . some members of the Guards wearing his majesty's uniform have degraded themselves in the royal park it is an appalling state of things . . . it behoves not only the regiment but the police to root out this vice. If it is allowed to become rampant it may cause the fall of this city and country.[23]

Wild's outburst constituted a very tangible sign of the fears generated when the soldier-hero encountered his mirror opposite. This "appalling state of things" threatened to overwhelm the nation. Wild's focus on seemingly innocuous codes of dress instantiated those anxieties underpinning his anger. For it was the guardsman's uniform that symbolized his iconic masculine status and the national traditions that it embodied. To engage in homosex while wearing "his majesty's uniform" was to degrade the individual, his regiment, and Britain itself. It was to erode the masculine qualities upon which Britain's strength depended. As with the "painted boy," the stakes were high, for if this "vice" were not "rooted out" it could spread contagionlike and "cause the fall of this city and country."

Facing these anxieties, many commentators simply denied the actuality of the guardsman's practices. His iconic status made it inconceivable that the soldier-hero could have homosex.[24] Ultimately, however, it was undeniable: guardsmen *did* have sex with men. And, as the War Office noted in 1955, this was a peculiarly metropolitan issue: "In London homosexuality is undoubtedly much more prevalent than elsewhere." While acknowledging that the "problem cannot be well expressed in statistics" due to "its essentially secretive nature," they deemed it "relevant to note that during 1954 . . . the Royal Military Police investigated 28 cases of sodomy and gross indecency in London . . . compared with one case in . . . Western Command and five in Scotland."[25]

Such patterns made London the spatial and symbolic focus for the guardsman-queer encounter, ensuring that the modern city exercised a powerful influence over the ways that that encounter was discursively produced. In London, where the guardsman's ceremonial and sexed body was simultaneously most evident, civil and military authorities and the popular press were forced into an uncomfortable engagement with his dissonant status as soldier-hero *and* rent boy. How could the embodiment of British manhood participate in homosex? How could this threat to the nation's social body be accommodated? How could hegemonic masculinities be protected? As they negotiated these disquieting questions, the pleasures and dangers of the modern metropolis loomed large. In striving to maintain the guardsman's status as soldier-hero, his sexed body was inscribed within a contradictory set of silences and evasions. Never denying the actuality of these encounters, defensive dominant narratives constructed the guardsman as an innocent abroad in the city and vulnerable to the temptations placed before him. Placed within wider axes of social power constituted at the interstices of class and age, the guardsman's sexual practices were justified and exculpated, and his masculine status secured, at the cost of rendering it inherently unstable.

The War Office thus outlined how

> the contamination of members of the armed forces stationed in London is a greater risk than that incurred in the provinces . . . there is in addition to [the guardsman's] separation from his family . . . an environment containing all shades of entertainment . . . at a very high cost. It is thus possible for him to be perpetually short of money . . . amidst attractions where complete supervision is impossible . . . soldiers have obviously succumbed to a temptation for easy money . . . [V]ice and target exist together in concentrated areas and circumstances which favour the practice of the former and render the latter more vulnerable.[26]

Contrasting sexual threat—the older, wealthy queer—with sexual vulnerability—the young guardsman—the War Office constituted the Guards as virtuous normal men exploited by vicious queers. This narrative of sexual danger interwove anxieties over class and generational difference into a broad critique of the city's effect on working-class men. In London the glittering temptations of the consumerist metropolis intersected with the realities of inequality. Transgressive sexual practices were a function of the guardsman's subordinate position within differentials of wealth, age, and status, his "vulnerability" to the suggestions of others. Within this volatile matrix, the queer became a near-apocalyptic threat, and London a disruptive space of immorality and danger.

The commercial organization of homosex thus constituted consumerist temptations as *the* defining feature of this vulnerability. In 1951 Robert B., a BBC official, was arrested with several Life Guardsmen in his Curzon Street flat. Robert had first met Corporal S. at a party in 1948. In 1950 Robert approached S. for "some company." S. took troopers to parties at Robert's flat, receiving almost £300 for "himself and the boys." Corporal W. had

been to the flat dozens of times with other troopers . . . after we had something to eat and drink we would leave B. with a trooper. Besides buying us
clothes, cigarettes and drinks he would nearly always fork out a fiver.[27]

Newspaper reports highlighted the draw of the metropolis and persistent
social inequalities, eliding sexual threat with social difference, consumerist
temptations, and the dangers of seeking a lifestyle above one's status.
Life Guards at Mayfair cocktail parties symbolized these risks, the disjunc-
tion between appropriate and inappropriate consumption mapped onto
the slide from virtue into vice: "These soldiers . . . would normally be drinking beer, but had been out in London drinking port, champagne and
brandy."[28]

Rather than vicious and depraved, such narratives depicted the guardsman as an innocent victim. This was a comforting fiction persistently reproduced for public consumption. The guardsman did not participate in
homosex because he wanted to, but for money and the pleasures it could
buy—his subordinate position seemingly precluding his capacity for moral
agency. Simultaneously emphasizing commercial transactions *and* dissonances of age and wealth, while remaining notably silent about the guardsman's agent role and desires and the ways that such practices were embedded
into everyday life rendered the guardsman-queer encounter an imagined
instance of corruption. "Young soldiers" were "perverted"; they were "led
away by older men," "contaminated," or "tempted to lend themselves to
these practices for money."[29] Such language instated power as the central
trope through which the state and the press negotiated the anxieties generated by these encounters. The notion of corruption pivoted upon a specific
geography of power, morality, and guilt—the contradistinction between the
predatory queer and his otherwise "normal" victim. When "men of means
and . . . position pay younger men of a different class to gratify them,"
argued Lord Chief Justice Goddard, *"it is the former who are the worst and . . .
greater danger."*[30]

These differential notions of guilt were reflected in sentencing policies
that defined the queer as a potent threat to British manhood while suggesting the guardsman's essential innocence. Robert B. received eighteen
months' imprisonment after the Curzon Street trial. George B., the trooper
involved, was bound over for two years.[31] Here, as for other crimes for which
guardsmen were tried, this sympathy was reinforced by recognition of their
brigade's reputation and individual service records—their status as soldier-
heroes. Within this imaginary landscape, magistrates were strikingly reluctant to impose the law's full punishment.[32]

These patterns embodied the confidence that guardsmen's actions were temporary aberrations; that they were "normal" men who could be redeemed as masculine citizens. After the Curzon Street case, the recorder addressed Robert on his "corruption of soldiers, otherwise reasonably decent young men." While he positioned Robert within potentially sympathetic medical etiologies of sexual difference—acknowledging his need for "psychiatric treatment"—the recorder determined that he endangered Britain's social body. It was "clear that you should be removed from the community."[33]

He addressed the trooper very differently. While acknowledging George's offence, he went some way to exonerating him of moral guilt in assuming that George had "been led into this." George should "take warning" though, lest he continued to slide into depravity. Masculinity here was not an innate given but to be achieved through determined struggle: "If you cleanse yourself by hard work, there is no reason why you should not return to the ranks of decent honest soldiers." Purified of the taint of homosex by the physicality of "hard work," George could once again reenter Britain's masculine elite. The threat to the guardsman's manhood, and therefore the nation, was never irreversible.[34] So powerful were assumptions of corruption that, after Robert's imprisonment, the recorder could remark that "the prime instigator has now been removed . . . it is unlikely that such conduct will happen again."[35] With the queer "removed" it was inconceivable that guardsmen would engage in homosex. Britain was safe.

As military and civil authorities and the press negotiated these anxieties, they found themselves adopting a position that was contradictory and unstable. Discourses of corruption and "normality" produced a comforting set of silences and evasions around the guards' sexual practices. Yet the implications of this were disquieting. To use the terms suggested by Eve Sedgwick, corruption invoked both minoritizing and universalizing discourses: homosex was securely confined to a tightly bounded subculture yet threatened to spread contagionlike into the ranks of "normal" men.[36] If guardsmen—like young workingmen more generally—*could* be corrupted, masculine "normality" became inherently vulnerable. Constantly imperiled, it demanded equally constant protection.

Military and civil authorities thus drew on the full panoply of disciplinary power in order to, in one senior officer's words, "protect the young soldier from contamination by other people."[37] After 1931, recruits underwent an extensive educational program of lectures designed to "creat[e] a public opinion in regiments entirely hostile to this type of offence."[38] This was supplemented by a pervasive network of surveillance. The Met and military police patrolled those public and commercial spaces where men interacted, placing certain venues "out of bounds" to soldiers.[39] Such official practices sought to establish an absolute spatial demarcation between predator and prey. If guardsmen could not be trusted to refuse the queer's advances, they were to be evacuated from those sites where they risked being "corrupted."

THE PEDOPHILE NARRATIVE

As this suggests, the danger of queer urban culture lay in the risk of otherwise "normal" men being seduced away from hegemonic masculinities—what, in 1932, Taylor Croft called queer men's "tendency to make converts." For Croft, there were two factors that made "normal" men vulnerable: class—as with the guardsman—and age. "Homosexuals," he observed, "are . . . constantly recruiting and can easily entice in working-class youths through presents and so on . . . This is the danger of this organised society . . . it should be watched and parents with young sons . . . should have a care."[40] Croft suggested that the queer's sexuality was rampant to the point where he could not but be drawn to younger men. Anxieties over the abuse of class power and the allure of consumerist temptations merged imperceptibly into fears surrounding adults' physical and moral power over boys and youths—what the *Law Journal* termed "a child's subordination to the suggestions of a determined elder."[41]

The correlation between "homosexuality" and intergenerational sex was, again, embedded in police practice. Given the difficulties in detecting private and consensual encounters, a significant proportion of sexual offenses cases followed complaints about an unwanted advance, often by youths or boys. Reported in papers like the *Illustrated Police News,* this was one of the dominant public images of queer life.[42] While many people disapproved of relationships between men and boys, however, those encounters possessed meanings that are very different from those today. Indeed, certain relationships were accepted in working-class neighborhoods, as I suggested in chapter 7. Even if other encounters generated considerable anger, they were considered dangerous for very different reasons. Given contemporary attitudes to childhood sexuality, it is challenging to recognize that the assumption that intergenerational sexual encounters *always* involve a predatory and dangerous adult—the pedophile—coercively "abusing" an innocent child emerged only in the 1920s and acquired hegemonic status as late as the 1950s.

In interwar London responses to intergenerational sex were ambiguous. Church Army Captain Hanmore's *The Curse of the Embankment* (1935) was, in part, an exposé of destitute youths acting as trade in London's public spaces.

For Hanmore, their older sexual partners were the "wreckers of young lives." What he labeled "the corruption of the young" was thus "a canker and a curse . . . a plague . . . to be greatly feared" because it endangered a future generation of Britons.[43] Despite this, Hanmore could not see these boys as simply innocent victims since they had *chosen* to engage in homosex. Such complicity was a sign of *their* delinquency and viciousness. In language normally reserved for "fallen" girls, he demanded a rural home for their "rescue, redemption and restoration," outside London's temptations, under medical supervision and under the guidance of "a Christian man with military training":

> 8 hours regular work per day would go far towards overcoming most weaknesses . . . Many young men could be usefully employed . . . working towards their own salvation . . . Christlike kindness and firmness has . . . by the grace of God, turned many from the evil of their ways and made them true MEN.[44]

Hanmore's notion of "corruption" apportioned moral guilt—"evil" and "weakness"—to *both* parties involved in homosex, regardless of age. The assumed delinquency of youth on which this depended was enshrined in the stated aims of the South London Committee for the Protection of Children: to help "victims of indecent assaults, children with specific diseases and children with bad habits, immoral tendencies or living in immoral surroundings." Child "victims" and those with "immoral tendencies" were considered equivalent categories of problematic deviance.[45]

These ambiguities were reflected in the sentencing policies of the Hampstead Petty Sessions, a court at the same jurisdictional level as the Metropolitan Magistrate. In 1918, for example, Joseph B.—a fifty-one-year-old dock laborer—and William B.—a twelve-year-old schoolboy—were arrested having sex on the Heath. *Both* were charged with outraging public decency. Joseph was fined £5. While William was found not guilty, he was remanded in a home for three weeks, before appearing before the Children's Court charged with "wandering and having a parent who does not exercise proper guardianship." He was convicted and sent to an industrial school until he was sixteen. The court's punitive actions simultaneously reflected William's presumed delinquency and an underlying assumption that his age somehow lessened his moral guilt.[46] Together with the strikingly light sentences passed on adults—only a fine in this case—such patterns highlight significant differences in interwar attitudes towards intergenerational sex. The relationships between boys and men, as Steven Maynard suggests, were regulated "not to protect innocent victims from abuse and exploitation by homosexual psychopaths but to prevent frivolous boys being lead astray by fallen men."[47]

By the late 1940s, that intergenerational sex involved an adult leading an already delinquent youth astray was almost unthinkable. In 1947, writing in the *Medico-Legal Journal,* G. D. Roberts constructed an image of the predatory and psychologically damaged pedophile in contradistinction to his vulnerable victim:

> Suppose one of our own children were assaulted by one of these persons suffering . . . from a disordered mind . . . suppose that one of these persons had decoyed the child, lured him and defiled him at the tender age of 6 or 8 or ten . . . although we endeavour to maintain the coolness and decorum of the advocate our blood sometimes boils when we think of the injury done to poor innocent children.[48]

Roberts' impassioned narrative and his subsequent demand for "revenge" drew on an image of childhood as "innocent," dependent, and needing protection. To "assault" a "child" was thus to transgress a fundamental boundary in modern British culture, and the man who would do so was a threatening, depraved figure increasingly set apart from the society he inhabited.

These understandings of innocent boyhood emerged in the late nineteenth century, acquiring increasing salience through education and child welfare policies and the work of organizations like the National Society for the Prevention of Cruelty to Children. In establishing this as the dominant framework for interpreting intergenerational sexuality and undermining the assumptions behind the sentencing policies discussed above, the 1920s were a turning point. Before the First World War, discourses of sexual corruption focused overwhelmingly on girls. The war disrupted established notions of masculinity while making it a precarious indicator of national strength. Set against anxieties surrounding women's social position and the Depression's cultural impact, male youth became increasingly problematic. More than ever, the state and voluntary organizations worried about boys' sexual practices. While "assaults" on girls still predominated in the courts, the relationships between boys and men were a growing component of public debates surrounding childhood and sexual danger.[49]

These debates were driven by the vociferous demands of purity organizations, anxious that the state act to protect Britain's future. In 1923, the Six Point Group held a public meeting on "child abuse" at Kingsway Hall, concluding that "a move should now be made to agitate for a more stringent administration of the law."[50] Such "agitation" utilized a stereotypical narrative of sexual danger—a paradigmatic "assault" that took place in the public leisure spaces where boys and men met. Persistent pressure from the

Central South London Free Church Council and the vigilance advocate F. N. Charrington regarding the "molestation of young persons in cinemas," for example, forced the LCC into ongoing investigations between 1915 and 1925. Charrington's reports codified the basis of modern understandings of intergenerational sex. Although his agents often observed boys willingly having sex with men, they refused to engage with these troubling implications. Assuming an essential childhood innocence, these ambiguous encounters were codified as "indecent assaults," "molestation," and "corruption." Writing in the *Church Times* (1916) a "parent" contrasted the youthful innocent with the vicious adult: "Children have fallen victims time and time again to men who for the vilest purposes frequent these shows."[51]

London's open spaces were considered similarly dangerous. Groups like the Hammersmith Juvenile Organisation Committee regularly forwarded "particulars of known cases of molestation of children" to the LCC and Home Office, demanding women police patrols to protect children. In part, such lobbying was driven by the need of women's police organizations to find a peacetime role. Yet it also reflected an increasing concern with Britain's racial future after the war.[52] The coding of public space as dangerous reshaped public understandings of good parenting and childhood freedom and the policy decisions made by municipal authorities. In 1923, for example, the secretary of the Hampstead Heath Protection Society noted how "the things that go on [on] the Heath . . . are such that . . . most careful parents would not allow their youngsters to sit on the Heath alone, I certainly never allow mine to go off the . . . paths."[53] By 1925 the Parks and Open Spaces Department was asking that the Education Department "arrange for children in the schools maintained by the Council be warned periodically against conversing with or accepting gifts from strangers in parks or open spaces." Through official warnings and regular newspaper reports, the public city was constructed as a threatening place, populated by dangerous men who preyed on vulnerable children.[54]

These debates culminated in the 1925 Departmental Committee on Sexual Offences against Young Persons, a response to fears that "indecent assaults" were increasing.[55] Their recommendations refracted the distinction between predatory adult and innocent child into legal practice. Indecent assault charges assumed both one party's physical aggression and the absence of consent. Gross indecency, by contrast, assumed consent and complicity— regardless of age. Drawing upon hegemonic notions of childhood innocence, the committee recommended that "for a male person to commit an act of gross indecency with a young person . . . under 16; that the young person shall not be prosecuted for being concerned in the offence." In contrast to

Hampstead's sentencing policies, their recommendations crystallized the assumption that boys did and could not consent to homosex with older men. They were de facto always victims of "abuse" and "assault." The dangers of "homosexuality" were remapped and dramatically enhanced through the public interventions of purity organizations.[56]

Paradoxically, these campaigns left other forms of intergenerational sex invisible. There was, for example, a resounding silence around sex *within* the family.[57] More notable was the absence of concerns over institutional relationships between men and boys, particular within the missions and settlements evangelical reformers had established in working-class neighborhoods since the 1870s. As Seth Koven suggests, religious motivations and a desire to protect boys from the city's temptations often merged with a powerful emotional and erotic attraction to these "rough lads." The combination of moral, social, institutional, and generational power, moreover, *could* leave youths vulnerable to adult men.[58]

The ties binding the child welfare lobby and the mission movement made this milieu problematic. Many social clubs were affiliated to the PMC and NVA. Many purity leaders—including Charrington, as superintendent of the Tower Hamlets Mission—were themselves youth workers.[59] Exposing sexual encounters here risked tainting ideas of Christian brotherhood, opening men's motives to suspicion. In 1920, Henry E. was tried for "improperly assault[ing] boys of tender years" while clearing away chairs at his Tottenham Mission Hall. All the elements of sexual danger were present. Yet organizations like the NVA never commented on such cases even though they appeared regularly in court.[60] Identifying London's public spaces as *the* locus of sexual danger deflected unwanted attention from the institutional relationships between middle-class men and working-class boys. In the 1940s, however, these silences vanished. Purity organizations lost influence, state youth services replaced voluntary institutions, and amidst a climate of heightened moral panic, the youth worker came under increasing public scrutiny.[61]

MORAL PANIC IN THE NEW JERUSALEM

After the Second World War fears surrounding "homosexuality" acquired a particularly electric resonance, and narratives of sexual danger as corruption predominated in public discourse. For many observers, the rapid social changes unleashed by the war seemed to have rendered Britain's stability problematic, destabilizing the critical interpretative categories—of masculinity, youth, and nationhood—within which narratives of sexual difference and danger were framed. When established notions of Britishness seemed threatened from every direction, queer urban culture was viewed as ever more dangerous, assuming a central symbolic position in the postwar politics of sexuality.

The pressures of war placed the integrity of the gendered national body under increasing threat. Overseas service and the ever-present reality of the male head of household's death disrupted the "natural" organization of the family—concerns intensified by women's growing independence and the number of "war babies" born out of wedlock. As in the 1920s, the consolidation of the family and established gender arrangements was thus central to postwar reconstruction, exemplified by new housing provision and the promotion of companionate marriage. Official anxieties were compounded in the late 1940s by rising divorce rates and unease over the national birthrate. The National Marriage Guidance Council (1948) and the Royal Commission on Marriage and Divorce (1951) were symptomatic responses to this perceived crisis. Moreover, rising rates of juvenile crime, dramatized by repeated panics surrounding metropolitan youth cultures, focused anxious attention upon young men's socialization into normative masculinities. That boys were growing up in female-dominated households, without suitable male role models, made their future cause for massive concern.[62] Anxieties surrounding the integrity of established gender roles were sharpened further by vociferous critiques of the transition from postwar austerity to 1950s affluence. Working-class prosperity and consumerism generated profound unease amongst many commentators, nostalgic for traditional forms of community. In Richard Hoggart's *The Uses of Literacy* (1957), affluence and Americanization threatened to rob the working class of its authenticity and undermine normative masculinities.[63]

Within this volatile climate, metropolitan "immorality" became a profound source of cultural disturbance. In 1954, for example, ex-CI Arthur Thorp argued that

> the West End of London spells VICE in searing capital letters. There's plenty of it to be found in other parts of the capital of course, and in other British cities, town and even villages. But for the black rotten heart of the thing look to London's golden centre.[64]

For Thorp, as for *John Bull* three decades earlier, London's public and commercial spaces were a sensitive proxy for the moral condition of Britain itself. Britain's declining imperial status invested these anxieties with further resonance, disrupting long-established notions of Britishness and making the spectacle of metropolitan vice ever more disquieting. "What goes on at the heart of the Empire," the *News of the World* admitted in 1953, "is more than enough to make the citizens of no mean city blush with shame."[65]

In the decade after the Second World War, the impact of war again focused attention on the "social problem" of queer urban culture. In the early 1950s, for the first time in three decades, tabloid newspapers began to conduct independent investigations into this phenomenon, their incipient panic fuelled by the spiraling numbers of arrests for sexual offences. Journalists like Douglas Warth at the *Sunday Pictorial*, for example, eagerly traversed London's queer spaces, mapping the "evil of homosexuality" in order to expose "an unnatural sexual vice which is getting a dangerous grip on this country."[66] A growing number of reports suggested that Britain's stability would be threatened if the state did not act decisively. In November 1953, for example, the home secretary David Maxwell-Fyffe called a meeting of metropolitan magistrates in response to the growing number of "moral offences in London." This was, one judge noted, "an indication of moral decadence that is wholly regrettable." A *News of the World* editorial—its first on this topic—responded: "The grip of this particular form of vice is tightening. Only the searchlight of public opinion will reveal the extent of this evil at our midst." They endorsed Maxwell-Fyffe's "anti-vice drive": "If London sets a good example the rest of the country would soon follow. As things are it too often brings a blush to provincial cheeks."[67]

These deep-rooted fears gained further impetus through the changing relationship between queer life and metropolitan culture. "In wartime London," recalled Rodney Garland in *The Heart in Exile* (1953), the "underground . . . came as near to the surface as perhaps it had ever before come in the course of English history." As Allied servicemen came to London in their thousands and the risk of death created a unique sense of release, commercial and public sites of sociability became increasingly popular, crowded, and—it seems—visible. For many men the war was a kind of sexual utopia, containing freedoms and possibilities absent both before and after.[68] Set against the backlash that followed, complained Quentin Crisp, "the horrors of peace were many."[69]

Queer urban culture thus entered the public gaze through the operations of the sexual offences laws because it was "discovered" as a source of moral danger and because it had become increasingly visible. If there are parallels between the anxious debates about "homosexuality" that permeated public life after *both* wars, however, the meanings of sexual difference, as well as the precise nature of the threat the queer posed to British society, were not the same in the 1950s as the 1920s. *John Bull*'s "Painted Boy Menace" was very different to the *Sunday Pictorial*'s "Evil Men." Narratives of sexual danger in post–Second World War London coalesced and solidified upon the figure of the predatory masculine queer—the man who preyed on young men and boys alike, the man who might seduce the nation's youth away from hegemonic masculinities, the man who threatened to destabilize the family. This was a narrative of corruption rather then effeminacy, emblematized by the activities of groups like the National Campaign to Protect Juveniles against Male Perverts, the increasing number of reports on intergenerational sexual encounters, and the public scandals surrounding the Brigade of Guards. As the Empire was fragmenting, youth and family life were becoming increasingly problematic, and comfortable assumptions of the ordered social body were eroding, these narratives of sexual danger acquired increasing resonance. The queer, a predatory and lustful danger to the nation and its manhood, embodied a wider postwar crisis of Britishness.[70]

CONCLUSION

The encounters between queer urban culture and the law ensured that public knowledge of "homosexuality" was framed by an overarching narrative of sexual danger. If that danger was located in different qualities and influences, these were all, nonetheless, underpinned by a common assumption: the queer threatened British society. Indeed, that threat was so pronounced as to warrant extremes of public vitriol, and what were, nominally, draconian forms of regulation. The operations of the law, in this schema, were imagined as protecting the national community against what was variously termed a "disease," a "plague," a "canker," and a "foreign" invasion. Narratives of the "painted boy menace" and corruption both pivoted on a series of rigid spatial and discursive oppositions between "normal" and queer, British and treacherous, moral and immoral, pure and diseased, the "good" and the "bad" subject. Called into being through a "dialectics of discovery," the spectacle of queer urban culture established the abject outside of Britishness. In this public domain, dominant moral codes and hegemonic notions of sexual and masculine "normality" were dramatized in opposition to a threatening other.[71]

I do not want to suggest that the courtroom, the newspaper, and the interventions of the state and purity organizations were the only sites at which knowledge of queer urban culture was produced or that public attitudes to "homosexuality" were marked by an ingrained hostility. Londoners encountered that culture directly, witnessing queer men walking their city's streets and socializing in its commercial venues. They heard music hall comedians tell jokes about "pansies" and saw drag acts perform in pubs and theatres. They saw plays and read published novels or exposés about—or even *by*—men like that. Just as often as they were angered and shocked, they were curious or amused. Yet the operations of the law, the subsequent reporting of those operations, and the responses of the state and the nation's self-appointed moral guardians played a hegemonic role in shaping public knowledge of who the queer was and what he represented. Whether articulated as the "effeminacy" that threatened to erode the "natural" differences between men and women, or as the risk to the nation's youth or working-men, that knowledge functioned to legitimate and sustain the operations of the sexual offences laws. Through these intersecting narratives of sexual danger, the queer was constructed as beyond the boundaries of national citizenship and therefore a fitting subject for social exclusion, legal repression, and as Karl B. discovered, immigration practices that marked the "sexual pervert" as an intolerable social presence—as un-British.

10

DARING TO SPEAK WHOSE NAME? QUEER CULTURAL POLITICS

I have no doubt that we shall win, but the road is long, and red with monstrous martyrdoms. Nothing but the repeal of the Criminal Law Amendment Act would do any good. That is essential.

OSCAR WILDE, 1898[1]

In 1967, as the Sexual Offences Bill he had sponsored was passed through the House of Lords, Lord Arran sought to mark the moment by looking back seventy years to this most famous of "martyrs." For Arran, the decriminalization of private sexual acts between consenting adult men represented the long-delayed achievement of the measure Wilde had deemed "essential": "Mr. Wilde was right: the road has been long and the martyrdoms many, monstrous and bloody. Today, please God! sees the end of that road." As he linked the legislative "victory" of 1967 to the decades of pain Wilde had anticipated in 1898, Arran evoked a teleological narrative of struggle, progress, and eventual liberation—crystallized through the spatial and temporal metaphor of the "road" to reform.[2]

For Arran—like many commentators at the time and since—the Sexual Offences Act, in particular, and the issue of "homosexuality" in general, became key motifs in confident and congratulatory narratives that defined postwar Britain as the "permissive society." Here legislative reform embodied a wider and more intangible sense of tolerance, liberalism, and respect for individual rights and freedoms. Recent obituaries of Roy Jenkins, for example, cohere around his representation as "the great reforming Home Secretary" of the twentieth century within Harold Wilson's Labour administration. Positioned within that wider raft of legislation over which Jenkins presided—abortion law reform, the relaxation of censorship—the Sexual Offences Act secures his near-iconic status as an agent of progressive cultural change.[3] The invocation of the act as somehow definitive of a historical era is, moreover, a point around which commentators from across the political spectrum unite. Whether seen as the embodiment of postwar liberalism or a dangerous sign of a nation in terminal moral decline, all assume the measure's powerful symbolic resonance.[4]

If homosexual law reform has assumed a central place in debates surrounding the "permissive society," "permissiveness" itself occupies a similar prominence in all queer histories, where Arran's linear narrative is aligned with the story of what Jeffrey Weeks terms a collective "coming out."[5] Although Weeks, Hyde, Jeffrey-Poulter, and Higgins dispute the relative importance of particular events, their stories share a familiar plot, chronology, and cast of characters. Through the "monstrous martyrdoms" between the acts, "we" struggled against a repressive state and society to produce the conditions of "our" own emancipation. The tragedy suffered by Wilde and countless others culminated in the unprecedented "witch hunt" of the 1950s, that, in turn, prompted the backlash leading to the Wolfenden Report of 1957 and the recommendation that the law be reformed. In a more tolerant climate the sober pressure-group politics of the Homosexual Law Reform Society (HLRS) secured the "victory" of 1967 but was quickly surpassed by the spectacular "stunts" of the Gay Liberation Front and the mature assertiveness of contemporary campaigning organizations like Pride and Stonewall. Here the "permissive society" and the Sexual Offences Act are, to paraphrase Chris Waters, milestones in "the forward march of homosexual emancipation."[6]

Against this Whiggish progressive history, I want to suggest an alternative reading of queer cultural politics in the early twentieth century, one that takes as its central focus the problematic unifying operations of Wilde's "we" and the "*Homosexual* Law Reform Society." For while the emergence of an assertive queer identity politics that challenged the cultural moorings of apparently punitive laws appeared unequivocally affirmative, it was consciously underpinned by powerful exclusionary trajectories that encapsulated the profound antagonisms *between* queer men explored in this book. As they deliberately challenged hegemonic pejorative notions of sexual difference and the legal prohibition of their right to privacy by publicly articulating a respectable "homosexual" subject—the deserving beneficiary of reform—queer men contested the meaning of their practices with those who represented the dominant moral order as well as with each other. The meanings of "we" and the "homosexual" for whom rights should be secured were neither self-evident nor inclusionary and, like teleological narratives of "emancipation," effaced—and continue to efface—multiple and inalienable sexual and social differences.

Rather than a point of fusion, the articulation of a "homosexual" subject around which an effective politics of identity could be mobilized was thus a central point of fissure. This respectable "homosexuality" was assembled from interwoven legal, scientific, and medical discourses and a particular moral politics of space. It was publicly and repeatedly articulated at disparate cultural sites: within the court, in medical journals, tabloids, and the respectable press, and particularly in the postwar decades, through novels, autobiography, sociological investigations, and direct testimony to the Wolfenden Committee and through the HLRS. In 1937, indeed, the Public Morality Council listed "the advocacy of homo-sexuality" as one of the "tendentious speeches" made at Speaker's Corner.[7] Never simply denying these differences nor subsuming them into the singular category "homosexual," this political project depended upon the recognition *and rejection* of practices positioned beyond the boundaries of respectability. In short, the "homosexual" was constituted through and within broader matrices of sexual difference, defined through his distance from places, practices, and people repudiated as abject, immoral, and dangerous.

If this project was successful in radically redrawing the relationship between law and morality, moving the discreet and respectable "homosexual" within the boundaries of social acceptability and formal citizenship, the "victory" of 1957 and 1967 was achieved precisely *because* it deliberately excluded those unable to fulfill the requirements of respectability. Those who inhabited the spaces beyond these parameters—the effeminate quean, the man driven by uncontrollable lust into the city's abject public spaces, the workingman moving between male and female partners, the pedophile—were left to face continued social opprobrium and the ever-increasing threat of arrest. Queer political interventions were thus about power. They were about elite men's privileged ability to access the sites of cultural and political influence and to create the "homosexual" in their own image, affirming and liberating a narrowly conceived conception of the self and engagement with the city, just as they excluded vibrant alternatives forged—primarily—by working-class men. The postwar accommodation between men like the members of the HLRS, medical and legal "experts," and the British state—symbolized by the Wolfenden Report and the Sexual Offences Act—cemented a growing division between the respectable "homosexual" and the disreputable queer.[8]

THE CONTRADICTIONS OF QUEER POLITICS

In March 1933, at the conclusion of a sensational Old Bailey trial, Ernest Wild, the recorder of London, was prompted into a characteristically intemperate diatribe:

> The peculiarity of sexual perverts is that not only do they not think they are in the wrong but they think they are right and they regard any kind of interference as an infringement of individual liberty. These people glory in their shame. Sometimes they are blatant with regard to it.[9]

Wild addressed a powerful public challenge to punitive laws that—nominally—suppressed queer lives which were, quite simply, "wrong." Before him were thirty-two "sexual perverts" on trial for "corrupting public morals" following their arrest in a Holland Park Avenue ballroom. The ballroom had been let for a series of dances by Austin S.—more commonly Lady Austin—a twenty-four-year-old barman, John P., a twenty-two-year-old waiter, and Betty, who ran other West London dance halls.[10] Publicized via word of mouth and a flyer advertising "Hotel Staff Dances" within a network of friends working in nearby hotels, the events were run "only for our love for each other."[11] In court, arresting officers described a "blatant" spectacle of sexual transgression: men had danced together, they had embraced, kissed, and been intimate; they had worn women's clothes and makeup and called themselves "Lady Austin's Camp Boys."[12]

Rather than cower before Wild's imposing wrath, these men refused to accept the pejorative notions of their practices embodied in the law. Instead, to Wild's amazement, they "gloried" in who they were. During the raid and subsequent court proceedings they produced a powerful critique of the laws of which they had fallen foul. As such, they articulated an oppositional politics of sexual difference in which they were moral, rather than immoral; they were citizens who claimed the rights innate to all Englishmen rather than threatening outsiders. David M. asked of one policeman:

> Surely in a free country we can do what we like? We know each other and are doing no harm . . . it is a pity these people don't understand our love. I am afraid a few will have to suffer yet before our ways are made legal.[13]

David's dismissal of pejorative conceptions of "our ways" and of the state's right to police them was echoed widely. During the raid, for example, Inspector Francis began to question Lady Austin. When a plainclothes constable passed by, Austin asked if he was a detective: "Fancy that, he is too nice. I could love him and rub his Jimmy for him for hours." After Francis had cautioned him, Austin continued:

> There is nothing wrong in that. You may think so but it is what we call real love man for man. You call us Nancies and bum boys but . . . before long our cult will be allowed in this country.[14]

Austin and David interwove the language of intimate privacy, liberal understandings of Britain's status as a "free country," and medical etiologies of sexual difference to challenge the law's moral foundations. This was a full-frontal attack on a law that was both unjust and—since their desires were innate—incapable of policing them into "normality." As Jimmy B. noted, "people would sympathize with us if they . . . knew we couldn't help it."[15]

The ballroom was thus a constitutive site of *difference,* positioning the Camp Boys in opposition to the "normal" world beyond. "We are all of our own class," Albert A. told officers.[16] The duchess echoed him: "We are a species of our own. You could tell us a mile off."[17] If "our own class" denoted common cultural practices—a queer way of being in the world—and "a species of our own" suggested commonalities of physiology and character, their conjunction invoked a queer subject that was essentialized and, as the Duchess asserted, self-evident. Moreover, as the language of mutual possession—"our own"—suggests, this was shared and unequivocally affirmative.[18]

Drawing upon circulating discourses of social, medical, and biological classification thus dismantled and reworked dominant power structures within which these men were marginalized. If denigrated as "Nancies," they themselves could celebrate their effeminacy. Questioned about the expression "Camp Boys," Austin replied that he "understood camp to mean beautiful and artistic."[19] Positioning themselves within a canonical queer history reinforced this process. Austin's keenly anticipated moment of reform was to be a "vindication of our patron saint, the glorious Oscar Wilde." Here the claim to privacy—carried into the courtroom—was a claim to the right to be "gloriously," "blatantly," and unequivocally *different.* The freedom from legal intervention was valorized as enabling that difference.[20]

These spectacular encounters with the law, reported at length in the popular press, thus mobilized a powerful articulation of queer citizenship that would never otherwise have entered the public domain. If the law brought queer urban culture into view to rid Britain of this contagion, it simultaneously provided a site at which to challenge those operations of power, enabling such critiques and shaping the terrain on which a queer politics of identity could develop. Ironically, the sexual offences laws generated the conditions of their own instability. For queer politics the criminal law was a paradoxically productive space.

Alongside such direct encounters, the *potential* threat of arrest sustained a more generalized critique of the sexual offences laws in the decades after the passage of the Criminal Law Amendment Act in 1885. Like the arguments explored above, this position cohered around the deployment of medical discourse and the assertion of the queer's right to privacy. Yet the relationship between these two positions was profoundly antagonistic. The Camp Boys' assertion of their right to visibly occupy commercial, private, and public space existed in persistent tension with a largely middle-class political culture of discretion that sought to evade the law by becoming invisible to it. What for the former was a claim to the inalienable right to public difference was for the latter the very opposite. Here the claim to privacy was predicated upon the refusal of difference—the notion that, apart from his sexual object choice, the "homosexual" was a "normal" man, and therefore no threat to British society. As such, this position was based upon the deliberate repudiation of such flamboyant public differences. Privacy was claimed through *both* the promise of social conformity *and* its valorization as constraining difference. Once granted, the "homosexual" would be able to live his life in complete accord with social norms, vanishing into the respectability of domesticity.

The most sophisticated version of this position, drawing on the earlier work of Carpenter, Symonds, and Ellis, was articulated in George Ives's *The Continued Extension of the Criminal Law* (1922) and Anomaly's *The Invert and His Social Adjustment* (1927).[21] By the 1920s Ives, a penal reformer, writer, and founder of the secretive Order of the Chaerona—what Matt Cook calls the first "pressure group for 'homosexual' men"—had been campaigning discreetly within elite circles for reform of the sexual offences laws for almost thirty years.[22] His 1922 work, and Anomaly's later text, to varying degrees, appropriated contemporary medical discourses and deployed a moral politics of space in order to distinguish the respectable "homosexual" from the repugnant queer. For both, it was the former who should be guaranteed rights and left alone to enjoy his pleasures in private, unmolested by the moral guardians of society.

This claim started from the premise that, as Ives argued, "homosexuality" has "a physiological basis . . . [and] is ever latent in the actual nature of man." Punitive legislation thus contradicted "all the fresh evidence furnished by modern science."[23] Such arguments were bolstered by a critical engagement with dominant notions of the queer's depravity and danger, embodying the antagonisms *between* queer men. Queer political interven-

tions, predicated upon the articulation of a respectable "homosexual" subject, operated as much through difference as commonality. For Anomaly,
cases involving men arrested in parks or urinals, the unashamedly effeminate, or indecent assault were "unpleasantly prominent" in the courts and
newspapers. The result was a popular image of "an abnormally lustful person of more or less insatiable and uncontrollable impulses." These were
"moral lepers, corrupt, obscene and monstrous."[24] As he admitted, "when
one realizes the assumptions upon which the laws . . . are based it is easy to
understand their draconian severity."[25]

Despite endorsing such notions, however, Anomaly simultaneously situated the "homosexual" *outside* these paradigms, thereby arguing for the
continued criminalization of public "vice" while still claiming his inalienable right to privacy. As such he articulated a dominant "homosexuality"
that was private and invisible—that could not be defined as a social problem: "The commonest cases are men who are aware of their condition [and]
are anxious to adjust themselves to society."[26] Difference was explicitly
repudiated: "The invert in his emotions differs but little from his normal
brother . . . that his sexual reactions are inverted does not necessarily
imply other deviations from the normal."[27] This was a statement of present fact and a promise for the future: the respectable would meet the grant-
ing of rights by assuming the responsibilities of citizenship. Anomaly
reinforced this argument, advising "the invert" to "adjust his movements
to those of the crowd."[28] Unequivocally, the argument for law reform was
"not intended as an argument in favor of the toleration of vice."[29] An-
ticipating Wolfenden, Anomaly concluded with his own vision of the future—the

> reasonable . . . hope that co-operation between justice and science will result
> in the drafting of recommendations which will be acted upon by those
> whose duty it is to reform our laws.[30]

As this invocation of "co-operation"—together with such men's involvement in the British Society for the Study of Sex Psychology (BSSSP)—
suggests, the medical and scientific professions were viewed as potentially
crucial allies in generating tolerance and understanding for the "homosexual."[31] Anomaly sought the authority afforded the expert by prefacing *The
Invert* with an introduction by Dr. R. H. Thouless. Basing his claims on "the
grounds of science," Thouless endorsed Anomaly's attempt to distance
the moral and discreet "invert"—whose desires were rooted "partly in heredi-
tary factors"—from the transgressive effeminacy of the Camp Boys or the
immorality and "perversion" of those arrested in public.[32] For him

the mere possession of the homosexual disposition is not a matter for moral condemnation at all. In a society made charitable by scientific knowledge the chaste invert would meet from the normally sexed the pity and sympathy given to the disabled instead of the shocked condemnation which is often his lot at the present time.[33]

Thouless continued: "The virtuous love of a homosexual is as clean, as decent and as beautiful a thing as the virtuous love of one normally sexed . . . at the same time homosexual vice is as foul and hideous as heterosexual vice."[34] The implications were clear: the private "homosexual" should no longer face the law's full wrath. In challenging the sexual offences laws, the respectable "homosexual" and the progressive "expert" forged a crucial, albeit precarious, alliance. An affirmative yet exclusive respectable "homosexual" politics and a potentially liberating medical etiology of sexual difference developed as adjacent and intersecting cultural formations from the 1920s onwards, sustaining an ongoing challenge to the state's right to intervene in men's private lives.

This challenge was further articulated in fictional form, particularly through the titles published by Reginald Caton's Fortune Press. Driven by commercial opportunism rather than campaigning zeal, the Fortune Press, nonetheless, presented an affirmative "homosexual" politics to a popular audience. Reginald Underwood's middlebrow fiction was, in this context, particularly important. Angry at the "harsh attitudes" of London's magistrates and inspired by his encounters with Edward Carpenter, in 1925 Underwood began working on a novel that would make modern "sexual psychology" accessible. The "task proved to be more formidable than I expected." After the *Well of Loneliness* trial in 1928, "no publisher would have anything to do with a book treating of sexual inversion." Deterred by the fear of legal action, Underwood waited five years before publishing *Bachelor's Hall* "quietly and discreetly" in 1934.[35]

Here, and in his later *Flame of Freedom* (1936), Underwood made an unabashed plea for understanding, acceptance, and reform on behalf of the respectable "homosexual." *Bachelor's Hall* was prefaced with a simple statement of intent. Underwood recognized that "I may be running full-tilt against some of the strongest prejudices and distastes known to society." Despite this, he challenged the "unduly harsh and entirely wrong judgments" law and the "popular mind" passed on the "homosexual." Invoking the authority of "scientific investigation," Underwood argued that this "anomaly by no means necessarily has its basis in mental, moral or even physical degeneracy." Distinguishing between the "emotional and affectional" expressions of same-sex desire and the "vulgar and blatant homosexual grossnesses . . . reported from police court proceedings," Underwood promised to demonstrate "that it is just as possible for all that is beautiful and of good report to spring from such an attachment . . . as from any ordinary and so-called normal love-match."[36]

Like the writing of Anomaly and Ives, Underwood's novels were underpinned by scientific etiologies of sexual difference which defined "homosexuality" as an inalienable and innate condition.[37] Like them, he utilized a particular moral politics of space to distance the respectable "homosexual" from the "vulgar and blatant . . . grossnesses" of the disreputable queer and make his case for social acceptance and legal reform. Unlike them, however, Underwood presented that case as a moving narrative of love between men. *Flame of Freedom,* for example, maps Julian Ferrers's metropolitan experiences. Initially, Julian falls for a female prostitute. Quickly, however, his feelings for her wane upon meeting Don in the Caledonian Market. Overwhelmed by a sense of "human affinity," Julian moves into Don's South Kensington flat. There he finds a "hitherto undreamed of spiritual reciprocity," a domestic relationship "almost like a married couple."[38] While stressing the chaste and "spiritual" nature of the relationship, *Flame of Freedom,* nonetheless, is permeated by repeated expressions of masculine intimacy. "My life wouldn't be worth tuppence without you," Julian blurts out: "There's nobody I-I-I love more than you." In a dramatic confrontation, he expresses his desire to marry Don, engaging "in a whole-hearted renunciation of everything in the world except Don himself."[39]

Throughout, Underwood deliberately contrasts the moral rectitude and respectability of same-sex love to the "sordid world" of public queer sociability and the "ordinary sexual or aesthetic magnetism" between men and women.[40] Julian, in particular, is physically repelled by both these phenomena. In Soho's "notorious" Juno's Tearooms, he finds the atmosphere brittle and "nasty." He feels "sick" at those men "got up with appallingly obvious cosmetics." He escapes this "unbearable" "den of ghouls," finding happiness in a private domestic realm.[41] The novel concludes with a "tremendous realization":"

> More than all he wanted Don . . . to feel the old spell of that elusive Jonathon . . . Don was unique. Don who had loved him, with a love passing the love of women . . . He began to feel conscious of an amazing calm pervading him, the ballast at last of definite and steady purpose.[42]

At the intersection between modern scientific knowledge and ideals of romantic love and privacy, Underwood dramatized the respectable "homosexuality" on which queer political interventions were based.

The direct impact of these pressures was muted. The writings of Ives or Anomaly never reached beyond elite circles, and BSSSP pamphlets and meetings only ever drew tiny progressive audiences. As Underwood's nagging anxieties and Ives's characteristic reticence suggest, set against the risk of imprisonment, the "homosexual's" social conformity and invisibility were powerful barriers to entering the political realm. Despite this, familiarity with these ideas seems to have grown, sustaining more tangible critiques of the sexual offences laws. Paradoxically, the public articulation of a political position predicated upon situating the "homosexual" within private space depended upon the prosecution of "respectable" men arrested in those very spaces mapped as abject and degenerate. Queer cultural politics acquired impetus only through the contentious politics of policing in the 1920s.

The massive increase in arrests for "street offences" in the decade after the First World War generated a series of outcries surrounding the apparent gap between the Met's working rules and the formal legal conventions within which they operated. This volatile climate sustained a generalized critique of law enforcement, through which queer men exploited the law's procedural morality, challenging individual prosecutions for importuning or gross indecency by exposing police malpractice.[43] Ives noted with bitter irony:

> So little . . . seems needed to constitute an offence that an alleged smile or wink or look may cause an arrest . . . any young person is at the mercy of any two detectives hunting in couples . . . [who have] a degree of unchecked authority which places the liberty of citizens entirely in their hands . . .[44]

These tensions culminated in Frank Champain's successful appeal against his conviction for importuning in 1927 after his defense counsel, the prominent barrister Henry Curtis-Bennett, mounted a ferocious attack on the arresting officer's actions. After the case, Mr. J. Chester wrote to the commissioner of police, condemning the "pack of lies" told by the officer involved as "most damnable to British Justice." Chester focused upon preventing the alleged fabrication of evidence, demanding that importuning statutes be made equivalent to those regulating female prostitution.

> I pray that the time will not be far off when that Bill is passed making it impossible for an arrest unless a member of the public comes forward to say he or she has been annoyed and also gives evidence.

While he withheld sympathy for the blackmailer or the "degraded young men who live on a kind of prostitution," Chester demanded protection for the "young innocent men . . . who do not do these things for a living." In this, he began to tentatively map the essential site and character of the

respectable "homosexual," locating this figure *outside* the promiscuous public realm and arguing that law reform would reduce the number of importuning cases. "As I have studied these man-woman characters intimately, I
know quite fully that they do not solicit as is said they do, in the streets, but
rather in a very much more different, sociable way."[45]

Chester's critique was further elaborated in London's courts, as elite men
drew upon this wider unease, together with medical etiologies of sexual difference, in seeking to evade imprisonment. It was Curtis-Bennett, acting in
a series of high-profile cases, who developed the most consistent version of
this position in what was a remarkable career as a queer defense lawyer. He
led the successful appeal of the Savoy Turkish Baths against the revocation
of their license; he defended workingmen involved in the most notorious
"pansy cases," including the Fitzroy Square and Adelphi Rooms "scandals,"
and one of the Camp Boys. Curtis-Bennett was, it seems, known as the man
to call for queer men in trouble with the law.[46] With some notable exceptions, his clients tended to be prominent and wealthy, exploiting class privilege to access legal representation and magisterial sympathy in ways that
most men could not. In 1932, for example, Curtis-Bennett had a solicitor's
six-month sentence for gross indecency waived since the "mental strain and
anguish" and collapse of his career was punishment enough.[47]

Primarily—as in Champain's case—Curtis-Bennett utilized attacks on
police practice and evidence of "good character."[48] From the late 1920s,
however, he and his clients began to work out the implications of medical
discourses, transforming a generalized critique into a direct courtroom
defense. The key moment here was the 1927 trial of Robert M., a former
Indian army major. When arrested for gross indecency, Robert approached
CI Gillian: "Look here—man to man . . . well you know some men are
inverts? I am one and I can't help it." He continued in a written statement:
"I am a Homo-sexualist, or invert." Through this frank confession of selfhood, Robert sought to mitigate the law's wrath, drawing upon medical etiologies of sexual difference in order to present his desires and conduct as
innate and inescapable—"I can't help it."[49]

In court, Curtis-Bennett elaborated upon this basic premise. His submission moved uneasily between environmental and medical etiologies but
hinged upon definitions of innate "homosexuality." Robert, he suggested,
was "suffering from a disease." He had

> served . . . in India for a considerable period. Whether this has affected his
> mind or not it was difficult to say, but he was undoubtedly a man of abnormal
> mentality. His condition called for institutional rather than penal treatment.

His argument was supported by the testimony and diagnosis of four medical "specialists": Theophilus Hislop, senior physician at the Bethlehem Hospital; Hugh Davis of the Camberwell House Institution, and the private practitioners James Russell and John Valentine Rees. If he would acquit, the judge was told, Robert would voluntarily become an "inmate" of Camberwell House.[50] While this defense failed, in 1930 Curtis-Bennett had a clergyman's sentence for importuning overturned on appeal, attributing his actions to a "malady."[51] By the 1940s the legal implications of scientific knowledge were clearly established. When, in 1944, defending a vicar charged with importuning, Frederick Levy argued that "the case was really one for a doctor's consulting room rather than a prison cell," the judge noted that such arguments were "getting more and more common."[52]

The relationship between respectable "homosexual" politics and the legal authorities was thus more complex than the simple opposition between a nascent emancipation movement and a repressive state. For if magistrates treated visibly transgressive practices with characteristic hostility, inflicting the law's full force on the effeminate and many of those arrested in public, their reactions to men who appeared otherwise conventionally respectable were more ambiguous, as likely to encompass sympathy and understanding as violent condemnation. The privileges of class could be a powerful force in attenuating the law's potential hostility. The legal establishment was thus never a static or united persecuting force but instead engaged in an ongoing dialogue with elite queer men, resulting in sympathetic noises—and occasional actions—by progressive magistrates influenced by medical opinion.

Throughout the 1920s, for example, Judge Atherley Jones—sitting at the Old Bailey—regularly acquitted defendants, much to the disquiet of senior police officers and civil servants. In part, his actions reflected a wider unease at the law's intervention into matters of private morality. Summing up a decision in 1922, he argued that "although people who tamper with young persons . . . ought to be punished very severely, cases of gross indecency between adult persons ought not to be brought to court but should be a matter for the men's consciences."[53] Presiding at Robert M.'s trial, moreover, Atherley Jones "agreed with [Curtis-Bennett's] remarks that it was more a medical than a criminal matter," noting, however, "that as the Law stood *at present* he was *obliged* to deal with it as a criminal matter." So pronounced was this sympathetic reputation that Curtis-Bennett "maneuvered successfully to have [Robert] dealt with by Judge Atherley Jones." As one senior Met officer noted with exasperation, "this nasty man would have received a sentence of penal servitude from almost any other Judge."[54]

Yet Atherley Jones was not alone in the judiciary in articulating such ideas. In 1932, for example, the chairman of the London Quarter Sessions, Cecil Whitely, gave a widely reported lecture on "The Problem of the Moral Pervert" at the Institute of Hygiene. Experience had lead Whitely to consider imprisonment "an altogether futile method of coping with this class of case." In such cases, he noted:

> It was essential to protect the public but the future of the condemned man had to be considered. The tragedy was that many of these men were of good social position and sometimes brilliant intellectually and with a long record of good service to their name.

Where men's claims to respectability were otherwise undoubted, Whitely suggested "an institution suitably equipped with medical staff where these unfortunate persons could receive skilled treatment." He concluded: "The subject seemed a matter for medical men rather than lawyers."[55] Likewise, Cecil Chapman, magistrate at several London courts, was a long-standing member of the BSSSP and was, as Laura Doan notes,

> well informed about sexual inversion as a medical category and not only shared the [BSSSP]'s disapproval of legislating sexual inversion between consenting adults but "denounced the senselessness and cruelty of the sentences passed on inverts."[56]

The North London magistrate Claud Mullins developed a similar relationship with the Institute for the Scientific Treatment of Delinquency in the 1930s. In dealing with queer offenders, Mullins regularly sought medical reports prior to sentencing and—if a favorable prognosis was indicated—made treatment a condition of probation.[57] For all these magistrates, the use of discretionary judicial powers, either in outright acquittals or in substituting probation and medical treatment for a penal sentence, embodied a veiled opposition to the sexual offences laws. As Chris Waters argues, "it was often . . . resistance to the harshness of the . . . laws that led [judges] . . . to collude . . . in keeping homosexual offenders out of prison."[58]

From the mid-1920s, increasing numbers of such cases were reported in criminological and medical journals, respectable papers like the *Times* and mass-circulation tabloids like the *News of the World*. The complex interactions between progressive medical opinion, unease surrounding police practices, respectable "homosexual" politics, and the operations of the laws thus sustained an emerging *public* critique of the sexual offences laws. If this focused upon individual cases, it nevertheless established continuities between the reforming positions mapped out by Ellis and Carpenter in the

1890s and those that would be articulated with increasing vociferousness after the Second World War.[59] However tentatively, however exclusively, however reliant upon mobilizing sympathy for the poor suffering "homosexual" rather than being unequivocally affirmative, however dependent on reinforcing the stigma attached to particular practices, however fraught with ambiguities, elite men were probing at the law's margins to construct a legitimate *private* space.

PERMISSIVENESS AND PRIVILEGE

It was in the 1950s and 1960s that these trajectories converged and the tensions and ambiguities inherent to queer political interventions solidified into a rigid bifurcation between the respectable and disreputable, the "homosexual"—beneficiary of law reform, and the queer—continued subject of social opprobrium and regulatory intervention. In postwar Britain, set against the profound anxieties surrounding queer urban culture and the growing intensity with which sexual offences were policed, those critiques of the law circulating between the wars acquired increasing public resonance. Particularly after the high-profile prosecutions of, amongst others, John Gielgud, Lord Montagu and Peter Wildeblood, respectable papers like the *Observer* and *New Statesman* began to react to the excesses of tabloid sensationalism, drawing upon progressive medical and legal opinion to demand a reasoned discussion of "homosexuality."[60] In 1954, responding *both* to wider cultural anxieties *and* that "considerable body of opinion which regards the existing law as . . . out of harmony with modern knowledge," the home secretary, David Maxwell-Fyfe, appointed the Departmental Committee on Homosexual Offences and Prostitution, chaired by John Wolfenden. In mapping "dangerous sexualities" through the evidence generated by official bureaucracies and "expert" witnesses, the committee sought to render them visible as a strategy in their effective regulation.[61]

Yet the committee and the debates that surrounded it simultaneously generated the discursive space that allowed elite "homosexual" men to challenge their association with pejorative notions of sexual difference, prompting a powerful political intervention that coalesced around opposition to the law. As the committee convened, its members were "approached by a number of homosexuals anxious to discuss their problems."[62] Captain L. H. Green, for example, sent Wolfenden copies of Symonds's *Problem in Modern Ethics* and Carpenter's *Intermediate Sex,* drawing attention to the latter's "sane and reasonable views." G. H. Macmillan offered to testify "as to the point of view of one who had experienced homosexuality." And Anatole

James highlighted blackmail cases, arguing that "the sooner the law is altered the better."[63]

The committee responded to these pressures by convening a series of panels through which to acquire such men's formal testimony. "The idea," noted the secretary, W. Conwy Roberts, "is to . . . see what a few ["homo-sexuals"] look and behave like."[64] Yet access to this forum was highly exclusive, embedded in the materiality of power, class, and privilege. Of the three men who eventually testified, Patrick Trevor-Roper was a Harley Street consultant; Carl Winter the director of the Fitzwilliam Museum in Cambridge; and Peter Wildeblood, the diplomatic correspondent for the *Daily Mail*.

All deliberately approached Wolfenden to counter what Winter termed the "disproportionate emphasis on ["homosexuality's"] more morbid aspects" and the negative implications of the law's salience in shaping public knowledge of sexual difference.[65] For Trevor-Roper:

> Several of us felt . . . that the homosexuals they would have to give evidence . . . would be the ones they could lay their hands on . . . who had been caught or . . . had been in prison or occasionally exhibitionists . . . We felt that they might not get a more considered view of people who are in fairly established jobs.[66]

While many men's claims to speak were rejected, since they were perceived as disreputable cranks, *these* men were able to draw upon the privileges of social connection and status and their evident distance from what Roberts termed "the seamier side of things."[67] All three approached Wolfenden through Goronwy Rees, a mutual acquaintance and committee member.[68] Those who dared to speak the name of "homosexuality"—those *allowed* to speak—were thus unequivocally respectable men "in responsible positions [who] had successfully concealed their inversion."[69] In providing an enabling space for queer politics, the Wolfenden Committee privileged certain voices at the same time as it silenced others.

While Leslie Moran thus discerns a pervasive distinction between that "canonical code" of homosexuality deployed by experts and the disruptive language of queer men, experts, committee members and witnesses were bound by shared cultural styles, interpersonal networks, and modes of representing the "homosexual."[70] Far from threatening "subaltern subjects," these deep-rooted commonalities placed the witnesses firmly within the boundaries of respectability. As Roberts commented of Winter, "he struck me as being a very decent sort of chap."[71] This cordial familiarity marked the proceedings. Before testifying, Wolfenden had lunch with Trevor-Roper and Winter at the University Club, where the atmosphere was "sympathetic." At the Home Office, Rees "gave us a very warm and encouraging entrance, saying that . . . he is entirely on our side."[72] While the disreputable queer was beyond acceptability, Wolfenden's encounter with these men eventually led him to criticize "the assumption we are dealing with 'queer people,' whereas it seems that many homosexuals are in other respects normal."[73]

The formal proceedings of a departmental committee thus provided a privileged political space within which to define the "homosexual" subject and the case for law reform. When isolated to individual court appearances, the claims of the "homosexual" could be easily dismissed as an attempt to evade justice, and the implications of medical etiologies were limited to a tenuous sympathy and the ad hoc substitution of probation and "treatment" for imprisonment. When made by those whose visible difference placed them beyond the pale, such claims were simply untenable. When confined to medical journals or elite texts this political position was unable to generate sufficient tangible momentum for law reform. While the arguments developed by Trevor-Roper, Winter, and Wildeblood were thus embedded in those delineated since the 1920s, the community they addressed and the position from which they spoke the word "homosexual' " had changed radically. In Wolfenden, the respectable "homosexual" spoke directly to representatives of the state granted the authority to recommend legislative change. Moreover, since—unequivocally in Trevor-Roper's and Winter's cases—he had come forward willingly rather than been forced into public scrutiny by the law, he spoke with particular moral authority.[74] More intangibly, the respectable "homosexual" addressed an interpretative community of *men like him,* sexual orientation excepted.

By narrating a singular "homosexual" subject through their written and oral testimony—elaborated, in Wildeblood's case, through his published autobiography *Against the Law*—these men developed a case for law reform that was simultaneously exclusionary and liberating. Their position hinged upon reconfiguring an impermeable and ineffable boundary between respectable and disreputable—public and private—with greater rigidity than had been the case between the wars. If all nodded towards existent critiques of policing, the earlier salience of such arguments was effaced as they sought to inscribe the "homosexual" firmly within private space. In this context, any plea on behalf of those arrested in public threatened to destabilize the respectable subject envisaged as the beneficiary of reform, eliding him with the abject realm mapped so assiduously by tabloid commentators. Rather, their arguments cohered around a dialogue between medical discourse and representations of urban life that mapped "homosexuality" as a privatized condition and set of cultural practices. As such, they articulated a map of desire in general, and of London in particular, that positioned space and subjectivity in dialectical relationship, "dramatiz[ing] [their] sense of self through a series of confessional statements about the acceptable places in which homosexuality could be represented and practiced."[75]

These interconnecting spatial domains pivoted upon a common narrative of sexual disclosure: the public statement of identity emblematized by Wildeblood's simple declaration that "I am homosexual."[76] Such a narrative tacitly recognized the social invisibility of the respectable "homosexual," reconfiguring the movement from secrecy to revelation common to tabloid exposés in order to articulate this subject's claims to privacy. For Wildeblood this marked the movement from darkness into light, from silence into knowledge—knowledge, moreover, over which he and men like him claimed authority. Journeying through the same urban landscape where politicians, tabloid journalists, and moral entrepreneurs saw only vice, corruption, and degeneracy, Wildeblood, Trevor-Roper, and Winter mapped an alternative world that remained hidden from this paranoid scrutiny, a queer world that was moral, discreet, and respectable—that could in no way be seen as a threat. Engaging in a broader discursive struggle over the representation of sexual difference, they suggested the parallel existence of two intersecting "undergrounds": that "discovered" by the Met and the *Sunday Pictorial* and that submerged beneath it—the more respectable queer world that the tabloid press never saw. Yet this was not the basis for asserting the "homosexual's" right to a public life but a necessary tactic to secure the foundations for a discreet *private* life. Rather than that affirmative claim to sexual difference made by men like the Camp Boys, freedom from the threat of exposure and law would allow the "homosexual" to retreat once more into silence. These men came out purely so that they could then retreat, constructing a respectable subject predicated upon the space of the middle-class home.

The broad conception of homosexuality as an "inherent biological characteristic"—uncontested throughout the proceedings—enabled them to define their desires as a privatized condition rather than a social problem.[77] Moreover, medical etiologies meshed neatly with the careful mapping of the public-private boundary through which they articulated the discretion that defined the "homosexual's" respectability. Drawing upon a middle-class moral politics of space, public queer life was represented through the tropes of promiscuity and abjection. In explicitly coding this as the realm of depravity and disorder, they—like Anomaly or Underwood before them—partially

endorsed circulating tabloid narratives. Wildeblood railed against "the promiscuous homosexual, who seeks his lover in the street."[78] He continued:

> You do not want people behaving badly in public. If you are going to have
> homosexuality . . . it might just as well be discreet . . . Soliciting, whether
> it is homosexual or heterosexual, is obviously a social nuisance and will have
> to be curbed.[79]

All public queer practices, particularly the use of streets and parks for sex
and sociability, were thus dangerous and immoral. This was mirrored by a
violent hostility towards those who exhibited their difference flamboyantly—the effeminate quean, whose body carried the indelible marks of
his sexual character. Trevor-Roper distanced himself from such men, noting how "most homosexuals dislike male effeminacy."[80] For Wildeblood
they were "deplored" by "homosexuals within the strict meaning of the
word . . . of necessity extremely cautious and discreet."[81]

This rigid spatial and moral distinction was mirrored by a careful
attempt to disassociate themselves from public images of the predatory
queer—the corrupter of otherwise "normal" men, youths, and boys—that
acquired such resonance after the Second World War. "Pedophilia" was, as
Wildeblood put it, "an entirely separate condition" to his own "homosexuality."[82] For Winter, it was "just as revoltingly strange" to men like him as
to society in general.[83] Moreover, since all three emphatically rejected the
argument that a "normal" man could be corrupted and denied any personal
attraction to such men, they effaced the threat of "homosexuality" spreading
contagionlike through British society.[84] "Homosexuality" was securely—
reassuringly—confined to both the private sphere and a tightly bounded
group of men like that. As Trevor-Roper noted, "my private life tends to be
virtually restricted to . . . the purely homosexual world."[85]

Partly, these disreputable practices were attributed to laws that produced
isolation and unhappiness, preventing men from leading ordered private
lives. Winter, for example, thought reform

> would make a great deal of difference to the attitude of a number of homo-
> sexuals . . . who are extremely embittered and rather exhibitionist . . . [in]
> protest against what they feel is an infringement against their security . . .
> the lunatic fringe of homosexuals, the same sort of absurd people who exist
> on the fringe of any group of persons.[86]

Yet despite this ambiguous plea for tolerance, they carefully distanced themselves from these "absurd people," defining their own respectability through
the repudiation of "the pathetically flamboyant pansy," "the corrupters of

youth," and the promiscuous who dared to transgress the public domain. The "homosexual" was both masculine and discreet. As Wildeblood argued,

> we do our best to look like everyone else and we usually succeed. That is why no one realizes how many of us there are . . . they behave more soberly and behave more conventionally in public than the normal men I know.[87]

The disreputable queer was displaced beyond the margins of respectable "homosexuality."

By establishing the spatial and cultural boundaries of "homosexuality" along a rigid division between public and private, Wildeblood, Trevor-Roper, and Winter began to define a subject who was far from depraved, possessing what Wildeblood termed an "austere and strict morality."[88] Winter made this explicit, as he described his own social life to Wolfenden.

> I have many [homosexual] friends . . . we are all completely at ease in one another's company and the world in which we live . . . We visit each other's houses, go abroad . . . [go to] art exhibitions and ballet and have a satisfactory life within this sphere.[89]

He thus found it unjust that behavior resulting from a medical condition

> should be regarded as criminal and [that] acts not harmful to other people, not publicly indecent should be punishable . . . That a man should have . . . everything smirched and destroyed because his sex life does not conform to the sex life of the majority of the population, seems to be grotesque.[90]

Winter mapped a lifestyle all the committee members could recognize, centered upon friendship networks and the middle-class home, far removed from tabloid revelations of West End immorality and that manifested in the courts. The life he produced for public consumption explicitly mirrored the wider behavioral and emotional codes associated with respectability, particularly the emphasis upon self-control, restraint, and discretion. Asked how he found partners, Trevor-Roper rejected the implication that he cruised parks, streets, and urinals: "One is introduced to them by other homosexuals."[91] Inhabiting the realm of domestic order and propriety meant "there is no evidence that [the "homosexual"] is less prone to the emotion of love than the heterosexual."[92]

In embedding the "homosexual" within this exclusive social and subjective geography and repudiating those people and practices who dared to transgress the public domain, Wildeblood, Winter, and Trevor-Roper were, in part, forging a contrived political fiction for a particular audience. Their testimony thus effaced problematic middle-class urban practices, deliberately overstressing the fixity of the public-private boundary in presenting themselves—and men like them—as unequivocally respectable. Wildeblood argued eloquently that

> I seek only to apply to my life the rules which govern the lives of all good men; freedom to chose a partner and . . . to live with him discreetly and faithfully . . . the right to choose the person whom I love.[93]

Yet in so doing, he neatly glossed over the question of where exactly he was going to *meet* that "partner." Both he—who had met the airman McNally in Piccadilly Circus subway—and Trevor-Roper—cautioned by a policeman in St. James's Park during the war—constructed a deafening silence around their own public practices.[94]

Their testimony was, moreover, striking for the complete invisibility of queer commercial venues. In part, this silence was a deliberate response to the ambivalent spatial position of the commercial domain, which existed precariously on the boundary between public and private, disreputable and respectable. Such venues were as likely to generate the flamboyant spectacle of the effeminate quean or the cruisy atmosphere of many pubs as discretion, restraint, and respectability. It was also, perhaps, sharpened by the increasingly vociferous critiques of the transition from austerity to affluence that marked 1950s Britain. The problematic dual status of consumerism and the queer "scene" threatened to disrupt the operations of respectable "homosexual" politics in ways that could not be tolerated.[95]

The legal reforms for which Wildeblood, Winter, and Trevor-Roper argued were thus limited: they asked only that the words "in private" be removed from section 11 of the Criminal Law Amendment Act, thereby decriminalizing encounters that took place in the home. At no point did they contemplate the legalization of public practices, a reconfigured relationship between the state and queer commercial venues, or the right to be visibly different.[96] As such they sought to remove the stigma and danger attached to otherwise respectable lives, legitimating and protecting a private "homosexual" realm of discretion, fidelity, and intimacy. All agreed that the laws regulating *public* sexual behavior should be retained—targeted at the disreputable queer who continued to transgress the public-private boundary. As Wildeblood noted, "if far-reaching changes in the law were to be recommended, they would . . . be principally concerned with . . . [those who] tend to live their lives with discretion and decency, neither corrupting others nor publicly flaunting their condition."[97] Regulation of the public-private boundary was displaced—in certain cases—onto the respectable subject. A situation where "there is no particular advantage in obeying the universal moral rule and ordering one's private life with discretion and fidelity" was to be replaced with a model of citizenship that carefully balanced rights and responsibilities.[98] This would, Winter suggested, allow men "to live perfectly ordered lives."[99]

In its own terms, this intervention was unequivocally successful. Moved by their compelling encounter with the respectable "homosexual" and the added impetus for reform generated by the testimony of a disparate range of medical and legal "experts," the Wolfenden Report, published in 1957, endorsed Wildeblood, Winter, and Trevor-Roper's claims. The report started from a basic conception of the law's purpose as being "to preserve public order and decency, to protect the citizens from what is offensive and injurious and to provide sufficient safeguards against the exploitation and corruption of others."[100] Acceptance of an innate "homosexual propensity" sustained their primary recommendation: private relationships between consenting adults should no longer be criminal: "We are charged not to enter into matters of private moral conduct except in so far as they directly affect the public good."[101]

Wedded to a notion of "personal and private responsibility" and oriented by a middle-class moral politics of space, the report thus partly displaced the regulation of public and private onto the respectable "homosexual" self. As the report spelled out, "this limited modification of the law should not be interpreted as indicating that the law can be indifferent to other forms of homosexual behaviour, or as a general license to homosexuals to behave as they please."[102] Articulating a space outside the law yet explicitly refusing to countenance a public queer realm and retaining statutory prohibitions on *public* sexual offences invested the respectable "homosexual" with legitimacy. The report endorsed his demand for social acceptance and formal citizenship, just as it contributed to the ever-greater stigmatization of the disreputable queer. As such, its conclusions embodied profound differences and antagonisms *between* queer men.

CONCLUSION

In making a political intervention on behalf of the middle-class "homosexual," Wildeblood, Winter, and Trevor-Roper were certainly not unique in postwar Britain. Rather, their testimony was one aspect of a wider politics that explicitly attempted to reassert discursive control over the queer subject, countering dominant narratives of depravity and degeneracy in order to establish an image of the respectable "homosexual" for whom tolerance and legal recognition should be granted. Such arguments permeated the public domain in ways that they never had between the wars, articulated with increasing insistence as a particular notion of sexual difference was produced and reproduced for public consumption through disparate politico-cultural practices. They were manifest, for example, in a series of published works—including Michael Schofield's pioneering sociological investigations, which were based upon interviews with a disparate group of queer men and framed within scientific etiologies of sexual difference, Wildeblood's moving auto-biographical writings, and popular novels like Rodney Garland's *The Heart in Exile* or Mary Renault's *The Charioteer*. And in 1961 they reached the big screen, framing the discussion of blackmail central to Basil Dearden's seminal film *Victim*.[103]

After 1957 these indirect pressures for reform acquired further impetus. For, if the Wolfenden Report did not change the law, it provided an authoritative focus for queer politics—an officially endorsed map of the future that had been lacking between the wars. In 1958 a group of middle-class men thus formed the HLRS, with the explicit intention of having Wolfenden's recommendations passed into law.[104] The society's work institutionalized the growing convergence between the politics of "respectable" homosexuality, progressive medical opinion, and liberal authority figures first established between the wars and reinforced in the debates surrounding Wolfenden. These disparate elements coalesced around the common policy of turning a blind eye to discreet, private liaisons between otherwise law-abiding males. The public support of medical and legal experts, writers like J. B. Priestley, and politicians like Roy Jenkins sustained *direct* pressure for reform. In 1967, after a series of abortive attempts to introduce legislation by sympathetic MPs, the Sexual Offences Act was passed through Parliament.[105]

Like the Wolfenden Report on which it was based, the Sexual Offences Act of 1967 embodied a respectable, yet highly exclusive, "homosexual" subject. For if law reform created a legitimate private "homosexual" space, for those who could or would not conform to such rigid models of desire it was at best irrelevant, at worst disastrous.[106] As David Bell and Jon Binnie suggest:

> The twinning of rights with responsibilities in the logic of citizenship is another way of expressing compromise—*we will grant you certain rights if (and only if) you match these by taking on certain responsibilities*. . . . This demands the circumspection of "acceptable" modes of being a sexual citizen . . . a modality . . . that is privatized, de-radicalized, de-erotized and *confined*.[107]

The act thus inscribed the "homosexual" firmly within the paradigm of heterosexual marriage as the central foundation of national citizenship. As such, it confirmed the stigmatization of sexual practices that transgressed the public realm. More tangibly, those who inhabited the spaces displaced to the margins of respectability—the men who frequented queer commercial venues, who cruised the public city, who were excluded from private space—continued to face the risk of arrest and imprisonment. The recorded incidence of indecency between men doubled between 1967 and 1977.[108] If private practices had been decriminalized, the boundaries between public and private were regulated with increasing vigor. Just in case the respectable "homosexual" did not willingly assume the responsibilities of citizenship by remaining discreet and invisible, the law would police him into confinement.

The narrowness of this legislation, moreover, represented more than simply the limitations of postwar liberal "tolerance." It was embedded in the limitations of the respectable "homosexual" imagination and in the harsh realities of power and social exclusion in postwar British society. That the claims of the "homosexual" subject became so persuasive hinged upon his rejection of public manifestations of sexual difference—upon accepting, even accentuating, a radical distinction between the respectable "homosexual" and the repugnant queer. By being discreet, the "homosexual" remained discrete from a realm repudiated as abject, acquiescing in the deliberate silencing and marginalization of those placed beyond the boundaries of social acceptability and formal citizenship. Respectability—the key to law reform—crystallized the antagonisms and contradictions characteristic of those modes of early twentieth-century queerness explored in this book.

CONCLUSION

How are we to understand the history of queer London in the period between the First World War and the publication of the Wolfenden Report?

In the first place, this was a distinctly *urban* queer culture. In the lives they forged in London's public, commercial, and residential spaces and in the ways in which they made sense of their desires and practices, men were never a distinct subculture somehow removed from the city, but an integral part of modern metropolitan life. Each day, whether walking the streets, relaxing at home, or meeting friends in a café, they utilized the characteristic forms of urban life to create the complex and vibrant forms of sociability and selfhood described here. They forged worlds with their own geographies and temporal rhythms, histories, and cultures, styles of behavior and language, ways of being, and modes of self-understanding which were, nonetheless, deeply embedded within the broader metropolitan landscape. Through such practices men negotiated their legal, spatial, and discursive marginalization, constructing queer lives *within* the city through what was—in one sense—a conflict *over* the city.[1] London exercised a profound influence upon the geography, culture, and politics of queer lives in the first half of the twentieth century but it was also itself irrevocably shaped by those lives. In part, this book has been a deliberate attempt to write queer men back into London's history and, in the process, to rewrite that history.

Yet if, as Cyril L.'s letter, with which this book began, suggests, many men represented London in these terms—as a productive and liberating turning point in their lives—queer urban culture was always far more ambiguous than such narratives allowed. London was never simply a space of affirmation and citizenship, of love and sociability, of rich and unproblematic lives. Men cried in the city. Men were afraid, lonely, guilty, and isolated. Men were arrested and imprisoned, attacked and blackmailed. Men took their own lives in the city. Queer lives were braced by these common and contradictory experiences, taking shape within a persistent tension between pleasure and danger. Those very spaces that offered sanctuary to some men at certain moments excluded other men at other times. As Cyril learned, urban life could be hell in the same way that it could often be wonderful.

Just as we need to recognize the vitality of queer urban culture, so we must also appreciate its exclusive and exclusionary nature. As the first half of this book suggests, men's experiences of London were fractured by powerful differences of class, gender, age, ethnicity, and place. Where men found sex and sociability, the lives they led, and the dangers they faced depended, crucially, on these broader social differences. The privileges of class, wealth, and status meant it was always middle-class men who were more likely to find privacy and safety, who were most likely to avoid arrest—however contradictory their experiences may have been. This is not to suggest that working-class men did not find sex and sociability in London's streets, cafés, and lodgings. They did—and the lives they forged there could be vibrant and fulfilling. But the contrast between the dockside pub and the prestigious Trocadero, the Bermondsey cottage and the bachelor chambers, embodies the radical differences that drove men apart.

This emphasis on men's divergent experiences of the city highlights the second theme running throughout this book: this was a distinctly *queer* urban culture. What do I mean by this? It was distinctly queer in the sense of being unfamiliar to a twenty-first-century observer. The world mapped in this book is not a *gay* world as we would currently understand it. The places are different: Soho has retained its importance, but today it seems almost impossible that Waterloo Road or Edgware Road could have been the site of equally important, diverse, extensive, and vital queer enclaves between the wars. And, crucially, the people are different: like Cyril, they live different lives and make sense of those lives in ways that can be disturbingly unintelligible. The historical task of recuperation—of finding "our" hidden history—is an inadequate paradigm within which to appreciate the complexities of the geography, culture, and politics of queer life in the first half of the twentieth century. Those very categories of identity—"gay" and "straight," "homo" and "heterosexual"—that have often been taken for granted since the 1970s are of limited use in understanding this history.

It was a distinctly *queer* urban culture, moreover, in the sense that it was created and inhabited by men who were irreducibly different from *each other*. It is impossible to discern a unitary and stable community in this world. Certainly, the men who frequented London's commercial venues or public cruising grounds were brought together through similar desires for homosex, erotic pleasure, sociability, or intimacy. But the meanings they invested in those desires, the ways in which they understood their practices, and the urban lives they forged differed sharply. Different modes of queerness—different ways of understanding sexual difference—converged at the same sites. Indeed, queer and "normal" converged at those sites, for definitions of masculine sexual "normality" within particular working-class cultures could encompass a remarkable range of sexual and emotional interactions between men. In moving through the city's diverse queer spaces, men forged unique pathways, individualized cognitive maps of metropolitan life and selfhood. If these pathways often overlapped and intersected, they were, nonetheless, different in their geographical organization and in what they meant to the men who created them.

When men encountered each other as they moved across London, they were just as likely to be reminded of their differences as to recognize their commonalities; just as likely to react with disdain and disgust as with desire and comradeship. This tension between distance and closeness—difference and sameness—was, moreover, integral to particular modes of self-understanding. Respectable "homosexuality" was predicated upon a disdainful repudiation of the quean's visible difference or the workingman's public sexual practices. Through his relationships with men the quean embodied broader understandings of his ineffably womanlike character. And in his same-sex encounters, the working-class "tough" enacted distinctive conceptions of manliness, status, and domination *against* other men. Queer urban culture was the site of diverse intersecting modes of queerness and "normality," coalescing around their desires for homosex, sociability, and intimacy.

These antagonisms crystallized in two prominent annual events: the Chelsea Arts Ball (fig. 14) and Lady Malcolm's Servants' Ball—both held at the Royal Albert Hall. The former, in particular, was a centerpiece in the metropolitan social calendar, a New Year's Eve costume ball that attracted massive media attention and crowds of up to 7,000 socialites, artists, and ordinary Londoners in elaborate fancy dress. These "true pageants" were, observed Kenneth Hare in 1926, notable for their "variety, inventiveness, vivacity and colour."[2] For many men, becoming part of this carnival generated a palpable sense of release. Hundreds of working-class queans flocked

Figure 14. Photograph, the Chelsea Arts Ball, 1926. Getty Images.

to both balls, discarding the masks they wore in everyday life, wearing drag, dressing outrageously, and socializing unashamedly while never appearing to be anything out of the ordinary. In so doing, they were further protected by the Albert Hall's unique legal status: it was outside the Met's operational sphere. For once, temporarily and locally, men could fully escape police surveillance.[3]

The results were spectacular. In 1934, one observer described "groups of men dressed in coloured silk blouses and tight-hipped trousers . . . lips . . . rouged and faces painted. By their attitude and general behaviour they were obviously male prostitutes."[4] The crowds included many of Lady Austin's Camp Boys: Austin himself received his camp name when he "went to a big ball at the Albert Hall in women's dress"; at another dance David M. was eckled for wearing an outfit he had worn previously at the Servants' Ball.[5] From at least the First World War, twice a year, men like Austin and David transformed their massed bodies into an unmistakable manifestation of queer urban culture, sufficiently visible that, in 1933, an anonymous letter writer could complain of "the disgraceful scenes of . . . Degenerate Boys and men in female attire parading about at Lady Malcolm's Servant's Ball."[6]

From the early 1930s the organizers of both events were increasingly exercised by these "disgraceful scenes," and a nagging sense that men's behavior was somehow out of control. In 1936, Lady Malcolm herself wrote cryptically—apparently in some desperation—to the *Times*:

> Each year I notice at the ball a growing number of people, who, to be frank, are not of the class for whom the ball is designed. It is what it is called—a servants' ball, and I am jealous that it shall go on deserving that name."[7]

Both balls employed private stewards to maintain "order" and exclude "undesirables." From 1933, having failed to secure a police presence, Malcolm employed two ex-CID officers to remove any identifiable "sexual perverts." From 1935 tickets were sold with the proviso that "NO MAN IMPERSONATING A WOMAN AND NO PERSON UNSUITABLY ATTIRED WILL BE ADMITTED" (fig. 15). On entry, men's costumes had to be approved by a "Board of Scrutineers." Whatever they tried, however, the organizers could neither keep the "Degenerate Boys" out nor adequately contain their visibility; indeed, they often struggled even to identify them amidst the fancy dressed crowds. In 1938, an observer thus described the "extraordinary number of undesirable men at this Ball who were unmistakably of the Homo-Sexual and male prostitute types."[8] Well into the 1950s, the balls remained, in Stephen's words, "a great Mecca for the gay world."[9]

Working-class men reappropriated two high-profile public events, creating a space at the center of metropolitan culture in which they could be together and socialize free of the constraints that braced everyday queer lives. It is, however, misleading to see the Albert Hall as simply a space of community and inclusion since the differences *within* this space suggest that Stephen's putative "gay world" was so fragmented as to undermine any notion of this as a singular unitary entity. While many respectable men attended the balls, they deliberately distanced themselves from what Emlyn Williams called "half-naked Chelsea riff-raff."[10] In part, this distance was physical—wealthier men tended to occupy the stalls or galleries, leaving the floor to the quean. In part,

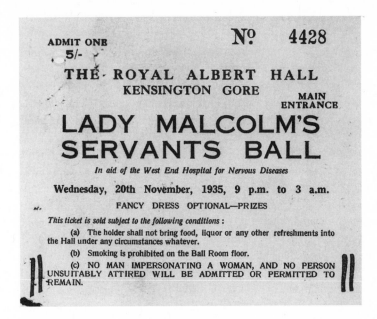

ADMIT ONE
5/-

N° 4428

THE ROYAL ALBERT HALL
KENSINGTON GORE

MAIN ENTRANCE

LADY MALCOLM'S SERVANTS BALL

In aid of the West End Hospital for Nervous Diseases

Wednesday, 20th November, 1935, 9 p.m. to 3 a.m.

FANCY DRESS OPTIONAL—PRIZES

This ticket is sold subject to the following conditions:

(a) The holder shall not bring food, liquor or any other refreshments into the Hall under any circumstances whatever.

(b) Smoking is prohibited on the Ball Room floor.

(c) NO MAN IMPERSONATING A WOMAN, AND NO PERSON UNSUITABLY ATTIRED WILL BE ADMITTED OR PERMITTED TO REMAIN.

Figure 15. Photograph, entrance ticket to Lady Malcolm's Servants' Ball, 1935. The National Archives of the UK (PRO), ref. no MEPO 2/3281. Material in the National Archives in the copyright of the Metropolitan Police is reproduced by permission of the Metropolitan Police Authority.

it was a matter of appearance: while men like Stephen—a civil servant—wore fancy dress, they avoided anything that might signal their sexual difference. Even in costume, the behavioral codes of discretion persisted: Stephen "dressed rather respectably . . . in an Arab costume."[11]

Of equal significance were those men who did *not* attend the balls—who were excluded from this imagined site of community. In part, these boundaries were a function of cost; particularly during the Depression, not everyone could afford a ticket. They also echoed differences of cultural practice and masculinity. Those workingmen who were so prominent in the public and commercial sites of queer sociability were conspicuous only by their absence from the theatrics of the Albert Hall. Set against the prescriptive demands of "normal" masculinity, such conduct marked an intolerable threat to a man's manliness, even if he were prepared to engage in homosex or enter into enduring same-sex relationships. In the internal segregation between modes of queerness and in the distinction between those men who flocked to the costume balls and those who held themselves distant, these social events embodied competing understandings of sexual difference and the unstable boundaries between difference and "normality" in the first half of the twentieth century.

By the 1940s, while the meanings of sexual difference continued to be fractured and contested, the boundaries between queer and "normal" were hardening, to preclude young workingmen's participation in queer urban culture. The cultural changes associated with affluence undermined the salience of the gendered opposition between man and quean to hegemonic understandings of male sexual practices. In this context, it was increasingly difficult for men to engage in homosex or emotional relationships with other men whilst considering themselves—and being considered by others—as "normal." In the middle of the twentieth century, through what we might call a process of privatization, queer London was, more than ever, inhabited by a narrowing group of men who explicitly thought of themselves as different, even though they may have disagreed profoundly about what exactly constituted that difference. In this drawn-out and contested historical process lies the emergence of the binary opposition between "homo" and "heterosexual" that shapes contemporary understandings of male sexual practices and identities.

This cultural privatization, moreover, had its corollary in the spatial reorganization of queer London. The Dilly Boy's disappearance and the urinal's declining importance embody a broad movement away from public forms of urban culture. As the first half of this book suggests, queer urban culture was privatized in the sense of becoming centered on the home, or particular semiprivate sites of commercial sociability. It was privatized in the sense of becoming increasingly hidden and invisible. And it was privatized in the sense of becoming physically separated from the sites of "normal" urban life. The growing number of exclusively queer commercial venues after the Second World War emblematized that broader cultural separation between queer and "normal." Indeed, as I have argued, the war—as well as the period that followed—was the key moment in both these changes. Many men thought of the war as queer London's "golden age," a frenetic time of sexual opportunity and social interaction in which the city was livelier than ever. Paradoxically, however, in figuring the queer as such a potent source of cultural danger, the war underpinned those police operations within which men and their meeting places retreated from visibility. The result of these interconnected processes was that by the 1950s, more than ever, queer urban culture was *both* discreet *and* discrete. It had not always been that way, and it would certainly not remain so.

This book ends at a deeply ambiguous moment in London's queer history: a moment of political "liberation," which excluded and stigmatized vibrant forms of queer urban culture; a moment at which enduring public practices and spaces coexisted in a precarious balance with the characteristic sites of contemporary consumerism; a moment at which trade and the quean—unfamiliar figures today—rubbed shoulders with the instantly recognizable "homosexual." Simultaneously, this moment was utopian and dystopian. As a renewed political activism intersected with the changing nature of modern metropolitan life, many men were able to construct private or semiprivate social networks in which it was possible to be intimately, discreetly, securely queer. Those same processes, however, threatened the very existence of alternative social forms, particularly that open, demotic public queer culture that visibly took hold in streets and parks, backstreet cafés and pubs. More than ever, people and places like *that* were forced to queer London's margins.

If you walk down St. Martin's Lane towards Trafalgar Square, just before the National Portrait Gallery comes into view you'll pass a narrow alleyway called Brydges Place on your left. Down here for decades was one of the "old-fashioned" cast-iron urinals; a noted site of sexual opportunity at London's heart. It was demolished in 1953, as part of the LCC and Met's "modernization" of the cityscape. Here, at almost exactly the same time, Ted Rodgers Bennett opened the Festival, an exclusive, self-consciously respectable, members' drinking and dining club behind an unmarked door.

In many ways the queer history of Brydges Place is the history of queer London. Here, we can see a movement from visibility to invisibility, from an open public sexual culture to an exclusive commercial sociability. Here we can see the relationship between police operations and changing geographies of queer lives. Here we can see the narrowing boundaries of masculine sexual "normality" and the increasingly rigid separation between queer and "normal." Here we can see how the privatization of queer urban culture was played out in one small alleyway. The Festival was safer than the urinal; it was certainly more comfortable. Yet it was by no means accessible to all men. Here, moreover, men were drawn from London's center into its shadows, from light into darkness, from being within the public city to being outside. The city still exerts a profound influence over the cultural and spatial organization of queer practices and identities, but its story is by no means solely that of liberation and affirmation. In exploring the history of queer London in the first half of the twentieth century, we should lament possibilities long lost as much as we celebrate opportunities newly acquired.

APPENDIX

Queer Incidents Resulting in Proceedings at the Metropolitan Magistrates' Courts
and City of London Justice Rooms, 1917–57

	Year								
COURT	1917	1922	1927	1932	1937	1942	1947	1952	1957
Bow Street	28	22	34	26	82	106	212	194	179
Clerkenwell	2	7	5	4	12	19	34	13	25
Greenwich	0	6	5	5	4	1	8	8	7
Guildhall	1	2	0	0	2	1	0	8	11
Lambeth	1	2	9	6	9	16	74	19	16
Mansion House	1	0	0	1	3	0	0	18	30
Marlborough Street	16	48	23	51	52	13	103	56	99
Marylebone	2	4	11	7	19	24	28	11	18
North London	1	9	1	12	16	7	15	11	11
Old Street	1	1	1	5	6	1	18	11	8
South Western	N/A	4	6	12	13	8	13	18	10
Thames	1	4	1	1	7	0	14	5	7
Tower Bridge	6	5	17	3	8	3	11	38	N/A
West London	2	4	14	6	2	6	100	168	63
Westminster	5	12	15	22	13	4	N/A	N/A	N/A
Woolwich	N/A	2	2	1	3	2	7	5	7
TOTAL	67	132	144	162	251	211	637	583	491

Sources: Registers of the London Metropolitan Magistrates' Courts and the City of London
Justice Rooms sampled at five-yearly intervals between 1917 and 1957. The year 1917 excludes
data for Woolwich and South Western; Westminster data unavailable from May 1942 onwards;
1957 excludes data for Tower Bridge; CLRO, GH: registers; CLRO, MH: registers; LMA, PS
BOW A1: 64–69, 83–88, 107–14, 137–44, 170–75, 196–201, 222–30, 251–60, 297–305;
LMA, PS BOW A2: 4, 5, 8–11, 24–25, 34–38, 51–57, 74–78; LMA, PS CLE A1: 43–46,
58–63, 68–73, 95–97, 111–15, 132–37, 153–60, 182–89, 205–21; LMA, PS GRE A1: 11–14,

21–24, 31–34, 39–42, 49–52, 59–62, 69–72, 79–82, 92–96; LMA, PS LAM A1: 33–36, 45–48, 61–64, 75–79, 95–98, 115–19, 134–39, 164–69, 194–99; LMA, PS MS A1: 35–39, 53–58, 79–84, 109–15, 154–61, 181–86, 202–8, 235–41, 267–73; LMA, PS MAR A1: 50–53, 68–73, 86–92, 110–15, 136–44, 162–68, 196–205, 234–42, 272–82; LMA, PS NLO A1: 19–22, 29–34, 43–46, 55–58, 67–72, 85–90, 107–12, 132–38, 155–60; LMA, PS OLD A1: 39–44, 57–60, 75–79, 90–94, 106–10, 124–28, 141–45, 162–65, 181–84; LMA, PS SWE A1: 6–11, 24–27, 40–45, 60–64, 80–84, 98–103, 120–23, 140–45; LMA, PS TH A1: 139–42, 157–62, 173–77, 187–203, 202–7, 222–27, 243–49, 269–75, 296–303; LMA, PS TOW A1: 133–38, 149–52, 163–66, 178–81, 193–06, 209–13, 223–26, 243–50; LMA, PS WLN A1: 201–5, 216–21, 232–37, 249–54, 270–75, 292–97, 320–27, 350–57, 380–86; LMA, PS WES A1: 88–92, 107–12, 127–31, 147–50, 165–69, 184–86; LMA, PS WOO A1: 3–6, 9–12, 15–18, 22–24, 29–32, 37–40, 45–48, 51–54.

Note—A queer incident is a single instance in which police apprehended one or more men who were subsequently charged with importuning, gross indecency, indecent assault, buggery, or a bylaw indecency offence. This definition excludes men charged with public order offences, where it is impossible to discern the nature of the incident leading to a charge. Figures include intergenerational sexual encounters, since the law made no formal distinction between the ages of concerned parties. Each incident could include multiple and varying numbers of offenders and offences, but represents a single moment of police intervention. This measure underestimates the intensity of police activity, ignoring occasions on which charges were not brought, or when men were informally warned or cautioned. There is no reason to assume significant chronological variations in such practices.

NOTES

INTRODUCTION

1. PRO, CRIM 1 735: Jack Neave and others, charged with keeping a disorderly house, exhibit 4: Cyril L. to Morris (undated 1934).

2. PRO, MEPO 3 758: "Caravan Club 81 Endell Street WC1: Disorderly House/Male Prostitutes," minute 8c: Cyril L. to Billy (16 August 1934).

3. Matt Cook, *London and the Culture of Homosexuality, 1885–1914* (Cambridge: Cambridge University Press, 2003), 2.

4. Armistead Maupin, *Tales of the City* (New York: Harper & Row, 1978). See also Neil Bartlett, *Mr. Clive and Mr. Page* (London: Serpent's Tail, 1996); and Alan Hollinghurst, *The Swimming Pool Library* (London: Penguin, 1988).

5. Michel Foucault, *The History of Sexuality,* vol. 1, *An Introduction,* trans. Robert Hurley (London: Allen Lane, 1979). For this queer urban history see, for example, Alan Berrube, *Coming Out Under Fire: The History of Gay Men and Women in World War Two* (New York: Free Press, 1990); George Chauncey, *Gay New York: The Making of the Gay Male World, 1890–1940* (London: Flamingo, 1995); Dan Healey, *Homosexual Desire in Revolutionary Russia: The Regulation of Sexual and Gender Dissent* (Chicago: University of Chicago Press, 2001); David Higgs, ed., *Queer Sites: Gay Urban Histories since 1600* (London and New York: Routledge, 1999); John Howard, "The Library, the Park and the Pervert: Public Space and Homosexual Encounter in Post World War Two Atlanta," *Radical History Review* 62 (1995): 166–87; Charles Kaiser, *The Gay Metropolis, 1940–1996* (London: Weidenfeld and Nicolson, 1998); Elizabeth Kennedy and Madeline Davis, *Boots of Leather, Slippers of Gold: The History of a Lesbian Community* (London and New York: Routledge, 1993); Steven Maynard, "'Horrible Temptations': Sex, Men and Working-Class Male Youth in Urban Ontario, 1890–1935," *Canadian Historical Review* 78, no. 2 (1997): 192–235; idem, "Through a Hole in the Lavatory Wall: Homosexual Subcultures, Police Surveillance and the Dialectics of Discovery, Toronto, 1890–1930," *Journal of the History of Sexuality* 5, no. 2 (1994): 207–42; Arne Nilsson, "Creating Their Own Private and Public: The Male Homosexual Life Space in a Nordic City during High Modernity," *Journal of Homosexuality* 35, nos. 3–4 (1998): 81–116; Marc Stein, *City of Brotherly and Sisterly Love: Lesbian and Gay Philadelphia, 1945–72* (Chicago: University of Chicago Press, 2000); and Gary Wotherspoon, *City of the Plain: History of a Gay Subculture* (Sydney: Hale and Iremonger, 1991).

6. Neil Bartlett, *Who Was That Man? A Present for Mr. Oscar Wilde* (London: Serpent's Tail, 1988).

7. See Rictor Norton, *Mother Clap's Molly House: The Gay Subculture in England, 1700–1830* (London: Gay Men's Press, 1992); Netta Murray Goldsmith, *The Worst*

of Crimes: Homosexuality and the Law in Eighteenth-century London (Aldershot: Ashgate, 1998); Randolph Trumbach, "Sodomy Transformed: Aristocratic Libertinage, Public Reputation and the Gender Revolution of the Eighteenth Century," *Journal of Homosexuality* 19, no. 2 (1990): 105–24, idem, *Sex and the Gender Revolution*, vol. 1, *Heterosexuality and the Third Gender in Enlightenment London* (Chicago: Chicago University Press, 1998); Harry Cocks, *Nameless Offences: Homosexual Desire in the Nineteenth Century* (London and New York: IB Tauris, 2003); Lewis Chester, David Leitch, and Colin Simpson, *The Cleveland Street Affair* (London: Weidenfeld and Nicolson, 1977); H. Montgomery Hyde, *The Cleveland Street Scandal* (London: W. H. Allen, 1976); Hugh David, *On Queer Street: A Social History of British Homosexuality, 1895–1995* (London: Harper Collins, 1997); H. Montgomery Hyde, *The Other Love: An Historical and Contemporary Survey of Homosexuality in Britain* (London: William Heinemann, 1970); Jeffrey Weeks, "Inverts, Perverts and Mary-Annes: Male Prostitution and the Regulation of Homosexuality in England in the Nineteenth and Early Twentieth Centuries," in *Hidden from History: Reclaiming the Gay and Lesbian Past*, ed. George Chauncey, Martin Duberman, and Martha Vicinus, 195–211 (Canada: New American Library, 1989); Jeffrey Weeks, *Coming Out: Homosexual Politics in Britain from the Nineteenth Century to the Present* (London: Quartet Books, 1977); Charles Upchurch, "Forgetting the Unthinkable: Cross Dressers and British Society in the Case of the Queen vs. Boulton and Others," *Gender and History* 12, no. 1 (2000): 127–54; Theo Aronson, *Prince Eddy and the Homosexual Underworld* (London: Murray, 1994); Cook, *London and the Culture of Homosexuality*, passim; Morris Kaplan, "Who's Afraid of Jack Saul? Urban Culture and the Politics of Desire in Late-Victorian London," *GLQ* 5, no. 3 (1999): 267–314; idem, "Did 'My Lord Gomorrah' Smile? Homosexuality, Class and Prostitution in the Cleveland Street Affair," in *Disorder in the Court: Trials and Sexual Conflict at the Turn of the Century,* ed. George Robb and Nancy Erber (New York: New York University Press, 1999); Gavin Brown, "Listening to Queer Maps of the City: Gay Men's Narratives of Pleasure and Danger in London's East End," *Oral History* (2001): 48–61.

8. Frank Mort and Lynda Nead, "Introduction: Sexual Geographies," *New Formations* 37 (1999): 6. See also, for example, Henri Lefebvre, *The Production of Space,* trans. David Nicholson-Smith (Oxford: Basil Blackwell, 1991); David Harvey, *The Condition of Postmodernity: An Enquiry into the Origins of Cultural Change* (Oxford: Basil Blackwell, 1989); Edward Soja, *Postmodern Geographies: The Reassertion of Space in Critical Social Theory* (London and New York: Verso, 1989); Michel de Certeau, *The Practice of Everyday Life,* trans. Steven Randall (Berkeley: University of California Press, 1984); Michael Keith and Steve Pile, eds., *Place and the Politics of Identity* (London and New York: Routledge, 1993); Erica Carter, James Donald, and Judith Squires, eds., *Space and Place: Theories of Identity and Location* (London: Lawrence and Wishart, 1993); Steve Pile and Nigel Thrift, eds., *Mapping the Subject: Geographies of Cultural Transformation* (London and New York: Routledge, 1995); Rob Shields, *Places on the Margin: Alternative Geographies of*

Modernity (London and New York: Routledge, 1991); David Sibley, *Geographies of Exclusion: Society and Difference in the West* (London and New York: Routledge, 1995); Frank Mort, *Cultures of Consumption: Masculinities and Social Space in Late Twentieth-Century Britain* (London and New York: Routledge, 1996); Matt Houlbrook, "Towards a Historical Geography of Sexuality," *Journal of Urban History* 27, no. 44 (2001): 497–504.

9. See Jan Lofstrom, "The Birth of the Queen/The Modern Homosexual: Historical Explanations Revisited," *Sociological Review* 45, no. 11 (1997): 24; John d'Emilio, *Sexual Politics, Sexual Communities: The Making of a Homosexual Minority in the United States, 1940–1970* (Chicago: University of Chicago Press, 1983); Weeks, *Coming Out,* passim.

10. Henning Bech, *When Men Meet: Homosexuality and Modernity,* trans. Teresa Mesquit and Tim Davies (Oxford: Polity Press, 1997), 98–99, 104–16. For contemporary explorations of this relationship see, for example, Gordon Brent Ingram, Anne-Marie Bouthilette, and Yolanda Retter, eds., *Queers In Space: Communities/Public Places/Sites Of Resistance* (Seattle: Bay Press, 1997); David Bell and Gill Valentine, eds., *Mapping Desire: Geographies of Sexuality* (London and New York: Routledge, 1995); Aaron Betsky, *Queer Space: Architecture and Same-Sex Desire* (New York: William Morrow and Co, 1997); and Stephen Whittle, ed., *The Margins of the City: Gay Men's Urban Lives* (Aldershot: Arena, 1994).

11. PRO: MEPO 3 758: minute 11a, statement of DC/E Daws; DS/E Stevenson: 29 August 1934; Minute 15a: DDI/E Campion to Supt.: 30 October 1934. See also LMA: ACC 2385 185: Calendars of Prisoners: CCC: 16 October 1934.

12. "Police Swoop on Club Dancers," *NW,* 23 September 1934, 18 "Vile Den of Iniquity," *IPN,* 8 November 1934, 6. "Caravan Club Case," *Times,* 27 October 1934, 14.

13. Scott Bravmann, *Queer Fictions of the Past: History, Culture and Difference* (Cambridge: Cambridge University Press, 1997), x, 9. Recent work has moved beyond the simple correlation between urbanization and a singular "homosexual" identity to explore the complexities of the interrelationships between sexual practices and urban culture. See, in particular, Cocks, *Nameless Offences;* Kaplan, "Who's Afraid of Jack Saul?" Cook, *London and the Culture of Homosexuality;* and Mark Turner, *Backward Glances: Cruising the Queer Streets of New York and London* (London: Reaktion, 2003).

14. PRO, MEPO 3 758: minute 8c: Cyril L. to Billy (undated 1934); ibid., minute 11a, DDI/E Campion to DPP: Insp./E Chedzoy; DC/E Daws; DS/E Mogford (29 August 1934).

15. Steven Maynard, "Respect your Elders: Know Your Past; History and the Queer Theorists," *Radical History Review* 75 (1999): 69–71.

16. While the spellings "queen" and "quean" were used interchangeably in the first half of the twentieth century, I have followed Eric Partridge's *Dictionary of the Underworld* (Hertfordshire: Wordsworth, 1995), 545–49, in using "quean" as the standard spelling throughout this book.

17. On this, see Chauncey, *Gay New York,* 13.

18. Joan Scott, "The Evidence of Experience," in *The Lesbian and Gay Studies Reader,* ed. Henry Abelove, Michele Aina Barale, and David Halperin (London and New York: Routledge, 1993), 399–401.

19. This argument draws upon queer theory's conceptualization of the multiplicity of sexual practices and subjectivities. See, for example, Steven Seidman, ed., *Queer Theory/Sociology* (Oxford: Blackwell, 1996); Michael Warner, ed., *Fear of a Queer Planet: Queer Politics and Social Theory* (Minneapolis: University of Minnesota Press, 1993); and Abelove et al., *Lesbian and Gay Studies Reader.*

20. See, for example, Brighton Ourstory Project, *Daring Hearts: Lesbian and Gay Lives of 50s and 60s Brighton* (Brighton: QueenSpark Books, 1992).

21. E. M. Forster, *Maurice* (London: Edward Arnold, 1971); and Quentin Crisp, *The Naked Civil Servant* (London: Jonathon Cape, 1968). John Howard, *Men Like That: A Southern Queer History* (Chicago: Chicago University Press, 2001) is a compelling reminder that not all queer history is urban history.

22. See, for example, Harold Acton, *Memoirs of an Aesthete* (London: Methuen and Co., 1948); Hugo Vickers, *Cecil Beaton: The Authorised Biography* (London: Weidenfeld and Nicolson, 1985); Philip Hoare, *Noel Coward: A Biography* (London: Sinclair Stevenson, 1995); Michael Davidson, *Some Boys* (London: David Bruce and Watson, 1970); Marie-Jacqueline Lancaster, ed., *Brian Howard: Portrait of a Failure* (London: Anthony Blond, 1968); Christopher Isherwood, *Christopher and His Kind, 1929–1939* (London: Eyre Methuen, 1977); and John Lehmann, *In the Purely Pagan Sense* (London: Blond and Briggs, 1976).

23. Robert Sinclair, *Metropolitan Man: The Future of the English* (London: George Allen and Unwin, 1937), 17–18.

24. Here I am influenced by Laura Doan's insistence on "a particularized national context and temporality" as a "new direction in lesbian historiography." See Doan, *Fashioning Sapphism: The Origins of a Modern English Lesbian Culture* (New York: Columbia University Press, 2001), xxiii. My sense of these particular differences draws on Chauncey, *Gay New York.*

25. The contemporary relationship between lesbianism and urban space is explored in Sally Munt, *Heroic Desire: Lesbian Identity and Cultural Spaces* (London: Cassell, 1998); Gill Valentine, "Heterosexing Space: Lesbian Perceptions and Experiences of Everyday Spaces," *Environment and Planning D: Society and Space* 11, no. 44 (1993): 395–413, idem, "Negotiating and Managing Multiple Sexual Identities: Lesbian Time Space Strategies," *Transactions of the Institute of British Geographers* 18, no. 2 (1993): 237–48, and idem, "Out and About: Geographies of Lesbian Landscapes," *International Journal of Urban and Regional Research* 19, no. 1 (1995): 96–112. For women's relationship with the city, see, for example, Judith Walkowitz, *City of Dreadful Delight: Narratives of Sexual Danger in Late-Victorian London* (London: Virago, 1998); Elizabeth Wilson, *The Sphinx in the City: Urban Life, the Control of Disorder and Women* (Berkeley: University of California Press, 1991); Erika Rappaport, *Shopping for Pleasure: Women in the Making of London's West End*

(Princeton: Princeton University Press, 2000); Deborah Parsons, *Streetwalking the Metropolis: Women, the City and Modernity* (Oxford: Oxford University Press, 2000); and Deborah Epstein Nord, *Walking the Victorian Streets: Women, Representation and the City* (Ithaca: Cornell University Press, 1995).

26. This summary draws upon Samuel Hynes, *A War Imagined: The First World War and English Culture* (London: Pimlico, 1992), 227–41; PRO: HO 144 1498: "The Black Book Mentioned in the Criminal Libel Case against Mr. Pemberton Billing MP" (1918); Philip Hoare, *Wilde's Last Stand: Decadence, Conspiracy and the First World War* (London: Duckworth, 1997); Lucy Bland, "Trial by Sexology? Maud Allan, Salome and the Cult of the Clitoris Case," in *Sexology in Culture: Labeling Bodies and Desires,* ed. Lucy Bland and Laura Doan (Oxford: Polity Press, 1998), 183–98.

27. See, in particular, Becky Conekin, Frank Mort, and Chris Waters, eds., *Moments of Modernity: Reconstructing Britain, 1945–1964* (London: Rivers Oram Press, 1999); Martin Daunton and Bernhard Rieger, eds., *Meanings of Modernity: Britain from the Late-Victorian Era to World War Two* (Oxford: Berg, 2001); Mica Nava and Alan O'Shea, eds., *Modern Times: Reflections on a Century of English Modernity* (London and New York: Routledge, 1996).

28. PRO, MEPO 3 758: minute 11a, DDI/E Campion to DPP: statements of Insp./E. Chedzoy; DC/E Daws; DS/E Mogford (29 August 1934).

CHAPTER 1

1. Liz Gill, "Lavender Linguistics," *Guardian,* 14 July 2003.

2. Cocks, *Nameless Offences,* chaps. 1 and 2.

3. *Public General Acts 44 and 45 Vict.* (London, 1861), 833, sec. 61 and 62; *Public General Acts 48–49 Vict.* (London, 1885), 6, sec. 11.

4. See, for example, PRO, HO 45 17520: "Bylaws, LCC Parks, Gardens and Open Spaces" (1931–38); Leon Radzinowicz, *Sexual Offences: A Report of the Cambridge Department of Criminal Science* (London: Macmillan, 1957), 358–59.

5. *Public General Acts 61–62 Vict.* (London, 1898), 221, sec. 1b; *Public General Acts, 2–3 Geo V.* (London, 1912), 91–92, sec. 5, 7.

6. This summary draws upon Frank Mort, *Dangerous Sexualities: Medico-Moral Politics in England since 1830* (London and New York: Routledge, 1987), 127–30; E. J. Bristow, *Vice and Vigilance: Purity Movements in England since 1700* (Dublin: Gill and Macmillan, 1977), 115–71; Hyde, *The Other Love,* 134–37; Weeks, *Coming Out,* 11–22; F. B. Smith, "Labouchere's Amendment to the Criminal Law Amendment Bill," *Historical Studies* 17, no. 67 (1976): 165–75; and Cook, *London and the Culture of Homosexuality,* 42–55.

7. Philip Hubbard, *Sex and the City: Geographies of Prostitution in the Urban West* (Aldershot: Ashgate, 1999), 103.

8. Leslie Moran, *The Homosexual(ity) of Law* (London and New York: Routledge, 1996), 56.

9. For the development of municipal government, see V. A. C. Gatrell, "Crime, Authority and the Policeman State," in *The Cambridge Social History of Britain,*

1750–1950, vol. 3, *Social Agencies and Institutions,* ed. F. M. L. Thompson (Cambridge: Cambridge University Press, 1993), 254; David Ascoli, *The Queens Peace: The Origins and Development of the Metropolitan Police, 1829–1979* (London: Hamish Hamilton, 1979); Clive Emsley, *The English Police: A Social History* (London: Longman, 1996); and Susan Pennybacker, *A Vision for London, 1889–1914: Labour, Everyday Life and the LCC Experiment* (London and New York: Routledge, 1995).

10. Nick Fyfe, "Space, Time and Policing: Towards a Conceptual Understanding of Police Work," *Environment and Planning D: Society and Space* 10, no. 4 (1992): 475–76.

11. PRO, DPP 6 66: "Homosexual Offences and Treatment of Persons Convicted of Prostitution and Soliciting for Immoral Purposes," MC to DPP (14 October 1954).

12. I discuss conditions of access to commercial venues, see pp.73–80. For the geography of policing, see Gatrell, "Crime, Authority and the Policeman State"; and Stephen Inwood, "Policing London's Morals: The Metropolitan Police and Popular Culture," *London Journal* (1990): 123–42. This focus was implicit within the law. Importuning was, de jure, a public order offence. Louise Jackson convincingly argues that the Criminal Law Amendment Act responded to men's visibility on London's streets. See Jackson, *Child Sexual Abuse in Victorian England* (London and New York: Routledge, 2000), 103–5.

13. See PRO, MEPO 3 2979: "Parliamentary Questions: Police Supervision of Hyde Park" (1936); PRO, MEPO 3 297: "Indecency Offences on Hampstead Heath" (1927); PRO, MEPO 3 248: on importuning (1915); PRO, MEPO 2 3231: "Immorality in Parks and Open Spaces" (1928–34).

14. PRO, MEPO 2 9367, "Vice at Piccadilly Circus and Surrounding Area," minute 4a, "Prostitutes, Homosexuals, Pornography and Rowdyism in the West End" (30 October 1952).

15. PRO, MEPO 3 990, "Use of Plainclothes Officers in Detecting Indecency Offences in Urinals," CCGRA (31 August 1933).

16. "Police Story of Scenes at a West End House," *Illustrated Police News* (hereafter *IPN*), 26 January 1933, 3.

17. PRO, MEPO 3 405, "Francis Champain: Importuning," Street Offences Committee: subcommittee, transcript of proceedings at the fifth meeting (5 January 1928), Q1–81.

18. Ibid., Q233, Q462.

19. Ibid., Q259–64.

20. "Shadowed in the Strand," *News of the World* (hereafter *NW*), 27 June 1926, 14; and "Artist Arrested," *NW*, 20 June 1926, 12. See also "Male Moral Perverts," *NW*, 28 August 1927, 8; "One of a Gang," *NW*, 3 October 1926, 3; "Court Denials of Former Oxford Man," *NW*, 3 October 1937, 8; and "London after Dark," *NW*, 25 December 1927, 15.

21. LMA, PS BOW A01 113 (November 1927).

22. LMA, PS BOW A01 107–114 (1927). See also "Ex-Officer to Appeal," *NW*, 28 March 1926, 10.

23. LMA, PS BOW A01 64–9 (1917); and LMA, PS BOW A01 83–8 (1922). See also Steve Herbert, "Police Subculture Reconsidered," *Criminology* 36, no. 2 (1998): 343–70. For an excellent evocation of police culture written by a queer officer, see Harry Daley, *This Small Cloud: A Personal Memoir* (London: Weidenfeld and Nicholson, 1986).

24. PRO, MEPO 3 405, transcript of proceedings (5 January 1928), Q614–15, Q30, Q572 and Q568–72, Q242–3 and Q466–9, Q573–86, Q205, Q644 and Q222, Q183–Q184, Q193–210.

25. "Police Begin Big West End 'Clean Up,'" *NW*, 31 January 1937, 8; LMA, PS BOW A01 170–5 (1937); LMA, PS BOW A02 8–11 (1937).

26. See appendix 1.

27. See David Sibley, *Geographies of Exclusion: Society and Difference in the West* (London and New York: Routledge, 1995); Philip Hubbard, "Red Light Districts and Toleration Zones: Geographies of Female Prostitution in England and Wales," *Area* 29, no. 2 (1997): 129–40.

28. See Mort, *Dangerous Sexualities*, 104–49; Stefan Petrow, *Policing Morals: The Metropolitan Police and the Home Office, 1870–1914* (Oxford: Clarendon Press, 1994), 117–66; and Lesley Hall, *Sex, Gender and Social Change in Britain since 1880* (London: Palgrave, 2002), 10–47. The relationship of these organizations to queer urban culture is discussed below, see pp. 57–60, 78–79, 104–5, 123–25, 214–15. See also LMA, A PMC 98 3: annual report (1933), 23–4; LMA, A PMC 98 7: annual report (1937); LMA, A PMC 98 8: annual report (1938); LMA, A PMC 4: executive committee minute book and agenda, chairman's notes (27 June 1940; 25 July 1940).

29. LMA, A PMC 42: patrolling officer's reports (July 1942).

30. LMA, A PMC 43: patrolling officer's reports (March 1955); LMA, A PMC 11: Parliamentary, Patrol and Propaganda (hereafter PPP) subcommittee minute book (November 1949 to January 1957); LMA, A PMC 12: PPP minute book (1957–64); LMA, A PMC 98 24, annual report (1954); LMA, A PMC 98 26, annual report (1956).

31. PRO, MEPO 3 405, transcript of proceedings (5 January 1928), Q678.

32. See Robert Fabian, *Fabian of the Yard* (Kingswood Surrey: Naldrett Press, 1950), 11–16; and Daley, *This Small Cloud,* passim.

33. PRO, HO 45 12633: "Appointing of a Commission to Consider the Law and Practice Relating to Soliciting," sections 85–86: Proceedings of the Street Offences Committee: Brigadier General Sir William Horwood (20 December 1927), Q2746–7.

34. Moran, *Homosexual(ity) of Law,* 143.

35. PRO, CRIM 1 2487: Aloysius B., charged with indecent assault, statement of DC 472/H Martin (2 October 1954). See also Peter Wildeblood, *Against the Law* (Harmondsworth: Penguin, 1955), 48; Crisp, *Naked Civil Servant,* 80–81; and Tom Driberg, *Ruling Passions* (London: Jonathon Cape, 1977), 147–48.

36. "Alleged Scenes at West End Dances," *NW,* 26 February 1933, 8.

37. Ibid. See also PRO, CRIM 1 640, Austin S. and (33) others charged with keeping a disorderly house, conspiracy to corrupt morals, transcript of statements

given before Magistrate at West London Police Court (4 January 1933), statements of PC 524/F Chopping.

38. PRO, CRIM 1 639: Austin S. and (33) others charged with keeping a disorderly house, conspiracy to corrupt morals (1933/1938), information of PC 139/F Labbatt.

39. Ibid.

40. Ibid., statement of PC 524/F Chopping. See also PRO, CRIM 1 639, copy depositions, statement of PC 524/F Chopping.

41. PRO, CRIM 1 639, information: statement of PC 139/F Labbatt.

42. "Alleged Scenes at West End Dances," NW, 26 February 1933, 8.

43. Frank Mort, "Mapping Sexual London: The Wolfenden Committee on Homosexual Offences and Prostitution, 1954–7," New Formations 37 (1999): 101–2.

44. See PRO, MEPO 3 990, Wontners solicitors to police (5 August 1933); PRO, MEPO 3 987, "Evidence in Importuning Cases": Insp. D Wright to SDI (16 October 1935); PRO, CRIM 1 547, Harold R.: charged with importuning (1931); PRO, MEPO 3 992, "Hugh C.: Persistent Importuner" (1935); PRO, MEPO 3 2330, "George B.: Importuning" (1943); PRO, HO 45 25622, "Definition of the Term 'Agent Provocateur': Memo on the Use of Agents Provocateurs by the DPP" (1945); and PRO, DPP 6 66, JB: 14 (October 1954).

45. These critiques focused upon the extent to which officers were implicated in the committal of an offence. See, for example, J. B. Lopian, "Crime, Police and Punishment, 1918–29: Metropolitan Experiences, Perceptions and Policies" (Ph.D. diss., University of Cambridge, 1986), 44; and Gatrell, "Crime, Authority and the Policeman State," 271–77. See also "Watchers at Victoria," NW, 28 March 1920, 4; and "Ex-Officer to Appeal," NW, 28 March 1926, 10.

46. See "Double Blue's Lapse," NW, 28 August 1927; "Another Case Dismissed on Appeal," Birmingham DM, 21 September 1927; "Where Justice Erred," NW, 25 September 1927, 6; and "Public Schoolmaster Charged with Serious Offence," IPN, 1 September 1927, 7.

47. Joynson-Hicks personally approached the barrister H. P. Macmillan, chairman of the Street Offences Committee. The other members of the subcommittee deputed to consider the case were the lawyers William Jowitt and Joseph Priestley. See PRO, HO 45 12633: section 85 (18 October 1927); and "Street Law Enquiry," NW, 16 October 1927, 8.

48. PRO, MEPO 3 405: transcript of proceedings (5 January 1928), Q117–8, 184, 295.

49. Ibid., attachment 35a, report of the subcommittee (28 January 1928).

50. Ibid., transcript of proceedings (5 January 1928), Q359–60.

51. Ibid., Q633.

52. Ibid., attachment 35a, report of the subcommittee (28 January 1928).

53. Ibid.

54. Ibid.

55. PRO, HO 45 25860: "Royal Commission on Police Powers and Procedures, 1929," pars. 57 and 119. In 1945, the DPP lent further sanction to such practices under the euphemistic rubric of "participatory evidence." See PRO, HO 45 25622 (1945).

56. PRO, HO 45 25860: RCPPP (1929), par. 102. See also PRO, MEPO 2 3231, "Immorality in Parks and Open Spaces" (1929); PRO, HO 144 7044; "Hyde Park Disturbance and Annoying and Insulting Behavior" (1908–27).

57. PRO, HO 45 14216: "Restrictions on Clubs," section 82, Powers of Entry into and Inspection of Certain Premises [extracts from the report of the RCPPP; 1929], par. 115.

58. PRO MEPO 3 990: Wontners Solicitors to Police: Magistrate's Remarks (30 August 1933).

59. Jeffrey Weeks and Kevin Porter, eds., *Between the Acts: Lives of Homosexual Men, 1885–1967* (London: Rivers Oram Press, 1999), 98.

60. "West End Nest of Vice Smoked Out," *NW*, 5 March 1933, 18.

61. For the RCPPP's recommendations, see PRO, HO 45 25860 (1929). For the de facto adoption of this procedure, see PRO, MEPO 3 248, minute 5: GCD to E Henry (22 April 1914).

62. PRO, MEPO 2 5962: "Procedures for Dealing with Disorderly Houses and Importuning" (1929–40); PRO: MEPO 2 3231: "Immorality in Parks and Open Spaces" (1929).

63. PRO, MEPO 3 2330: minute 6a, Supt./C Franklin to SCC (16 October 1943).

64. Mrs. C. Neville-Rolfe, "Sex Delinquency," in *The New Survey of London Life and Labour,* vol. 9, *Life and Leisure,* ed. Sir Hubert Llewellyn Smith (London: P. S. King and Son, 1935), 322. This trend was echoed by the dramatic decline in arrests for female prostitution in 1923 and 1929, following the furor surrounding the Fitzroy and Savidge cases. See PRO, HO 144 7044, section 40: Immorality in Hyde Park: Forwards copy of note of Conference held on 24 July 1923; PRO, HO 45 24902: "1929 Street Offences Bill/1928 Public Places (Order and Decency) Bill"; PRO, MEPO 2 3231: minute 13a, Supt./A J. Thornton (29 August 1929). For Joynson-Hicks's concerns, see "Hyde Park Charges," *NW,* 1 July 1929, 3.

65. PRO, HO 45 24960: "Homosexual Offences Conference" (1931).

66. PRO, MEPO 3 405: transcript of proceedings (5 January 1928), Q530–57.

67. PRO, HO 45 24960 (1931). In 1952, Commander Sheldon similarly responded to pressure from the British Travel and Holidays Association to "clean up" the West End: "I am reluctant to push for any drastic action against homosexuals which would only lead to complaints as it has done in the past." PRO, MEPO 2 9367, minute 5, Commander 1 R Sheldon (31 October 1952).

68. PRO, HO 45 24960 (1931).

69. PRO, MEPO 2 9367: minute 4a: "Prostitutes, Homosexuals, Pornography and Rowdyism in the West End" (30 October 1952).

70. Neville-Rolfe, "Sex Delinquency," 322.

71. Pamela Cox, *Bad Girls: Gender, Justice and Welfare in Britain, 1900–1950* (London: Palgrave, 2003), 17. See also Howard Taylor, "Rationing Crime: The Political Economy of Criminal Statistics since the 1850s," *Economic History Review* 51 (1998): 569–90.

72. I discuss this methodological approach in appendix 1 below. It has a deflationary impact on official criminal statistics. In an indexed comparison between 1937 and 1952—in which 1937 equals 100—the number of homosexual offences known to the police in the Metropolitan Police District rose from 100 to 342. The number of queer incidents resulting in legal proceedings increased to 232. These data are drawn from LMA, LCC PH GEN 19: Papers of Dr. Letitia Fairfield: "Homosexuality: Analysis by Police Districts of Homosexual Offences, 1937–53," table 1 (appendix), 329.

73. "War and Nightlife," *NW,* 25 February 1940, 6.

74. Since first sketched by Montgomery Hyde in 1970, this narrative has been uncritically reproduced, often near verbatim. See, for example, Hyde, *Other Love,* 213–15; Patrick Higgins, *Heterosexual Dictatorship: Male Homosexuality in Post-War Britain* (London: Fourth Estate, 1996); and David, *On Queer Street,* 163–64.

75. Michael S., interview by the author, July 1999.

76. PRO, HO 345 7: CHP 10: John Nott-Bower.

77. Jeffrey Weeks, *Sex, Politics and Society: The Regulation of Sexuality since 1800* (London: Longman, 1996), 240.

78. "Judges Are Shocked," *NW,* 1 November 1953, 2, emphasis added. For this retrospective distortion of source material, see also Hyde, *Other Love,* 213–15; and Weeks, *Coming Out,* 158–59.

79. Higgins, *Heterosexual Dictatorship,* 175.

80. PRO, HO 45 24960 (1931).

81. PRO, DPP 6 66: JB memo (14 October 1954).

82. PRO, HO 345 7: CHP 10: John Nott-Bower.

83. LMA, PS WLN A1 320–7 (1947); LMA, PS WLN A1 257–37 (1952); LMA, PS WLN A1 380–6 (1957).

84. See appendix 1.

85. "Sequel to Serious Charge," *IPN,* January 17 1935, 8. For the annotation of court registers with "reported to have committed suicide," see LMA, PS MAR A1 053 (28 June 1917).

INTRODUCTION TO PART 2

1. Hunter Davies, ed., *The New London Spy: A Discreet Guide to the City's Pleasures* (London: Anthony Blond, 1966), 222.

2. Michael Schofield, *Sociological Aspects of Homosexuality: A Comparative Study of Three Types of Homosexuals* (London: Longmans, 1965), 25–26, 79; and Gordon Westwood [pseud. Michael Schofield], *A Minority: A Report on the Life of the Male Homosexual in Great Britain* (London: Longmans, 1960).

3. NSA, C456 123 2–4: John Chesterman. See also NSA, C456 03 02: John Alcock; NSA, C456 122 01–08: Michael James; NSA: C547 43, Richard; NSA, C456 49: Frank Birkhill.

4. This discussion draws upon wider debates in history and human geography. See, in particular, Lynda Nead, *Victorian Babylon: People, Streets and Images in Nineteenth Century London* (New Haven and London: Yale University Press, 2000); Simon Gunn, *The Public Culture of the Victorian Middle Class: Ritual and Authority and the English Industrial City, 1840–1914* (Manchester: Manchester University Press, 2000); Rappaport, *Shopping for Pleasure;* Parsons, *Streetwalking the Metropolis;* Walkowitz, *City of Dreadful Delight;* and Nava and O'Shea, *Modern Times.*

CHAPTER 2

1. Robert Hutton, *Of Those Alone* (London: Sidgwick and Jackson, 1958), 9–10.

2. H. V. Morton, *The Nights of London* (London: Methuen and Co., 1932), 5. See also Walkowitz, *City of Dreadful Delight,* 46–50; and Rappaport, *Shopping for Pleasure.*

3. Hutton, *Of Those Alone,* 9–10.

4. Thomas Burke, *The London Spy: A Book of Town Travels* (London: Thornton Butterworth, 1922), 51–54.

5. Ruth Bowley, "Amusements and Entertainments," in *The New Survey of London Life and Labour,* vol. 9, *Life and Leisure,* ed. Sir Hubert Llewellyn Smith (London: P. S. King and Son, 1935), 51–52.

6. Thomas Burke, *The Streets of London through the Centuries* (London: B. T. Batsford, 1943), 134.

7. PRO, MEPO 3 2979: "Police Supervision of Hyde Park," minute 2a: DDI Kidd to Supt. (20 February 1936). See also "Hyde Park Arrest," *NW,* 8 January 1922, 5; PRO, MEPO 2 3231: "Immorality in Parks and Open Spaces" (1929); "Hyde Park after Dark," *NW,* 26 April 1931, 5; and "Hyde Park Scene," *NW,* 19 January 1936, 10.

8. Hutton, *Of Those Alone,* 9–10.

9. LMA, A PMC 98 9: annual report (1939), 26–27.

10. Xavier Mayne [pseud. Edward Prime Stevenson], *The Intersexes: A History of Similisexualism as a Problem in Social Life* (New York: Arno Press, 1975), 427–28.

11. Westwood [pseud. Schofield], *A Minority,* 83–84, 92.

12. NSA, C547 06: John Alcock.

13. PRO, MEPO 3 923: "Harry Raymond and Others Operating as a Blackmail Gang in Leicester Square," 203 UNC 1970, minute 9a, Insp. Parker to Supt./C (23 September 1937), which includes the statement of Ashley P. See also "Stories of Meeting in Piccadilly," *NW,* 23 September 1934, 4; and "I Talked with a Stranger," *NW,* 26 August 1951, 3.

14. LMA, PS HAM A 37: Ernest R., charged with importuning (22 May 1935).

15. See Matthew Hilton, *Smoking in British Popular Culture, 1800–2000* (Manchester and New York: Manchester University Press, 2000); "Men Lured to

Room," *NW,* 17 April 1934, 6; Peter Wildeblood, *A Way of Life* (London: Weidenfeld and Nicholson, 1956), 41; Angus Wilson, *Hemlock and After* (Harmondsworth: Penguin, 1962), 33–36, 107; Rodney Garland, *The Heart in Exile* (London: W. H. Allen, 1953), 62; LMA, PS HAM A 40: John L., charged with importuning (19 October 1938); and LMA, PS LAM B1 033: Cecil A., charged with importuning (3 August 1927).

16. "Clergyman Fined," *NW,* 4 June 1922, 6.

17. PRO, HO 345 12, CHP TRANS 8: PC Butcher and Darlington (7 December 1954).

18. PRO, HO 345 14, CHP TRANS 32: two witnesses called by the chairman (28 July 1955); PRO, HO 345 13, CHP TRANS 24: Peter Wildeblood (27 April 1955).

19. NSA, C547 06: John Alcock. This discussion of street life draws upon Chauncey, *Gay New York,* 189–90.

20. E. Hanmore, *The Curse of the Embankment: And the Cure* (London: P. S. King and Sons, 1935), 27, 70, 94; Driberg, *Ruling Passions,* 76; and Michael Davidson, *The World, the Flesh and Myself: The Autobiography of Michael Davidson* (London: Arthur Barker, 1962), 134–35.

21. NSA, C547 15: Pat.

22. "Shadowed in Strand," *NW,* 27 June 1926, 14; and "Three Men in a Flat," *NW,* 15 June 1930, 11.

23. "MP Changes Plea to Not Guilty," *NW,* 11 January 1953, 9; "MP to Appeal," *NW,* 25 January 1953, 7; PRO, HO 345 12: CHP TRANS 8: PC Butcher and Darlington (7 December 1954).

24. NSA, C547 06: John Alcock.

25. PRO, MEPO 2 1192: "Conditions in the Vicinity of the Union Jack Club" (1908–12).

26. "Waterloo Road Pests Sentenced," *IPN,* 30 April 1925, 7. A character in Reginald Underwood, *Flame of Freedom* (London: Fortune Press, 1936), 131, 162–79, calls Waterloo Road that "notoriously unsavoury spot." See also "Disgusting Scenes at a Night Coffee Stall," *IPN,* 11 August 1927, 4; "Waterloo Road Pests," *IPN,* 7 May 1925, 7; LMA, PS TOW B1 173: Harry M., charged with importuning (29 October 1927); LMA, PS TOW B1 168: Reginald S., charged with importuning (29 April 1927), and Horace D., charged with importuning (18 April 1927); LMA, PS TOW B01 167: Arthur C., charged with importuning (14 April 1927); LMA, PS TOW B01 165: John E., outraging public decency (17 March 1926); LMA, PS TOW B1 164: Joseph P., charged with importuning (17 January 1927); and LMA, PS TOW B01 049: Lewis H./William S., charged with importuning (24 December 1922).

27. PRO, CRIM 1 1194: Ronald G. and Michael R., charged with attempted buggery (28 May 1940), statement of John G.

28. LMA, PS TH A1 206 (3 January 1938).

29. LMA, PS TH A1 189 (2 May 1932). Other niches included a disused house in Tufton Street or beneath railway arches in Tower Street (Southwark). LMA, PS

WES A1 109 (19 May 1922); LMA, PS TOW A1 180 (10 September 1932); and LMA, PS LAM A1 138 (15 September 1947).

30. For the queer history of London's urinals and its relationship to developments in municipal sanitation, see Randolph Trumbach, "London," in *Queer Sites: Gay Urban Histories since 1600,* ed. David Higgs (London and New York: Routledge, 1999), 89–109; M. J. D. Roberts, "Public and Private in Early Nineteenth Century London: The Vagrant Act of 1822 and Its Enforcement," *Social History* 13, no. 3 (1988): 273–94; Pennybacker, *A Vision for London,* 192; and Angus McLaren, *The Trials of Masculinity: Policing Sexual Boundaries 1870–1930* (Chicago: University of Chicago Press, 1997), 194.

31. PRO, CRIM 1 906: Albert W. and Frederick C., charged with gross indecency (14 December 1937), statement of PS 106/S. Lawlor.

32. PRO, MEPO 3 990: "Use of Plainclothes Officers in Detecting Indecency Offences in Urinals," ADI/G Pierson to Supt./M (30 August 1933).

33. Ibid., DS G. Trucker to DDI (25 August 1933).

34. Weeks and Porter, *Between the Acts,* 175.

35. Michael S., interview.

36. See, for example, LMA, A PMC 42: patrolling officer's reports (4 March 1947, 23 August–18 September 1943); "Watchers at Victoria," *NW,* 28 March 1920, 4; "Gave Notice of Appeal," *NW,* 18 June 1922, 5; and "After an Operation," *NW,* 11 October 1931, 14.

37. Other urinals included, for example, those attached to the Tavern (Kennington), Plough and Harrow (King Street), the Constitution (Kings Road St. Pancras), or the Red Cow (Colet Gardens). See, for example, LMA, PS BOW A01 198 (15 July 1942); LMA, PS LAM A1 118 (9 December 1942); LMA, PS GRE A1 021 (20 December 1921); LMA, PS CLE A1 080 (19 September 1927); LMA, PS WES A1 109 (22 May 1922); LMA, PS WLN A1 324 (23 September 1947); and LMA, PS WLN A1 293 (6 April 1942).

38. See, for example, CLRO, MH: William R., charged with gross indecency (31 August 1952); CLRO, MH: Arthur R., charged with importuning (13 November 1952); CLRO, MH: William F., charged with importuning (14 January 1952); CLRO, MH: Jonathan N., charged with importuning (11 September 1957); CLRO, MH: Donald T., charged with importuning (12 September 1957); CLRO, MH: Samuel H., charged with importuning (12 September 1957); and CLRO, MH: Charles B., charged with importuning (24 September 1957).

39. LMA, PS OLD A1 142 (26 August 1947). See also LMA, PS OLD A1 109 (July, September, November 1937); LMA, PS OLD A1 144/145 (1947); LMA, PS OLD A1 163–65; LMA, PS OLD A1 165 (August, October, December 1952); and LMA, PS OLD A1 181 (January–March 1957).

40. LMA, PS BOW A1 143 (November 1932).

41. Driberg, *Ruling Passions,* 88, 147–48.

42. Emlyn Williams, *Emlyn: An Early Autobiography, 1927–1935* (London: Bodley Head, 1973), 18.

43. *For Your Convenience: A Learned Dialogue Instructive to all Londoners and London Visitors Overheard in the Theleme Club and Taken Down Verbatim by Paul Pry* (London: George Routledge and Sons, 1937), 1, 2, and 16. See also Houlbrook, "For Whose Convenience? Gay Guides, Cognitive Maps and the Construction of Homosexual London, 1918–67," in *Identities in Space: Contested Terrains in the Modern City since 1850,* ed. Simon Gunn and R. J. Morris (Aldershot: Ashgate, 2001), 165–86.

44. *For Your Convenience,* 36. Driberg reviewed the book for the *New Statesman* in 1937 and apparently knew "Pry's" identity. Driberg, *Ruling Passions,* 88. Burke's other works include *London in My Time* (London: Rich and Cowan, 1934), and *City of Encounters: A London Divertissement* (London: Constable and Company, 1932).

45. Ibid., 15, 20, 5. For the open secret, see Alan Sinfield, "Closet Dramas: Homosexual Representation and Class in Post-War British Theatre," *Genders* 9 (1990): 119–21.

46. Ibid., 9–10. "Busies" and "Dicks" are plainclothes detectives.

47. Ibid., 68.

48. Ibid., 55–56.

49. Ibid., 20.

50. Ibid., 52–53.

51. Ibid., 27.

52. See the monthly police returns presented to the Parks and Open Spaces Committee in the following: LCC, MIN 8932 (23 July 1920); LCC, MIN 8933 (September 1920); LCC, MIN 8773 (11 March 1921); LCC, MIN 8945 (June 1923); LCC, MIN 8954 (26 June 1925); LCC, MIN 8954 (19 June 1925); LCC, MIN 8955 (9 October 1925); LCC, MIN 8973 (26 April 1929); LCC, MIN 8983 (27 February 1931); LCC, MIN 8984 (27 March 1931); and LCC, MIN 8984 (1 May 1931).

53. LMA, PS HAM A 26 (August 1919).

54. LMA, PS MS A1 109–15 (January–December 1932).

55. Williams, *Emlyn,* 13. See also LMA, PS HAM A 34: Edward P. and George P., charged with gross indecency (2 June 1930).

56. PRO, MEPO 3 248: "Importuning: Right to be Dealt with by Jury": Insp. A Brennan (7 April 1915).

57. Ibid.

58. See, for example, PRO, MEPO 2 5815: "Hyde Park Prostitution/Indecency and Disorderly Conduct" (28 April 1903); PRO, CRIM 1 480 (1929), statement of PC 504/B Wardle; PRO, HO 144 7044: "Hyde Park Disturbance and Annoying and Insulting Behaviour" (1908–27), sec. 167700/24 (27 March 1922), sec. 167700/23 (9 March 1922); PRO, HO 45 24960: "Homosexual Offences Conference" (11 May 1931).

59. See, for example, LMA, PS HAM 37: Arthur E., charged with importuning (22 May 1935). See also LMA, PS HAM A 40: Herbert T., charged with importuning (21 December 1938); ibid., John B., charged with importuning (25 June 1939); ibid., John L., charged with importuning (19 October 1938); LMA, PS HAM 37: Ernest R., charged with importuning (22 May 1935); ibid., Harry W., charged with

importuning (30 April 1935); and LMA, PS HAM A 38: Ramsey M., charged with importuning (15 July 1937).

60. PRO, CRIM 1 480: statement of Stephen L.

61. LMA, PS HAM A 32: Leslie B. and William C., charged with indecency (23 November 1926). See also PRO, CRIM 1 433: John S. and William H., charged with buggery (1 June 1928); LMA, PS HAM A 26: Joseph B. and William B., charged with outraging public decency (19 October 1918); LMA, PS HAM A 34: James G. and Arthur C., charged with gross indecency (24 June 1931).

62. Stephen Humphries, *A Secret World of Sex: Forbidden Fruit; The British Experience, 1900–50* (London: Sidgwick and Jackson, 1988), 208.

63. Crisp, *Naked Civil Servant,* 155; Daley, *This Small Cloud,* 213; LMA, PS SWE A1 081 (20 April 1942); LMA, PS SWE A1 083 (2 November 1941, 5 November 1942, and 7 November 1942); LMA, PS SWE A1 100 (18 June 1947); LMA, PS SWE A1 120 (19 May 1952); LMA, PS SWE A1 121(2 April 1952).

64. NSA, C444 03 30a–32a: Alex Purdie.

65. Russell Davies, ed., *The Kenneth Williams Diaries* (London: HarperCollins, 1994), 60, 78–79, 100, 133.

66. Davidson, *World, the Flesh and Myself,* 121–22; see also Davidson, *Some Boys,* 101–5.

67. James Gardiner, *A Class Apart: The Private Pictures of Montague Glover* (London: Serpents Tail, 1992), 66.

68. Davidson, *World, the Flesh and Myself,* 121–22; PRO, HO 45 16223: "Powers under the Hyde Park Regulations: Park Regulations Amendment Act" (1926).

69. LMA, A PMC 11: PPP subcommittee minute book (14 September 1953).

70. Westwood, *A Minority,* 89–90. See also James Kirkup, *A Poet Could Not But Be Gay: Some Legends of My Lost Youth* (London: Peter Owen, 1991), 118; NSA, C456 122 02: Michael James; and Garland, *Heart in Exile,* 26.

71. LMA, Public Morality Council: 33rd annual report (1932), 33.

72. PRO, HO 345 7, CHP 17: memorandum submitted by Paul Bennett, metropolitan magistrate for Marlborough Street, emphasis added.

73. PRO, MEPO 2 1691: "Immorality in Cinematograph Halls," minute 1: MRA to Sir E. Henry (18 May 1916).

74. Ibid., Supt./J West (25 March 1916).

75. For a sample of these cases, see LMA, PS WES A1 164 (30 January 1937); LMA, PS BOW A01 111 (5 September 1927); LMA, PS MAR A1 236 (21 January 1952); LMA, PS CLE A1 112 (1 June 1937, 22 June 1937); LMA, PS LAM A1 063 (15 November 1927); LMA, PS NLO A1 111 (24 October 1947); LMA, PS OLD A1 164 (20 November 1952); LMA, PS SWE A1 009 (20 May 1922); LMA, PS TH A1 159 (1 September 1922); LMA, PS WES A1 90 (31 August 1917); PRO, CRIM 1 880: Alfred Y, charged with indecent assault (1936) is a more detailed account.

76. Weeks and Porter, *Between the Acts,* 151; Rappaport, *Shopping for Pleasure,* 178–206; Tracy Davis, "Indecency and Vigilance in the Music Halls," in *British*

Theatre in the 1890s: Essays on Drama and the Stage, ed. Richard Foulkes (Cambridge: Cambridge University Press, 1992), 111–31; and Pennybacker, *Vision for London,* 227–40.

77. Hutton, *Of Those Alone,* 36–37.

78. Taylor Croft, *The Cloven Hoof: A Study of Contemporary London Vices* (London: Denis Archer, 1932), 66.

79. "Wickedest Gang in London," *John Bull* (hereafter *JB*), 25 July 1925, 11.

80. Humphries, *Secret World,* 206–7. See also the case in the Prince of Wales in LMA, PS BOW A1 111 (5 September 1927); and "Author Acquitted," *NW,* 16 October 1927, 15.

81. PRO, HO 45 24570: "Improper Behaviour in London Cinemas," sec. 176622/5, Attendance and Molestation of Children at Cinematograph performances (13 May 1916).

82. LMA, PS BOW A01 113 (30 November 1927); PRO, HO 45 24570: sec. 176622/10, report of the commissioner (18 July 1916); G. M., 6 September 1916. For the Prince of Wales and Collins, see Weeks and Porter, *Between the Acts,* 92–94; Davidson, *World, the Flesh and Myself,* 168; and LMA, PS NLO A1 058 (20–27 September 1932).

83. Public Morality Council: 36th annual report (1935), 32.

84. "The Passing of an Empire," *NW,* 23 January 1927, 1. For NVA opposition to the renewal of the licenses of the Pavilion, Alhambra, and Empire, see FL, NVA, volume 6, box 194: executive minutes (26 September 1916, 28 November 1916). For the expansion of cinema going, see Jeffrey Richards, *The Age of the Dream Palace: Cinema and Society in Britain, 1930–39* (London and New York: Routledge, 1989).

85. See PRO, HO 45 24570 (1909–21); and PRO, MEPO 2 1691 (1912–16). Charrington was superintendent of the Tower Hamlets Mission and a member of the National Vigilance Association and the Central South London Free Church Council. For his career campaigning against public "vice," see William Fishman, *The Streets of East London* (London: Duckworth, 1992), 64–67; and G. Thorne, *The Great Acceptance: The Life Story of FN Charrington* (London: Hodder and Stoughton, 1912).

86. PRO, HO 45 24570: sec. 176622/10: report of the commissioner of police (18 July 1916): G. M., 6 September 1916; ibid., sec. 176622/4: report of agent of Mr. Charrington (15 April 1916).

87. Ibid.

88. Ibid., sec. 176622/10: report of the commissioner of police (18 July 1916); H. M. Charrington to Mr. Aitken (3 October 1916).

89. PRO, MEPO 2 1691 (1912–16); PRO, HO 45 24570: section 176622/4: report of agent of Mr. Charrington (15 April 1916).

90. See PRO, MEPO 2 1691: 976726: Supt./J West (25 March 1916); PRO: HO 45 24570: sec. 176622/12: Lighting of Cinemas (30 July 1917); ibid., sec. 176622/11: Cinematograph Arrangements: Improvements In (6 December 1916); ibid., sec. 176622/10: report of the commissioner of police (18 July 1916): H. M. Charrington to Mr. Aitken (3 October 1916).

91. "Cinema Pest Caught," *NW,* 7 February 1937, 3.

92. LMA, PS BOW A01 197 (8 June 1942).

93. LMA, PS BOW A01 171 (1 April 1937). For men's use of the Eros News Cinema (Piccadilly) and Praed Street News Theatre, see LMA, PS BOW A02 009 (22 March 1937); and LMA, PS MAR A1 236 (21 January 1952). For other West End and suburban cinemas including the Odeon and Cameo (Leicester Square), the Trocadero (Old Kent Road), or Trinity (Southwark), see Davies, *Kenneth Williams,* 22, 62; LMA, PS BOW A01 175 (23 December 1937); LMA, PS WES A1 90 (31 August 1917); LMA, PS SWE A1 098 (22 January 1947); LMA, PS TH A1 204 (16 July 1937); LMA, PS LAM A1 063 (15 November 1927); LMA, PS TOW A1 196 (11 October 1937); LMA, PS TOW A1 245 (20 May 1952); and LMA, PS TOW A1 248 (2 Aug. 1952; 25 Aug. 1952).

94. Davies, *Kenneth Williams,* 73. See also Margaret O'Brien and Allen Eyles, *Enter the Dream House: Memories of Cinemas in South London from the Twenties to the Sixties* (London: BFI, 1993), 105; LMA, PS BOW A01 301 (17 July 1957); LMA, PS BOW A01 251 (16 January 1952); and LMA, PS BOW A02 055 (8 September 1952).

95. LMA, GLC DG EL 3 W19: Biograph Cinema.

96. PRO, MEPO 2 5815: GR 26 PA 199: Hyde Park Policing: H. G. Peel to HM Office of Works (1 July 1922). For these anxieties and the deployment of National Union of Women's Workers patrols, see PRO, HO 45 141896: "Indecency on Hampstead Heath" (1906–19); LMA, LCC MIN 8714 (24 November 1919, 11 April 1919, 11 July 1919, 25 July 1919, 10 October 1919, 18 June 1920, 8 July 1920, 23 June 1922, 7 July 1922, and 13 July 1923); LMA, LCC MIN 8945: Hampstead Heath Protection Society (30 June 1923); LMA, LCC MIN 8932: Deptford Council of Christian Churches (8 July 1920); PRO, MEPO 2 1708: "Indecency in Hyde Park—Women Patrol Witnesses" (1915–16).

97. For wider attempts to order public space, see Pennybacker, *Vision for London,* 191–201, 210–40. Chauncey, *Gay New York,* 203–4.

98. LMA, A PMC 43: patrolling officer's report (30 July 1950).

99. PRO, HO 345 7; PRO, CHP 10: memorandum submitted by Sir John Nott-Bower; PRO, MEPO 2 5815: GR 139605: Supt./A Bean to commissioner (28 April 1903), sec. 139605/8: Supt./G Wall to commissioner (9 November 1912); and PRO, HO 144 7044 (1908–27).

100. For the salience of these injunctions to officers' decision making, see PRO, MEPO 3 990: PC 528/M Cooper (25 August 1933); PRO, CRIM 1 547: Harold R., charged with importuning, PC 208/C McKechnie (11 March 1931); PRO, CRIM 1 617: Charles P. and Ralph B., charged with gross indecency: PC 660/L Knight (13 September 1932); PRO, CRIM 1 2187: James L., charged with importuning: PC 258/C Renshaw (13 November 1951).

101. PRO, CRIM 1 2487: Aloysius B., charged with importuning: PC 552/H Ramskill (12 October 1954), statement of accused.

102. PRO, MEPO 3 405: Francis Champain, charged with indecency (1927), attachment 35a: Street Offences Committee, report of the subcommittee (28

January 1928). For the surprising frequency of this defense, see LMA, PS HAM A 42: FG D: Indecency (26 August 1942); LMA, PS LAM B1 273: Edward F. and Ernest D., charged with indecency (16 July 1937); "Dismissed the Charge," *NW,* 21 March 1926, 9; and "Priest Bound Over," *NW,* 14 May 1944, 2.

103. LMA, LCC MIN 8715 (16 July 1926).

104. PRO, HO 45 16223: "Powers under the Hyde Park Regulations," sec. 509445/8: Office of Work Minutes (21 May 1928).

105. LMA, LCC MIN 8715 (16 October 1925); LMA, LCC MIN 8955: Mrs. J. Davidson to Council (2 September 1925); ibid., Chief Officer's Report (16 October 1925).

106. PRO, HO 345 12: CHP TRANS 12, PC/C Butcher (7 December 1954), Q635, 7.

107. LMA, LCC MIN 8715 (1 April 1927), item 28; and LMA, LCC MIN 8781 (18 July 1930). In 1930, they asked the Hampstead MBC to conduct the requisite work: LMA, LCC MIN 8715: agenda item 14: Hampstead Heath Convenience (18 July 1930).

108. LMA, LCC MIN 8715 (31 January 1930).

109. LMA, LCC MIN 8717 (3 December 1948, 27 January 1950).

110. LMA: A PMC 11: PPP subcommittee minute book (17 November 1949), 1950–53.

111. LMA, LCC MIN 8717 (2 April 1946); LMA, LCC MIN 8717 (8 October 1948), item 45: Urgent Repair Works; LMA, LCC MIN 8718 (5 October 1951).

112. Between April 1930 and December 1932, seventy men were arrested around the Adelphi. PRO, MEPO 2 4309: "Adelphi Estate Bill," minute 3a: Abstract of evidence given by ASDI Woods (17 July 1933).

113. Ibid., minute 1a: Mr. L. Fladgate to H. M. Howgrave (secretary NSY): 14 July 1933.

114. PRO: HO 345 7: CHP 11: memorandum submitted by Harold Sturge, metropolitan magistrate, Old Street.

115. PRO, HO 345 12: CHP TRANS 8, Q633, 3.

116. Anomaly, *The Invert and His Social Adjustment* (London: Balliere Tindall and Cox, 1948), 7–8. For this mapping of urban types onto urban spaces, see David Sibley, *Geographies of Exclusion: Society and Difference in the West* (London and New York: Routledge, 1995), 9–10.

117. Weeks and Porter, *Between the Acts,* 92–94.

118. *Walking after Midnight: Gay Men's Life Stories,* Hall-Carpenter Archives, Gay Men's Oral History Group (London and New York: Routledge, 1989), 34.

119. LMA, PS LAM B1 410: Arthur C., charged with importuning (13 May 1942).

120. Hutton, *Of Those Alone,* 43.

121. LMA: PS HAM 37: Harold C., charged with importuning (8 May 1935).

122. *Walking after Midnight,* 34.

123. Williams, *Emlyn,* 18; Croft, *Cloven Hoof,* 61, 65; and Michael S., interview.

124. Hyde, *The Other Love*, 207.

125. James Polchin, "Having Something to Wear: The Landscape of Identity on Christopher Street," in *Queers in Space: Communities/Public Places/Sites of Identity*, ed. Gordon Ingram, Anne-Marie Bouthilette, and Yolanda Retter (Seattle: Bay Press, 1997), 388–89.

126. PRO, MEPO 3 2331: "Gross Indecency/Importuning: Legal Aid in Cases Likely to Cause Publicity" (1943).

127. *For Your Convenience*, 66–67.

128. Gordon Westwood [pseud. Michael Schofield], *Society and the Homosexual* (London: Victor Gollancz, 1952), 121.

129. Ibid., 74.

130. CLRO, MH/GH (1952, 1957).

131. CLRO, GH (22 August 1952).

132. Hyde, *Other Love*, 206.

133. Westwood, *A Minority*, 74.

CHAPTER 3

1. Williams, *Emlyn*, 8, 75, 139 142, 149.

2. Ibid., 12, 204, 205.

3. Ibid., 13.

4. Charlie was the piano player. PRO, MEPO 3 758: "Caravan Club, 81 Endell Street WC1: Disorderly House/Male Prostitutes," minute 8c, SDI Campion to Supt. (16 August 1934).

5. Westwood [pseud. Schofield], *Society and the Homosexual*, 126.

6. PRO, CRIM 1 903: Billie Joice and others charged with keeping a disorderly house, application at Bow Street Police Court (14 November 1936), statement of DS Miller NSY.

7. See B. D. Nicholson, "Drink," in *The New Survey of London Life and Labour*, vol. 9, *Life and Leisure*, ed. Sir Hubert Llewellyn-Smith (London, 1935), 254.

8. PRO, CRIM 1 633: Laurence B., charged with gross indecency (1933), exhibit 1: diary of Sidney C. See also PRO, MEPO 3 923: "Harry Raymond and Others Operating as a Blackmail Gang in Leicester Square," minute 13b, statement of Ian F. (26 November 1937); PRO, MEPO 3 362: Roland B., "Attempted Murder of Philip E.," 202 UNE 1151 Insp. Bradley to insp. (26 August 1929).

9. Croft, *The Cloven Hoof*, 66.

10. The customers of the Running Horse in Shepherd's Market included women in collar, tie, and evening dress, and one man "of very effeminate appearance . . . his face was powdered, lips rouged, hair dyed blonde, wearing a small black hat in feminine style over the left eye and high-heeled shoes. He was wearing his overcoat in the form of a ladies cape." PRO, MEPO 2 4485: "Running Horse Public house: Permitting Drunkenness/Disorderly Conduct of Undesirables," minute 63a, SDI/C Buller (31 July 1937), and PS 44/C Gowen (1 March 1937).

11. Williams, *Emlyn*, 18.

12. Croft, *The Cloven Hoof*, 66; *The Blue Guide: Muirhead's London and Its Environs* (London: Macmillan, 1922), 22; "Brazen Blackmail Gang," *JB*, 30 May 1925, 13; and PRO, MEPO 3 923: minute 13a, statement of John O. (23 October 1937).

13. Williams, *Emlyn*, 17. Ives is quoted in Cook, *London and the Culture of Homosexuality*, 26. See Chauncey, *Gay New York*, 163.

14. PRO, MEPO 3 758: minute 8a, PC 453/E Mortimer (26 July 1934). See also, for example, "Caravan Club Case," *Times*, 27 October 1934, 14; and "Sensational Court Sequel to Club Raid," *NW*, 26 August 1934, 1.

15. PRO, CRIM 1 387: Bobby B. and (11) others, charged with keeping a disorderly house: exhibit 10, Bill to Bert L. (7 January 1927). See also PRO, CRIM 1 903 (1936–37); "Sinks of Iniquity," *NW*, 29 January 1933, 8; LMA, LCC MIN 4386: commissioner of police to LCC: 2 Archer Street Notting Hill and 50 Baker Street (14 December 1932); Croft, *The Cloven Hoof*, 67; and Weeks and Porter, *Between the Acts*, 10.

16. Wildeblood, *Against the Law*, 40. See also Lehmann, *In the Purely Pagan Sense*, 52–33, 127–28, 162–65; Garland, *The Heart in Exile*, 40–49, 237–40; Wildeblood, *A Way of Life* (London: Weidenfeld and Nicholson, 1956), 31–40; Daniel Farson, *Soho in the Fifties* (London: Michael Joseph, 1988), 74–99; NSA, C456 06 01: Bernard Dobson; and NSA, C456 88 2: David Godin.

17. PRO, MEPO 3 4485: minute 63a, statement of PS 44/C Gowen; minute 7b, statement of PS Gavin (24 August 1936).

18. Peter Parker, *Ackerley: A Life of J. R. Ackerley* (London: Constable, 1988), 112–13; and Kirkup, *A Poet Could Not But Be Gay* (London: Constable, 1991), 194–96.

19. Michael Wishart, *High Diver* (London: Quartet Books, 1978), 65; Hoare, *Noel Coward*, 156–57; Philip Hoare, *Serious Pleasures: The Life of Stephen Tennant* (London: Hamish Hamilton, 1990), 244, 255; and Vickers, *Cecil Beaton*, 236.

20. LMA, ACC 3527 232: M. Joseph, *Goodbye Piccadilly 1960*.

21. LMA, ACC 3527: James Agate, *Trocadero 1896–1946*, 10; Cook, *London and the Culture of Homosexuality*, 145.

22. Williams, *Emlyn*, 151–52, 204–5. See also Bryan Connon, *Beverley Nichols: A Life* (London: Constable, 1991), 64.

23. "A New Song for Maurice," *Evening Standard*, 14 November 1931, 10.

24. Hutton, *Of Those Alone*, 38.

25. Ibid.

26. NSA, C547 11: John Alcock; NSA, C444 03 30a–32a: Alex Purdie; Margaret Drabble, *Angus Wilson: A Biography* (London: Secker and Warburg), 133; and Lancaster, *Brian Howard*, 426.

27. PRO, MEPO 3 4485: minute 63a, statement of PS 44/C Gowen (1 March 1937).

28. Sydney Moseley, *The Night Haunts of London* (London: Stanley Paul and Co., 1920), 43.

29. Croft, *The Cloven Hoof,* 66.

30. PRO, MEPO 3 629: "Melodies Bar Club: Liquor Offences," minute 10: WC Carter A1 (13 February 1940); "Sinks of Iniquity," *NW,* 29 January 1933, 8; LMA, LCC MIN 11097: solicitor's report on unlicensed public dancing (23 February 1927).

31. PRO, HO 345 7: CHP 10, John Nott-Bower.

32. PRO, HO 345 12: CHP TRANS 7, John Nott-Bower (7 December 1954).

33. PRO, HO 345 7: CHP 10, John Nott-Bower.

34. See, for example, LMA, PS TOW B1 168: Reginald S., charged with importuning (29 April 1927); LMA, PS BOW B1 168: Horace D., charged with importuning (18 April 1927); LMA, PS TOW B1 164: Joseph P., charged with importuning (17 January 1927).

35. PRO, MEPO 2 4485: minute 2a, SDI Gavin to supt. (14 August 1936); and minute 63b, report of supt. C. (3 August 1937).

36. Action for harboring prostitutes under section 76 of the 1910 Licensing Act was impossible—prostitution was de jure a female offence. There were no grounds for individual prosecutions for gross indecency. Ibid., minutes 3, 8, 9, 10, 14, 27, 28, and 36 (1936–37).

37. Ibid., minute 47, WAC1 (16 January 1937); and minute 54, JND (24 February 1937).

38. Ibid., minutes 56, 58, 62, 86, 87a, 91, and 95a (1937–38).

39. "West End Public House Pests," *NW,* 25 October 1953, 4; "Fitzroy Man Fine," *Daily Express,* 1 December 1955; LMA, A PMC 43: patrolling officer's reports (25 October 1949); "Coffee Stall in Soho," *NW,* 3 January 1955, 5; and "Van Parked off Piccadilly Circus," *NW,* 25 February 1951, 3.

40. "Mayfair's Bohemian Clean-up," *Daily Mail,* 23 September 1936.

41. For official anxieties surrounding these constraints, see PRO, HO 144 22487: "Clubs Registration Bill" (1939); PRO, HO 45 18810: "Proposed Legislation for Clubs: 1936–41"; PRO, HO 45 18488: "Bottle Parties: 1932–40"; PRO, HO 45 16205: "Police Supervision of Nightclubs, 1924–35"; and PRO, HO 45 14216: "Restrictions on Nightclubs" (1926–31).

42. PRO, MEPO 923: 203 UNC 1936, minute 11a, DS Banhill to DDI (24 April 1937).

43. PRO, MEPO 3 758, minute 13b, Holborn town clerk to commissioner (17 August 1934); minute 8a, Anon to Lord Trenchard (11 August 1934).

44. PRO, MEPO 2 4485: minute 1, C2 (4 August 1936); PRO, MEPO 3 629: SDI/C Gavin to Supt./C (26 January 1939); and PRO, HO 345 8: CHP 47, War Office, appendix A, "Homosexuality in London."

45. LMA, PMC, 31st annual report (1930), 26.

46. LMA, PMC, 34th annual report (1933), 23–4. See also PMC, 35th Annual report (1934).

47. Including Sam's Café (Rupert Street) in 1941, the Bouchin Street Coffee Stall in 1949–50, and several all-night cafes in 1955–56. See LMA, A PMC 41:

patrolling officer's reports (November 1941); LMA, A PMC 43: patrolling officer's report (25 October 1949, 30 July 1950); LMA, A PMC 80, Mr. Tomlinson to Lady Coleville, letter dated 29 August 1955.

48. LMA, A PMC 4: executive minute book and agenda (31 October 1940); and LMA, A PMC 41: patrolling officer's reports (August–November 1941).

49. Ibid. (November 1941).

50. Ibid. (27 June 1944).

51. Ibid. (20 January 1943).

52. The phrase is from Farson, *Soho in the Fifties,* 22–23. See also "Prisoners in Dock Numbered," *ES,* 20 February 1933, 8; and "Numbered Prisoners at Old Bailey," *MA,* 21 February 1933, 3.

53. "Dance Hall Orgies," *NW,* 23 January 1927, 4.

54. PRO, MEPO 2 4485: minute 39a, SDI/C Welley (16 December 1936).

55. PRO, HO 345 7: Sir John Nott-Bower. On this, see Chauncey, *Gay New York,* 336–37.

56. "Raid on a Public House," *NW,* 13 September 1953, 7; "West End Public House Pests," *NW,* 25 October 1954, 4.

57. "Sinks of Iniquity," *NW,* 29 January 1933, 8.

58. PRO, CRIM 1 735: Rex vs. Jack Neave and others, charged with keeping a disorderly house (1934); PRO, MEPO 3 758 (1934); and "Caravan Club Disclosures," *NW,* 28 October 1934, 19. Known as "Iron Foot Jack," Neave was a well-known Soho character into the 1950s, living as a strongman, club manager, antique dealer, con artist, and street phrenologist. He acquired a remarkable degree of literary fame, including a published biography: Mark Benney, *What Rough Beast? A Biographical Fantasia on the Life of Professor J. R. Neave, Otherwise Known as Iron Foot Jack Neave* (London: Peter Davies, 1939). Neave was also "the Professor" in George Scott Moncrieff, *Café Bar* (London: Wishart and Co., 1932). Farson, *Soho in the Fifties,* 92–93, describes one of his scams.

59. "Numbered Prisoners on their Defence," *NW,* 24 January 1937, 19; and PRO, CRIM 1 903 (1936). For Barnes, see NSA, B1143 4: 1; The Black Sheep of the Family; Paul Bailey, *Three Queer Lives: An Alternative Biography of Fred Barnes, Naomi Jacob and Arthur Marshall* (London: Hamish Hamilton, 2001).

60. PRO, MEPO 2 4485: minute 63a, statement of PS 44/C Gowen (1 March 1937).

61. Ibid., minute 63a, PC 82/C Hoare (8, 6 March 1937); and PS 44/C Gowen (1 March 1937).

62. Michael S., interview.

63. *Walking after Midnight,* 12.

64. NSA, C444 03 30a–32a: Alex Purdie.

65. "Raid on a Public House," *NW,* 13 September 1953, 7; and "West End Public House Pests," *NW,* 25 October 1954, 4.

66. PRO, MEPO 2 4485: minute 63a, statement of PC 82/C Hoare (8 March 1937).

67. Ibid., minute 46a, statement of Insp. C. Weston (15 January 1937).

68. Alkarim Jivani, *It's Not Unusual: A History of Gay and Lesbian Life in the Twentieth Century* (London: Michael O'Mara, 1997), 52; and "Wickedest Gang in London," *JB*, 25 July 1925, 11.

69. Williams, *Emlyn*, 17. The Corner House's daytime and late night clientele was similarly different: PRO. MEPO 3 362: Insp. Bradley (26 August 1929); PRO, PCOM 9, 31: "Note of the West London Mission Social Welfare and Rescue Department" in "Reports to the Prison Commissioners" (26 November 1928).

70. "West End Nest of Vice Smoked Out," *NW*, 5 March 1933, 18.

71. See "Nightclub Disclosure," *NW*, 12 August 1928, 9; and FL, NVA: case files C107: Sergeant Goddard Bribery (1928).

72. Hugh David, *The Fitzrovians: A Portrait of Bohemian Society, 1900–1955* (London: Michael Joseph, 1988), 241. See also LMA, A PMC 41: patrolling officer's report (June 1941); Wildeblood, *Against the Law*, 40; Michael S., interview.

73. Weeks and Porter, *Between the Acts*, 174; Farson, *Soho in the Fifties*, 40–45, 71–72; NSA, C456 122 01 02: Michael James; NSA, C547 43: Richard; NSA, C547 06 C1: Unnamed Manager of A&B Club; Lehmann, *In the Purely Pagan Sense*, 210–12; and Garland, *Heart in Exile*, 128.

74. NSA, C547 06 C1: Unnamed Manager of A&B Club; NSA, C547 15: Pat.; NSA, C547 11: John Alcock; NSA, C547 21: interview with unnamed male; Michael S., interview; Weeks and Porter, *Between the Acts*, 174, 183.

75. Crisp, *Naked Civil Servant*, 84.

76. Quotation from NSA, C456 122 02: Michael James; see also Lehmann, *In the Purely Pagan Sense*, 210–12; Garland, *Heart in Exile*, 128; NSA, C547 06 C1: unnamed manager of A&B Club; NSA, C456 31 01: Tom Cullen; NSA, C456 89 01: Patrick Trevor-Roper; and NSA, C547 15: Pat.

77. Westwood [pseud. Schofield], *A Minority*, 130–1. For the Spartan's similar clientele, see NSA, C456 122 02: Michael James.

78. NSA, C547 11: John Alcock.

79. NSA, C456 71 01: Antony Grey.

80. PRO, HO 345 12, CHP TRANS 7: John Nott-Bower.

81. NSA, C547 11: John Alcock.

82. See, for example, PRO, CRIM 1 758: Harry H. and Henry E., charged with gross indecency (1935); NSA, C444 03 30a–32a: Alex Purdie; Weeks and Porter, *Between the Acts*, 138, 140, 174–75; Garland, *Heart in Exile*, 182; Davies, *Kenneth Williams Diaries*, 60, 71; and Michael Nelson, *A Room in Chelsea Square* (London: Cape, 1958), 128.

83. LMA, ACC 3527 233: untitled newspaper cutting from the *Caterer*, January 1909; "Front of the House," *Lyons Journal*, December 1949; and John Kings, "The Four Corners of London," n.d.

84. Judith Walkowitz, " 'The 'Vision of Salome': Cosmopolitanism and Erotic Dancing in Central London, 1908–1918," *American Historical Review* 108, no. 2 (2003): 338.

85. "Caravan Club Scene," *NW*, 26 August 1934, 3.

86. PRO, MEPO 2 10108: "Allegations that the Café Royal is Frequented by Known Prostitutes and Confidence Tricksters," minute 1: Supt./C Whitstable (25 February 1920).

87. Burke, *London Spy,* 301–2.

88. See, for example, Connon, *Beverley Nichols,* 51, 54–55; Michael de la Noy, *The Journals of Denton Welch* (London: Alison and Busby, 1984), 77; PRO, MEPO 3 923, 203 UNC 1970: minute 9a, statement of Edward S. (1 September 1937). Metropolitan bohemia and elite queer circles also overlapped in venues like Elsa Lanchester's Cave of Harmony Club (Charlotte Street) and Ivor Novello and Constance Collier's Fifty-Fifty. Terry Castle, *Noel Coward and Radclyffe Hall: Kindred Spirits* (New York: Columbia University Press, 1996), 20; and Richard Huggett, *Binkie Beaumont: Eminence Grise of the West End Theatre, 1933–73* (London: Hodder and Stoughton, 1989), 77–78. Similar networks existed in 1950s Soho venues like the Colony Room and Gargoyle. Farson, *Soho in the Fifties,* 45–51; David, *The Fitzrovians,* passim; and Michael Luke, *David Tennant and the Gargoyle Years* (London: Weidenfeld and Nicholson, 1991).

89. Burke, *London Spy,* 10–12; "Artist Arrested," *NW,* 20 June 1926, 12; "Shadowed in Strand," *NW,* 27 June 1926; "Believed the Sailor," *NW,* 21 May 1922, 5; and LMA, PS TOW B1 168: Reginald S., charged with importuning (29 April 1927).

90. Weeks and Porter, *Between the Acts,* 95, 174, 184; PRO, MEPO 3 923, 203 UNC 1970: minute 9a, Insp. Parker to Supt./C (23 September 1937).

91. "The Passing of an Empire," *NW,* 23 January 1927, 1.

92. Venues like Fortes Café and the Queen's Bar remained popular into the 1950s: NSA, C547 11: John Alcock; LMA, A PMC 80: Mr. L. J. to Mr. Tomlinson (1 June 1955); and "MP to Appeal against Bow Street Conviction," *NW,* 25 January 1953, 7.

93. Baedecker, *London and Its Environs: Handbook for Travellers* (Leipzig: Karl Baedecker, 1923), 308.

94. Drabble, *Angus Wilson,* 28; PRO, CRIM 1 387: exhibit 10, Eric to Peter P. (29 November 1926); PRO, CRIM 1 633: exhibit 1, diary of Sidney C. (3 April 1932); and Davies, *Kenneth Williams,* 58, 70.

95. For the Standard, see NSA, C456 06 1: Bernard Dobson; and NSA, C456 123: John Chesterman.

96. See Mort, *Cultures of Consumption,* 151–54; Judith Summers, *Soho: A History of London's Most Colourful Neighbourhood* (London: Bloomsbury, 1989); and Arthur Tietjen, *Soho: London's Vicious Circle* (London: Allan Wingate, 1956), 123–24.

97. "An Alien's Audacity," *JB,* 16 October 1926, 15; and Crisp, *Naked Civil Servant,* 33.

98. See "Van Parked off Piccadilly Circus," *NW,* 25 February 1951, 3; LMA, A PMC 80: Mr L. J. to Mr. Tomlinson (1 June 1955; 2 August 1955); and "Coffee Stall in Soho," *NW,* 3 January 1955. There were similar clusters of venues in other "bohemian" locales, particularly Fitzrovia, Seven Dials, and Shepherd's Market—

frequented by a "cosmopolitan set of undesirables" and "homo-sexual perverts." See PRO, MEPO 3 629: Melodies Bar Club, result of inside observation, SDI Gavin to Supt. (6 November 1939); ibid., SDI Gavin to Supt./C on alleged irregularities (26 October 1939); Burke, *London Spy,* 303; and Weeks and Porter, *Between the Acts,* 139–40.

99. Burke, *London Spy,* 182–99; James Bone, *The London Perambulator* (London: Jonathon Cape, 1931), 149–51; "Grave Miscarriage of Justice," *JB,* 24 January 1925, 11; PRO, MEPO 3 923: 203 UNC 1970, minute 13b, statement of Ian F. (21 October 1937); "Blackmail Most Foul," *JB,* 27 February 1926, 18; LMA, PS TOW B01 167: Arthur C., charged with importuning (14 April 1927); and LMA, PS TOW B1 168: Reginald S., charged with importuning (29 April 1927).

100. See, for example, Kate Meyrick, *Secrets of the 43 Club* (Dublin: Parkgate Publications, 1994), passim; Sidney Felstead, *The Underworld of London* (London: John Murray, 1923), 3–9; H. V. Morton, *The Nights of London* (London: Methuen and Co., 1932), 98–100, 167–70; and Moseley, *Night Haunts of London,* 14–21.

101. Westwood, *A Minority,* 73. See also NSA, C456 123 4: John Chesterman; NSA: C547 15: Pat; Michael S., interview.

102. LMA, A PMC 80: Mr. L. J. to Mr. Caughlin (1 July 1955). See also, for example, Burke, *London Spy,* 187–88, 199–200; NSA, C457 11: John Alcock; Williams, *Emlyn,* 378–79; and "Charlie Brown Passes," *NW,* 12 June 1932, 14.

103. Williams, *Emlyn,* 156; LMA, PS TOW B1 168: Horace D., charged with importuning (18 April 1927); LMA, PS TOW B1 164: Joseph P., charged with importuning (17 January 1927); LMA, PS TOW B1 049: Lewis H. and William S., charged with importuning (24 December 1922); LMA, PS TOW B1 167: Arthur C.. charged with importuning (14 April 1927); LMA, PS TOW B1 168: Reginald S., charged with importuning (29 April 1927).

104. Peter Alexander, *William Plomer: A Biography* (Oxford: Oxford University Press, 1989), 181; Lehmann, *In the Purely Pagan Sense,* 127–29; PRO, MEPO 3 362: "Roland B., Attempted murder of Philip E.," Insp. Bradley to Insp. (26 August 1929). For the Alexandra, see PRO, MEPO 3 404: "Gross Indecency with Boys," 213/IMP/203: Sir Charles H. and Major M.: Alleged Sodomites (27 February 1923).

105. Garland, *Heart in Exile,* 57–58.

106. LMA, LCC MIN 11088: solicitor's report on the Adelphi Rooms (16 June 1926); and LMA, LCC MIN 11066: SDI/D Bailey (10 May 1924).

107. Burke, *London Spy,* 303. See also Weeks and Porter, *Between the Acts,* 95.

108. PRO, MEPO 3 404: 213 / IMP / 716, Robert M., sentenced on charges of gross indecency, minute 11s: result of observation upon Major M. (April 1927).

109. "Plague Spot Raided," *NW,* 27 February 1927. This account draws upon "Dance Hall Sensation," *NW,* 5 December 1926, 13; "Dance Hall Decorum," *NW,* 12 December 1926, 11; "Dance Hall Orgies," *NW,* 23 January 1927, 4; "Alleged Scandalous Scenes in a Dance Hall," *IPN,* 16 December 1926, 4; "Alleged Disgraceful Orgies at a West End Dance," *IPN,* 9 December 1926, 4; and LMA: LCC MIN 11097: solicitor's report: "Adelphi Rooms: Unlicensed public dancing"

(23 February 1927). See also the 1927 raid on a party in Fitzroy Square, attended by many men who also frequented the Adelphi Rooms: PRO, CRIM 1 387 1927: exhibit 10, Leslie K. to Bobby B. (29 January 1926).

110. Richard Smith, "Ron Storme: Obituary," *Guardian,* 2 December 2000, 28; and NSA, C547 07: Tricky Dicky. I draw here on Chauncey, *Gay New York,* 8–9.

111. Stephen Whittle, "Consuming Differences: The Collaboration of the Gay Body with the Cultural State," in *The Margins of the City: Gay Men's Urban Lives,* ed. Whittle (Aldershot: Ashgate, 1994), 27–38; and David Bell and Jon Binnie, *The Sexual Citizen: Queer Politics and Beyond* (Oxford: Polity, 2000), 96–107.

CHAPTER 4

1. LMA, LCC MIN 9621: special meeting (16 October 1931) "Incidents at Baths," *NW,* 18 October 1931, 7; and "LCC and Turkish Baths," *Times,* 25 November 1931, 15.

2. Michael S., interview.

3. Weeks and Porter, *Between the Acts,* 163.

4. Bartlett, *Mr. Clive and Mr. Page.*

5. NSA, C547 15: Pat.

6. Bermondsey Metropolitan Borough Council, *Public Baths and Washhouses. Souvenir of the Opening of the New Central Baths* (London: MBC publication, 1927), 1–14. See also Agnes Campbell, *Report on Public Baths and Washhouses in the United Kingdom* (Edinburgh: Carnegie United Kingdom Trust, 1918).

7. Jerry White, *Rothschild Buildings: Life in an East End Tenement Block; 1887–1920* (London: Routledge and Kegan Paul, 1980), 48.

8. Sam Lambert, ed., *London Night and Day* (London: Architectural Press, 1951), unpaginated. This overview draws upon Malcolm Shifrin's superb Web site, http://www.victorianturkishbath.org (accessed April 2004). See also the records of the Board of Trade's Companies Registration Office: PRO, BT 31 3253 19102: Savoy Turkish Bath Company Ltd. (1883); PRO, BT 31 2882 15942: Woolwich Turkish Hot and Cold Bath Company Ltd. (1881); PRO, BT 31 2902 16125: Finsbury Park Turkish Baths Company Ltd. (1881); PRO, BT 31 6516 45844: Earls Court Turkish Bath Company Ltd. (1895); Baedecker, *London and Its Environs,* 17; LMA, LCC PC MASS 21: case file for Savoy Turkish Baths Company, notepaper (15 August 1916); LMA,: LCC MIN 9818: Inspection of Turkish Baths (6 February 1931).

9. Mayne [pseud. Stevenson], *The Intersexes,* 440, 513. Mayne's suggestion is echoed in Ian Anstruther, *Oscar Browning: A Biography* (London: John Murray, 1983), 138–41; and Aronson, *Prince Eddy and the Homosexual Underworld,* 72–73, 197.

10. Shifrin, *Victorian Turkish Baths;* LMA, LCC MIN 9642 (1 February 1948); LMA, LCC MIN 9913: new application for licence (1 September 1948); NSA, C547 15: Pat; Michael S., interview.

11. See Seth Koven, "From Rough Lads to Hooligans: Boy Life, National Culture and Social Reform," in *Nationalisms and Sexualities,* ed. Andrew Parker,

Mary Russo, Doris Somner and Patricia Yaeger (London and New York: Routledge, 1992); and Cocks, *Nameless Offences,* 157–98.

12. A. J. Langguth, *Saki: A Life of Hector Hugh Munro* (London: Hamish Hamilton, 1981), 187.

13. *Walking After Midnight,* 67. For men's appropriation of YMCA facilities in American cities, see Chauncey, *Gay New York,* 151–58; John Gustav-Wrathall, *Take the Young Stranger by the Hand: Same Sex Relationships and the YMCA* (Chicago and London: University of Chicago Press, 1999).

14. "Incidents at Baths," *NW,* 18 October 1931, 7.

15. Stevenson also identified a vapor bath frequented by "uraniads" (lesbians) on Ladies' Days. Mayne [pseud. Stevenson], *Intersexes,* 440, 513.

16. Connon, *Beverley Nichols,* 61.

17. Hutton, *Of Those Alone,* 53.

18. Michael S., interview.

19. Garland, *The Heart in Exile,* 238. See also NSA, C547 21: unnamed Male interviewee; Weeks and Porter, *Between the Acts,* 163–64.

20. Davies, *Kenneth Williams Diaries,* 143. See also LMA, PS TOW A1225 (6 October 1947), in which a man was arrested for indecent assault at Bermondsey Baths.

21. LMA, PS GRE A1 079 (1 February 1952).

22. *Walking After Midnight,* 67; NSA: C456 90 01: Tony Garrett. Duncan Grant visited the baths regularly while living nearby in Fitzroy Street in the 1930s: Frances Spalding, telephone conversation with the author, 14 June 1999.

23. Michael S., interview.

24. Davies, *New London Spy,* 226.

25. NSA, C547 15: Pat.

26. Ibid.

27. This description is taken from LMA, LCC MIN 9905: chief officer's report (8 August 1947).

28. LMA, LCC MIN 9618: special meeting (11 April 1930).

29. "Turkish Bath Scene," *NW,* 11 May 1930, 5.

30. NSA, C547 15: Pat.

31. LMA, LCC MIN 9618: special meeting (11 April 1930).

32. NSA, C547 15: Pat. For the Imperial, see NSA, C456 03 02: John Alcock.

33. Ibid.

34. LMA, LCC MIN 9618: special meeting (11 April 1930).

35. Ibid.

36. NSA, C547 15: Pat.

37. *Baedecker's London and Its Environs,* 17.

38. Lambert, *London Night and Day.*

39. NSA, C456 03 02: John Alcock.

40. "Accused Major in the Box," *Evening Standard,* 15 February 1933, 4.

41. Alexander, *William Plomer,* 158.

42. Michael S., interview.

43. Ibid.

44. Rupert Hart-Davis, *Hugh Walpole: A Biography* (London: Rupert Hart-Davis, 1952), 167, 193.

45. LMA, LCC MIN 9621: special meeting (16 October 1931).

46. NSA C456 03 02: John Alcock.

47. PRO, CRIM 1 633: Lawrence B.: Buggery, charged with gross indecency (1933), statement of Sidney C.

48. Humphrey Carpenter, *Benjamin Britten: A Biography* (London: Faber, 1992), 107.

49. LMA, PS GRE A1 079 (1 February 1952).

50. Davies, *New London Spy,* 226. In 1927, the Turkish Baths at Bermondsey, charged 3s 6d on weekdays and 2s 6d on a Saturday. The Russian baths were cheaper: 1 shilling. Metropolitan Borough of Bermondsey, *Public Baths,* 23–24.

51. Weeks and Porter, *Between the Acts,* 163.

52. Davies, *New London Spy,* 226.

53. In Weeks and Porter, *Between the Acts,* 163.

54. LMA, PS CLE A1 185 (10 May 1952).

55. Shifrin, *Victorian Turkish Baths.*

56. Weeks and Porter, *Between the Acts,* 162.

57. "Turkish Baths Secrets," *NW,* 13 September 1930, 9. See also "Turkish Bath Scene," *NW,* 11 May 1930, 5.

58. LMA, LCC MIN 9618: special meeting (11 April 1930).

59. NSA: C547 15: Pat.

60. Michael S., interview.

61. NSA: C547 15: Pat.

62. LMA, LCC MIN 9905: report by chief officer (15 October 1947).

63. Davies, *New London Spy,* 133.

64. LMA, LCC MIN 9823: letter in respect of the Savoy case (25 November 1931).

65. See PRO, J 13 18484: Supreme Court of Judicature: Higher Court of Justice: Companies Court (Winding Up Proceedings): case of Nevill's Turkish Baths Ltd. (1947).

66. Davies, *New London Spy,* 133. For the baths' place within this cosmopolitan milieu, see Jeffrey Bernard, *Low Life* (London: Duckworth, 1986), 31–32.

67. LMA, LCC MIN 9618: special meeting (11 April 1930); "Turkish Bath Scene," *NW,* 11 May 1930, 5. See also LMA, LCC MIN 9572: agendas (7 October 1916, 23 January 1920).

68. "LCC and Turkish Baths," *Times,* 25 November 1931, 15. "Incidents at Baths," *NW,* 18 October 1931, 7.

69. LMA, LCC MIN 9823: letter in respect of the Savoy case (25 November 1931).

70. For the NVA's "systematic visitation" of "massage establishments," their lobbying of the Met, LCC, and Home Office, and the introduction of the General Powers Acts, see PRO, HO 45 17371: "By-Laws: LCC Massage Establishments"

(1916–38); LMA, LCC MIN 9572: agendas: 1915–22; FL, NVA: correspondence files, box 107: S85, "Massage and Other Establishments: Correspondence and Proof of Evidence re: 1930–1"; William Coote, *A Romance of Vigilance* (London: National Vigilance Association, 1916), 131–32; FL, NVA, executive minutes, vol. 6, box 194 (26 May 1914, 27 July 1915, 31 October 1916). These powers were widely deployed against establishments suspected of permitting heterosexual impropriety: see, for example, LMA, PC MASS 1 9 (14 April 1943); LMA, LCC MIN 9599 (6 February 1920, 5 March 1920); and LMA, LCC MIN 9609 (15 May 1925).

71. FL, NVA, correspondence files, box 107: S85, unsigned to Herbert Bryant (22 December 1930).

72. Michael S., interview.

73. LMA, LCC MIN 9818: chief officer's report: Inspection of Turkish Baths (6 February 1931).

74. Ibid.

75. "Turkish Bath Scene," *NW,* 11 May 1930, 5.

76. FL, NVA, correspondence files, box 107: S85, unsigned to Herbert Bryant (22 December 1930).

77. LMA, LCC MIN 9576 (30 April 1941).

78. LMA, LCC PC MASS 1 8: Massage etc Establishments: record of special cases: Jermyn Street Turkish Baths Ltd: (1947); LMA, LCC MIN 9913: chief officer's report (3 October 1948); LMA, LCC MIN 9640 (25 June 1947); LMA, LCC MIN 9641 (15 October 1947); LMA, LCC MIN 9905: chief officer's report (15 October 1947); and LMA, LCC MIN 9913: chief officer's report (13 October 1948).

79. LMA, LCC MIN 9913: chief officer's report (13 October 1948); and LMA, LCC MIN 9643 (13 October 1948).

80. LMA, LCC MIN 9572: agendas, 1915–22; LMA, LCC MIN 9598: January 1917–December 1918. See also LMA, LCC MIN 9614: chief officer's report (17 February 1928); LMA, LCC MIN 9609: chief officer's report: complaint against the Savoy Turkish Baths (20 November 1925). For an overview of the regulation of the Savoy in this period, see LMA, LCC MIN 9573: agendas, 1923–31. The 1917 incident was alluded to by Captain Spencer in his cross-examination during the "Black Book" trial, though there is little evidence to support his claim that the Admiralty "conducted a very thorough campaign" to "stamp out" such practices. See Hoare, *Wilde's Last Stand,* 123; PRO, HO 144 1498: "The Black Book Mentioned in the Criminal Libel Case against Mr. Pemberton Billing MP" (1918); and "Mr. Billing's Defence," *Times,* 31 May 1918.

81. LMA, LCC MIN 9814: solicitor's papers (9 May 1930); LMA, LCC MIN 9617: Savoy case, special investigation (18 October 1929); ibid., Chief Officer's Report (29 November 1929). LMA: LCC MIN 9619 (25 July 1930).

82. The details of the case are taken from LMA: LCC MIN 9618: special meeting (11 April 1930); and ibid., special meeting (9 May 1930). It was widely reported. See "Turkish Baths Secrets," *NW,* 13 September 1930, 9; and "Turkish Bath Scene," *NW,* 11 May 1930, 5.

83. LMA, LCC MIN 9822 (16 October 1931); LMA, LCC MIN 9621: special meeting (16 October 1931).

84. Ibid. See also "Incidents at Baths," *NW,* 18 October 1931, 7.

85. "Alleged Incident at Turkish Baths," *IPN,* 22 October 1931, 3.

86. For the appeal hearing, see LMA, LCC MIN 9823 (27 November 1931); and "LCC and Turkish Baths," *Times,* 25 November 1931, 15.

87. LMA, LCC MIN 9577: opposed application for a licence (8 October 1952).

88. LMA, LCC PC MASS 18: case number ML 5318: A. B. W., Pavinsky's' Beauty Parlour, 41 Belsize Park Gardens NW3 (1952). Albert's premises appear to have already attracted official attention: LMA, LCC MIN 9577: chief officer's report: suitability of a licensee (30 April 1952).

89. LMA, LCC PC MASS 18: case number ML 5318 (1952).

90. LMA, LCC MIN 9647 (8 October 1952).

CHAPTER 5

1. James Bone, *The London Perambulator* (London: Jonathan Cape, 1931), 116–7.

2. Ibid., 120. For the association between Englishness and domesticity between the wars, see Alison Light, *Forever England: Femininity, Englishness and Conservatism between the Wars* (London and New York: Routledge, 1991). See also Moran, *Homosexual(ity) of Law,* 56.

3. Davidson, *World, The Flesh and Myself,* 134–35.

4. PRO, HO 345 8, CHP 61: memo submitted by the Law Society.

5. LMA, PS TOW A1 243 (17 January 1952).

6. "Man's Grave Offences," *IPN,* 8 March 1934, 4.

7. "Plague Spot Raided," *NW,* 27 February 1927, 13.

8. LMA, PS MAR A1 053 (28 June 1917); LMA, PS MAR A1 089 (13 June 1927); LMA, PS BOW A1 141 (6 July 1932); LMA, PS BOW A2 005 (12 July 19320; LMA, PS CLE A1 114 (2 October 1937); LMA, PS WES A1 186 (11 May 1942); LMA, PS BOW A01 255 (13 August 1952); LMA, PS TOW A1 243 (7 January 1952).

9. See, for example, Paul Groth, *Living Downtown: The History of Residential Hotels in the United States* (Berkeley: University of California Press, 1994); and Howard Chudacoff, *The Age of the Bachelor: Creating an American Subculture* (Princeton: Princeton University Press, 1999).

10. See Leonore Davidoff, "The Separation of Home and Work? Landladies and Lodgers in Nineteenth- and Twentieth-Century England," in *Fit Work for Women,* ed. Sandra Burman (London: Croom Helm, 1979), 64–97; Martin Daunton, *House and Home in the Victorian City: Working Class Housing, 1850–1914* (London: Edward Arnold, 1983); Andrzej Olechnowicz, *Working-Class Housing in England between the Wars: The Becontree Estate* (Oxford: Clarendon Press, 1997); and Patricia Garside, *The Conduct of Philanthropy: The William Sutton Trust, 1900–2000* (London: Athlone Press, 2000).

11. Sinclair, *Metropolitan Man,* 105.

12. Westwood [pseud. Schofield], *A Minority,* 180.

13. Chris Hamnett and Bill Randolph, *Cities, Housing and Profits: Flat Break Up and the Decline of Private Renting* (London: Hutchinson, 1988), 7–8, 215.

14. *The Blue Guide,* 17.

15. Ben Weinrebe and Christopher Hibbert, *The London Encyclopaedia* (London: Papermac, 1983), 351–52.

16. LMA, LCC MIN 4386: agenda papers (8 July 1931).

17. *The Blue Guide,* 11, 15, 17. See also *Baedecker's London and Its Environs,* 11.

18. PRO, MEPO 3 362: "Roland B., charged with attempted murder of Philip E." (1929–31).

19. Hart-Davis, *Hugh Walpole,* 240; Maureen Borland, *Wilde's Devoted Friend: A Life of Robert Ross, 1869–1918* (London: Leonard Publishing, 1990); John Stuart Roberts, *Siegfried Sassoon, 1886–1967* (London: Richard Cohen Books, 1999), 65–67; and Marek Kohn, *Dope Girls: The Birth of the British Drug Underground* (London: Lawrence and Wishart, 1992), 77.

20. J. R. Ackerley, *My Father and Myself* (London: Bodley Head, 1968), 123.

21. LMA, PS WES A1 89 (2 January 1917); Adrian Wright, *John Lehmann: A Pagan Adventure* (London: Duckworth, 1998), 119; and Richard Huggett, *Binkie Beaumont: Eminence Grise of the West End Theatre, 1933–1973* (London: Hodder and Stoughton, 1989), 260.

22. Hamnett and Randolph, *Cities, Housing and Profits,* 17–27; Gavin Weightman and Steve Humphries, *The Making of Modern London, 1914–1939* (London: Sidgwick and Jackson, 1984), 34; and Donald Olsen, *The Growth of Victorian London* (Harmondsworth: Penguin, 1976), 90–91, 116–20.

23. Weinrebe and Hibbert, *London Encyclopaedia,* 223; and Drabble, *Angus Wilson,* 143.

24. Isherwood, *Christopher and His Kind,* 83.

25. Felstead, *Underworld of London,* 64.

26. Ibid., 129. See also Olsen, *Growth of Victorian London,* 77–78, 131–40, 149, 168, and 174–79.

27. "Police Begin Big West End 'Clean Up,'" *NW,* 31 January 1937, 8. See also "Stories of Meeting in Piccadilly," *NW,* 23 September 1934, 4; Crisp, *The Naked Civil Servant,* 50; "Adventure of Mr. H.," *NW,* 27 April 1930, 6; and "Three Men in a Flat," *NW,* 15 June 1930, 11.

28. Hoare, *Noel Coward,* 61; Hutton, *Of These Alone,* 207; *Walking After Midnight,* 11; Bernard in Porter and Weeks, *Between the Acts,* 154; and Williams, *Emlyn,* 245. See also "Shadowed in Strand," *NW,* 27 June 1926, 14.

29. PRO, HO 345 7 CHP 5: Sir Laurence Dunne.

30. "Dance Hall Sensation," *NW,* 5 December 1926, 13; PRO, MEPO 3 362: minute 9e: Insp. Bradley to insp. (26 August 1929).

31. See "Man at Food of Bed," *NW,* 15 March 1953, 9; "Police Begin Big West End 'Clean Up,'" *NW,* 31 January 1937, 8; LMA, ACC 2385 191: calendars of prisoners, CCC (12 January 1937).

32. Alexander, *William Plomer,* 161, 163, 196, 239. See also Connon, *Beverley Nichols,* 57; LMA, ACC 2385 183: calendars CCC (7 February 1933); PRO, MEPO 3 923, 203 UNC 1970: minute 13b: statement of Ian F.; PRO, CRIM 1 461: Charles R, charged with buggery (19 March 1929).

33. Quoted in Nigel Nicolson, ed., *The Sickle Side of the Moon: The Letters of Virginia Woolf: Volume 5, 1932–35* (London: Hogarth Press, 1979), 261–22. See also Parker, *Ackerley,* 164; Alexander, *William Plomer,* 195–96; and Hugh David, *Stephen Spender: A Portrait with Background* (London: Heinemann, 1992), 181.

34. LMA, PS MAR A1 053 (28 June 1917).

35. See Davidson, *World, the Flesh and Myself,* 134–55; and "Caravan Club Scene," *NW,* 26 August 1934, 3.

36. NSA, C547 11: John Alcock.

37. See NSA, C547 43: *Richard;* NSA, C456 123 4: John Chesterman; NSA, C456 122 2: Michael James; and Sebastian Faulks, *The Fatal Englishman: Three Short Lives* (London: Constable, 1991), 245.

38. Burke, *City of Encounters,* 26–27.

39. Westwood [pseud. Schofield], *A Minority,* 181, emphasis added.

40. George Orwell, *Down and Out in Paris and London* (London: Secker and Warburg, 1949), 210.

41. Lionel Rose, *Rogues and Vagabonds: Vagrant Underworld in Britain, 1815–1985* (London and New York: Routledge, 1988), 63, 71–72; Morton, *Nights of London,* 44; and Orwell, *Down and Out,* 129–37.

42. Sir Hubert Llewellyn-Smith, "Introduction," *The New Survey of London Life and Labour: Volume 1* (London: P. S. King and Sons, 1930), 23.

43. Orwell, *Down and Out,* 203–4. See also Frank Gray, *The Tramp: His Meaning and Being* (London: J. M. Dent and Sons, 1931), 157–71.

44. Rose, *Rogues and Vagabonds,* 60–75; Pennybacker, *A Vision for London,* 183–90.

45. Rose, *Rogues and Vagabonds,* 60.

46. Michael Sheridan, *Rowton Houses, 1892–1954* (London: Rowton Houses Ltd, 1956); and "Wonderful Rowton Houses," *IPN,* 24 June 1926, 2.

47. PRO, MEPO 3 362: attached: Rex vs. B. and M., summary of report on statements: Insp. Bradley to Insp.: statements of William O.; Wilfred T.; Joseph M.; Charles P.; James M. (26 August 1929).

48. PRO, MEPO 3 990: "Use of Plainclothes Offices in Detecting Indecency Offences in Urinals," Wontners Solicitors to Supt. (5 August 1933).

49. "Caught Red-Handed," *IPN,* 21 January 1932, 7.

50. PRO, CRIM 1 1194: John G. and Michael R. charged with attempted buggery (1940).

51. "Coffee Stall Meeting," *NW,* 12 March 1922, 3.

52. Orwell, *Down and Out,* 147.

53. LMA, PS WOO A1 010 (6 July 1927).

54. LMA, PS CLE A1 114 (2 October 1937); LMA, PS TH A1 177 (12 November 1927). See also PRO, HO 144 1098: "Long Sentences for Sexual Offenders," memo to home secretary (21 September 1910).

55. PRO, HO 144 22298: "Criticism of Elderly Judge's Treatment of Homosexual Offences" (1922–8), minute 2: Messrs. Wontners to home secretary.

56. LMA, PS TOW A1 193 (6 March 1937).

57. Orwell, *Down and Out*, 158.

58. Ibid., 160.

59. NSA, 90 02: Tony Garrett.

60. *Walking after Midnight*, 61.

61. *The Blue Guide*, 319.

62. Jivani, *It's Not Unusual*, 66; and Weeks and Porter, *Between the Acts*, 10–11, 99. See also "Believed the Sailor," *NW*, 21 May 1922, 5; "Bogus Naval Man," *NW*, 20 December 1925, 4; and "Caravan Club Scene," *NW*, 26 August 1934, 3.

63. LMA, PS TOW A1 249 (6 November 1952).

64. PRO, AIR 20 9061: "Air Ministry: Union Jack Club and Hostel," minute 101a: extract from minutes of SCWF meeting (21 April 1953).

65. Ibid.

66. NSA, C547 11: John Alcock.

67. PRO, MEPO 3 923, 203 UNC 1970: minute 9a, statement of Edward S. (11 September 1937); and *The Blue Guide*, 20.

68. Jivani, *It's Not Unusual*, 69; Davidson, *World, the Flesh and Myself*, 82; and "Edinburgh Man Convicted on Grave Charges," *IPN*, 8 March 1928, 8.

69. PRO, CRIM 1 1194: John G. (1940).

70. "Hotels on Our Blacklist," *JB*, 30 January 1926.

71. "The Greed of Gleed," *JB*, 26 December 1925; "Midnight Horrors," *JB*, 27 March 1926, 13; "Hotels on Our Blacklist," *JB*, 30 January 1926; and "An Edgware Road House of Ill Fame," *IPN*, 24 December 1925, 7.

72. "Queenie at It Again," *JB*, 20 June 1925; PRO, HO 45 24649: Queenie Gerald: Conviction for Keeping a Disorderly House (1913–27).

73. "Strand District "Hotels" Used for Improper Purposes," *IPN*, 24 June 1926, 7; "Two Vile Hotels," *JB*, 3 July 1926, 8; and "Evil of the Strand," *NW*, 20 June 1926, 4.

74. NSA, C547 15: Pat.

75. See "Advertised for Youth," *NW*, 26 July 1925, 12; Wildeblood, *A Way of Life*, 41; Michael S., interview; and PRO, MEPO 3 923, 203 UNC 1970: minute 11c, Harold G.

76. LMA, PS BOW A01 069 (13 October 1917).

77. LMA, PS BOW A01 083 (19 January 1922); and PRO, HO 144 22298: minute 430 931 1: Wontners's Solicitors to home secretary (29 March 1922).

78. LMA, PS BOW A01 173 (15 June 1937); LMA: PS BOW A01 297 (18 February 1957); and Drabble, *Angus Wilson*, 28. See also LMA, PS BOW A01 170 (1 March 1937); and "Pageboy's Story of Visits to Hotel," *NW*, 7 March 1937, 15.

79. NSA, C547 15: Pat.

80. Cecil Chapman, *The Poor Man's Court of Justice: Twenty-Five Years as a Metropolitan Magistrate* (London: Hodder and Stoughton, 1926), 90.

81. Ibid., 95.

82. Ibid., 94. See also PRO, MEPO 2 1192, "Local Supervision: Conditions in the Vicinity of the Union Jack Club" (1908–12); PRO, MEPO 2 431: "MR JD Bairstow (Central South London Free Church Council): Brothels in Vicinity of the Union Jack Club" (1908–12).

83. "Hotels on Our Blacklist," *JB*, 30 January 1926; PRO, HO 45 22676: "Disorderly Houses: Metropolitan Police Powers of Prosecution" (1907–49); PRO, MEPO 2 5962: "Procedures for Dealing with Disorderly Houses and Importuning," minute 64: MRA (20 February 1940); ibid., minute 67a, HGG M Division to ACC (7 March 1940).

84. PRO, MEPO 3 923: 203 UNC 1970: minute 11c, statement of Harold G.

85. "Stories of Meeting in Piccadilly," *NW*, 23 September 1934, 4.

86. LMA, PS TOW B01 049: Lewis H. and William S., charged with importuning (24 December 1922).

87. Ibid.

88. PRO, HO 45 24570: "Improper Behaviour in London Cinemas," minute 10: GM after visit from Mr. Charrington and Mr. Crowley (6 September 1916).

89. For Aplin's, see "Two Vile Hotels," *JB*, 3 July 1926, 8; "Evil of the Strand," *NW*, 20 June 1926, 4. For the law, see PRO, MEPO 2 5962 (1933–47); PRO, HO 45 2267 (1907–49); Judith Walkowitz, *Prostitution and Victorian Society: Women, Class and the State* (Cambridge: Cambridge University Press, 1980); and Petrow, *Policing Morals*, 147–66.

90. LMA, PS BOW A01 173 (15 June 1937). See also LMA, PS BOW A01 069 (13 October 1917); LMA, PS BOW A01 222 (16 January 1947); and LMA, PS BOW A01 297 (18 February 1957).

91. "A Gap in the Law," *NW*, 9 March 1930, 9; and "Shocking Story of Man and Two Boys," *IPN*, 13 March 1930, 3.

92. Martin Daunton, "Housing," in *The Cambridge Social History of Britain, 1750–1950: Volume Two*, ed. F. M. L. Thompson (Cambridge: Cambridge University Press, 1996), 195.

93. Wildeblood, *A Way of Life*, 142.

94. PRO, MEPO 2 4485: minute 63b, report of Supt. C. (8 September 1935).

95. Williams, *Emlyn*, 118.

96. NSA, C456 49: Frank Birkhill.

97. "Adventure of Mr. H.," *NW*, 27 April 1930, 6.

98. NSA, C54 11: John Alcock.

99. Westwood [pseud. Schofield], *A Minority*, 178.

100. Emlyn Williams, *George: An Early Autobiography* (London: Hamish Hamilton, 1961), 443–44; and Williams, *Emlyn*, 18–19, 61–62, 115–18, 128, 172, 245–46.

101. PRO, MEPO 2 4485: minute 63b, report of Supt. C. (8 September 1935); and "Caravan Club Scene," *NW,* 26 August 1934, 3.

102. LMA: PS BOW A01 141: 6 July 1932. LMA: PS BOW A02 005: 12 July 1932.

103. Westwood [pseud. Schofield], *A Minority,* 178.

104. LMA, A PMC 80: "Homosexuality": L. J. to Caughlin (1 July 1955); ibid., L. J. to Tomlinson (1 June 1955).

105. Ibid., L. J. to Lady Coleville (7 July 1955).

106. Ibid., L. J. to Caughlin (1 July 1955); and L. J. to Lady Coleville (19 October 1955).

107. Schofield, *Sociological Aspects Of Homosexuality,* 26.

108. Ibid., 79.

109. Ibid., 106–7.

110. Westwood [pseud. Schofield], *Society and the Homosexual,* 132.

111. John Tosh, *A Man's Place: Masculinity and the Middle-Class Home in Victorian England* (New Haven and London: Yale University Press, 1999), 13.

112. Huggett, *Binkie Beaumont,* 327–28, 338. See also Davies, *Kenneth Williams Diaries,* 42, 51–52; Wildeblood, *A Way of Life,* 85–95; Vickers, *Cecil Beaton,* 85–97; and Hoare, *Noel Coward,* 73, 80, 87–88, 109.

113. NSA, C547 11: John Alcock.

114. Sharon Marcus, *Apartment Stories: City and Home in Nineteenth Century Paris and London* (Berkeley: University of California Press, 1999), 3.

115. PRO, MEPO 2 4485: minute 23a: statement of PC 144/C Medhurst (26 October 1936).

116. PRO, MEPO 3 362: "Roland B.: Attempted Murder of Philip E." (1929–31); "Brutal Attack on Man in Mayfair Flat," *IPN,* 22 August 1929, 2; "Mayfair Flat Outrage," *IPN,* 5 September 1929, 5; "Met in Piccadilly," *NW,* 8 September 1929, 6; and "Upheaval in Flat," *NW,* 1 September 1929, 12.

117. See, for example, "A Flat in Disorder," *NW,* 17 May 1925, 5; and "Man Attacked and Robbed in a Pimlico Attic," *IPN,* 27 November 1930, 4.

118. "Money or Exposure," *NW,* 11 March 1928, 3. For blackmail see, for example, PRO, MEPO 3 923: minute 9a, Insp. Parker to Supt C. (23 September 1937); "Parted with £10000," *NW,* 10 April 1927, 6; and "Adventure of Mr. H.," *NW,* 27 April 1930, 6.

119. Marcus, *Apartment Stories,* 12, 85–87.

120. "Mayfair Flat Outrage," *IPN,* 5 September 1929, 5.

121. Croft, *The Cloven Hoof,* 67–68.

122. NSA, C547 11: John Alcock. See also NSA, C547 21, unnamed male interviewee; and Lionel Fielden, *The Natural Bent* (London: Andre Deutsch, 1960), 58.

123. LMA, ACC 2385 171: calendars: CCC (8 February 1927).

124. PRO, CRIM 1 387 (8 February 1927): statements of PS 42/D Spencer; PC 504/D Gavin.

125. "Plague Spot Raided," *NW,* 27 February 1927, 13.

126. PRO, CRIM 1 387: information and complaint of CI/D Sygrove (8 November 1927).

127. NSA, C547 15: Pat. Contemporary novels support his suggestion: Mary Renault, *The Charioteer* (London: Longmans, 1962), 130–77; Lehmann, *In the Purely Pagan Sense*, 33–35; Angus Wilson, *Hemlock and After*, 100–2.

128. "Brazen Blackmail Gang," *JB*, 30 May 1925, 13.

129. PRO, CRIM 1 906: Billie Joice and others, charged with keeping a disorderly house: statement of DS Murray (12 November 1937).

130. PRO, CRIM 1 387: Supt. D. Collins.

131. Ibid.

132. See PRO, CRIM 1 387: legal arguments before the recorder (18 February 1927).

133. PRO, MEPO 2 3281: "Lady Malcolm's Servant's Ball," 26 PP 2694: minute 9b: PC 488/B Adams to SDI (23 November 1932).

134. PRO, CRIM 1 480: Herbert W., charged with attempting to procure an act of gross indecency (1929), statement of Mr. L.

135. Garland, *The Heart In Exile*, 106.

INTRODUCTION TO PART 3

1. PRO, CRIM 1, 903: Billie Joice and others, charged with keeping a disorderly house, depositions and application at Bow Street Police Court: statement of DS Murray (14 November 1936); "Numbered Prisoners on Their Defence," *NW*, 24 January 1937, 19.

2. Steven Maynard, "'Respect your Elders: Know Your Past': History and the Queer Theorists," *Radical History Review* 75 (1999): 69–71.

3. Partridge, *Dictionary of the Underworld*, 545–49.

4. Westwood [pseud. Schofield], *Minority*, 35.

5. See, for example, Weeks and Porter, *Between the Acts*, 49, 95; and Davidson, *World, the Flesh and Myself*, 134. The increasing use of "gay" after the Second World War reflected the influence of U.S. servicemen. Weeks and Porter, *Between the Acts*, 158; D. J. West, *Homosexuality: A Frank and Practical Guide to the Social and Medical Aspects of Male Homosexuality* (Harmondsworth: Pelican Books, 1960), 50–51; and Wildeblood, *Against the Law*, 29.

6. See also PRO, CRIM 1, 639: Austin S. and (33) others, charged with keeping a disorderly house, statement of PC 139/F Labbatt; Weeks and Porter, *Between the Acts*, 49, 158; and Davies, *Kenneth Williams Diaries*, 25, 31, 52.

CHAPTER 6

1. PRO, CRIM 1, 387: Robert B. and others, charged with keeping a disorderly house (1927), statements of PS 42/D Spencer and PC 504/D Gavin.

2. "Dance Hall Orgies," *NW*, 23 January 1927, 4.

3. "Brazen Blackmail Gang," *JB,* 30 May 1925, 13; "A Modern Gomorrah," *JB,* 13 June 1925, 18; and "Wickedest Gang in London," *JB,* 25 July 1925, 11. See also Daley, *This Small Cloud,* 156.

4. Judith Butler, *Gender Trouble: Feminism and the Subversion of Identity* (London and New York: Routledge, 1990); and Susan Bordo, *Unbearable Weight: Feminism, Western Culture and the Body* (Berkeley: University of California Press, 1993), 38. See also Ruth Ford, "The Man-Woman Murderer: Sex Fraud, Sexual Inversion and the Unmentionable Article in 1920s Australia," *Gender and History* 12, no. 1 (2000): 158–96; and Marjorie Garber, *Vested Interests: Cross-Dressing and Cultural Anxiety* (Harmondsworth: Penguin, 1993).

5. NSA, C547 11: John Alcock. See, for example, the occupations of men arrested for sexual or public order offences in LMA, A PMC 41 48: patrolling officer's reports (December 1941); LMA, ACC 2385 191: calendars of prisoners, CCC (12 January 1937); LMA, ACC 2385 185: CCC calendars (16 October 1934); LMA, ACC 2385 183: CCC calendars (7 February 1933); and LMA, ACC 2385 171: CCC calendars (8 February 1927).

6. NSA: C444 03 48a–49a: John Alcock; NSA, C456 03 01: John Alcock.

7. Crisp, *Naked Civil Servant,* 61.

8. Ibid. See also Chauncey, *Gay New York,* chapter 2.

9. Susanne Davis, "Sexuality, Performance and Spectatorship in Law: The Case of Gordon Lawrence, Melbourne 1888," *Journal of the History of Sexuality* 7, no. 3 (1997): 405.

10. Anomaly, *Invert,* 9. See also Reginald Underwood, *Hidden Lights* (London: Fortune Press, 1937), 147–53.

11. PRO, MEPO 3, 405: "Francis Champain: Indecency," minute 4a, Mr. J. Chester to the commissioner of police (27 September 1927).

12. NSA, C456 03 02: John Alcock.

13. Croft, *Cloven Hoof,* 67.

14. LMA, A PMC 80: Mr. L. J. to Tomlinson (1 June 1955); PRO, HO 345 12: CHP TRANS 8, PC/C Butcher (7 December 1954), 645, 12; Crisp, *Naked Civil Servant,* 164; PRO, MEPO 2, 4485: "Running Horse Public House: Permitting drunkenness/disorderly conduct of undesirables," minute 7c: PC 144/C Medhurst (21 August 1936); PRO, CRIM 1, 639: Austin S. and (33) others, charged with keeping a disorderly house (1933/1938), statement of PC 139/F Labbatt; PRO, CRIM 1, 735 Jack Rudolph Neave and others, charged with keeping a disorderly house (1934), statement of PC/E Mortimer; PRO, MEPO 3, 758: Caravan Club, 91 Endell Street WC1, charged with disorderly house/male prostitutes, statement of DS/E Mogford (25 August 1934).

15. PRO, CRIM 1, 387: exhibit 10, F. E. M. to Bobby B. (21 March [year not noted]).

16. Ibid., F. E. M. to Bobby B. (7 November 1923); and ibid., F. E. M. to Bobby B. (21 March [year not noted]).

17. NSA, C456 03 02: John Alcock.

18. Weeks and Porter, *Between the Acts,* 125.

19. James Curtis, *What Immortal Hand* (London and Toronto: William Heinemann, 1939), 10. For these slang terms, see Partridge, *Dictionary of the Underworld,* 462, 496, 524–25, 527; PRO, CRIM 1, 387: information; PRO, CRIM 1, 903: Billie Joice and others, charged with keeping a disorderly house; application at Bow Street Police Court (14 November 1936), statement of DS/E Murray; PRO, MEPO 3, 758: Insp. E. Pollock (25 August 1934); Moncrieff, *Café Bar;* James Spenser, *The Gilt Kid* (London: Jonathon Cape, 1936); and Renault, *Charioteer,* 53.

20. LMA, PS TOW B01 049: Lewis H. and William S., charged with importuning (24 December 1922). See also the incident recounted in Daley, *This Small Cloud,* 122, 171.

21. "Numbered Prisoners at Old Bailey," *MA,* 21 February 1933, 3.

22. "West End Nest of Vice Smoked Out," *NW,* 5 March 1933, 18. See also "Improper Performance in West London," *Times,* 28 February 1933, 9; "Prisoners in Dock Numbered," *ES,* 20 February 1933, 8; and "Alleged Scenes at West End Dances," *NW,* 26 February 1933, 8. The emergence of these connections in the late nineteenth century is discussed in Alan Sinfield, *The Wilde Century: Effeminacy, Oscar Wilde and the Queer Moment* (New York: Columbia University Press, 1994); Joseph Bristow, *Effeminate England: Homoerotic Writing after 1885* (New York: Columbia University Press, 1995); and Ed Cohen, *Talk on the Wilde Side: Towards a Genealogy of a Discourse on Male Sexualities* (London and New York: Routledge, 1993).

23. NSA, C444 03 30a–32a: Alex Purdie.

24. PRO, CRIM 1, 639: copy depositions, statement of PC 314/F Haylock, 54.

25. Ibid., statement of PS 32/F Spiers, 2–3.

26. Ibid., statement of PC 441/F Whitcombe, 5.

27. See, for example, "Masquerade for Bet," *NW,* 20 July 1947, 3; "Sinks of Iniquity," *NW,* 29 January 1933, 8; "Dance Hall Orgies," *NW,* 23 January 1927, 4; and "Dance Hall Sensation," *NW,* 5 December 1926, 13.

28. Croft, *Cloven Hoof,* 63. Similarly, Croft noted, "'Lesbians wear clothes which are as a rule of set outline, neatly tailored and masculine" (81). For lesbian forms of self-presentation, see, for example, PRO, MEPO 2, 4485: minute 63a, statement of PC 82/C Hoare (31 July 1937); NSA, C456 86 03,: Olive Agar; and Davies, *New London Spy,* 233–34.

29. PRO, MEPO 2, 4485: minute 7a, statement of Insp. C. Gavin (22 August 1936); and Reginald Underwood, *Flame of Freedom* (London: Fortune Press, 1936), 200. On this point, see Chauncey, *Gay New York,* 51.

30. Christopher Breward, "Fashion and the Man: From Suburb to City Street; The Spaces of Masculine Consumption, 1870–1914," *New Formations,* 37 (1999): 49. See also Breward, *The Hidden Consumer: Masculinities, Fashion and City Life, 1860–1914* (Manchester and New York: Manchester University Press, 1999).

31. PRO, CRIM 1, 633: Laurence B., charged with buggery (1933), exhibit 1, diary of Sidney C. For the appropriation of these items, see, for example, Williams, *Emlyn,* 37; PRO, CRIM 1, 387, depositions: statement of PC/D Gavin (8 February

1927); PRO, MEPO 3, 758: minute 8b, statement of PC 453/E Mortimer (26 July 1934); Ackerley, *My Father and Myself,* 136–37.

32. See, for example, PRO, MEPO 2, 4485: minute 63a, statement of PS 44/C Gowen (25 February 1937); PRO, MEPO 3, 758: minute 11a, statement of SDI/E Campion to DDI (29 August 1934); ibid., minute 8b, statement of PC 453/E Mortimer (26 July 1934); PRO, CRIM 1, 903: application at Bow Street Police Court (14 November 1936), DS Miller NSY; LMA, A PMC 80: Mr. L. J. to Caughlin (13 June 1955).

33. Williams, *Emlyn,* 11; "Numbered Prisoners on their Defence," *NW,* 24 January 1937, 19; and PRO, CRIM 1, 903 (1937), DS Murray. See also "Raid on a Public House," *NW,* 13 September 1953, 7; NSA: C547 15: Pat; NSA, C456 49: Frank Birkhill; and Chauncey, *Gay New York,* 52.

34. Hoare, *Noel Coward,* 140.

35. Croft, *Cloven Hoof,* 68.

36. David, *Stephen Spender,* 67.

37. Westwood [pseud. Schofield], *Minority,* 62–63.

38. See Shaun Cole, "Invisible Men: Gay Men's Dress in Britain, 1950–1970," in *Defining Dress: Dress as Object, Meaning and Identity,* ed. Elizabeth Wilson and Amy de la Haye (Manchester and New York: Manchester University Press, 1999), 143–54; and Cole, *Don We Now Our Gay Apparel: Gay Men's Dress in the Twentieth Century* (Oxford: Berg, 2000).

39. Croft, *Cloven Hoof,* 67. The relationship between cosmetics and gender identities is discussed in Kathy Peiss, "Making Faces: The Cosmetics Industry and the Cultural Construction of Gender, 1890–1930," in *Genders,* 7 (1990): 143–69; and Peiss, "Of Men and Make-up: The Gender of Cosmetics in Twentieth Century America," in *The Material Culture of Gender,* ed. Kenneth Ames and Katherine Martinez (New York: Norton, 1997).

40. Quoted in Jivani, *It's Not Unusual,* 22.

41. NSA, C444 03 30a–32a: Alex Purdie.

42. See, for example, Hanmore, *Curse of the Embankment,* 27; PRO, CRIM 1, 639, information: statement of PC 139/F Labbatt: 2; PRO, CRIM 1, 633 (1933), statement of Albert W.; LMA, PS HAM 37: Harold C., charged with importuning (8 May 1935); PRO, MEPO 3, 758: statement of DS/E Mogford (25 August 1934); PRO, MEPO 2, 4485: minute 63a, PS 44/C Gowen (6 March 1937); Insp. C. Forrest (7 March 1937).

43. See, for example, Crisp, *Naked Civil Servant;* Williams, *Emlyn,* 118; PRO, MEPO 2, 4485: minute 7c, statement of PC 144/C Medhurst (24 August 1936); and PRO, CRIM 1, 903: application at Bow Street Police Court (14 November 1936), statement of DS Miller NSY.

44. Burke, *London Spy,* 303; "Rouged Rogues," *JB,* 3 January 1925, 10; and "A Modern Gomorrah," *JB,* 13 June 1925, 18.

45. Moseley, *Night Haunts of London,* 47, 150. See also "A New Peril to Women," *JB,* 10 January 1925, 16.

46. Crisp, *Naked Civil Servant,* 28.

47. See, for example, Croft, *Cloven Hoof*, 62–63; PRO, CRIM 1, 633: exhibit 6, statement of Winifred P; PRO, CRIM 1, 1041 (1938); statement of PC 407/C Hooper; PRO, CRIM 1, 903: application at Bow Street Police Court (14 November 1936), statement of DS/E Murray; "Life in the Early Hours in a Soho Café," *NW*, 1 September 1957, 9; PRO, CRIM 1, 639, information: statement of PC 139/F Labbatt: 2; and PRO, CRIM 1, 639: statement of PC Edward Walker.

48. Burke, *London Spy*, 302.

49. Crisp, *Naked Civil Servant*, 70–71. See Chauncey, *Gay New York*, 25.

50. "One of a Gang," *NW*, 3 October 1926, 3.

51. NSA, C456 03 02: John Alcock; NSA: C444 03 48a–49a: John Alcock.

52. PRO, CRIM 1, 903: exhibit 7 (1937); "Numbered Prisoners on Their Defence," *NW*, 24 January 1937, 19.

53. Westwood [Schofield], *Minority*, 211.

54. PRO, CRIM 1, 735: statement of PC/E Mortimer (1934).

55. PRO, MEPO 3, 758: minute 8b, statement of PC 453/E Mortimer (26 July 1934). See Chauncey, *Gay New York*, 290; and Esther Newton, *Mother Camp: Female Impersonators in America* (Englewood Cliff: Prentice Hall, 1972).

56. NSA, C444 03 30a–32a: Alex Purdie.

57. Peter Gurney, "'Intersex' and 'Dirty Girls': Mass Observation and Working-Class Sexuality in England in the 1930s," *Journal of the History of Sexuality* 8, no. 2 (1997): 289.

58. PRO, MEPO 2, 4485, minute 63a, PC 82/C Hoare (31 July 1937).

59. Williams, *Emlyn*, 91, 311.

60. NSA, C444 03 30a–32a: Alex Purdie.

61. Ibid.

62. PRO, MEPO 2, 4485: minute 23b: Insp. C. Gavin (9 September 1936).

63. I draw here upon Peter Bailey's notion of "parasexuality": "an extensive ensemble of sites, practices and occasions that mediate across the frontiers of the putative public/private divide." See Bailey, "Parasexuality and Glamour: The Victorian Barmaid as Cultural Prototype," *Gender and History* 2, no. 2 (1990): 148–49.

64. Eric Partridge, *Slang Today and Yesterday* (London: George Routledge and Sons, 1933), 139, 152–53, 223, 249, 266, 276; Paul Baker, *Polari: The Lost Language of Gay Men* (London and New York: Routledge, 2002); L. J. Cox and R. J. Fay, "Gayspeak, the Linguistic Fringe: Bona Polari, Camp, Queerspeak and Beyond," in *The Margins of the City: Gay Men's Urban Lives*, ed. Stephen Whittle (Aldershot: Ashgate, 1994).

65. Weeks and Porter, *Between the Acts*, 174–75.

66. NSA, C456 03 02: John Alcock.

67. Quoted in David, *On Queer Street*, 200.

68. "Brazen Blackmail Gang," *JB*, 30 May 1925, 13. See also the "winks and backslang" prostitutes used to deceive customers described in Moseley, *Night Haunts of London*, 47.

69. NSA, C444 03 30a–32a: Alex Purdie.

70. Croft, *Cloven Hoof,* 65.

71. NSA, C444 03 30a–32a: Alex Purdie. There are glossaries in NSA, C456 03 02: John Alcock; Croft, *Cloven Hoof,* 65; Westwood, *Minority,* 208; and Baker, *Polari,* appendix.

72. PRO, CRIM 1, 1041: statement of PC 144/C Medhurst (11 October 1938).

73. See, for example, NSA, C456 49: Frank Birkhill; NSA, C547 15: Pat; PRO, MEPO 2, 9367: "Vice at Piccadilly Circus and Surrounding Area," minute 4a: Chief Supt. C. Walters to commissioner: "Prostitutes, Homosexuals, Pornography and Rowdyism on the West End" (30 October 1952); PRO, MEPO 2, 4485, minute 7b, statement of John Gavin (24 August 1936); PRO, HO 345 12, CHP TRANS 8, PC/C Butcher (7 December 1954); Weeks and Porter, *Between the Acts,* 140, 185–87; "Film Artist Accused," *NW,* 11 December 1932, 8; "Blackmailed Mr. W.," *NW,* 29 January 1933, 16; and "Male Moral Perverts," *NW,* 28 August 1927, 8.

74. Daley, *This Small Cloud,* 156–57. See also PRO, MEPO 2, 9367: minute 4a (30 October 1952); Crisp, *Naked Civil Servant,* passim; NSA, C547 15: Pat.; Michael S., interview.

75. "Rouged Rogues," *JB,* 3 January 1925, 10.

76. "One of a Gang," *NW,* 3, October 1926, 3, emphasis added.

77. Crisp, *Naked Civil Servant,* 91. See also "Puzzle for Police Who Kept Watch on a Club," *NW,* 31 October 1954, 2; LMA, A PMC 80: L. J. to Tomlinson (1 June 1955).

78. PRO, MEPO 2, 4485: minute 7b, statement of Insp. C Gavin (24 August 1936). See also PRO, MEPO 3, 758: minute 8b, statement of PS 13/E Miller (26 July 1934).

79. William Norwood East and W. H. de B. Hubert, *Report on the Psychological Treatment of Crime* (London: HMSO, 1939), 89.

80. See, for example, PRO, MEPO 2, 4485: minute 7c, PC 144/C Medhurst (21 August 1936); PRO, CRIM 1, 735 PS 13/E Miller (1934).

81. Michael S., interview.

82. NSA, C456 49: Frank Birkhill.

83. "One of a Gang," 3; PRO, CRIM 1, 1041: PC 407/C Hooper; statement of the accused; CAA 1097: Particulars of Trial Form II (11 October 1938).

84. Charles Upchurch, "Forgetting the Unthinkable: Cross-Dressers and British Society in the Case of the Queen vs. Boulton and Others," *Gender and History* 12, no. 1 (2000): 128–29. Of the incidents resulting in proceedings before the Bow Street magistrate when C Division intensified its activities during the 1937 Coronation, sixty-two arose on Piccadilly or in the Circus and only eleven in Soho. See LMA, PS BOW A1 170–75; LMA, PS BOW A2 8–11 (1937).

85. "Weeping Men in the Dock," *Daily Mail,* 28 February 1933, 7; "West End Nest of Vice Smoked Out," *NW,* 5 March 1933, 18; For the advertising leaflet, see PRO, CRIM 1, 638, attachment 7.

86. Crisp, *Naked Civil Servant,* 50–52.

87. PRO, MEPO 2, 4485: minute 63a, statement of PC 82/C Hoare (8 March 1937).

88. Ibid., statement of PS 44/C Gowen (26 February 1937).

89. PRO, CRIM 1, 903: statement of DS Miller (12 January 1937). See Chauncey, *Gay New York,* chapter 1.

90. NSA, C444 03 30a–32a: Alex Purdie; NSA, Testimony Films, "A Secret World of Sex: The Other Love" [transcript of notes from screened program].

91. Weeks and Porter, *Between the Acts,* 176.

92. "848.14: London's Clubs and Cabaret No. 6—The Anchor Cabaret (1926)," at http://www.britishpathe.com (accessed Oct. 20, 2004).

93. "Songs in the Saloon Bar," *NW,* 26 September 1954, 3; James Gardiner, *Who's a Pretty Boy Then? One Hundred and Fifty Years of Gay Life in Pictures* (London: Serpent's Tail, 1997), 61; NSA, C547 11: John Alcock; NSA, C444 03 30a–32a: Alex Purdie; Davies, *Kenneth Williams Diaries,* 21, 25, 51–52, 80; Jivani, *It's Not Unusual,* 14–15.

94. See Gurney, "'Intersex' and 'Dirty Girls,'" 280–87.

95. "Sensational Court Sequel to Club Raid," *NW,* 26 August 1934, 1

96. "76 Discharged in Club Case," *NW,* 9 September 1934, 8.

97. Ibid.

98. Mervyn Harris, *The Dilly Boys: Male Prostitution in London* (London: Croom Helm, 1973).

99. NSA, C456 03 02: John Alcock. See also NSA, C547 43: Richard.

100. I draw here upon interviews with Alcock conducted over the past twenty years. See NSA, C456 03 02: John Alcock; NSA, C547 11: John Alcock; NSA, C547 06: John Alcock; and NSA, C444 03 48a–49a: John Alcock.

101. See, for example, PRO, HO 45 25033: "Cases of Masquerading: Males in Female Attire and Females in Male Attire," Norman Haire to Oliver Stanley (6 August 1937). For Hull, see Angus McLaren, *The Trials of Masculinity: Policing Sexual Boundaries, 1870–1930* (Chicago and London: University of Chicago Press, 1997), 208–29.

102. "In an Eerie Half World between the Sexes," *NW,* 3 November 1957, 3. See also "Man Who Worked as a Waitress," *NW,* 7 October 1951, 2; "He Gave His Name as Sonia," *NW,* 22 December 1957, 5; "PC's Suspicions Were Aroused During Car Ride," *NW,* 21 October 1956, 10; "Surprise for the Police in Mayfair," *NW,* 19 December 1954, 2; "A Figure in the Shadows," *NW,* 29 August 1957, 8; "The Clue of the Slight Moustache," *NW,* 22 September 1957, 5; and "Surprise for Women PC," *NW,* 15 January 1956, 9.

103. PRO, MEPO 2, 4485: minute 2a: ASDI Gavin to Supt. C (14 August 1936).

104. LMA, A PMC 80: undated news clipping from the *Daily Telegraph* (1957).

CHAPTER 7

1. Humphries, *The Secret World of Sex,* 40, 144, 204, 206–7.

2. Jivani, *It's Not Unusual,* 66–67.

3. LMA, PS TOW B1 168: Reginald S., charged with importuning (29 April 1927); See also LMA, PS TOW B1 168: Horace D., charged with importuning (18

April 1927); LMA, PS TOW B01 167: Arthur C., charged with importuning (14 April 1927); LMA, PS TOW B01 049: Lewis H. and William S., charged with importuning (24 December 1922).

4. Humphries, *Secret World of Sex,* 202, 206–7.

5. PRO, HO 345 9: CHP 64, Dr. F. G. Jefferies, St. Mary's: "VD and the Homosexual."

6. PRO, CRIM 1, 480: Herbert W., charged with attempting to procure an act of gross indecency (November 1929), statement of Mr. L.

7. Croft, *The Cloven Hoof,* 65; Westwood [pseud. Schofield], *A Minority,* 208.

8. See B. D. Nicholson, "Drink," 254.

9. See Alyson Brown and David Barrett, *Knowledge of Evil: Child Prostitution and Child Sexual Abuse in Twentieth-Century England* (Cullompton and Devon: Willan Publishing, 2002), 5–7.

10. Simon Raven, "Boys Will Be Boys: The Male Prostitute in London," *Encounter* 15, no. 5 (1960): 19–24.

11. Lehmann, *In the Purely Pagan Sense,* 54–55.

12. See James Gardiner, *A Class Apart: The Private Pictures of Montague Glover* (London: Serpent's Tail, 1992); Alexander, *William Plomer,* 182–87; Peter Quennell, *A Lonely Business: A Self-Portrait of James Pope-Hennessy* (London: Weidenfeld and Nicholson, 1981).

13. LMA, PS TOW B1 164: Joseph P., charged with importuning (17 January 1927).

14. Chauncey, *Gay New York,* 97.

15. Andrew Davies, "Street Gangs, Crime and Policing in Glasgow during the 1930s: The Case of the Beehive Boys," *Social History* 23, no. 3 (1998): 251–67; Joanna Bourke, *Working Class Cultures in Britain, 1890–1960: Gender, Class and Ethnicity* (London and New York: Routledge, 1994), 42–43, 130; Steve Humphries and Pamela Gordon, *A Man's World: From Boyhood to Manhood, 1900–60* (London: BBC Books, 1996).

16. S. F. Hatton, *London's Bad Boys* (London: Chapman and Hall, 1931), 46.

17. Humphries, *Secret World of Sex,* 29–30, 141, 147; Joanne Jones, "'She Resisted with All Her Might': Sexual Violence against Women in Late-Nineteenth Century Manchester and the Local Press," in *Everyday Violence in Britain, 1850–1950,* ed. Shani d'Cruze (London: Longman, 2000), 104–18.

18. Humphries, *Secret World of Sex,* 15–28, 95; Judy Giles, "Playing Hard to Get: Working-class Women, Sexuality and Respectability in Britain, 1918–1940," *Women's History Review* 1, no. 2 (1992): 239–55.

19. John Marshall, "Pansies, Perverts and Macho Men: Changing Conceptions of Male Homosexuality," in *The Making of the Modern Homosexual,* ed. Ken Plummer (London: Hutchinson, 1981), 147.

20. Williams, *Emlyn,* 19.

21. PRO, HO 345 9: CHP 83, summary of data from prison commissioners' questionnaire.

22. Westwood [pseud. Schofield], *A Minority,* 152–53.

23. PRO, CRIM 1, 480: statement of PC 504/B Wardle (November 1929).

24. PRO, MEPO 3, 990: "Use of Plainclothes Officers in Detecting Indecency Offences in Urinals" (30 August 1933). See also LMA, PS LAM B1 273: Edward F. and Ernest D., charged with indecency (16 July 1937); and PRO, MEPO 3, 992: "Hugh C. Persistent Importuner" (1935).

25. LMA, PS TOW B01 040: Richard K. and Waldemar C., charged with gross indecency (5 March 1917).

26. Ackerley, *My Father and Myself,* 126–28.

27. Parker, *Ackerley,* 133.

28. Wildeblood, *A Way of Life,* 151.

29. T. C. Worsley, *Fellow Travellers* (London: GMP, 1984), 46–47, 62–65; David, *Stephen Spender,* 64, 164–67.

30. Weeks and Porter, *Between the Acts,* 129.

31. PRO, CRIM 1, 1194: Ronald G. and Michael R., charged with attempted buggery (1940).

32. Crisp, *Naked Civil Servant,* 61–62. See also "Man Who Worked as a Waitress," *NW,* 7 October 1951, 2.

33. Marshall, "Pansies, Perverts and Macho Men," 136.

34. LMA, PS TOW B01 167: Walter S., charged with indecency (21 April 1927). See also LMA, PS TOW B01 165: John E., charged with outraging public decency (17 March 1926).

35. George Orwell, *Down and out in Paris and London* (London: Secker and Warburg, 1949), 203–4.

36. Joseph Flynt, "Homosexuality among Tramps," in Havelock Ellis, *Studies in the Psychology of Sex,* vol. 1, *Sexual Inversion* (London: Wilson and Macmillan, 1897), 256–57. See also "Coffee Stall Meeting," *NW,* 12 March 1922, 3; Steve Humphries and Pamela Gordon, *Forbidden Britain: Our Secret Past, 1900–1960* (London: BBC Books, London, 1994), 35–36.

37. Hatton, *London's Bad Boys,* 72–73.

38. PRO, CRIM 1, 433: John S. and William H., charged with buggery (1928), DS Ellis.

39. PRO, HO 144 22298: "Criticism of Elderly Judge's Treatment of Homosexual Offences," sec. 430931/2: Home Office Report: Thomas R. and Philip T. (6 December 1927).

40. Wal Hannington, *The Problem of the Distressed Areas* (London: Victor Gollancz, 1937), 116–23. See also Keith Laybourn, *Britain on the Breadline: A Social and Political History of Britain, 1918–39* (London: Sutton Publishing, 1990); and Nigel Gray, *The Worst of Times: An Oral History of the Great Depression in Britain* (London: Wildewood House, 1985), 104, 110.

41. Mrs. C. Neville-Rolfe, "Sex Delinquency," in Llewellyn Smith, *New Survey,* 291–322.

42. Hanmore, *The Curse of the Embankment,* 27.

43. PRO, HO 345 16: CHP TRANS 54, Dr. D. Carroll et al. for the Institute for the Study and Treatment of Delinquency, 4578 6 (1 February 1956).

44. Davidson, *World, the Flesh and Myself,* 94.

45. "Major in the Dock," *NW,* 17 April 1927, 11; and "Veteran Major's Sin," *NW,* 29 May 1927, 11. See also "Man with a Degree," *NW,* 31 January 1932, 16; and "Rector in Role of Prosecutor," *NW,* 11 November 1934, 6.

46. PRO, MEPO 3, 923: "Harry Raymond and Others Operating as a Blackmail Gang in Leicester Square," sec. 203 UNC 1970, minute 11c: statement of Harold G. (10 July 1932). See also Lee Bartlett, ed., *Letters to Christopher: Stephen Spender's Letters to Christopher Isherwood, 1929–1939* (Santa Barbara: Black Sparrow Press, 1980), 57.

47. Westwood [pseud. Schofield], *Society and the Homosexual,* 118.

48. Croft, *The Cloven Hoof,* 68.

49. I discuss this further in Matt Houlbrook "Soldier Heroes and Rent Boys: Homosex, Masculinities and Britishness in the Brigade of Guards, c.1900–1960," *Journal of British Studies* 42, no. 3 (2003): 351–88. For the Royal Navy, see "Believed the Sailor," *NW,* 21 May 1922, 5; PRO, MEPO 2, 4485 (1936); LMA, PS TOW B1 168 (29 April 1927); LMA, PS TOW B1 168 (18 April 1927); LMA, PS TOW B01 167 (14 April 1927).

50. Partridge, *Dictionary of the Underworld,* 524. For such incidents, see, for example, "Committed for Trial on Blackmail Charge," *IPN,* 13 March 1924, 7; "Hard Labour and 'Cat' for Two Guardsmen," *IPN,* 26 February 26 1931, 3; "Bail for Two Guardsmen," *The People,* 25 January 1931; "A Flat in Disorder," *NW,* 17 May 1925, 5; "Artist in Bandages," *NW,* 31 May 1925, 5; and "They Slink in the Darkest Places," *NW,* 27 May 1951, 5.

51. For the "Squint Eyed Sheikh's" blackmail of a retired Indian Army captain, see PRO, MEPO 3, 372: Conspiracy and Demanding Money by Threats to Accuse of Crime (1927); "Posters for Captain," *NW,* 17 April 1927, 11; "Parted with £10000," *NW,* 10 April 1927, 6; "Life for Blackmailer," *NW,* 29 May 1927, 6; "Amazing Blackmail Plot," *JB,* 25 June 1927, 20; and "The £10000 Blackmail Case," *IPN,* 2 June 1927, 8. See also Harry Raymond's "nefarious game" of blackmail in PRO, MEPO 3, 923 (1937–39); "Britain's Sinister Blackmail Racket Smashed," *NW,* 5 December 1937, 10; and "Blackmailed Mr. W.," *NW,* 29 January 1933, 16. Angus McLaren hints at these patterns but fails to consider tabloid newspapers—a characteristic site of the blackmail narrative—in his analysis: McLaren, *Sexual Blackmail: A Modern History* (Cambridge Mass.: Harvard University Press, 2002), 105–43.

52. "Bogus Naval Man," *New of the World,* 20 December 1925, 4. See also "Unwelcome Visitor," *NW,* 30 October 1955, 4; "Moral Murder," *NW,* 30 July 1922, 4, 12; and "Adventure of Mr. H.," *NW,* 27 April 1930, 6.

53. PRO, MEPO 3, 362: Roland B., "Attempted Murder of Philip E.," minute 9a: Insp. Bradley to insp. (26 August 1929).

54. See, for example, "A Mystery of Mayfair," *NW,* 18 August 1929, 5; "Brutal Attack on Man in Mayfair Flat," *IPN,* 22 August 1929, 2; and "Mayfair Flat Outrage," *IPN,* 5 September 1929, 5.

55. PRO, MEPO 3, 362, minute 9a, Insp. Bradley to insp. (26 August 1929); "Met in Piccadilly," *NW,* 8 September 1929, 6; "Upheaval in Flat," *NW,* 1 September 1929, 12; and "Flat Victim's Ordeal," *NW,* 15 September 1929, 6.

56. Crisp, *Naked Civil Servant,* 65–68.

57. "Steamer" derived from "steam tug"—rhyming slang for mug. See Partridge, *Dictionary of the Underworld,* 356, 433, 462, 525, 527, 748; Robert Fabian, *Fabian of the Yard* (Kingswood Surrey: Naldrett Press, 1950), 184–86; Moncrieff, *Café Bar;* Spenser, *The Gilt Kid;* Jim Phelan, *Lifer* (London: Peter Davies, 1938); D. S. Alexander Black, "Criminal Slang," *Police Journal* (March 1943); Curtis, *What Immortal Hand;* PRO, MEPO 3, 362: minute 9a: Insp. Bradley to insp. (26 August 1929); and Ackerley, *My Father and Myself,* 136, 139, 190–92.

58. Judith Butler, *Bodies That Matter: On the Discursive Limits of "Sex"* (London and New York: Routledge, 1993), 226.

59. PRO, MEPO 3, 404: "Gross Indecency with Boys," sec. 213 / IMP / 290: Robert M., Complaints from GPO regarding Alleged Familiarity with Messenger Boys (28 November 1923).

60. Westwood, *A Minority,* 155.

61. See "Three Men in a Flat," *NW,* 15 June 1930, 11; and "Secret Name in Charge," *NW,* 6 March 1932, 16.

62. See "Hyde Park after Dark," *NW,* 26 April 1931, 5; "In Hyde Park," *Emp,* 26 April 1931, 12; "Dangers of Hyde Park," *DE,* 23 April 1931, 7; "Night Perils of Hyde Park," *MA,* 23 April 1931, 8; "Perils of Hyde Park after Nightfall," *IPN,* 30 April 1931, 5; and PRO, HO 45 24960: "Homosexual Offences Conference" (11 May 1931).

63. Weeks, "Inverts, Perverts and Mary Annes," 195.

64. See the contemporary descriptions in Hatton, *London's Bad Boys;* and Curtis, *What Immortal Hand.* See also Anna Davin, *Growing up Poor: Home, School and Street in London, 1870–1914* (London: Rivers Oram Press, 1996), 63–84; and Harry Hendrick, *Images of Youth: Age, Class and the Male Youth Problem, 1880–1920* (Oxford: Clarendon Press, 1990).

65. I draw here upon Maynard, "'Horrible Temptations,'" 196.

66. PRO, HO 144 7044: "Hyde Park Disturbance and Annoying and Insulting Behaviour," sec. 24, Case of Colonel Alfred R. (27 March 1922); and ibid., sec. 23, Alfred R., appeal to the king (9 March 1922). See also LMA, PS MS A1 53: Alfred R. and Albert T., charged with gross indecency (6 January 1922).

67. PRO, CRIM 1, 898: Colin E., charged with attempt to procure an act of gross indecency, statement of Colin E. 1 December 1936). For these suggestions, see also PRO, MEPO 3, 994: "Mitford B.: Attempt to Procure Gross Indecency," minute 3a: PS Sowell to DDI (17 September 1936).

68. LMA, LCC MIN 9911: complaint from Mr. C. E. H. (7 July 1947). See also PRO, CRIM 1, 880: Alfred Y., charged with indecent assault (1936); and PRO, CRIM 1, 2343: R., charged with buggery/indecent assault (1953).

69. For these different sites of encounter, see, for example, PRO, CRIM 1, 897: M., charged with indecent assault (1937); PRO, CRIM 1, 1200: Charles W., charged with buggery (1940); PRO, HO 144 22298: sec. 3, statement of Leo D. (23 May 1928). LMA: PS HAM A 33: Horace G., charged with indecent assault (14 December 1927); PRO, MEPO 3, 995: "George B.: Charged with Importuning a Boy aged 9" (1937).

70. PRO, CRIM 1, 898 (1937), exhibit 2. See also PRO, CRIM 1, 352: Stanley J., charged with indecent assault/gross indecency (1926).

71. LMA, PS HAM A 35: Bert V. and Frederick F., charged with indecency (30 June 1932).

72. LMA, PS HAM A 38: Edward R., charged with indecent assault (11 September 1936).

73. "Pageboy's Story of Visits to Hotel," *NW*, 7 March 1937, 15; and "Headmaster Put in Care of Bishop," *NW*, 18 April 1937, 4. See also "Tale of Cellar Stray," *NW*, 8 September 1944, 2; and "Vicar in Custody," *NW*, 24 September 1944, 5.

74. PRO, CRIM 1, 461: Charles R., charged with buggery (1929), John D.; Annie D.

75. Davidson, *Some Boys*, 176.

76. Geoffrey Crossick, *An Artisan Elite in Victorian Society: Kentish London, 1840–80* (London: Croom Helm, 1978).

77. LMA, PS MS A1 79: Henry P., charged with importuning (17 January 1927).

78. PRO, CRIM 1, 323: Eric R. and William M., charged with gross indecency (1925).

79. Wright, *John Lehmann*, 62–63.

80. Many workingmen remained friends with former partners after marrying. See Davidson, *Some Boys*, 214–15; and Parker, *Ackerley*, 241–57.

81. Court registers only record defendants' name and age systematically. Occupations and addresses were recorded at various times and in various courts. No note was made of a man's ethnicity or nationality. Some indication can be derived from names, though this is highly problematic. Newspapers rarely referred to ethnicity or nationality, basing their reports on near-verbatim transcriptions of court cases in which ethnicity was rarely mentioned.

82. See, for example, LMA, PS TH A1 144: Solomon M., charged with importuning (8 April 197); LMA, PS TH A1 247: Moss C.. charged with indecent assault (20 September 1947); LMA, PS TH A1 204: James G., charged with gross indecency (1 March 1937); LMA, PS TH A1 189: Joseph I., charged with gross indecency (2 May 1932); LMA, PS OLD A1 141, Michael M., charged with gross indecency (31 March 1947); LMA, PS OLD A1 142: Aaron G., charged with gross indecency (26 August 1947); LMA, PS OLD A1 144: Hyman P., charged with outraging public decency (8 October 1947); LMA, PS OLD A1 144: Sidney F., charged with importuning (17 October 1947); LMA, PS OLD A1 108: David L., charged with

indecent assault (26 April 1937); LMA, PS OLD A1 090: Joseph M., charged with gross indecency (19 February 1932).

83. "Life for Blackmailer," *NW,* 29 May 1927, 6. Jewish men's participation in homosex is partially suggested in "Moral Murder," *NW,* 1 April 1928, 13.

84. The only references I know of are Dudley Cave in *Walking after Midnight,* 25; and Parker, *Ackerley,* 95. For similar patterns in New York, see Chauncey, *Gay New York,* 72–76.

85. Chauncey, *Gay New York,* 72–76. For London's Jewish neighborhoods, see White, *Rothschild Buildings;* and V. D. Lipman, *A History of the Jews in Great Britain since 1858* (Leicester: Leicester University Press, 1990).

86. "A Black Betrayal," *JB,* 25 July 1927, 13.

87. Kohn, *Dope Girls;* and Lucy Bland, "The Trial of Madame Fahmy: Orientalism, Violence, Sexual Perversity and the Fear of Miscegenation," in d'Cruze, *Everyday Violence,* 185–97.

88. See the arrest of George H.—a ship's fireman—and Mohammed K.—an engine room hand—on South West India Dock Quay. LMA, PS TH A1 206 (3 January 1938). See also PRO CRIM 1, 2565: Aaron M. and Gordon P., charged with gross indecency (1955); LMA, PS TH A1 157–62 (1922); LMA, PS TH A1 173–77 (1927); LMA, PS TH A1 187-203 (1932); LMA, PS TH A1 202-7 (1937); LMA, PS TH A1 2227 (1942); LMA, PS TH A1 243-9 (1947); LMA, PS TH A1 269-75 (1952); LMA: PS TH A1 296-303 (1957); PRO, CRIM 1, 897: M., charged with importuning/attempting to procure an act of gross indecency (1936).

89. PRO, CRIM 1, 903: Billie Joice and others, charged with keeping a disorderly house (1937); "Opium Traffic," *IPN,* June 4 1925, 7; "Opium Charge against Coloured Men," *IPN,* June 11 1925, 7; "Six Month's Hard for Trafficker in Drugs," *IPN,* July 16 1925, 8; and "A Black Betrayal," *JB,* 25 July 1927, 13.

90. Underwood, *Flame of Freedom,* 184. For black men's participation in queer urban life, see also Samuel Selvon, *The Lonely Londoners* (London: Alan Wingate, 1956); Andrew Salkey, *Escape to an Autumn Pavement* (London: Hutchinson, 1960); and PRO: CO 876 247: "Report on Coloured People in Stepney by Derek Bamuta" (1949–50).

91. The descriptions are from Westwood, *A Minority,* 73, 119. See also Crisp, *Naked Civil Servant,* 52–53; Douglas Sutherland, *Portrait of a Decade: London Life, 1945–55* (London: Harrap, 1988), 177; and Quennell, *A Lonely Business,* 177; newspapers regularly reported Irishmen being arrested on Piccadilly. See, for example, "Four Men for Trial," *NW,* 3 April 1932, 17; "Secret Name in Charge," *NW,* 6 March 1932, 16; and "Stories of Meeting in Piccadilly," *NW,* 23 September 1934, 4.

92. NSA, C547 11: John Alcock.

93. See Humphries and Gordon, *Forbidden Britain,* 146, 177; Orwell, *Down and Out,* passim; Donald MacRaild, *Irish Migrants in Modern Britain, 1750–1922* (Basingstoke: Macmillan, 1999); and Lyn Lees, *Exiles of Erin: Irish Migrants in Victorian London* (Manchester: Manchester University Press, 1979).

94. See, for example, PRO, CRIM 1, 2548: Thomas C. and Frederick M., charged with gross indecency (1954), PC 104/E McClaren.

95. Garland, *The Heart in Exile,* 99–102.

96. PRO, HO 345 7: CHP 5: Laurence Dunne: Chief Metropolitan Magistrate, memo submitted to Wolfenden Committee.

97. Mervyn Harris, *The Dilly Boys: Male Prostitution in London* (London: Croom Helm, 1973); and Barbara Gibson, *Male Order: Life Stories from Boys Who Sell Sex* (London: Cassell, 1995).

98. See Bill Osgerby, *Youth in Britain Since 1945* (Oxford: Blackwell, 1998). The classic contemporary studies of affluence and youth culture are Mark Abrams, *The Teenage Consumer* (London: Press Exchange, 1959); and John Goldthorpe et al., *The Affluent Worker in the Class Structure* (London: Cambridge University Press, 1969);

99. Bourke, *Working-Class Cultures,* 30–34. This account draws upon McKibbin, *Classes and Cultures,* 296–98; J. Finch and Penny Summerfield, "Social Reconstruction and the Emergence of Companionate Marriage, 1945–59," in *Marriage, Domestic Life and Social Change,* ed. David Clark (London and New York: Routledge, 1991), 7–32.

100. Garland, *Heart in Exile,* 224.

101. Ibid., 180.

102. Westwood, *A Minority,* 89–90; and Eliot George, *The Leather Boys* (London: Anthony Blond, 1961). For the depiction of this figure, see also NSA, C456 122 01-08: Michael James; Michael S., interview; Kirkup, *A Poet Could Not But Be Gay,* 118; and Garland, *Heart in Exile,* 26, 136, 180.

CHAPTER 8

1. NSA, C444 03 39a-40a: Dudley Cave. For such attitudes see, for example, Marshall, "Pansies, Perverts and Macho Men," 147; Westwood [pseud. Schofield], *A Minority,* 87; Isherwood, *Christopher and His Kind,* 28; and Vickers, *Cecil Beaton,* 23.

2. NSA: C456 89 01: Patrick Trevor-Roper.

3. Westwood [Schofield], *Society and the Homosexual,* 131. See also Chauncey, *Gay New York,* 99–100.

4. Foucault, *History of Sexuality.* For debates surrounding sexology's influence in Britain see, for example, Lucy Bland and Laura Doan, eds., *Sexology in Culture: Labelling Bodies and Desires* (Oxford: Polity Press, 1998); Weeks, *Coming Out,* 23–31; McLaren, *Trials of Masculinity,* 133–232; Sheila Jeffreys, *The Spinster and Her Enemies: Feminism and Sexuality, 1880–1930* (London: Pandora, 1985); Lillian Faderman, *Surpassing the Love of Men: Romantic Friendship and Love between Women from the Renaissance to the Present* (New York: William Morrow, 1981); and Chris Waters, "Disorders of the Mind, Disorders of the Body Social: Peter Wildeblood and the Making of the Modern Homosexual," in *Moments of Modernity: Reconstructing Britain, 1945–1964,* ed. Becky Conekin, Frank Mort, and Chris Waters (London and New York: Rivers Oram Press, 1999), 135–51. The most sophisticated recent work is Oosterhuis, *Stepchildren of Nature.*

5. Havelock Ellis, *The Psychology of Sex* (London: William Heinemann, 1939), 197.

6. Anomaly, *The Invert,* 9–10.

7. Ellis, *Psychology Of Sex,* 204–5.

8. PRO, HO 345 9: CHP 84, Dr. R. Sessions Hodge, Neuro-Psychiatric Department, Musgrave Park Hospital, Taunton.

9. Norwood East and de B. Hubert, *Report on the Psychological Treatment of Crime,* 88.

10. PRO, HO 45 25306: Departmental Committee on Homosexual Offences and Prostitution 1954–6, "Memorandum of the National Council of Social Services and the National Association for Mental Health."

11. PRO, HO 345 1: *Report of the Committee on Homosexual Offences and Prostitution* (London: HMSO, 1957), 73.

12. See Simon Gunn, "The Public Sphere, Modernity and Consumption: New Perspectives on the History of the English Middle Class," in *Gender, Civic Culture and Consumerism: Middle-Class Identity in Britain, 1800–1940,* ed. Alan Kidd and David Nicholls (Manchester: Manchester University Press, 1999), 18–19.

13. Fielden, *The Natural Bent,* 73. See also Lehmann, *In the Purely Pagan Sense,* 7; PRO, CRIM 1 633: Laurence B., charged with buggery (1933): Sidney C. Medical discourses are summarized in West, *Homosexuality,* 92–137.

14. Anomaly, *The Invert,* 72.

15. NSA, C456 49: Frank Birkhill.

16. Oosterhuis, *Stepchildren of Nature,* 231–35. See also Tosh, *A Man's Place,* 4; Leonore Davidoff, Megan Doolittle, Janet Fink and Katherine Holden, *The Family Story: Blood, Contract and Intimacy, 1830–1950* (London and New York: Longman, 1999); Leonore Davidoff and Catherine Hall, *Family Fortunes: Men and Women of the English Middle Class, 1750–1850* (London: Hutchinson, 1987); Antony Giddens, *The Transformation of Intimacy: Sexuality, Love and Eroticism in Modern Times* (Oxford: Polity Press, 1992).

17. Marie Stopes, *Married Love: A New Contribution to the Solution of Sex Difficulties* (London: Fifield, 1918); Lesley Hall, *Hidden Anxieties: Male Sexuality, 1900–1950* (Cambridge: Polity Press, 1991), 65–86; Marcus Collins, *Modern Love: An Intimate History of Men and Women in Twentieth Century Britain* (London: Atlantic Books, 2003), 39–56.

18. See Harold Perkin, *The Rise of Professional Society: England since 1880* (London: Routledge, 1987); McKibbin, *Classes and Cultures,* 52–62; Susan Kingsley Kent, *Sex and Suffrage in Britain, 1860–1914* (London: Routledge, 1990); Walkowitz, *City of Dreadful Delight,* 41–80; Lucy Bland, *Banishing the Beast: English Feminism and Sexual Morality, 1885–1914* (London: Penguin, 1995); Jill Greenfield, Sean O'Connell, and Chris Reid, "Gender, Consumer Culture and the Middle-Class Male, 1918–39," in Kidd and Nicholls, *Gender, Civic Culture and Consumerism,* 188; and Peter Bailey, "White Collars, Grey Lives? The Lower Middle Class Re-visited," *Journal of British Studies* 38, no. 3 (1999): 281.

19. A James Hammerton "The English Weakness? Gender, Satire and "Moral Manliness" in the Lower Middle Class, 1870–1920," in Kidd and Nicholls, *Gender, Civic Culture and Consumerism,* 178. See also Joanna Bourke, *Dismembering the Male: Men's Bodies, Britain and the Great War* (London: Reaktion Books, 1999), 153–70; and Alison Light, *Forever England: Femininity, Literature and Conservatism between the Wars* (London and New York: Routledge, 1991).

20. For the use of letters as evidence see, for example, PRO, CRIM 1 2424: Cecil W., charged with importuning: R. to Cecile (2 June 1954). For these changes, see Harry Cocks, "Calamus in Bolton: Spirituality and Homosexual Desire in Late-Victorian England," *Gender and History* 13, no. 2 (2001): 191–223; Jeffrey Richards, "'Passing the Love of Women': Manly Love and Victorian Society," in *Manliness and Morality: Middle-Class Masculinity in Britain and America, 1800–1940,* ed. James Mangan and J. A. Walvin (Manchester and New York: Manchester University Press, 1987), 92–122.

21. Quoted in Weeks, *Coming Out,* 81. For Carpenter's work see, for example, Carpenter, *Iolaus: An Anthology of Friendship* (London: Swan Sonnenschein and Co., 1902); Carpenter, *Homogenic Love and Its Place in a Free Society* (Manchester: Labour Press Society, 1894); Carpenter, *The Intermediate Sex: A Study of Some Transitional Types of Men and Women* (London: Swan Sonnenschein and Co., 1908); and Carpenter, *Love's Coming of Age* (Manchester: Labour Press, 1906). For Symonds, see Phyllis Grosskurth, *John Addington Symonds: A Biography* (New York: Arno Press, 1975); Phyllis Grosskurth, ed., *The Memoirs of John Addington Symonds* (London: Hutchinson, 1984); Symonds, *A Problem in Greek Ethics* (New York: Haskell House, 1971); Symonds, *A Problem in Modern Ethics* (New York: B. Blom, 1971); and Sam Brinkley, "The Romantic Sexology of John Addington Symonds," *Journal of Homosexuality* 40, no. 1 (2000): 79–103.

22. See Suzanne Rait, "Sex, Love and the Homosexual Body in Early Sexology," in Bland and Doan, *Sexology in Culture,* 155–56.

23. Wright, *John Lehmann,* 114. See also Ackerley, *My Father and Myself,* 113; Renault, *The Charioteer,* 114; Frances Spalding, *Dance till the Stars Come Down: A Biography of John Minton* (London: John Curtis/Hodder and Stoughton, 1991), 51.

24. Hutton, *Of Those Alone,* 12, 50.

25. Williams, *Emlyn,* 163. See also Underwood, *Hidden Lights,* 93, 153; NSA, C456 070 01: Alan MacGregor; Drabble, *Angus Wilson,* 195–97; NSA, C444 03 39a-40a: Dudley Cave; and Huggett, *Binkie Beaumont,* 228–29, 326–27, 338.

26. For example: Weeks and Porter, *Between the Acts,* 146.

27. NSA, C456 71 01-3: Antony Grey.

28. Westwood, *A Minority,* 124.

29. Ellis, *Psychology Of Sex,* 215–16. See also Oosterhuis, *Stepchildren of Nature,* 249.

30. Anomaly, *The Invert,* 96–97.

31. Williams, *Emlyn,* 148–63.

32. Ibid., 210.

33. Williams, *Emlyn,* 340–41.

34. Ibid., 347.

35. Ibid., 367.

36. Martin Francis, "Tears, Tantrums and Bared Teeth: The Emotional Economy of Three Conservative Prime Ministers, 1951–1963," *Journal of British Studies* 41, no. 3 (2002): 355. On the behavioral and emotional conventions of middle-class masculinity see also, for example, Frank Mort, "Social and Symbolic Fathers and Sons in Postwar Britain," *Journal of British Studies* 38, no. 2 (1999), 353–84; Marcus Collins, "The Fall of the English Gentleman: The National Character in Decline, c. 1918–1970," *Historical Research* 75, no. 187 (2002): 90–111; and Breward, *The Hidden Consumer.*

37. Anomaly, *The Invert,* 135–36.

38. Ibid.

39. Cole, "Invisible Men," 144; Cole, *Don We Now Our Gay Apparel;* NSA, C547 15: Pat; and NSA, C444 03 39a-40a: Dudley Cave, 22.

40. West, *Homosexuality,* 40.

41. See Fielden, *Natural Bent,* 126; Westwood, *A Minority,* 171; Wildeblood, *Against the Law,* 188; and Wildeblood, *Way of Life,* 23.

42. Weeks and Porter, *Between the Acts,* 138–39.

43. Wildeblood, *Against the Law,* 37. See also Williams, *Emlyn,* 199; Westwood, *A Minority,* 185; Barrie Penrose and Simon Freeman, *Conspiracy of Silence: The Secret Life of Anthony Blunt* (London: Grafton Books, 1987), 333–34.

44. NSA, C456 71 01-3: Antony Grey.

45. Westwood, *A Minority,* 75.

46. Anomaly, *The Invert,* 53, 133.

47. Tosh, *A Man's Place,* 13.

48. NSA, C456 123 2: John Chesterman. Queer reading practices are discussed in Christopher Craft, *Another Kind of Love: Male Homosexual Desire in English Discourse, 1850–1920* (Berkeley and London: University of California Press, 1994); Mark Mitchell and David Leavitt, eds., *Pages Passed from Hand to Hand: The Hidden Tradition of Homosexual Literature in English from 1748 to 1914* (London: Chatto and Windus, 1998).

49. Carpenter, *Iolaus;* Davidson, *World, the Flesh and Myself,* 130–31; Underwood, *Hidden Lights,* 154–55. See also Ackerley, *My Father and Myself,* 118; Christopher Reed, "Making History: The Bloomsbury Group's Construction of Aesthetic and Sexual Identity," *Journal of Homosexuality* 27, nos. 1–2 (1994): 189–224; Weeks and Porter, *Between the Acts,* 45–46, 78, 139.

50. Timothy d'Arch Smith, *Love in Earnest: Some Notes on the Lives of English "Uranian" Poets from 1889 to 1930* (London: Routledge and Kegan Paul, 1970), 21, 140, 148.

51. Anomaly, *The Invert,* chapter 8. For Hellenism's influence on elite men, see Linda Dowling, *Hellenism and Homosexuality in Victorian Oxford* (Ithaca: Cornell University Press, 1994); and Cook, *London and the Culture of Homosexuality,* chap. 5.

52. Mary Renault, *The Charioteer* (London: Longmans, 1953); Angus Wilson, *Hemlock and After* (Harmondsworth: Penguin, 1962); and Michael Nelson, *A Room in Chelsea Square* (London: Cape, 1958). See also James Barr, *Quatrefoil* (London: Vision, 1953); and Arthur Anderson Peters, *Finistere* (London: Victor Gollancz, 1951).

53. Croft, *The Cloven Hoof,* 59–65. For the "homosexuals in history" tradition, see Ackerley, *My Father and Myself,* 118; and Lancaster, *Brian Howard,* 325.

54. "Double Blue's Lapse," *NW,* 28 August 1927.

55. "Another Case Dismissed on Appeal," *Birmingham DM,* 21 September 1927.

56. Ibid.

57. PRO, MEPO 3, 405: 1927, attachment 35a: Confidential Street Offences Committee: Report of the Sub-committee. For the "character" defense, see "Hyde Park Arrest," *NW,* 8 January 1922, 5; "Shadowed in Strand," *NW,* 27 June 1926, 14; "Dismissed the Charge," *NW,* 21 March 1926, 9; PRO, HO 144 22298: "Criticism of Elderly Judge's Treatment of Homosexual Offences" (1922–28).

58. PRO, MEPO 3, 923: "Harry Raymond and Others Operating as a Blackmail Gang in Leicester Square": 203 UNC 1970, minute 15c: DDI C Parker to Supt. (14 December 1937); ibid., minute 13b: statement of Ian F. ibid., minute 11d: DDI Parker to Supt. (14 October 1937); ibid., minute 11c: Harold G.; ibid., minute 9a: Insp. Parker to Supt. C (23 September 1937).

59. Alexander, *William Plomer,* 244.

60. Desmond Curran and Dennis Parr, "Homosexuality: An Analysis of 100 Male Cases Seen in Private Practice," *British Medical Journal,* 6 April 1957, 797–801, 800–1. See also, for example, Driberg, *Ruling Passions,* 88; Fred Sommer, "Anthony Blunt and Guy Burgess: Gay Spies," *Journal of the History of Homosexuality,* 29, no. 4 (1995): 279–80; John Lahr, ed., *The Orton Diaries* (London: Methuen, 1986); and NSA: C456 070 01: Alan MacGregor.

61. PRO, MEPO 3, 405: transcript of proceedings: 5 January 1928: Q450-52. For the centrality of these sartorial codes to conventions of social investigation see, for example, Orwell, *Down and Out in Paris and London,* 128–29.

62. Anomaly, *The Invert,* 171. See, for example, Driberg, *Ruling Passions,* 13; Quennell, *A Lonely Business;* and Lancaster, *Brian Howard.*

63. Lehmann, *In the Purely Pagan Sense,* 129, 164; and 54, 127, 162–63, 249, 251. See also Douglas Blair Turnbaugh, *Private: The Erotic Art of Duncan Grant, 1885–1978* (London: Gay Men's Press, 1989); Simon Watney, *The Art of Duncan Grant* (London: John Murray, 1990); Hoare, *Serious Pleasures,* 232–35; and Gardiner, *A Class Apart,* 40–66.

64. Michael S., interview.

65. Lehmann, *In the Purely Pagan Sense,* 50–51, emphasis added.

66. For the wider resonance of this eroticization of the working-class body within bourgeois culture see, for example, Grosskurth, *Memoirs of John Addington Symonds;* E. M. Forster, *Maurice* (Harmondsworth: Penguin, 1972); George Orwell, *Road to Wigan Pier* (London: Victor Gollancz, 1937); and D. H. Lawrence, *Lady Chatterley's Lover* (London, Penguin, 1961).

67. See Peter Stallybrass and Allon White, *The Politics and Poetics of Transgression* (London: Methuen, 1986).

68. Bartlett, *Letters to Christopher*, 45.

69. Ackerley, *My Father and Myself*, 136.

70. Lehmann, *In the Purely Pagan Sense*, 129.

71. Ibid., 52.

72. Ibid., 245–46.

73. Parker, *Ackerley*, 114.

74. King, *My Sister and Myself*, 46–48.

75. Parker, *Ackerley*, 114; King, *My Sister and Myself*, 52.

76. Davidson, *World, The Flesh and Myself*, 134.

77. Ackerley, *My Father and Myself*, 110.

78. Lehmann, *In the Purely Pagan Sense*, 210.

79. Ackerley, *My Father and Myself*, 123.

80. Ibid., 216.

81. Williams, *Emlyn*, 28.

82. Westwood, *A Minority*, 79.

83. Weeks and Porter, *Between the Acts*, 164.

84. LMA, A PMC 80: "Homosexuality": L. J. to Lady Coleville (7 May 1955); ibid., L. J. to Tomlinson (1 June 1955); ibid., L. J. to Caughlin (13 June 1955); ibid., L. J. to Caughlin (1 July 1955); ibid., L. J. to Lady Coleville (7 July 1955); ibid., L. J. to Caughlin (12 July 1955); ibid., L. J. to Tomlinson (2 August 1955); ibid., Tomlinson to Lady Coleville (29 August 1955).

85. Garland, *Heart in Exile*. All page number are from the 1995 edition published by Millivres Books.

CHAPTER 9

1. PRO, MEPO 3, 1006: "Karl B. Moral Pervert/Refused Permission to Land," minute 15a: F. J. Rolfe CI Immigration Branch HO to Immigration Office (13 July 1937). See also minute 20a: Sergt. G. Brown (21 June 1937); minute 1a, statement of PS Allen (Port of Harwich Metropolitan Police), special report (7 December 1934).

2. Ibid., minute 1a (7 December 1934).

3. For the role of the press in shaping public knowledge of "homosexuality," see, for example, Waters, "Disorders of the Mind, Disorders of the Body Social," 138–139; Cook, *London and the Culture of Homosexuality*, 90, 98; and Cocks, *Nameless Offences*.

4. Maynard, "Through a Hole in the Lavatory Wall," 207–42. See also Hubbard, *Sex and the City*.

5. "A Modern Gomorrah," *JB*, 13 June 1925, 18. Begbie was well known for his reflections on contemporary British culture, as well as for being a writer for Methuen and Mills and Boon. See, for example, Begbie, *The Mirrors of Downing Street: Some Political Reflections* (London: Mills and Boon, 1920); Begbie, *Broken*

Lights: A Short Study in the Variety of Christian Opinion (London: Mills and Boon, 1926); and Joseph McAleer, *Passion's Fortune: The Story of Mills and Boon* (Oxford: Oxford University Press, 1999), 15, 52–54, 190, 293.

6. For the "Black Book" trial see above, pages 10–11.

7. "Wickedest Gang in London: The Painted Boy Menace," *JB*, 25 July 1925, 11; and "Blackmail Most Foul," *JB*, 27 February 1926, 18.

8. "Rouged Rogues," *JB*, 3 January 1925, 10.

9. "Brazen Blackmail Gang," *JB*, 30 May 1925, 13.

10. Ibid. See also "Blackmail Most Foul," *JB*, 27 February 1926, 18.

11. "Who's Gagging the Yard?" *JB*, 12 December 1925.

12. "A Modern Gomorrah," *JB*, 13 June 1925, 18. See Andy Croll, "Street Disorder, Surveillance and Shame: Regulating Behaviour in the Public Spaces of the Late-Victorian British town," *Social History* 24, no 3 (1999): 252.

13. "Who's Gagging the Yard?" *JB*, 12 December 1925. See also "Wickedest Gang in London," *JB*, 25 July 1925, 11.

14. I draw here upon Sibley, *Geographies of Exclusion*, 24–86. For the influence of this language on judicial representations of queer urban culture, see the comments of Ernest Wild, recorder of London, in "Plague Spot Raided," *NW*, 27 June 1927, 13; and "West End Nest of Vice Smoked Out," *NW*, 5 March 1933, 18.

15. See Daniel Pick, *Faces of Degeneration: A European Disorder, c. 1848–1918* (Cambridge: Cambridge University Press, 1989).

16. Susan Kingsley Kent, *Making Peace: The Reconstruction of Gender in Interwar Britain* (Princeton: Princeton University Press, 1993), 2. See also Bourke, *Dismembering the Male*; Susan Grayzel, *Women's Identities at War: Gender, Motherhood and Politics in Britain and France During the First World War* (Chapel Hill and London: University of North Carolina Press, 1999); Nicoletta Gullace, *"The Blood of Our Sons": Men, Women and the Renegotiation of British Citizenship during the Great War* (Basingstoke: Palgrave Macmillan, 2002); Kohn, *Dope Girls*; Angela Woollacott, "'Khaki Fever' and Its Control: Gender, Class, Age and Sexual Morality on the British Homefront in the First World War," *Journal of Contemporary History* 29 (1994): 325–47; Philippa Levine, "'Walking the Streets in a Way No Decent Women Should': Women Police in World War I," *Journal of Modern History* 66 (1994): 34–78; Sandra Gilbert and Susan Gubar, "Soldier's Heart: Literary Men, Literary Women and the Great War," in *Behind the Lines: Gender and the Two World Wars*, ed. Margaret Higonnet (New Haven: Yale University Press, 1987); Jill Greenfield, Sean O'Connell, and Chris Reid, "Fashioning Masculinity: *Men Only*, Consumption and the Development of Marketing in the 1930s," *Twentieth Century British History* 10, no. 4 (1999): 457–76.

17. "The Languid Youth," *JB*, 17 October 1925, 30.

18. Moseley, *Night Haunts of London*, 43.

19. For example: "Out with Their Names," *JB*, 28 November 1925, 20; "Nightclub Revelations," *JB*, 19 July 1925, 13; "A Black Betrayal," *JB*, 25 July 1925, 15; "Was He Murdered?" *JB*, 28 May 1927, 25; "The Greed of Gleed," *JB*,

26 December 1925, 8; "Hotels on Our Blacklist," *JB*, 30 January 1926; and "Aristocratic Drug Fiend," *JB*, 13 March 1926, 13.

20. Douglas Goldring, *The Nineteen Twenties: A General Survey and Some Personal Memories* (London: Nicholson and Watson, 1945). See, for example, Moseley, *Night Haunts;* Felstead, *The Underworld of London;* Hubert Stringer, *Moral Evil in London* (London: Chapman and Hall, 1925); and Croft, *The Cloven Hoof.*

21. Graham Dawson, *Soldier Heroes: British Adventure, Empire and the Imagining of Masculinities* (London and New York: Routledge, 1994), 2. I explore these themes in greater depth in Houlbrook, "Soldier Heroes and Rent Boys: Homosex, Masculinities and Britishness in the Brigade of Guards c.1900–1960," *Journal of British Studies* 42, no. 3 (2003): 351–88.

22. "In Hyde Park," *Emp,* 26 April 1931, 12; "Hyde Park after Dark," *NW,* 26 April 1931, 5; "Perils of Hyde Park after Nightfall," *IPN,* 30 April 1931, 5; and "Night Perils of Hyde Park," *MA,* 23 April 1931, 8.

23. "Hyde Park after Dark," *NW,* 26 April 1931, 5.

24. See "We Expose a Blackmail Gang," *JB,* 16 November 1929, 8.

25. PRO, HO 345 8, CHP 47: memorandum submitted by the War Office.

26. Ibid.

27. "This Was the Story of a Lost Soul," *NW,* 15 April 1951, 2; "Five Troopers Punished by Court Martial," *NW,* 29 April 1951, 2; PRO, HO 345 12: CHP TRANS 6, testimony of Theobald Mathew, director of public prosecutions (7 December 1954); PRO: HO 345 14: CHP TRANS 7, testimony of Sir John Nott-Bower, commissioner of police for the metropolis, et al. (7 December 1954).

28. "Five Troopers Punished," *NW,* 29 April 1951, 2.

29. "This Was the Story of a Lost Soul," *NW,* 15 April 1951, 2; "Perils of Hyde Park after Nightfall," *IPN,* 30 April 1931, 5; "Night Perils of Hyde Park," *MA,* 23 April 1931, 8; "Hyde Park after Dark," *NW,* 26 April 1931, 5; and "Men Who Prey on Guardsmen," *NW,* 4 November 1956, 1.

30. PRO, HO 345 7: CHP 12, memorandum submitted by Lord Chief Justice Goddard, emphasis added.

31. "This Was the Story of a Lost Soul," *NW,* 15 April 1951, 2. For these sentencing patterns, see LMA, PS MS A1 55 (16 May 1922); LMA, PS MS A1 35 (12 February 1917); LMA, PS MS A1 79 (18 March 1927); LMA, PS MS A1 83 (5 September 1927); LMA, PS MS A1 110 (11 April 1932); LMA, PS MS A1 160 (16 November 1937); LMA, PS BOW A01 067 (8 August 1917).

32. See, for example, "South-Western: Prison for Guardsman," *IPN,* 22 October 1925, 7; "Ex-Guardsman's Good War Record Reduces His Fine," *IPN,* 27 January 1927, 7.

33. "This Was the Story of a Lost Soul," *NW,* 15 April 1951, 2.

34. Ibid.

35. "Five Troopers Punished by Court Martial," *NW,* 29 April 1951, 2.

36. Eve Kosofsky Sedgwick, *Epistemology of the Closet* (Berkeley: University of California Press, 1990).

37. PRO, HO 45 24960: "Homosexual Offences Conference" (7 May 1931). The conference on "homosexual offences in which soldiers . . . might be concerned" was convened by the director of public prosecutions following the furor surrounding Cecil E. It was attended by officers from London District Command and the Judge-General's Office, as well as representatives from the Met and DPP's office.

38. Ibid. See also Alan Roland, *Guardsman: An Autobiography* (London: Museum Press, 1955), 107–8; PRO, HO 345 8: CHP 47, memorandum submitted by the War Office.

39. PRO, HO 45 24960 (7 May 1931); PRO, HO 345 8: CHP 47; PRO, HO 345 13: CHP TRANS 25 (25 May 1955).

40. Croft, *The Cloven Hoof,* 60–61, 68–69.

41. "Sexual Offences against Young Persons," *Law Journal,* 6 March 1926, 215.

42. See, for example, "Marylebone: Scoutmaster Committed for Trial on Serious Charge," *IPN,* 8 December 1927, 7; "Solicitor Convicted on a Disgraceful Charge," *IPN,* 3 November 1927, 3; and "Baptist Minister Committed for Trial on Serious Charge," *IPN,* 6 January 1927, 7.

43. Hanmore, *Curse of the Embankment,* 27–28.

44. Ibid., 32–33. See also FL, NVA: case files, C85 box 117: John William B. (1928).

45. FL, NVA: correspondence files: S46b box 104: Seventeenth Report of the South London Committee for the Protection of Children (February 1932).

46. LMA, PS HAM A 26: Joseph B. and William B., charged with outraging public decency (19 October 1918). See also LMA, PS HAM A 35: Bert V. and Frederick F., charged with indecency (30 June 1932); and LMA, PS HAM A 26: Robert B. and Robert A., charged with gross indecency (2 September 1918).

47. Maynard, "'Horrible Temptations,'" 235. For such assumptions see Hatton, *London's Bad Boys,* 60, 93.

48. Quoted in William Norwood East, "The Sociological Aspects of Homosexuality: A Discussion," *Medico Legal Journal* (1947): 21.

49. See, for example, Jackson, *Child Sexual Abuse in Victorian England,* passim; Bland, *Banishing the Beast;* and Linda Mahood and B. Littlewood, "The 'Vicious Girl' and the 'Street-corner Boy': Sexuality and the Gendered Delinquent in the Scottish Child-saving Movement, 1850–1940," *Journal of the History of Sexuality* 4 (1993): 17–42. For anxieties over "attempts to effeminise young manhood," see Hatton, *London's Bad Boys,* 23; and Hendrick, *Images of Youth.*

50. FL, NVA: correspondence files, S46b box 104: Six Point Group to NVA Secretary (4 October 1923).

51. "The Child and the Cinema," *Church Times,* 25 August 1916. See also, for example, LMA, LCC MIN 10709: agenda (24 April 1918); LMA, LCC MIN 10999: NUWW: Report of Women's Patrols on London Cinemas (20 April 1918); LMA, LCC MIN 10751: minutes (10 February and 24 February 1926): LMA, LCC MIN 11085: report by clerk of council: Sexual Offences Against Young Persons (24 February 1926): PRO, MEPO 2, 1691: "Immorality in Cinematograph Halls"

(1912–16); PRO, HO 45 24570: "Improper Behaviour in London Cinemas" (1909–21); FL, NVA: executive minutes, volume 7, box 195 (26 April 1921); and "Barred from Cinema," *IPN*, 10 November 1932, 3.

52. LMA, LCC MIN 8714: agenda (11 April 1919; 13 July 1923).

53. LMA, LCC MIN 8945: J. G. Pearce to committee (30 June 1923).

54. LMA, LCC MIN 8776: minutes (13 November 1925). See also LMA, LCC MIN 8974: Deputation of the Women's Freedom League; report of chief officer (10 May 1929); and "Untitled," *IPN*, 10 May 1923, 8.

55. "Sexual Offences against Young Persons," *Law Journal*, 6 March 1926, 215.

56. *Report of the Departmental Committee on Sexual Offences against Young Persons* (London: HMSO, 1925); FL, NVA: correspondence files, S46 box 104: Assaults: Departmental Committee 1932: (2) Summary of Recommendations of Departmental Committee on Sexual Offences against Young Persons. After 1925, organizations like the NVA intensified their campaigns "with a view to forcing Government to introduce legislation to deal more effectively with these cases." Ibid., NVA to F. James (Reformatory and Refuge Union) 24 February 1932; FL, NVA: executive minutes, volume 11, box 195 (28 June 1932; 29 April 1934).

57. Jackson, *Child Sexual Abuse*, passim. The exceptions to this pattern were concerns surrounding incest. See V. Bailey and S. Blackburn, "The Punishment of Incest Act 1908: A Case Study of Law Creation," *Criminal Law Review* (1979): 708–18; Anthony Wohl, "Sex and the Single Room: Incest among the Victorian Working Classes," in Wohl, *The Victorian Family: Structure and Stresses* (London: Croom Helm, 1978), 197–216.

58. Koven, "From Rough Lads to Hooligans"; George Chauncey, "Christian Brotherhood or Sexual Perversion? Homosexual Identities and the Construction of Sexual Boundaries in the World War One Era," *Journal of Social History* 19, no. 2 (1985): 182–211.

59. Fishman, *Streets of East London,* 64–67; G. Thorne, *The Great Acceptance: The Life Story of F. N. Charrington* (London: Hodder and Stoughton, 1912).

60. "Missionary and Boys," *NW,* 14 November 1920, 2. See also "Grave Charges against a Cub-Master," *IPN,* 28 September 1922, 7; "Serious Charge and Sentence on Captain of Church Lad's Brigade," *IPN,* 24 July 1924, 8; "Serious Charge against Assistant Scoutmaster," *IPN,* 13 June 1929, 3; and "Three Month's Hard Labour for Ex-Boys Brigade Officer," *IPN,* 9 May 1929, 3.

61. See, for example, PRO, HO 345 8, CHP 79: Association of Heads and Association of Managers of Approved Schools; PRO: HO 345 8, CHP 65: Standing Conference of National Voluntary Youth Organisations; PRO: HO 345 7, CHP 32, Minister of Education on the Misconduct of Teachers; and PRO, HO 345 12: CHP TRANS 14, Mr. Francis Morgan, legal adviser, Boy Scouts Organisation (3 February 1955).

62. See, for example, Pat Thane, "Population Politics in Post-War British Culture," in Conekin et al, *Moments of Modernity,* 114–33; Judy Giles, "Help for Housewives: Domestic Service and the Reconstruction of Domesticity in Britain,

1940–50," *Women's History Review* 10, no. 2 (2001): 299–324; Weeks, *Sex, Politics and Society,* 232–48; Tim Newburn, *Permission and Regulation: Law and Morals in Post War Britain* (London and New York: Routledge, 1992), 164; *The Report of the Royal Commission on Population* (London: HMSO, 1949); *The Report of the Royal Commission on Marriage and Divorce* (London: HMSO, 1951); and Bill Osgerby, *Youth in Britain since 1945* (Oxford: Blackwell, 1998), 17–82.

63. Richard Hoggart, *The Uses of Literacy* (London: Chatto and Windus, 1957). See also Abrams, *Teenage Consumer;* Goldthorpe et al., *The Affluent Worker;* Vernon Bogdanor and Robert Skidelsky, eds., *The Age of Affluence, 1951–1963* (London: Macmillan, 1970); and Ina Zweiniger-Bargeilowska, *Austerity in Britain: Rationing, Controls, and Consumption, 1939–1955* (Oxford: Oxford University Press, 2000).

64. "Thorp of the Yard: Vice!" *NW,* 11 April 1954, 7.

65. "This Isn't the London We Love," *NW,* 13 September 1953, 4. For contemporary reflections on this urban malaise, see Tietjen, *Soho;* Sutherland, *Portrait of a Decade,* 67–68, 176–88.

66. "Evil Men," *Sunday Pictorial,* 25 May 1952, 6, 15; 1 June 1952, 12; 8 June 1952, 12.

67. "Judges Are Shocked" and "An Evil in our Midst," *NW,* 1 November 1953, 2, 6.

68. Garland, *Heart in Exile,* 41.

69. Crisp, *Naked Civil Servant,* 105–73. See also Jivani, *It's Not Unusual,* 56–84; Lehmann, *In the Purely Pagan Sense,* 130–78; NSA, C547 43: Richard; NSA, C547 11: John Alcock; NSA, C456 89 01: Patrick Trevor-Roper; NSA, C456 06 01-2: Bernard Dobson; NSA: C456 03 02: John Alcock; Weeks and Porter, *Between the Acts,* passim.

70. Chris Waters, "'Dark Strangers' in our Midst: Discourses of Race and Nation in Britain, 1947–1963," *Journal of British Studies* 36, no. 2 (1997): 207–38, offers a different perspective on this crisis.

71. For the interconnections between national citizenship and notions of normative sexualities, see Kevin Grant, "'Bones of Contention': The Repatriation of the Remains of Roger Casement," *Journal of British Studies* 41, no. 3 (2002): 329–54; and Carolyn Dean, *The Frail Social Body: Pornography, Homosexuality and Other Fantasies in Interwar France* (Berkeley: University of California Press, 2000).

CHAPTER 10

1. Oscar Wilde to George Ives, quoted in Hyde, *The Other Love,* 2.

2. Quoted in Antony Grey, *Quest for Justice: Towards Homosexual Emancipation* (London: Sinclair-Stevenson, 1992), 125.

3. See, for example, Mary Liddell, "Give Us Back Our Freedom," *Observer,* 12 January 2003; and "Lord Jenkins of Hillhead," *Guardian,* 6 January 2003. For wider discussions of the "permissive society," see Newburn, *Permission and Regulation;* Cate

Haste, *Rules of Desire: Sex in Britain, World War One to the Present* (London: Pimlico, 1992), 139–251; and Arthur Marwick, *The Sixties: Cultural Revolution in Britain, France, Italy and the United States, c. 1958–c. 1971* (Oxford: Oxford University Press, 1991).

4. See Newburn, *Permission and Regulation,* passim.

5. Weeks, *Coming Out.*

6. Waters, "Disorders of the Mind," 134. See also Weeks, *Coming Out;* Hyde, *Other Love;* Stephen Jeffrey-Poulter, *Queers, Peers and Commons: The Struggle for Gay Law Reform from the 1950s to the Present* (London: Routledge, 1991); and Higgins, *Heterosexual Dictatorship.*

7. LMA, A PMC 98 7: annual report (1937). Patrick Higgins is thus simply wrong in asserting that "no one, in public at least, called for a reform of the laws in Britain until the autumn of 1953," in Higgins, *Heterosexual Dictatorship,* 3.

8. For the continued salience of these distinctions, see Anna-Marie Smith, *New Right Discourse on Race and Sexuality, Britain 1968–1990* (Cambridge: Cambridge University Press, 1994).

9. "West End Nest of Vice Smoked Out," *NW,* 5 March 1933. For Wild, see Robert Blackham, *Sir Ernest Wild KC* (London: Rich and Cowan, 1935).

10. "Improper Performances in West London," *Times,* 28 February 1933, 9; "Raid on a Dance," *NW,* 8 January 1933, 9; Weeks and Porter, *Between the Acts,* 97–98.

11. PRO, CRIM 1, 639: Austin S. and (33) others, charged with disorderly house, conspiracy to corrupt morals: depositions to Central Criminal Court (7 February 1933), statement of CI/F Smith: 22; PC 314/F Haylock: 53; William H.: 57; PRO, CRIM 1, 638: attachment 7; and "Masquerade Denied," *NW,* 29 January 1933, 6.

12. I discuss this case further in Matt Houlbrook, " 'Lady Austin's Camp Boys': Constituting the Queer Subject in 1930s London," *Gender and History* 14, no. 1 (2002): 31–61.

13. PRO, CRIM 1, 639: copy depositions: statement of PS 40/F Robbings: 49–50.

14. Ibid., statement of SDDI/F Francis, 29.

15. Ibid., statement of PC 139/F Labbatt, 9–10.

16. Ibid., statement of SDDI F Francis, 29.

17. Ibid., statement of PS 30/F Don, 32.

18. "Police Story of Scenes at a West End House," *IPN,* 26 January 1933.

19. "Alleged Scenes at West End Dances," *NW,* 26 February 1933.

20. PRO, CRIM 1, 639: copy depositions: statement of SDDI F Francis: 29. See also Jack Neave's defense of his right to run a queer commercial venue from the "scientific point of view," using the language of phrenology and "psychology." PRO, MEPO 3, 758: "Caravan Club: Disorderly House/Male Prostitutes," minute 11a (29 August 1934); and "Caravan Club Disclosures," *NW,* 28 October 1934.

21. George Ives, *The Continued Extension of the Criminal Law* (London: J. E. Francis, 1922); and Anomaly, *The Invert.* For this earlier work, see Havelock Ellis,

Studies in the Psychology of Sex; Symonds, *A Problem in Modern Ethics;* and Carpenter, *The Intermediate Sex.*

22. See Cook, *London and the Culture of Homosexuality,* 1, 32–33, 44, 138–50; Cook, "'A New City of Friends': London and Homosexuality in the 1890s," *History Workshop Journal* 56 (2003): 33–58.

23. Ives, *Continued Extension,* 21, 25.

24. Anomaly, *The Invert,* 7–8.

25. Ibid., 67.

26. Ibid., 140.

27. Ibid., 72.

28. Ibid., 126, 139.

29. Ibid., 32.

30. Ibid., 138.

31. For the BSSSP, with which Carpenter, Ellis, and Ives were all involved, and its discreet campaigning for law reform, see Weeks, *Coming Out,* 128–67; Lesley Hall, "'Disinterested Enthusiasm for Sexual Misconduct': The British Society for the Study of Sex Psychology, 1913–47," *Journal of Contemporary History* 30 (1995): 665–86; David Weigle, "Psychology and Homosexuality: The British Sexological Society," *Journal of the History of the Behavioral Sciences* 31 (1995): 137–48.

32. Anomaly, *The Invert,* xi.

33. Ibid., xv.

34. Ibid., xxiii–xxiv.

35. Underwood, *Hidden Lights* (London: Fortune Press, 1937), 152–75; Gregory Woods, *A History of Gay Literature: The Male Tradition* (New Haven: Yale University Press, 1998), 10; and Timothy d'Arch Smith, *R. A. Caton and the Fortune Press: A Memoir and a Hand-List* (London: Bertram Rota, 1983).

36. Underwood, *Bachelor's Hall* (London: Fortune Press, 1934), 7–8.

37. See, for example, the rector who voices Edward Carpenter's words in attributing homosexual desire to a "feminine soul enclosed in a male body." Underwood, *Bachelor's Hall,* 153.

38. Underwood, *Flame of Freedom,* 67, 104.

39. Ibid., 210, 231.

40. Ibid., 44, 192.

41. Ibid., 197–200.

42. Ibid., 237–38. *Bachelor's Hall* similarly maps Adrian Byfield's passionate, romantic, and spiritual love affair with Ronald, which ends with the latter's tragic suicide. See Underwood, *Bachelor's Hall,* passim. For similar fictionalized pleas for social acceptance see A. T. Fitzroy, *Despised and Rejected* (London: C. W. Daniel, 1918); and Radclyffe Hall, *The Well of Loneliness* (London: Jonathon Cape, 1928).

43. See PRO, MEPO 3, 2330 (1943); PRO, MEPO 3, 989: "Persons Frequenting Urinals Apparently for Improper Purposes" (1937–39); PRO, MEPO 3, 987 (1935); and PRO, MEPO 3, 2331: "Gross indecency/importuning" (1943).

44. Ives, *Continued Extension,* 8.

45. PRO, MEPO 3, 405: "Francis Champain: Indecency," minute 4a: Mr. J. Chester to the commissioner of police (27 September 1927).

46. Curtis-Bennett's public life, including his involvement in Champain's case, is described in Roland Wild and Derek Curtis-Bennett, *"Curtis": The Life of Sir Henry Curtis-Bennett KC* (London: Cassell, 1937). For the Savoy case, see pages 106–8 above. See also "Plague Spot Raided," *NW,* 27 February 1927, 13; "Dance Hall Orgies," *NW,* 23 January 1927, 4; and "Numbered Prisoners at Old Bailey," *MA,* 21 February 1933, 3.

47. "Wrecked His Career," *NW,* 15 May 1932. The men represented by Curtis-Bennett included a respected author, a public school games master, an independent gentleman, an ex-army officer and solicitor's clerk, and an ex-army major and stockbroker. See PRO, MEPO 3, 994: "Mitford B.," minute 9a: Mr. Kendal to Brig. James Whitehead (14 November 1936); "Two Men Acquitted," *NW,* 8 May 1932; "Gave Notice of Appeal," *NW,* 18 June 1922; "Ex-Officer to Appeal," *NW,* 28 March 1926; and "Jury Upholds the Honour of Major," *NW,* 19 February 1933.

48. For the "good character" defense, see "Hyde Park Arrest," *NW,* 8 January 1922; "Artist Arrested," *NW,* 20 June 1926; "Dismissed the Charge," *NW,* 21 March 1926; and "Gave Notice of Appeal," *NW,* 18 June 1922.

49. PRO, MEPO 3, 404: "Gross Indecency with Boys," 213 / IMP / 716: Robert M.: sentenced upon charges of gross indecency: minute 11a: CI CID Gillian to Supt (7 April 1927); ibid., minute 11K: statement of Robert M. (4 April 1927).

50. Ibid., minute 22a, Inspector A. Cornelius to Supt. (27 May 1927); "Major in the Dock," *NW,* 17 April 1927; and "Veteran Major's Sin," *NW,* 29 May 1927.

51. "Conviction to Stand," *NW,* 21 September 1930.

52. "Vicar in Custody," *NW,* 24 September 1944.

53. PRO, HO 144 22298: "Criticism of Elderly Judge's Treatment of Homosexual Offences" (1922–28), section 430931 / 1: John B. (28 February 1922).

54. PRO, MEPO 3, 404: 213/IMP/716: minute 22a: Inspector A. Cornelius to Supt. (27 May 1927); ibid., CI Gillian to Supt. (27 May 1927); ibid., minute 24: ACC (3 June 1927); ibid., minute 26: ACC GRA (8 June 1927).

55. Cecil Whitely, "The Problem of the Moral Pervert," *Medical Press,* 15 July 1932; Whitely, "The Problem of the Moral Pervert," *Journal of the Institute of Hygiene* (April 1933).

56. Doan, *Fashioning Sapphism,* 48. The quotation is from George Ives's journal notes on Chapman's comments at a 1914 BSSSP meeting.

57. Chris Waters, "Edward Glover, the Institute for the Scientific Treatment of Delinquency and the Question of Homosexual Law Reform in Mid-20th Century Britain" (unpublished paper).

58. Waters, "Edward Glover." Such judicial critiques increasingly influenced the policy positions of organizations like the National Vigilance Association. FL, NVA: executive minutes, volume 11, box 195 (28 June 1932); ibid., volume 10, box 196 (26 November 1935).

59. These continuities were reinforced by the personal and institutional ties between the BSSSP and men like Norman Haire and Edward Glover and the ISTD. See Chris Waters, "Havelock Ellis, Sigmund Freud and the State: Discourses of Homosexual Identity in Interwar Britain," in *Sexology in Culture: Labelling Bodies and Desires*, ed. Lucy Bland and Laura Doan (Oxford:, Polity Press, 1998), 165–79.

60. See "Severity Misplaced," *Observer*, 21 October 1956; NSA, C456 93 01: CH Rolfe.

61. For the debates over Wolfenden's appointment, see Higgins, *Heterosexual Dictatorship*, 3–12; John Wolfenden, *Turning Points* (London: Bodley Head, 1976), 129–46; and Mort, "Mapping Sexual London," 92–113. The committee's papers are contained in PRO, HO 345 1–20: Departmental Committee on Homosexual Offences and Prostitution (1954–57).

62. PRO, HO 345 2: correspondence: undated and unsigned memo.

63. Ibid., J. A. Newsom (22 August 1956); W. Conwy Roberts (8 August 1955); G. H. Macmillan (1 July 1955); and Anatole James (30 May 1955).

64. Ibid., Roberts (28 June 1955).

65. PRO, HO 345 14, CHP TRANS 32: two witnesses called by the chairman (28 July 1955), 32.

66. NSA, C456 89 01: Patrick Trevor-Roper.

67. PRO, HO 345 2: correspondence, Roberts (15 December 1953).

68. NSA, C456 89 01: Patrick Trevor-Roper.

69. PRO, HO 345 2: correspondence: undated and unsigned memo.

70. Moran, *Homosexual(ity) of Law*, 102–7; and Mort, "Mapping Sexual London," 108–9.

71. PRO, HO 345 2: correspondence, Roberts (15 December 1954).

72. NSA, C456 89 01: Patrick Trevor-Roper.

73. PRO, HO 345 4: correspondence: chairman's comments on Roberts's memo.

74. Wildeblood's circumstances were more complex, since he volunteered to give evidence while serving an eighteen-month prison sentence for gross indecency. Wildeblood, *Against the Law*.

75. Mort, "Mapping Sexual London," 109.

76. Wildeblood, *Against the Law*, 7.

77. For Trevor-Roper's and Winter's use of medical discourses, see PRO, HO 345 8: CHP 53; CHP 70: memorandum submitted by Mr. C. W.

78. Wildeblood, *Against the Law*, 175.

79. PRO, HO 345 13, CHP TRANS 24: Peter Wildeblood (24 May 1955): 1892 11, 1896 12. See also PRO, HO 345 8, CHP 69: memorandum submitted by witness from 28 July 1954.

80. PRO, HO 345 8, CHP 53.

81. Ibid., CHP 51: memorandum submitted by Peter Wildeblood.

82. PRO, HO 345 15, CHP TRANS 24: 1854a 1.

83. PRO, HO 345 14, CHP TRANS 32: 2612, 12.

84. PRO, HO 345 8, CHP 54; CHP 51.

85. PRO, HO 345 14, CHP TRANS 32: 2619, 16.

86. Ibid., 2622 18.

87. Wildeblood, *Against the Law,* 13.

88. Ibid., 17.

89. PRO, HO 345 14, CHP TRANS 32: 2597, 5–6.

90. Ibid.

91. Ibid., 2619, 16.

92. PRO, HO 345 8, CHP 53.

93. Wildeblood, *Against the Law,* 175.

94. Compare Wildeblood's public statements with reports of his trial: "All Day Hearing of Montagu Case," *NW,* 24 January 1954; PRO, HO 345 8: CHP 51; and PRO, HO 345 13: CHP TRANS 24. There are similar gaps between Trevor-Roper's testimony and his later recollections. See NSA, C456 89 01: Patrick Trevor-Roper; PRO, HO 345 8: CHP 53; and PRO, HO 345 14: CHP TRANS 32.

95. See, for example, Hoggart, *Uses of Literacy.*

96. PRO, HO 345 14: CHP TRANS 32: 2600, 7.

97. PRO, HO 345 8: CHP 51.

98. Ibid.

99. PRO, HO 345 14: CHP TRANS 32; PRO, HO 345 15: CHP TRANS 24.

100. PRO, HO 345 1: *Report of the Departmental Committee on Homosexual Offences and Prostitution* (London: HMSO, 1957), 10.

101. Ibid., 9, 12.

102. Ibid., 9, 24, 44.

103. See, for example, Westwood [Schofield], *Society and the Homosexual;* Westwood, *A Minority;* Wildeblood, *A Way of Life;* Renault, *The Charioteer;* Wilson, *Hemlock and After;* Garland, *The Heart in Exile;* and Homosexual Law Reform Society, *Homosexuals and the Law* (London: HLRS, 1959). For *Victim,* see John Hill, *Sex, Class and Realism: British Cinema, 1956–1963* (London: BFI Publishing, 1997), 90–94; and Stephen Bourne, *Brief Encounters: Lesbians and Gays in British Cinema; 1930–71* (London and New York: Cassell, 1996), 155–62.

104. For the HLRS, see Grey, *Quest for Justice,* passim; PRO, HO 291 125: 1960–4.

105. PRO, HO 291 123: "General notes on Homosexual Offences and Prostitution" (1957–58); PRO, FD 23 1893: "Homosexuality: 1958–62"; PRO, HO 291 125 (1960–1964); PRO, PREM 13 1563: "Law Relating to Homosexual Offences" (1965–67); PRO, HO 291 129: "Sexual Offences Bill" (1966–67); and PRO, HO 291 130: "Suggestion for Extending Provision Requiring DPP's Consent" (1967).

106. On this point, see the memoirs of two men who certainly did not meet the demands of respectability: Driberg, *Ruling Passions;* and Crisp, *Naked Civil Servant,* 207.

107. Bell and Binnie, *The Sexual Citizen,* 2–3, emphasis added.

108. Newburn, *Permission and Regulation,* 62.

CONCLUSION

1. I draw here upon Michel de Certeau's contrast between "strategic mapping"—the behaviors that municipal authorities and planners seek to impose on urban subjects—and "urban practices"—the "pedestrian speech acts" through which subjects compose their own individuated narratives of life in the city. See de Certeau, *The Practice of Everyday Life,* trans. Steven Randall (Berkeley: University of California Press, 1984), 30–37, 92–101.

2. Kenneth Hare, *London's Latin Quarter* (London: John Lane/Bodley Head, 1926), 94.

3. For the debates over the Albert Hall's legal position and the Met's unwillingness to assume responsibility for its supervision, see PRO, MEPO 2, 3281: "Lady Malcolm's Servants' Ball: Annual Albert Hall Demanding Unusual Treatment and Supervision" (1930–38); PRO, MEPO 2, 3278: "Chelsea Arts Ball: Commissioners Ruling on Duty and Cost" (1933–39).

4. Ibid., 26 PP 3067: "Supt. B.: Lady Malcolm's Ball: Observation on Male Prostitutes," minute 4a: SDI Baxter to Supt. (16 November 1934). The crowds at the Chelsea Arts Ball were similar: see Williams, *Emlyn,* 309. The balls are discussed in William Gaunt, *Chelsea* (London: B. T. Batsford, 1954), 147–48; Thea Holne, *Chelsea* (London: Hamish Hamilton, 1972), 247–48; Tom Cross, *Artists and Bohemians: 100 Years with the Chelsea Arts Club* (London: Quiller Press, 1992), 6–21, 59–70, 112–22.

5. PRO, CRIM 1, 639: Austin S. and others, charged with keeping a disorderly house (1933–38), copy depositions: statement of PS 40/F Robbings; and "Alleged Scenes at West End Dances," *NW,* 26 February 1933, 8.

6. PRO, MEPO 2, 3281: 26 PP 2694: Sir Ian Malcolm Asks for Services of 2 PCs on Gratuity, minute 16a: anon. to Trenchard (14 November 1933).

7. "The Servants' Ball," *Times,* 19 November 1936, 10.

8. See PRO, MEPO 2, 3281: PP 3067, minute 2: HF A1 (20 November 1934); attached is a ticket for Lady Malcolm's Servant's Ball (20 November 1935); ibid., minute 44a, ASDI-B Green to Supt. (26 November 1938); ibid., 26 PP 2694: minute 16b: Supt. J. Howell to ACC (14 November 1933).

9. Weeks and Porter, *Between the Acts,* 142.

10. Williams, *Emlyn,* 308.

11. Weeks and Porter, *Between the Acts,* 142–43. See also Rupert Hart-Davis, *Hugh Walpole: A Biography* (London: Rupert Hart-Davis, 1952), 110; Phillip Hoare, *Serious Pleasures: The Life of Stephen Tennant* (London: Hamish Hamilton, 1990), 109; Lancaster, ed., *Brian Howard,* 130–31; and Michael Luke, *David Tennant and the Gargoyle Years* (London: Weidenfeld and Nicolson, 1991), 110.

BIBLIOGRAPHY

PRIMARY SOURCES

Corporation of London Record Office
Registers and minutes: Mansion House and Guildhall Justice Rooms
Fawcett Library, London
National Vigilance Association papers
London Metropolitan Archive
Metropolitan Magistrates Courts registers and minutes:
Hampstead Petty Sessions PS HAM A1
Lambeth PS LAM A1, B1
Tower Bridge PS TOW A1, B1
Registers:
Bow Street PS BOW A1 / A2
Clerkenwell PS CLE A1
Greenwich PS GRE A1
Marylebone PS MAR A1
Marlborough Street PS MS A1 / A2
North London PS NLO A1
Old Street PS NLO A1
South Western PS SWE A1
Thames PS TH A1
Westminster PS TOW A1
West London PS WLN A1
Woolwich PS WOO A1
London County Council
Agendas, minutes, and presented papers of Entertainments (Licensing), Public Control, Public Health, Parks and Open Spaces, Theatres and Music Halls
Calendars of Prisoners: Central Criminal Court: ACC 2385
Public Morality Council papers: A / PMC / 1–98
Public Record Office, The National Archives, London
Central Criminal Court: depositions, indictments and calendars: CRIM 1 / CRIM 2 / CRIM 4
Director of Public Prosecutions Papers: DPP 6
Home Office Papers: HO 45 / HO 144 / HO 345
Metropolitan Police Papers: MEPO 2 / MEPO 3
Prison Commissioner Papers: PCOM 9
Parliamentary Papers
Report of the Royal Commission on Police Powers and Procedures: 1929

Report of the Street Offences Committee: 1927

Report of the Departmental Committee on Sexual Offences against Young Persons: 1925

Report of the Departmental Committee on Homosexual Offences and Prostitution: 1957

Newspapers

Daily Express, Daily Mail, Empire News, Evening Standard, Illustrated Police News, John Bull, Morning Advertiser, News of the World, The Times

ORAL TESTIMONIES

Hall-Carpenter Oral History Project

NSA, C456 86 01–7: Olive Agar, b. 1916 (May 1990)

NSA, C456 03 02: John Alcock, b. 1927 (July 1985)

NSA, C456 126 1–3: Bette Bourne, b. 1939 (March 1994)

NSA, C456 15: Diana Chapman, b. 1928 (September 1985)

NSA, C456 123 1–9: John Chesterman, b. 1935 (September 1993)

NSA, C456 31 01–2: Tom Cullen, b. 1913

NSA, C456 06 01–2: Bernard Dobson, b. 1927 (September 1985)

NSA, C456 90 01: Tony Garrett, b. 1929 (August 1990)

NSA, C456 88 1–3: David Godin, b. 1936 (June 1990)

NSA, C456 71 01–3: Antony Grey, b. 1927 (February 1990)

NSA, C456 122 01–08: Michael James, b. 1941 (August 1993)

NSA, C456 070 01: Alan MacGregor, b. 1930/1 (February 1990)

NSA, C456 49: Frank Birkhill, b. 1907 (January 1986)

NSA, C456 93 01: C. H. Rolfe, b. 1901 (August 1990)

NSA, C456 68 01–3: Rene Sawyer, b. 1936 (January 1990)

NSA, C456 89 01: Patrick Trevor-Roper, b. 1916 (August 1990).

Interviews conducted by Tony Dean

NSA, C547 11: John Alcock

NSA, C547 06: John Alcock

NSA, C547 21: Anonymous

NSA, C547 05: Anonymous

NSA, C547 14: Anonymous

NSA, C547 09: Anonymous

NSA, C547 07: Tricky Dicky

NSA, C547 06 C1: Unnamed Manager of A&B Club

NSA, C547 15: Pat

NSA, C547 43: Richard

Interviews in Domino film, *The Secret World of Sex*

NSA, C444 03 48a-49a: John Alcock

NSA, C444 03 39a-40a: Dudley Cave

NSA, C444 03 30a-32a: Alex Purdie

NSA, B1143/4: 1: "The Black Sheep of the Family"
Michael S. b.1919: interviewed by Matt Houlbrook (July 1999)

PUBLISHED SOURCES

Abelove, Henry, Michele Aina Barale, and David Halperin, eds. *The Lesbian and Gay Studies Reader*. London and New York: Routledge, 1993.

Abrams, Mark. *The Teenage Consumer*. London: Press Exchange, 1959.

Ackerley, J. R. *My Father and Myself*. London: Bodley Head, 1968.

Acton, Harold. *Memoirs of an Aesthete*. London: Methuen and Co., 1948.

———. *More Memoirs of an Aesthete*. London: Methuen and Co., 1970.

Alexander, Peter. *William Plomer: A Biography*. Oxford: Oxford University Press, 1989.

Anomaly. *The Invert and His Social Adjustment*. London: Balliere, Tindall and Cox, 1927.

Anonymous. "Prison and After: The Experiences of a Former Homosexual." *Howard Journal* 9, no. 2 (1955): 118–24.

Anstruther, Ian. *Oscar Browning: A Biography*. London: John Murray, 1983.

Aronson, Theo. *Prince Eddy and the Homosexual Underworld*. London: Murray, 1994.

Ascoli, David. *The Queen's Peace: The Origins and Development of the Metropolitan Police, 1829–1979*. London: Hamish Hamilton, 1979.

Baedecker's London and Its Environs: Handbook for Travellers. Leipzig: Karl Baedecker, 1923.

Bailey, Paul. *Three Queer Lives: An Alternative Biography of Fred Barnes, Naomi Jacob and Arthur Marshall*. London: Hamish Hamilton, 2001.

Bailey, Peter. "Parasexuality and Glamour: The Victorian Barmaid as Cultural Prototype." *Gender and History* 2, no. 2 (1990): 148–72.

———. "White Collars, Grey Lives? The Lower Middle Class Re-visited." *Journal of British Studies* 38, no. 3 (1999): 281–90.

Bailey, V., and S. Blackburn. "The Punishment of Incest Act 1908: A Case Study of Law Creation." *Criminal Law Review* (1979): 708–18.

Baker, Paul. *Polari: The Lost Language of Gay Men*. London and New York: Routledge, 2002.

Barr, James. *Quatrefoil*. London: Vision, 1953.

Bartlett, Lee, ed. *Letters to Christopher: Stephen Spender's Letters to Christopher Isherwood, 1929–1939: With "The Line of the Branch: Two Thirties Journals."* Santa Barbara: Black Sparrow Press, 1980.

Bartlett, Neil. *Mr. Clive and Mr. Page*. London: Serpent's Tail, 1996.

———. *Who Was That Man? A Present for Mr. Oscar Wilde*. London: Serpent's Tail, 1988.

Bech, Henning. *When Men Meet: Homosexuality and Modernity*. Trans. Teresa Mesquit and Tim Davies. Cambridge: Polity Press, 1997.

Begbie, Harold. *Broken Lights: A Short Study in the Variety of Christian Opinion*. London: Mills and Boon, 1926.

————. *The Mirrors of Downing Street: Some Political Reflections*. London: Mills and Boon, 1920.

Bell, David, and Jon Binnie. *The Sexual Citizen: Queer Politics and Beyond*. Oxford: Polity Press, 2000.

Bell, David and Gill Valentine, eds. *Mapping Desire: Geographies of Sexuality*. London and New York: Routledge, 1995.

Benney, Mark. *What Rough Beast? A Biographical Fantasia on the Life of Professor JR Neave, otherwise known as Iron Foot Jack Neave*. London: Peter Davies, 1939.

Bernard, Jeffrey. *Low Life*. London: Duckworth, 1986.

Berrube, Alan. *Coming Out Under Fire: The History of Gay Men and Women in World War Two*. New York: Free Press, 1990.

Betsky, Aaron. *Queer Space: Architecture and Same Sex Desire*. New York: William Morrow and Co., 1997.

Binkley, Sam. "The Romantic Sexology of John Addington Symonds." *Journal of Homosexuality* 40, no. 1 (2000): 79–103.

Black, DS Alexander. "Criminal Slang." *Police Journal* (March 1943).

Blackham, Robert. *Sir Ernest Wild, K.C.* London: Rich and Cowan, 1935.

Bland, Lucy. "Trial by Sexology? Maud Allan, Salome and the 'Cult of the Clitoris' Case." In *Sexology in Culture: Labelling Bodies and Desires,* ed. Lucy Bland and Laura Doan, 183–98. Oxford: Polity Press, 1998.

————. *Banishing the Beast: English Feminism and Sexual Morality, 1885–1914*. London: Penguin, 1995.

Bogdanor, Vernon, and Robert Skidelsky, eds. *The Age of Affluence, 1951–1963*. London: Macmillan, 1970.

Bone, James. *The London Perambulator*. London: Jonathan Cape, 1931.

Bordo, Susan. *Unbearable Weight: Feminism, Western Culture and the Body*. Berkeley: University of California Press, 1993.

Borland, Maureen. *Wilde's Devoted Friend: A Life of Robert Ross, 1869–1918*. London: Leonard Publishing, 1990.

Bourke, Joanna. *Dismembering the Male: Men's Bodies, Britain and the Great War*. London: Reaktion Books, 1999.

————. *Working-Class Cultures in Britain, 1890–1960: Gender, Class and Ethnicity*. London and New York: Routledge, 1994.

Bourne, Stephen. *Brief Encounters: Lesbians and Gays in British Cinema, 1930–71*. London and New York: Cassell, 1996.

Bowley, Ruth. "Amusements and Entertainments." In *The New Survey of London Life and Labour*. Vol. 9, *Life and Leisure,* ed. Sir Hubert Llewellyn Smith. London: P. S. King and Son, 1935.

Bravmann, Scott. *Queer Fictions of the Past: History, Culture and Difference*. Cambridge: Cambridge University Press, 1997.

Breward, Christopher. "Fashion and the Man: From Suburb to City Street: The Spaces of Masculine Consumption, 1870–1914." *New Formations* 37 (1999): 49.

————. *The Hidden Consumer: Masculinities, Fashion and City Life, 1860–1914*. Manchester and New York: Manchester University Press, 1999.

Brighton Ourstory Project. *Daring Hearts: Lesbian and Gay Lives of '50s and '60s Brighton*. Brighton: QueenSpark Books, 1992.

Bristow, E. J. *Vice and Vigilance: Purity Movements in England since 1700*. Dublin: Gill and Macmillan, 1977.

Bristow, Joseph. *Effeminate England: Homoerotic Writing after 1885*. New York: Columbia University Press, 1995.

Brown, Alyson and Barrett, David. *Knowledge of Evil: Child Prostitution and Child Sexual Abuse in Twentieth-Century England*. Cullompton and Devon: Willan Publishing, 2002.

Brown, Gavin. "Listening to Queer Maps of the City: Gay Men's Narratives of Pleasure and Danger in London's East End." *Oral History* (spring 2001): 48–61.

Buckle, Richard, ed. *Self-Portrait with Friends: The Selected Diaries of Cecil Beaton, 1926–1974*. London: Weidenfeld and Nicolson, 1979.

Burke, Thomas. *City of Encounters: A London Divertissement*. London: Constable and Co., 1932.

————. *English Night Life: From Norman Curfew to Present Black Out*. London: BT Batsford Ltd., 1943.

————. *For Your Convenience: A Learned Dialogue, Instructive to All Londoners and London Visitors Overheard in the Theleme Club and Taken Down Verbatim by Paul Pry*. London: Routledge, 1937.

————. *London in My Time*. London: Rich and Cowan, 1934.

————. *The London Spy: A Book of Town Travels*. London: Thornton Butterworth, 1922.

Burton, Peter. *Parallel Lives*. London: Gay Men's Press, 1985.

Butler, Judith. *Bodies That Matter: On the Discursive Limits of "Sex."* London and New York: Routledge, 1993.

————. *Gender Trouble: Feminism and the Subversion of Identity*. London and New York: Routledge, 1990.

Callow, Simon. *Charles Laughton: A Difficult Actor*. London: Mandarin, 1990.

Campbell, Agnes. *Report on Public Baths and Wash-houses in the United Kingdom*. Edinburgh: Carnegie United Kingdom Trust, 1918.

Carpenter, Edward. *Homogenic Love and Its Place in a Free Society*. Manchester: Labour Press Society, 1894.

————. *Iolaus: An Anthology of Friendship*. London: Swan Sonnenschein and Co., 1902.

————. *Love's Coming of Age*. Manchester: Labour Press, 1906.

————. *The Intermediate Sex: A Study of Some Transitional Types of Men and Women*. London: Swan Sonnenschein and Co., 1908.

Carpenter, Humphrey. *Benjamin Britten: A Biography*. London: Faber, 1992.

Carter, Erica, Donald James, and Judith Squires, eds. *Space and Place: Theories of Identity and Location*. London: Lawrence and Wishart, 1993.

Carter, Miranda. *Anthony Blunt: His Lives*. London: Macmillan, 2001.

Castle, Terry. *Noel Coward and Radclyffe Hall: Kindred Spirits*. New York: Columbia University Press, 1996.

Chapman, Cecil. *The Poor Man's Court of Justice: Twenty-Five Years as a Metropolitan Magistrate*. London: Hodder and Stoughton, 1926.

Chauncey, George. *Gay New York: The Making of the Gay Male World, 1890–1940*. London: Flamingo, 1995.

———. "Christian Brotherhood or Sexual Perversion? Homosexual Identities and the Construction of Sexual Boundaries in the World War One Era." *Journal of Social History* 19, no. 2 (1985): 182–211.

Chester, Lewis, David Leitch, and Colin Simpson. *The Cleveland Street Affair*. London: Weidenfeld and Nicolson, 1977.

Chudacoff, Howard. *The Age of the Bachelor: Creating an American Subculture*. Princeton: Princeton University Press, 1999.

Cocks, Harry. *Nameless Offences: Homosexual Desire in the Nineteenth Century*. London and New York: IB Tauris, 2003.

———. "Calamus in Bolton: Spirituality and Homosexual Desire in Late-Victorian England." *Gender and History* 13, no. 2 (2001): 191–223.

Cohen, Ed. *Talk on the Wilde Side: Towards a Genealogy of a Discourse on Male Sexualities*. London and New York: Routledge, 1993.

Cole, Shaun. "Invisible Men: Gay Men's Dress in Britain, 1950–1970." In *Defining Dress: Dress as Object, Meaning and Identity*, ed. Elizabeth Wilson and Amy de la Haye, 143–54. Manchester and New York: Manchester University Press, 1999.

———. *Don We Now Our Gay Apparel: Gay Men's Dress in the Twentieth Century*. Oxford and New York: Berg, 2000.

Collins, Marcus. *Modern Love: An Intimate History of Men and Women in Twentieth Century Britain*. London: Atlantic Books, 2003.

———. "The Fall of the English Gentleman: The National Character in Decline, c. 1918–1970." *Historical Research* 75, no. 187 (2002): 90–111.

Connon, Bryan. *Beverley Nichols: A Life*. London: Constable, 1991.

Cook, Matt. *London and the Culture of Homosexuality, 1885–1914*. Cambridge: Cambridge University Press, 2003.

———. "'A New City of Friends': London and Homosexuality in the 1890s." *History Workshop Journal* 56 (2003): 33–58.

Cox, L. J., and R. J. Fay. "Gayspeak, the Linguistic Fringe: Bona Polari, Camp, Queerspeak and Beyond." In *The Margins of the City: Gay Men's Urban Lives*, ed. Stephen Whittle, 103–118. Aldershot: Ashgate, 1994.

Cox, Pamela. *Bad Girls: Gender, Justice and Welfare in Britain, 1900–1950*. London: Palgrave, 2003.

Craft, Christopher, *Another Kind of Love: Male Homosexual Desire in English Discourse, 1850–1920*. Berkeley and London: University of California Press, 1994.

Crisp, Quentin. *The Naked Civil Servant*. London: Jonathon Cape, 1968.

Croft, Taylor. *The Cloven Hoof: A Study of Contemporary London Vices*. London: Denis Archer, 1932.

Crofte-Cooke, Rupert. *The Verdict of You All*. London: Secker and Warbourg, 1955.

Croll, Andy. "Street Disorder, Surveillance and Shame: Regulating Behaviour in the Public Spaces of the Late-Victorian British Town." *Social History* 24, no. 3 (1999): 250–68.

Cross, Tom. *Artists and Bohemian: 100 Years with the Chelsea Arts Club*. London: Quiller Press, 1992.

Crossick, Geoffrey. *An Artisan Elite in Victorian Society: Kentish London, 1840–80*. London: Croom Helm, 1978.

Culleton, Claire. *Working-Class Culture, Women and Britain, 1914–1921*. London: Macmillan, 2000.

Curran, Desmond, and Denis Parr. "Homosexuality: An Analysis of 100 Male Cases seen in Private Practice." *British Medical Journal* (6 April 1957): 797–801.

Curtis, James. *What Immortal Hand*. London: Nicolson and Watson, 1939.

D'Arch Smith, Timothy. *Love in Earnest: Some Notes on the Lives of English "Uranian" Poets from 1889 to 1930*. London: Routledge and Kegan Paul, 1970.

———. *R. A. Caton and the Fortune Press: A Memoir and a Hand-List*. London: Bertram Rota, 1983.

d'Emilio, John. *Sexual Politics, Sexual Communities: The Making of a Homosexual Minority in the United States, 1940–1970*. Chicago: University of Chicago Press, 1983.

Daley, Harry. *This Small Cloud: A Personal Memoir*. London: Weidenfeld and Nicolson, 1986.

Daunton, Martin and Bernhard Rieger, eds. *Meanings of Modernity: Britain from the Late-Victorian Era to World War Two*. Oxford: Berg, 2001.

Daunton, Martin. "Housing." In *The Cambridge Social History of Britain, 1750–1950*, vol. 2, *People and Their Environment*, ed. F. M. L. Thompson. Cambridge: Cambridge University Press, 1996.

———. *House and Home in the Victorian City: Working Class Housing, 1850–1914*. London: Edward Arnold, 1983.

David, Hugh. *On Queer Street: A Social History of British Homosexuality, 1895–1995*. London: Harper Collins, 1997.

———. *Stephen Spender: A Portrait with Background*. London: Heinemann, 1992.

———. *The Fitzrovians: A Portrait of Bohemian Society, 1900–55*. London: Michael Joseph, 1988.

Davidoff, Leonore. "The Separation of Home and Work? Landladies and Lodgers in Nineteenth and Twentieth Century England," in *Fit Work for Women*, ed. Sandra Burman, 64–97. London: Croom Helm, 1979.

Davidoff, Leonore, and Catherine Hall. *Family Fortunes: Men and Women of the English Middle Class, 1750–1850*. London: Hutchinson, 1987.

Davidoff, Leonore, Megan Doolittle, Janet Fink, and Katerine Holden, eds. *The Family Story: Blood, Contract and Intimacy, 1830–1950*. London and New York: Longman, 1999.

Davidson, Michael. *Some Boys*. London: David Bruce and Watson, 1970.

———. *The World, the Flesh and Myself: The Autobiography of Michael Davidson*. London: Arthur Barker, 1962.

Davidson, Roger. "'This Pernicious Delusion': Law, Medicine and Child Sexual Abuse in Early-Twentieth-Century Scotland." *Journal of the History of Sexuality* 10, no. 1 (2001): 62–76.

Davies, Andrew. "Street Gangs, Crime and Policing in Glasgow During the 1930s: The Case of the Beehive Boys." *Social History* 23, no. 3 (1998): 251–67.

———. "Youth Gangs, Masculinity and Violence in Late-Victorian Manchester and Salford." *Journal of Social History* 32, no. 2 (1998): 349–70.

Davies, Hunter, ed. *The New London Spy: A Discreet Guide to the City's Pleasures*. London: Anthony Blond, 1966.

Davies, Russell, ed. *The Kenneth Williams Diaries*. London: Harper Collins, 1994.

Davin, Anna. *Growing up Poor: Home, School and Street in London, 1870–1914*. London: Rivers Oram Press, 1996.

Davis, Susanne. "Sexuality, Performance and Spectatorship in Law: The Case of Gordon Lawrence, Melbourne 1888." *Journal of the History of Sexuality* 7, no. 3 (1997): 389–408.

Davis, Tracy. "Indecency and Vigilance in the Music Halls." In *British Theatre in the 1890s: Essays on Drama and the Stage,* ed. Richard Foulkes, 111–31. Cambridge: Cambridge University Press, 1992.

Dawson, Graham. *Soldier Heroes: British Adventure, Empire and the Imagining of Masculinities*. London and New York: Routledge, 1994.

De Certeau, Michel. *The Practice of Everyday Life*. Trans. Steven Randall. Berkeley: University of California Press, 1984.

De la Noy, Michael. *Denton Welch: The Making of a Writer*. London: Viking, 1984.

———. *The Journals of Denton Welch*. London: Alison and Busby, 1984.

Dean, Carolyn. *The Frail Social Body: Pornography, Homosexuality and Other Fantasies in Interwar France*. Berkeley: University of California Press, 2000.

Doan, Laura. *Fashioning Sapphism: The Origins of a Modern English Lesbian Culture*. New York: Columbia University Press, 2001.

———. "'Acts of Female Indecency': Sexology's Intervention in Legislating Lesbianism." In *Sexology in Culture: Labelling Bodies and Desires,* ed. Lucy Bland and Laura Doan, 199–213. Oxford: Polity Press, 1998.

Donahue, Joseph. "The Empire Theatre of Varieties Licensing Controversy of 1894: Testimony of Laura Ormiston-Chant before the Theatres and Music Halls Licensing Committee." *Nineteenth Century Theatre* 15, no. 1 (1987): 50–60.

Dowling, Linda. *Hellenism and Homosexuality in Victorian Oxford*. Ithaca: Cornell University Press, 1994.

Drabble, Margaret. *Angus Wilson: A Biography*. London: Secker and Warburg, 1995.

Driberg, Tom. *Ruling Passions*. London: Jonathon Cape, 1977.

East, W. Norwood, and W. H. de B. Hubert. *Report on the Psychological Treatment of Crime*. London: HMSO, 1939.

East, W. Norwood. "The Sociological Aspects of Homosexuality: A Discussion." *Medico-Legal Journal* (1947): 11–23.

———. *Medical Aspects of Crime*. London: J. and A. Churchill Ltd., 1936.

———. *Society and the Criminal*. London: HMSO, 1949.

Edelman, Lee. *Homographesis: Essays in Gay Literary and Cultural Theory*. London and New York: Routledge, 1994.

Ellis, Henry Havelock. *Studies in the Psychology of Sex*, vol. 1, *Sexual Inversion*. London: Wilson and Macmillan, 1897.

———. *The Psychology of Sex*. London: William Heinemann, 1939.

Emsley, Clive. *The English Police: A Social History*. London: Longman, 1996.

Evans, David. *Sexual Citizenship: The Material Construction of Sexualities*. London and New York: Routledge, 1993.

Fabian, Robert. *Fabian of the Yard*. Kingswood Surrey: Naldrett Press, 1950.

———. *London after Dark*. London: Naldrett Press, 1954.

Faderman, Lillian. *Surpassing the Love of Men: Romantic Friendship and Love between Women from the Renaissance to the Present*. New York: William Morrow, 1981.

Fallowell, Duncan. "The Spies Who Loved Me." *Sunday Times Magazine*, 7 April 1991, 18–22.

Farson, Daniel. *Never a Normal Man*. London: HarperCollins, 1997.

———. *The Gilded Gutter Life of Francis Bacon*. New York: Pantheon Books, 1993.

———. *Soho in the Fifties*. London: Michael Joseph, 1988.

Faulks, Sebastian. *The Fatal Englishman: Three Short Lives*. London: Vintage, 1997.

Felski, Rita. Introduction to *Sexology in Culture: Labelling Bodies and Desires*, ed. Lucy Bland and Laura Doan, 1–8. Oxford: Polity Press, 1998.

Felstead, Sidney Theodore. *The Underworld of London*. London: John Murray, 1923.

Fiber, Sally, with Clive Powell-Willams. *The Fitzroy: The Autobiography of a London Tavern*. Sussex: Temple House Books, 1995.

Fielden, Lionel. *The Natural Bent*. London: Andre Deutsch, 1960.

Finch, J. and Penny Summerfield. "Social Reconstruction and the Emergence of Companionate Marriage, 1945–59." In *Marriage, Domestic Life and Social Change*, ed. David Clark, 7–32. London and New York: Routledge, 1991.

Fishman, William. *The Streets of East London*. London: Duckworth, 1992.

Fitzroy, A. T. *Despised and Rejected*. London: C. W. Daniel, 1918.

Ford, Ruth. "The Man-Woman Murderer: Sex Fraud, Sexual Inversion and the Unmentionable Article in 1920s Australia." *Gender and History* 12, no. 1 (2000): 158–96.

Forster, E. M. *Maurice*. London: Edward Arnold, 1971.

Foucault, Michel. *The History of Sexuality*, vol. 1, *An Introduction*. Trans. Robert Hurley. London: Allen Lane, 1979.

Fowler, David. *The First Teenagers: The Lifestyle of Young Wage Earners in Interwar Britain*. London: Woburn Press, 1995.

Francis, Martin. "Tears, Tantrums and Bared Teeth: The Emotional Economy of Three Conservative Prime Ministers, 1951–1963." *Journal of British Studies* 41, no. 3 (2002): 354–87.

Fyfe, Nick. "Space, Time and Policing: Towards a Conceptual Understanding of Police Work." *Environment and Planning D: Society and Space* 10, no. 4 (1992): 469–81.

Garber, Marjorie. *Vested Interests: Cross-Dressing and Cultural Anxiety.* Harmondsworth: Penguin, 1993.

Gardiner, James. *A Class Apart: The Private Pictures of Montague Glover.* London: Serpent's Tail, 1992.

———. *Who's A Pretty Boy Then: One Hundred and Fifty Years of Gay Life in Pictures.* London: Serpent's Tail, 1997.

Garland, Rodney. *The Heart in Exile.* London: W. H. Allen, 1953.

Garside, Patricia. *The Conduct of Philanthropy: The William Sutton Trust, 1900–2000.* London: Athlone Press, 2000.

Gatrell, V. A. C. "Crime, Authority and the Policeman State." In *The Cambridge Social History of Britain: 1750–1950,* vol. 3, *Social Agencies and Institutions,* ed. F. M. L. Thompson. Cambridge: Cambridge University Press, 1993.

Gaunt, William. *Chelsea.* London: B. T. Batsford, 1954.

George, Eliot. *The Leather Boys.* London: Anthony Blond, 1961.

Gibson, Barbara. *Male Order: Life Stories from Boys Who Sell Sex.* London: Cassell, 1995.

Giddens, Anthony. *The Transformation of Intimacy: Sex, Love and Eroticism in Modern Societies.* Stanford: Stanford University Press, 1993.

Gilbert, Sandra, and Susan Gubar. "Soldier's Heart: Literary Men, Literary Women and the Great War," In *Behind the Lines: Gender and the Two World Wars,* ed. Margaret Higonnet. New Haven: Yale University Press, 1987.

Giles, Judy. "Help for Housewives: Domestic Service and the Reconstruction of Domesticity in Britain, 1940–50." *Women's History Review* 10, no. 2 (2001): 299–324.

———. "Playing Hard to Get: Working-class Women, Sexuality and Respectability in Britain, 1918–1940," *Women's History Review* 1, no. 2 (1992): 239–55.

———. *Women, Identity and Private Life in Britain, 1900–50.* Basingstoke: Macmillan, 1995.

Goldring, Douglas. *The Nineteen Twenties: A General Survey and Some Personal Memories.* London: Nicholson and Watson, 1945.

Goldsmith, Netta Murray. *The Worst of Crimes: Homosexuality and the Law in Eighteenth-century London.* Aldershot: Ashgate, 1998.

Goldthorpe, John et al. *The Affluent Worker in the Class Structure.* London: Cambridge University Press, 1969.

Grant, Kevin. "'Bones of Contention': The Repatriation of the Remains of Roger Casement." *Journal of British Studies* 41, no. 3 (2002): 329–54.

Gray, Frank. *The Tramp: His Meaning and Being*. London and Toronto: J. M. Dent and Sons, 1931.

Gray, Nigel. *The Worst of Times: An Oral History of the Great Depression in Britain*. London: Wildewood House, 1985.

Grayzel, Susan. *Women's Identities at War: Gender, Motherhood and Politics in Britain and France During the First World War*. Chapel Hill and London: University of North Carolina Press, 1999.

Greenfield, Jill, Sean O'Connell, and Chris Reid. "Gender, Consumer Culture and the Middle-Class Male, 1918–39." In *Gender, Civic Culture and Consumerism: Middle-Class Identity in Britain, 1800–1940*, ed. Alan Kidd and David Nicholls, 183–97. Manchester and New York: Manchester University Press, 1999.

———. "Fashioning Masculinity: *Men Only*, Consumption and the Development of Marketing in the 1930s." *Twentieth-Century British History* 10, no. 4 (1999): 457–76.

Grey, Antony. *Quest for Justice: Towards Homosexual Emancipation*. London: Sinclair Stevenson, 1992.

Grosskurth, Phyllis, ed. *The Memoirs of John Addington Symonds*. London: Hutchinson, 1984.

———. *Havelock Ellis: A Biography*. London: Quartet, 1981.

———. *John Addington Symonds: A Biography*. New York: Arno Press, 1975.

Groth, Paul. *Living Downtown: The History of Residential Hotels in the United States*. Berkeley: University of California Press, 1994.

Gullace, Nicoletta. *"The Blood of Our Sons": Men, Women and the Renegotiation of British Citizenship during the Great War*. New York: Palgrave Macmillan, 2002.

Gunn, Simon. *The Public Culture of the Victorian Middle-class: Ritual, Authority and the English Industrial City, 1840–1914*. Manchester: Manchester University Press, 2000.

———. "The Public Sphere, Modernity and Consumption: New Perspectives on the History of the English Middle Class." In *Gender, Civic Culture and Consumerism: Middle-Class Identity in Britain, 1800–1940*, ed. Alan Kidd and David Nicholls. Manchester and New York: Manchester University Press, 1999.

Gurney, Peter. "'Intersex' and 'Dirty Girls': Mass Observation and Working-Class Sexuality in England in the 1930s." *Journal of the History of Sexuality* 8, no. 2 (1997): 256–90.

Gustav-Wrathall, John. *Take the Young Stranger by the Hand: Same Sex Relationships and the YMCA*. Chicago: University of Chicago Press, 1999.

Hall, Lesley. *Sex, Gender and Social Change in Britain since 1880*. London: Palgrave, 2002.

———. "'Disinterested Enthusiasm for Sexual Misconduct': The British Society for the Study of Sex Psychology, 1913–47." *Journal of Contemporary History* 30 (1995): 665–86.

———. *Hidden Anxieties: Male Sexuality, 1900–1950*. Oxford: Polity Press, 1991.

Hall, Radclyffe. *The Well of Loneliness*. London: Jonathon Cape, 1928.

Hammerton, A. James. "Pooterism or Partnership? Marriage and Masculine Identity in the Lower Middle Class, 1870–1920." *Journal of British Studies* 38, no. 3 (1999): 291–321.

———. "The English Weakness? Gender, Satire and 'Moral Manliness' in the Lower Middle Class, 1870–1920." In *Gender, Civic Culture and Consumerism: Middle-Class Identity in Britain, 1800–1940*, ed. Alan Kidd and David Nicholls, 164–82. Manchester and New York: Manchester University Press, 1999.

Hamnett, Chris, and Bill Randolph. *Cities, Housing and Profits: Flat Break Up and the Decline of Private Renting*. London: Hutchinson, 1988.

Hanmore, E. *The Curse of the Embankment: And the Cure*. London: P. S. King and Sons, 1935.

Hannington, Wal. *The Problem of the Distressed Areas*. London: Victor Gollancz, 1937.

Hare, Kenneth. *London's Latin Quarter*. London: John Lane the Bodley Head, 1926.

Harris, Mervyn. *The Dilly Boys: Male Prostitution in London*. London: Croom Helm, 1973.

Hart-Davis, Rupert. *Hugh Walpole: A Biography*. London: Rupert Hart-Davis, 1952.

Harvey, David. *The Condition of Postmodernity: An Enquiry into the Origins of Cultural Change*. Oxford: Basil Blackwell, 1989.

Haste, Cate. *Rules of Desire: Sex in Britain; World War One to the Present*. London: Pimlico, 1992.

Hatton, S. F. *London's Bad Boys*. London: Chapman and Hall, 1931.

Healey, Dan. *Homosexual Desire in Revolutionary Russia: The Regulation of Sexual and Gender Dissent*. Chicago: University of Chicago Press, 2001.

Hendrick, Harry. *Images of Youth: Age, Class and the Male Youth Problem, 1880–1920*. Oxford: Clarendon Press, 1990.

Herbert, Steve. "Police Subculture Reconsidered." *Criminology* 36, no. 2 (1998): 343–70.

Higgins, Patrick. *Heterosexual Dictatorship: Male Homosexuality in Post-War Britain*. London: Fourth Estate, 1996.

Hill, John. *Sex, Class and Realism: British Cinema, 1956–1963*. London: BFI Publishing, 1997.

Hilton, Matthew. *Smoking in British Popular Culture, 1800–2000*. Manchester and New York: Manchester University Press, 2000.

Hoare, Philip. *Noel Coward: A Biography*. London: Sinclair Stevenson, 1995.

———. *Serious Pleasures: The Life of Stephen Tennant*. London: Hamish Hamilton, 1990.

———. *Wilde's Last Stand: Decadence, Conspiracy and the First World War*. London: Duckworth, 1997.

Hodges, Andrew. *Alan Turing: The Enigma of Intelligence*. London: Unwin Paperbacks, 1985.

Hollinghurst, Alan. *The Swimming Pool Library*. London: Chatto and Windus, 1988.

Holne, Thea. *Chelsea*. London: Hamish Hamilton, 1972.

Homosexual Law Reform Society. *Homosexuals and the Law*. London: HLRS, 1959.

Houlbrook, Matt. "Daring to Speak Whose Name? Queer Cultural Politics, 1920–1967." In *The Permissive Society and Its Enemies,* ed. Marcus Collins. London: Rivers Oram Press, 2006.

———. "Soldier Heroes and Rent Boys: Homosex, Masculinities and Britishness in the Brigade of Guards, c.1900–1960." *Journal of British Studies* 42, no. 3 (2003): 351–88.

———. "'Lady Austin's Camp Boys': Constituting the Queer Subject in 1930s London." *Gender and History* 14, no. 1 (2002): 31–61.

———. "For Whose Convenience? Gay Guides, Cognitive Maps and the Construction of Homosexual London, 1917–67." In *Identities in Space: Contested Terrains in the Western City since 1850,* ed. S. Gunn and R. J. Morris, 165–86. Aldershot: Ashgate, 2001.

———. "Towards a Historical Geography of Sexuality." *Journal of Urban History* 2, no. 4 (2001): 497–504.

———. "The Private World of Public Urinals: London, 1918–57." *London Journal* 25, no. 1 (2000): 52–70.

Howard, John. *Men Like That: A Southern Queer History.* Chicago: Chicago University Press, 2001.

———. "The Library, the Park and the Pervert: Public Space and Homosexual Encounter in Post World War Two Atlanta." *Radical History Review* 62 (1995): 166–87.

Hubbard, Philip. *Sex and the City: Geographies of Prostitution in the Urban West.* Aldershot, Ashgate, 1999.

———. "Red Light Districts and Toleration Zones: Geographies of Female Prostitution in England and Wales." *Area* 29, no. 2 (1997): 129–40.

Huggett, Richard. *Binkie Beaumont: Eminence Grise of the West End Theatre, 1933–1973.* London: Hodder and Stoughton, 1989.

Humphries, Steve and Pamela Gordon. *A Man's World: From Boyhood to Manhood, 1900–60.* London: BBC Books, 1996.

———. *Forbidden Britain: Our Secret Past, 1900–1960.* London: BBC Books, 1994.

Humphries, Steve, and John Taylor. *The Making of Modern London, 1945–85.* London: Sidgwick and Jackson, 1986.

Humphries, Steve. *Hooligans or Rebels? An Oral History of Working-Class Childhood and Youth, 1889–1939.* Oxford: Blackwell, 1995.

———. *A Secret World of Sex: Forbidden Fruit; The British Experience, 1900–1950.* London: Sidgwick and Jackson, 1988.

Hutton, Robert. *Of Those Alone.* London: Sidgwick and Jackson, 1958.

Hyde, H. Montgomery. *The Cleveland Street Scandal.* London: W. H. Allen, 1976.

———. *The Other Love: An Historical and Contemporary Survey of Homosexuality in Britain.* London: William Heinemann, 1970.

Hynes, Samuel. *A War Imagined: The First World War and English Culture.* London: Pimlico, 1992.

Ingram, Gordon Brent, Anne-Marie Bouthilette, and Yolanda Retter, eds. *Queers in Space: Communities/Public Place/Sites Of Resistance.* Seattle: Bay Press, 1997.

Inwood, Stephen. "Policing London's Morals: The Metropolitan Police and Popular Culture," *London Journal,* 1990, 123–42.

Isherwood, Christopher. *Christopher and His Kind, 1929–1939.* London: Eyre Methuen, 1977.

Ives, George. *The Continued Extension of the Criminal Law.* London: JE Francis, 1922.

Jackson, Louise. *Child Sexual Abuse in Victorian England.* London and New York: Routledge, 2000.

Jarman, Derek, *At Your Own Risk: A Saint's Testament.* London: Hutchinson, 1992.

Jeffery-Poulter, Stephen. *Peers, Queers and Commons: The Struggle for Gay Law Reform from 1950 to the Present.* London: Routledge, 1991.

Jeffreys, Sheila. *The Spinster and Her Enemies: Feminism and Sexuality, 1880–1930.* London: Pandora, 1985.

Jivani, Alkarim. *It's Not Unusual: A History of Lesbian and Gay Life in the Twentieth Century.* London: Michael O'Mara Books, 1997.

Kaiser, Charles. *The Gay Metropolis, 1940–1996.* London: Weidenfeld and Nicolson, 1998.

Kaplan, Morris. "Who's Afraid of John Saul? Urban Culture and the Politics of Desire in Late-Victorian London." *GLQ* 5 (3) 1999, 267–314.

———. "Did 'My Lord Gomorrah' Smile? Homosexuality, Class and Prostitution in the Cleveland Street Affair." In *Disorder in the Court: Trials and Sexual Conflict at the Turn of the Century,* ed. George Robb and Nancy Erber. New York: New York University Press, 1999.

Keith, Michael and Pile, Steve, eds. *Place and the Politics of Identity.* London and New York: Routledge, 1993.

Kennedy, Elizabeth Lapovsky and Madeleine Davis. *Boots of Leather, Slippers of Gold: The History of a Lesbian Community.* London and New York: Routledge, 1993.

Kent, Susan Kingsley. *Making Peace: The Reconstruction of Gender in Interwar Britain.* Princeton, NJ, Princeton University Press, 1993.

———. *Sex and Suffrage in Britain, 1860–1914.* London: Routledge, 1990.

King, Francis. *My Sister and Myself: The Diaries of J. R. Ackerley.* London: Hutchinson, 1982.

Kirkup, James. *A Poet Could Not But Be Gay: Some Legends of My Lost Youth.* London: Peter Owen, 1991.

Kohn, Marek. *Dope Girls: The Birth of the British Drug Underground.* London: Lawrence and Wishart, 1992.

Koven, Seth. "From Rough Lads to Hooligans: Boy Life, National Culture and Social Reform," in Andrew Parker, Mary Russo, Doris Somner and Patricia Yaeger (eds.), *Nationalisms and Sexualities.* London and New York: Routledge, 1992.

Lahr, John. *Prick Up Your Ears: The Biography of Joe Orton.* London: Allen Lane, 1978.

Lambert, Sam, ed. *London Night and Day.* London: The Architectural Press, 1951.

Lancaster, Marie Jacqueline, ed. *Brian Howard: Portrait of a Failure.* London: Anthony Blond, 1968.

Lanchester, Elsa. *Elsa Lanchester: Herself.* New York: St. Martins, 1983.

Langguth, AJ. *Saki: A Life of Hector Hugh Munro.* London: Hamish Hamilton, 1981.

Langhamer, Clare. *Women's Leisure in England, 1920–60.* Manchester and New York: Manchester University Press, 2000.

Laybourn, Keith. *Britain on the Breadline: A Social and Political History of Britain, 1918–39.* London: Sutton Publishing, 1990.

Lees, Lyn. *Exiles of Erin: Irish Migrants in Victorian London.* Manchester: Manchester University Press, 1979.

Lefebvre, Henri. *The Production of Space.* Trans. Donald Nicholson-Smith. Oxford: Basil Blackwell, 1991.

Lehmann, John. *In the Purely Pagan Sense.* London: Blond and Briggs, 1976.

Levine, Philippa. "'Walking the Streets in a Way No Decent Women Should': Women Police in World War I." *Journal of Modern History* 66 (1994): 34–78.

Light, Alison. *Forever England: Femininity, Englishness and Conservatism between the Wars.* London and New York: Routledge, 1991.

Lipman, V. D. *A History of the Jews in Great Britain since 1858.* Leicester, Leicester University Press, 1990.

Llewellyn Smith, Sir Hubert, ed. *The New Survey of London Life and Labour,* vol. 9, *Life and Leisure.* London: P. S. King and Son, 1935.

Lofstrom, Jan. "The Birth of the Queen / The Modern Homosexual: Historical Explanations Revisited." *Sociological Review* 45, no. 1 (1997): 24–41.

Lopian, J. B. "Crime, Police and Punishment 1918–29: Metropolitan Experiences, Perceptions and Policies." Ph.D. diss., University of Cambridge, 1986.

Luke, Michael. *David Tennant and the Gargoyle Years.* London: Weidenfeld and Nicolson, 1991.

MacRaild, Donald. *Irish Migrants in Modern Britain, 1750–1922.* Basingstoke: Macmillan, 1999.

Mahood, Linda, and B. Littlewood. "The 'Vicious Girl' and the 'Street-Corner Boy': Sexuality and the Gendered Delinquent in the Scottish Child-saving Movement, 1850–1940." *Journal of the History of Sexuality* 4 (1993): 17–42.

Marcus, Sharon. *Apartment Stories: City and Home in Nineteenth Century Paris and London.* Berkeley, University of California Press, 1999.

Marshall, John. "Pansies, Perverts and Macho Men: Changing Conceptions of Male Homosexuality." In *The Making of the Modern Homosexual,* ed. Ken Plummer. London: Hutchinson, 1981.

Marwick, Arthur. *The Sixties: Cultural Revolution in Britain, France, Italy and the United States, c.1958–c.1971.* Oxford: Oxford University Press, 1991.

Maupin, Armistead. *Tales of the City.* New York: Harper & Row, 1978.

Maynard, Steven. "'Respect Your Elders: Know Your Past': History and the Queer Theorists." *Radical History Review* 75 (1999): 56–78.

————. "'Horrible Temptations': Sex, Men and Working-Class Male Youth in Urban Ontario, 1890–1935." *Canadian Historical Review* 78, no. 2 (1997): 192–235.

————. "Through a Hole in the Lavatory Wall: Homosexual Subcultures, Police Surveillance and the Dialectics of Discovery, Toronto, 1890–1930." *Journal of the History of Sexuality* 5, no. 2 (1994): 207–42.

Mayne, Xavier [pseud. Edward Prime Stevenson]. *The Intersexes: A History of Similisexualism as a Problem in Social Life.* 1908. New York: Arno Press, 1975.

McAleer, Joseph. *Passion's Fortune: The Story of Mills and Boon.* Oxford: Oxford University Press, 1999.

McKibbin, Ross. *Classes and Cultures: England 1918–1951.* Oxford: Oxford University Press, 1998.

McLaren, Angus. *Sexual Blackmail: A Modern History.* Cambridge Mass.: Harvard University Press, 2002.

————. *The Trials of Masculinity: Policing Sexual Boundaries, 1870–1930.* Chicago: University of Chicago Press, 1997.

Metropolitan Borough of Bermondsey. *Public Baths and Washhouses: Souvenir of the Opening of the New Central Baths.* September 24th 1927.

Meyrick, Kate. *Secrets of the 43 Club.* Dublin, Parkgate Publications, 1994.

Mitchell, Mark and David Leavitt, eds. *Pages Passed from Hand to Hand: The Hidden Tradition of Homosexual Literature in English from 1748 to 1914.* London: Chatto and Windus, 1998.

Moran, Leslie. *The Homosexual(ity) of Law.* London and New York: Routledge, 1996.

Mort, Frank and Lynda Nead. "Introduction: Sexual Geographies." *New Formations* 37 (1999): 6.

Mort, Frank. "Mapping Sexual London: The Wolfenden Committee on Homosexual Offences and Prostitution, 1954–7." *New Formations* 37 (1999): 92–113.

————. "Social and Symbolic Fathers and Sons in Postwar Britain." *Journal of British Studies,* 38, no. 2 (1999): 353–84.

————. *Cultures of Consumption: Masculinities and Social Space in Late Twentieth Century Britain.* London and New York: Routledge, 1996.

————. *Dangerous Sexualities: Medico-Moral Politics in England since 1830.* London and New York: Routledge, 1987.

Morton, H. V. *The Nights of London.* London: Methuen and Co., 1932.

Moseley, Sydney. *The Night Haunts of London.* London: Stanley Paul and Co., 1920.

Munt, Sally. *Heroic Desire: Lesbian Identity and Cultural Spaces.* London: Cassell, 1998.

Nava, Mica and Alan O'Shea, eds. *Modern Times: Reflections on a Century of English Modernity.* London: Routledge, 1996.

Nead, Lynda. *Victorian Babylon: People, Streets and Images in Nineteenth Century London.* New Haven and London: Yale University Press, 2000.

Nelson, Michael. *A Room in Chelsea Square.* London: Cape, 1958.

Neville-Rolfe, Mrs C. "Sex Delinquency." In *The New Survey of London Life and Labour,* vol. 9, *Life and Leisure,* ed. Sir Hubert Llewellyn Smith. London: P. S. King and Son, 1935.

Newburn, Tim. *Permission and Regulation: Law and Morals in Postwar Britain*. London and New York: Routledge, 1992.

Newton, Esther. *Mother Camp: Female Impersonators in America*. Englewood Cliff New Jersey, Prentice Hall, 1972.

Nicholson, B. D. "Drink." In *The New Survey of London Life and Labour*, vol. 9, *Life and Leisure*, ed. Sir Hubert Llewellyn Smith. London: P. S. King and Son, 1935.

Nicolson, Nigel, ed. *The Sickle Side of the Moon: The Letters of Virginia Woolf; Volume 5, 1932–5*. London: Hogarth Press, 1979.

Nilsson, Arne. "Creating Their Own Private and Public: The Male Homosexual Life Space in a Nordic City During High Modernity." *Journal of Homosexuality* 35, nos. 3–4 (1998): 81–116.

Nord, Deborah Epstein, *Walking the Victorian Streets: Women, Representation and the City*. London and Ithaca, Cornell University Press, 1995.

Norton, Rictor. *Mother Clap's Molly House: The Gay Subculture in England 1700–1830*. London: Gay Men's Press, 1992.

Nottingham, Chris. *The Pursuit of Serenity: Havelock Ellis and the New Politics*. Amsterdam, Amsterdam University Press, 1999.

O'Brien, Margaret and Allen Eyles, eds. *Enter the Dream House: Memories of Cinemas in South London from the Twenties to the Sixties*. London: British Film Institute, 1993.

Olechnowicz, Andrzej. *Working-Class Housing in England between the Wars: The Becontree Estate*. Oxford: Clarendon Press, 1997.

Olsen, Donald. *The Growth of Victorian London*. Harmondsworth, Penguin, 1976.

Oosterhuis, Harry. *Stepchildren of Nature: Krafft-Ebing, Psychiatry and the Making of Sexual Identity*. Chicago: University of Chicago Press, 2000.

Orwell, George. *Down and Out in Paris and London*. London: Secker and Warburg, 1949.

Osgerby, Bill. *Youth in Britain since 1945*. Oxford: Blackwell, 1998.

Parker, Peter. *Ackerley: A Life of J. R. Ackerley*. London: Constable, 1988.

Parsons, Deborah. *Streetwalking the Metropolis: Women, the City and Modernity*. Oxford: Oxford University Press, 2000.

Partridge, Eric. *A Dictionary of Slang and Unconventional English*. London: Routledge and Kegan Paul. 1984.

———. *The Dictionary of the Underworld*. Hertfordshire, Wordsworth Editions, 1995.

Pearson, John. *The Profession of Violence: The Rise and Fall of the Kray Twins*. London: Granada Publishing, 1985.

Peiss, Kathy. "Making Faces: The Cosmetics Industry and the Cultural Construction of Gender, 1890–1930." *Genders* 7 (1990): 143–69.

———. "Of Men and Make-up: The Gender of Cosmetics in Twentieth Century America." In *The Material Culture of Gender*, ed. Kenneth Ames and Katherine Martinez. New York: Norton, 1997.

Pennybacker, Susan. *A Vision for London, 1889–1914: Labour, Everyday Life and the LCC Experiment*. London and New York: Routledge, 1995.

Penrose, Barrie, and Simon Freeman. *Conspiracy of Silence: The Secret Life of Anthony Blunt*. London: Grafton Books, 1987.

Perkin, Harold. *The Rise of Professional Society: England since 1880*. London: Routledge, 1987.

Peters, Arthur Anderson. *Finistere*. London: Victor Gollancz, 1951.

Petrow, Stefan. *Policing Morals: The Metropolitan Police and the Home Office, 1870–1914*. Oxford: Clarendon Press, 1994.

Phelan, Jim. *Lifer*. London: Peter Davies, 1938.

Pick, Daniel. *Faces of Degeneration: A European Disorder, c. 1848–1918*. Cambridge: Cambridge University Press, 1989.

Pile, Steve, and Nigel Thrift. *Mapping the Subject: Geographies of Cultural Transformation*. London and New York: Routledge, 1995.

Quennell, Peter, ed. *A Lonely Business: A Self-Portrait of James Pope-Hennessy*. London: Weidenfeld and Nicolson, 1981.

Radzinowicz, Leon. *Sexual Offences: A Report of the Cambridge Department of Criminal Science*. London: Macmillan, 1957.

Rait, Suzanne. "Sex, Love and the Homosexual Body in Early Sexology." In *Sexology in Culture: Labelling Bodies and Desires,* ed. Lucy Bland and Laura Doan, 150–64. Oxford: Polity Press, 1998

Rappaport, Erika. *Shopping for Pleasure: Women in the Making of London's West End*. Princeton University Press, Princeton New Jersey, 2000.

Raven, Simon. "Boys Will be Boys: The Male Prostitute in London." *Encounter* 15, no. 5 (1960): 19–24.

Reed, Christopher. "Making History: The Bloomsbury Group's Construction of Aesthetic and Sexual Identity." *Journal of Homosexuality* 27, nos. 1–2 (1994): 189–224.

Renault, Mary. *The Charioteer*. London: Longmans, 1953.

Richards, Jeffrey. *The Age of the Dream Palace: Cinema and Society in Britain, 1930–39*. London: Routledge, 1989.

———. "'Passing the Love of Women': Manly Love and Victorian Society." In *Manliness and Morality: Middle-Class Masculinity in Britain and America, 1800–1940,* ed. James Mangan and J. A. Walvin, 92–122. Manchester and New York: Manchester University Press, 1987.

Roberts, John Stuart. *Siegfried Sassoon, 1886–1967*. London: Richard Cohen Books, 1999.

Roberts, M. J. D. "Public and Private in Early Nineteenth Century London: The Vagrant Act of 1822 and Its Enforcement." *Social History* 13, no. 3 (1988): 273–94.

Roland, Alan. *Guardsman: An Autobiography*. London: Museum Press, 1955.

Rose, Lionel. *Rogues and Vagabonds: Vagrant Underworld in Britain, 1815–1985*. London and New York: Routledge, 1988.

Rowbotham, Sheila and Jeffrey Weeks. *Socialism and the New Life: The Personal and Sexual Politics of Edward Carpenter and Havelock Ellis*. London: Pluto Press, 1977.

Salkey, Andrew. *Escape to an Autumn Pavement*. London: Hutchinson, 1960.

Schofield, Michael. *Sociological Aspects of Homosexuality: A Comparative Study of Three Types of Homosexuals*. London: Longmans, 1965.

Scott Moncrieff, George. *Café Bar*. London: Wishart and Co., 1936.

Sedgwick, Eve Kosofsky. *Between Men: English Literature and Male Homosocial Desire*. New York: Columbia University Press, 1985.

———. *Epistemology of the Closet*. Berkeley, University of California Press, 1990.

Seidman, Steven, ed. *Queer Theory / Sociology*. Oxford: Blackwell, 1996.

Selvon, Samuel. *The Lonely Londoners*. London: Alan Wingate, 1956.

Senellick, Laurence. "Mollies or Men of Mode? Sodomy and the Eighteenth Century London Stage." *Journal of the History of Sexuality* 1, no. 1 (1990): 33–67.

Sheridan, Michael. *Rowton Houses, 1892–1954*. London: Rowton Houses Ltd, 1956.

Shields, Rob. *Places on the Margin: Alternative Geographies of Modernity*. London and New York: Routledge, 1991.

Shifrin, Malcolm. *Victorian Turkish Baths*. Http://www.victorianturkishbath.org (accessed April 2004).

Sibley, David. *Geographies of Exclusion: Society and Difference in the West*. London and New York: Routledge, 1995.

Sinclair, Robert. *Metropolitan Man: The Future of the English*. London: George Allen and Unwin, 1937.

Sinfield, Alan. *The Wilde Century: Effeminacy, Oscar Wilde and the Queer Moment*. London: Cassell, 1994.

———. "Closet Dramas: Homosexual Representation and Class in Post-War British Theatre." *Genders* 9 (1990): 112–31.

———. "Private Lives / Public Theatre: Noel Coward and the Politics of Homosexual Representation." *Representations* 36 (1991): 43–63.

Smith, F. B. "Labouchere's Amendment to the Criminal Law Amendment Bill." *Historical Studies* 17, no. 67 (1976): 165–75.

Smith, Malcolm. *Democracy in a Depression: Britain in the 1920s and 1930s*. Cardiff, University of Wales Press, 1998.

Soja, Edward. *Postmodern Geographies: The Reassertion of Space in Critical Social Theory*. London and New York: Verso, 1989.

Sommer, Fred. "Anthony Blunt and Guy Burgess: Gay Spies." *Journal of Homosexuality* 29, no. 4 (1995): 275–80.

Spalding, Frances. *Dance till the Stars Come Down: A Biography of John Minton*. London: John Curtis/Hodder and Stoughton, 1991.

———. *Duncan Grant*. London: Chatto and Windus, 1997.

Spenser, James. *The Gilt Kid*. London: Jonathon Cape, 1936.

Stafford Clark, David. "Homosexuality." *Medico Legal Journal* 25, no. 2 (1957): 76.

Stallybrass, Peter and Allon White. *The Politics and Poetics of Transgression*. London: Methuen, 1986.

Stein, Marc. *City of Brotherly and Sisterly Love: Lesbian and Gay Philadelphia, 1945–72*. Chicago: University of Chicago Press, 2000.

Stopes, Marie. *Married Love: A New Contribution to the Solution of Sex Difficulties*. London: Fifield, 1918.

Stringer, Hubert. *Moral Evil in London*. London: Chapman and Hall, 1925.

Summers, Judith. *Soho: A History of London's Most Colourful Neighbourhood*. London: Bloomsbury, 1989.

Sutherland, Douglas. *Portrait of a Decade: London Life, 1945–55*. London: Harrap, 1988.

Symonds, John Addington. *A Problem in Greek Ethics*. New York: Haskell House, 1971.

———. *A Problem in Modern Ethics*. New York: B. Blom, 1971.

Taylor, Howard. "Rationing Crime: The Political Economy of Criminal Statistics since the 1850s." *Economic History Review* 51 (1998): 569–90.

Thane, Pat. "Population Politics in Post-War British Culture." In *Moments of Modernity: Reconstructing Britain, 1945–64*, ed. Becky Conekin, Frank Mort and Chris Waters, 114–33. London: Rivers Oram, 1994.

The Blue Guide: Muirhead's London and Its Environs. London: Macmillan, 1922.

The Report of the Departmental Committee on Homosexual Offences and Prostitution. London: HMSO, 1957.

The Report of the Royal Commission on Marriage and Divorce. London: HMSO, 1951.

The Report of the Royal Commission on Population. London: HMSO, 1949.

Thorne, G. *The Great Acceptance: The Life Story of F. N. Charrington*. London: Hodder and Stoughton, 1912.

Tietjen, Arthur. *Soho: London's Vicious Circle*. London: Allan Wingate, 1956.

Tosh, John. *A Man's Place: Masculinity and the Middle-Class Home in Victorian England*. New Haven: Yale University Press, 1999.

Trumbach, Randolph. "Sex, Gender and Sexual Identity in Modern Culture: Male Sodomy and Female Prostitution in Enlightenment London." *Journal of the History of Sexuality* 2, no. 2 (1991): 186–203.

———. "Sodomy Transformed: Aristocratic Libertinage, Public Reputation and the Gender Revolution of the 18th Century." *Journal of the History of Homosexuality* 19, no. 2 (1990): 105–24.

———. *Sex and the Gender Revolution*, vol. 1, *Heterosexuality and the Third Gender in Enlightenment London*. Chicago: Chicago University Press, 1998.

Turnbaugh, Douglas Blair. *Private: The Erotic Art of Duncan Grant, 1885–1978*. London: Gay Men's Press, 1989.

Turner, Mark. *Backward Glances: Cruising the Queer Streets of New York and London*. London: Reaktion, 2003.

Underwood, Reginald. *Bachelor's Hall*. London: Fortune Press, 1934.

———. *Flame of Freedom*. London: Fortune Press, 1936.

———. *Hidden Lights*. London: Fortune Press, 1937.

Upchurch, Charles. "Forgetting the Unthinkable: Cross-Dressers and British Society in the Case of the Queen vs. Boulton and Others." *Gender and History* 12, no. 1 (2000): 127.

Valentine, Gill. "Children should be Seen and not Heard: The Production and Transgression of Adults' Public Space." *Urban Geography* 17, no. 3 (1996): 205–20.

———. "Heterosexing Space: Lesbian Perceptions and Experiences of Everyday Spaces." *Environment and Planning D: Society and Space* 11, no. 4 (1993): 395–413.

———. "Negotiating and Managing Multiple Sexual Identities: Lesbian Time Space Strategies." *Transactions of the Institute of British Geographers* 18, no. 2 (1993): 237–48.

———. "Out and About: Geographies of Lesbian Landscapes." *International Journal of Urban and Regional Research* 19, no. 1 (1995): 96–112.

Vickers, Hugo. *Cecil Beaton: The Authorised Biography.* London: Weidenfeld and Nicolson, 1985.

Walking after Midnight: Gay Men's Life Stories. Hall-Carpenter Archives, Gay Men's Oral History Group. London: Routledge, 1989.

Walkowitz, Judith. *City of Dreadful Delight: Narratives of Sexual Danger in Late-Victorian London.* London: Virago, 1998.

Ward, Lock. *A Pictorial and Descriptive Guide to London.* London: Ward Lock, 51st Edition.

Warner, Michael, ed. *Fear of a Queer Planet: Queer Politics and Social Theory.* Minneapolis: University of Minnesota Press, 1993.

Waters, Chris. "'Dark Strangers' in our Midst: Discourses of Race and Nation in Britain, 1947–1963," *Journal of British Studies* 36, no. 2 (1997): 207–38.

———. "Disorders of the Mind, Disorders of the Body Social: Peter Wildeblood and the Making of the Modern Homosexual." In *Moments of Modernity: Reconstructing Britain, 1945–1964,* ed. Becky Conekin, Frank Mort and Chris Waters, 135–51. London and New York: Rivers Oram Press, 1999.

———. "Havelock Ellis, Sigmund Freud and the State: Discourses of Homosexual Identity in Interwar Britain." In *Sexology in Culture: Labelling Bodies and Desires,* ed. Lucy Bland and Laura Doan, 165–79. Oxford: Polity Press, 1998.

Watney, Simon. *The Art of Duncan Grant.* London: John Murray, 1990.

Weeks, Jeffrey, and Kevin Porter, eds. *Between the Acts: Lives of Homosexual Men: 1885–1967.* London: Rivers Oram Press, 1998.

Weeks, Jeffrey. "Inverts, Perverts and Mary-Annes: Male Prostitution and the Regulation of Homosexuality in England in the Nineteenth and Early Twentieth Centuries." In *Hidden from History: Reclaiming the Gay and Lesbian Past,* ed. George Chauncey, Martin Duberman and Martha Vicinus, 195–211. Canada: New American Library, 1989.

———. *Sex, Politics and Society: The Regulation of Sexuality since 1800.* London: Longman, 1989.

———. *Coming Out: Homosexual Politics in Britain from the Nineteenth Century to the Present.* London: Quartet Books, 1977.

Weightman, Gavin, and Steve Humphries. *The Making of Modern London, 1914–1939.* London: Sidgwick and Jackson, 1984.

Weightman, Gavin. *Bright Lights, Big City: London Entertained, 1830–1950*. London: Collins and Brown, 1992.

Weigle, David. "Psychology and Homosexuality: The British Sexological Society." *Journal of the History of the Behavioral Sciences* 31 (1995): 137–48.

Weinrebe, Ben, and Christopher Hibbert. *The London Encyclopaedia*. London: Papermac, 1983.

West, D. J. *Homosexuality: A Frank and Practical Guide to the Social and Medical Aspects of Male Homosexuality*. London: Duckworth, 1955.

Westwood, Gordon [pseud. Michael Schofield]. *A Minority: A Report on the Life of the Male Homosexual in Great Britain*. London: Longmans, 1960.

———. *Society and the Homosexual*. London: Victor Gollancz, 1952.

Wheen, Francis. *Tom Driberg: His Life and Indiscretions*. London: Chatto and Windus, 1990.

White, Jerry. *Rothschild Buildings: Life in an East End Tenement Block, 1887–1920*. London Routledge and Kegan Paul, 1980.

———. *The Worst Street in North London: Campbell Bunk, Islington between the Wars*. London: Routledge and Kegan Paul, 1986.

Whitely, Cecil. "The Problem of the Moral Pervert: Discussion at the Institute of Hygiene." *Medical Press* (15 July 1932).

———. "The Problem of the Moral Pervert." *Journal of the Institute of Hygiene* (April 1933).

Whittle, Stephen, ed. *The Margins of the City: Gay Men's Urban Lives*. Aldershot: Ashgate, 1994.

Wild, Roland, and Curtis-Bennett, Derek. *"Curtis": The Life of Sir Henry Curtis-Bennett KC*. London: Cassell, 1937.

Wildeblood, Peter. *A Way of Life*. London: Weidenfeld and Nicolson, 1956.

———. *Against the Law*. London: Weidenfeld and Nicolson, 1955.

Williams, Emlyn. *Emlyn: An Early Autobiography, 1927–1935*. London: Bodley Head, 1973.

———. *George: An Early Autobiography*. London: Hamish Hamilton, 1961.

Wilson, Angus. *Hemlock and After*. London: Secker and Warburg, 1952.

Wilson, Elizabeth. *The Sphinx in the City: Urban Life, the Control of Disorder and Women*. Berkeley, University of California Press, 1991.

Wishart, Michael. *High Diver*. London: Quartet Books, 1978.

Wolfenden, John. *Turning Points: The Memoirs of Lord Wolfenden*. London: Bodley Head, 1976.

Woods, Gregory. *A History of Gay Literature: The Male Tradition*. New Haven, Yale University Press, 1998.

Woollacott, Angela. "'Khaki Fever' and Its Control: Gender, Class, Age and Sexual Morality on the British Homefront in the First World War." *Journal of Contemporary History* 29 (1994): 325–47.

Worsley, Thomas Cuthbert. *Flannelled Fool: A Slice of Life in the Thirties*. London: Hogarth, 1985.

————. *Fellow Travellers*. London: Gay Men's Press, 1984.

Wotherspoon, Gary. *City of the Plain: History of a Gay Subculture*. Sydney, Hale and Iremonger, 1991.

Wright, Adrian. *John Lehmann: A Pagan Adventure*. London: Duckworth, 1998.

Zweiniger-Bargeilowska, Ina. *Austerity in Britain: Rationing, Controls, and Consumption, 1939–1955*. Oxford: Oxford University Press, 2000.

INDEX

Numbers in italic indicate figures.